SEVEN SEAS ENTERTAINMENT PRESENTS

Monster Musume

story and art by **OKAYADO**

VOLUME 3

TRANSLATION
Ryan Peterson

ADAPTATION
Shanti Whitesides

LETTERING AND LAYOUT
Ma. Victoria Robado

LOGO DESIGN
Courtney Williams

COVER DESIGN
Nicky Lim

PROOFREADER
Janet Houck

MANAGING EDITOR
Adam Arnold

PUBLISHER
Jason DeAngelis

MONSTER MUSUME NO IRU NICHIJO VOLUME 3
© OKAYADO 2013
Originally published in Japan in 2013 by TOKUMA SHOTEN PUBLISHING
CO., LTD., Tokyo. English translation rights arranged with TOKUMA SHOTEN
PUBLISHING CO., LTD., Tokyo, through TOHAN CORPORATION, Tokyo.

Seven Seas books may be purchased in bulk for educational, business, or
promotional use. For information on bulk purchases, please contact Macmillan
Corporate & Premium Sales Department at 1-800-221-7945 (ext 5442)
or write specialmarkets@macmillan.com.

Seven Seas and the Seven Seas logo are trademarks of
Seven Seas Entertainment, LLC. All rights reserved.

ISBN: 978-1-626920-31-6

Printed in Canada

First Printing: May 2014

10 9 8 7 6 5 4 3 2 1

FOLLOW US ONLINE: www.gomanga.com

READING DIRECTIONS

This book reads from *right to left*, Japanese style.
If this is your first time reading manga, you start
reading from the top right panel on each page and
take it from there. If you get lost, just follow the
numbered diagram here. It may seem backwar
first, but you'll get the hang of it! Have fun!!

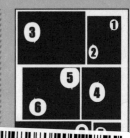

W9-CHF-975

Mero's Mermaid Mysteries

HEIGHT: 178CM
WEIGHT: 49KG
BUST: 85
WAIST: 55
HIP: 92

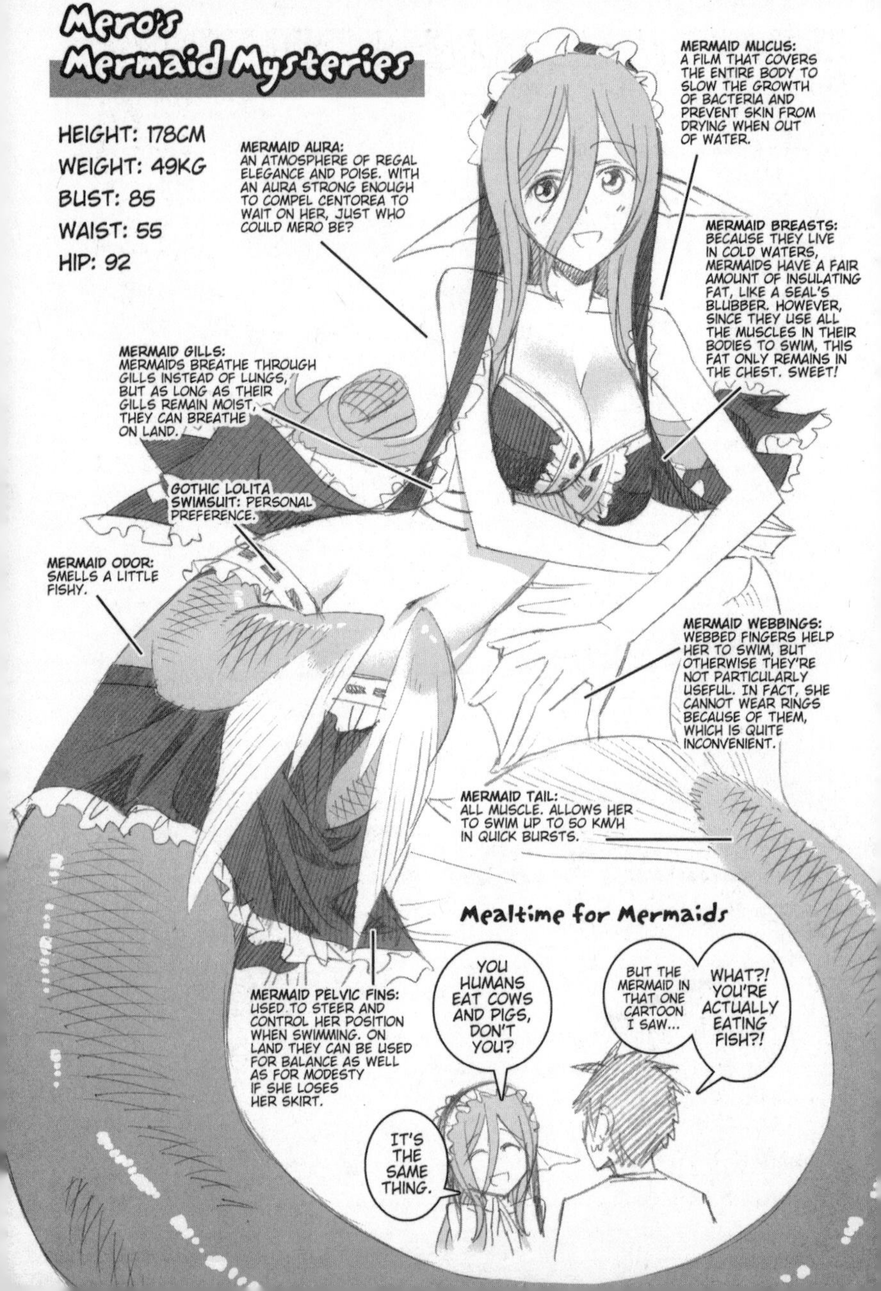

MERMAID MUCUS: A FILM THAT COVERS THE ENTIRE BODY TO SLOW THE GROWTH OF BACTERIA AND PREVENT SKIN FROM DRYING WHEN OUT OF WATER.
MERMAID AURA: AN ATMOSPHERE OF REGAL ELEGANCE AND POISE. WITH AN AURA STRONG ENOUGH TO COMPEL CENTOREA TO WAIT ON HER, JUST WHO COULD MERO BE?
MERMAID BREASTS: BECAUSE THEY LIVE IN COLD WATERS, MERMAIDS HAVE A FAIR AMOUNT OF INSULATING FAT, LIKE A SEAL'S BLUBBER. HOWEVER, SINCE THEY USE ALL THE MUSCLES IN THEIR BODIES TO SWIM, THIS FAT ONLY REMAINS IN THE CHEST. SWEET!
MERMAID GILLS: MERMAIDS BREATHE THROUGH GILLS INSTEAD OF LUNGS, BUT AS LONG AS THEIR GILLS REMAIN MOIST, THEY CAN BREATHE ON LAND.
GOTHIC LOLITA SWIMSUIT: PERSONAL PREFERENCE.
MERMAID ODOR: SMELLS A LITTLE FISHY.
MERMAID WEBBINGS: WEBBED FINGERS HELP HER TO SWIM, BUT OTHERWISE THEY'RE NOT PARTICULARLY USEFUL. IN FACT, SHE CANNOT WEAR RINGS BECAUSE OF THEM, WHICH IS QUITE INCONVENIENT.
MERMAID TAIL: ALL MUSCLE. ALLOWS HER TO SWIM UP TO 50 KM/H IN QUICK BURSTS.
MERMAID PELVIC FINS: USED TO STEER AND CONTROL HER POSITION WHEN SWIMMING. ON LAND THEY CAN BE USED FOR BALANCE AS WELL AS FOR MODESTY IF SHE LOSES HER SKIRT.
Mealtime for Mermaids
WHAT?! YOU'RE ACTUALLY EATING FISH?!
BUT THE MERMAID IN THAT ONE CARTOON I SAW...
YOU HUMANS EAT COWS AND PIGS, DON'T YOU?
IT'S THE SAME THING.

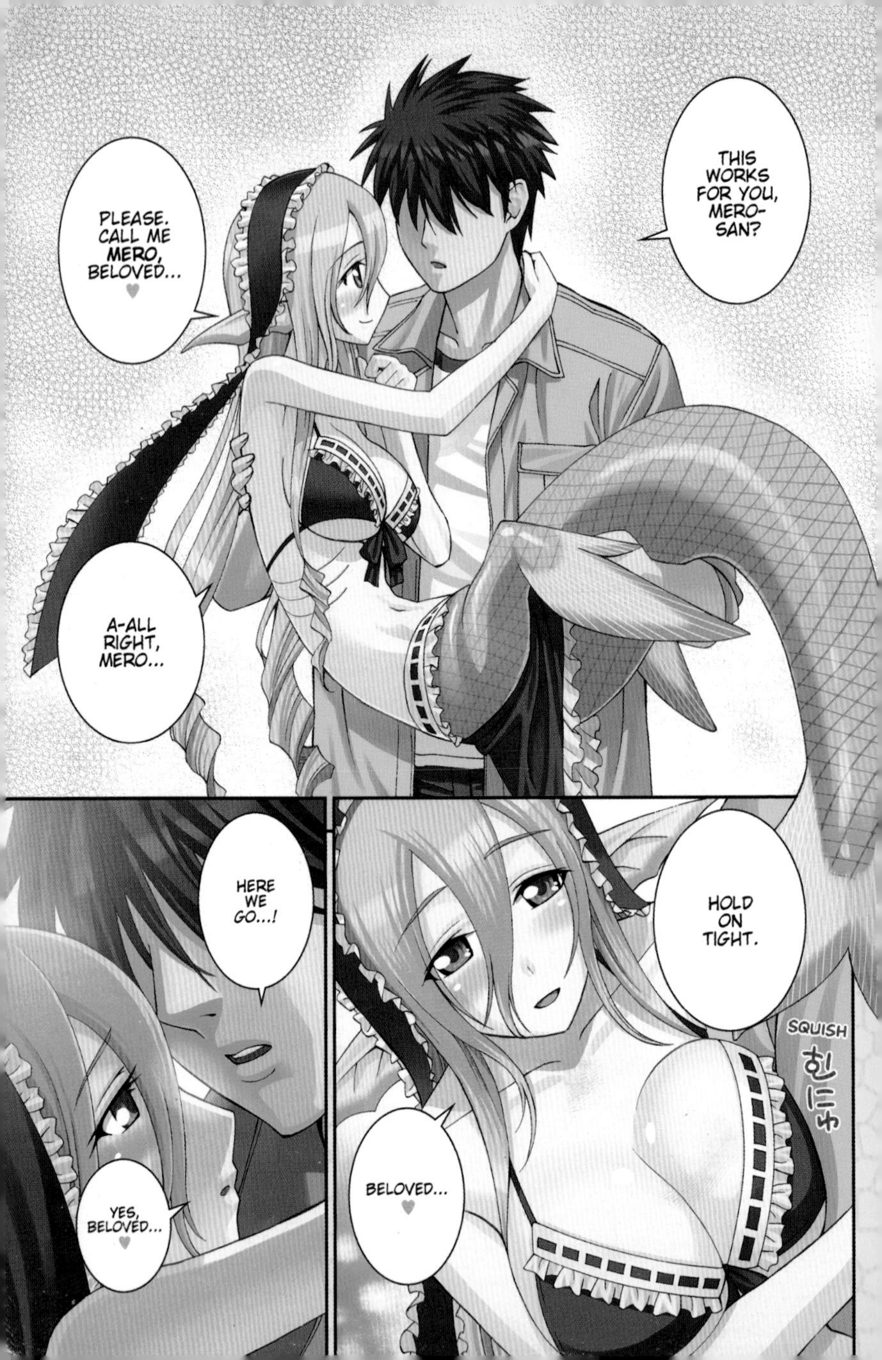
THIS WORKS FOR YOU, MERO-SAN?
PLEASE. CALL ME MERO, BELOVED... ♥
A-ALL RIGHT, MERO...
HOLD ON TIGHT.
SQUISH
むにゅ
BELOVED... ♥
HERE WE GO...!
YES, BELOVED... ♥

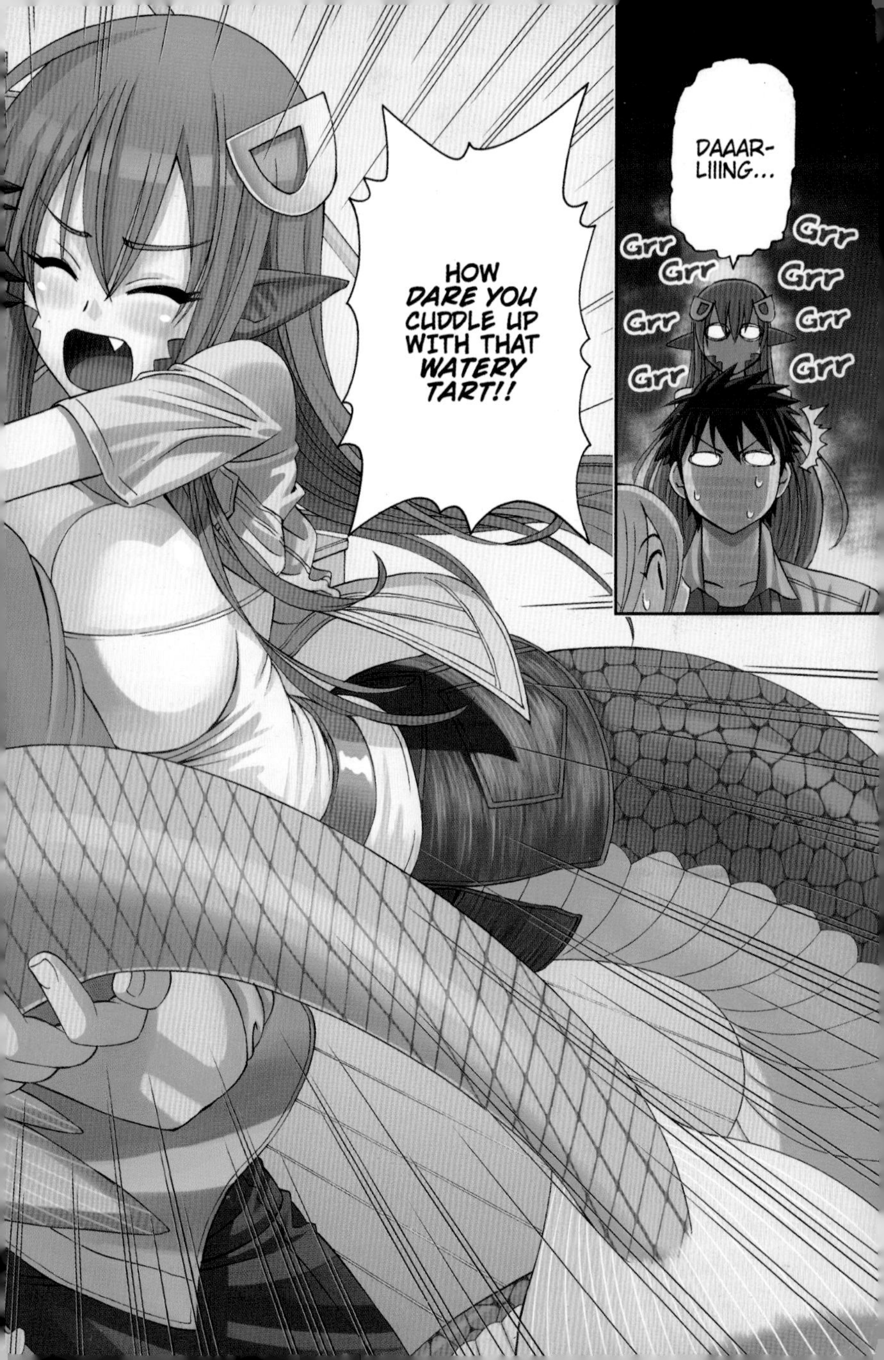
DAAAR-
LIIING...
Grr Grr Grr Grr Grr Grr Grr Grr
HOW *DARE YOU* CUDDLE UP WITH THAT *WATERY TART!!*

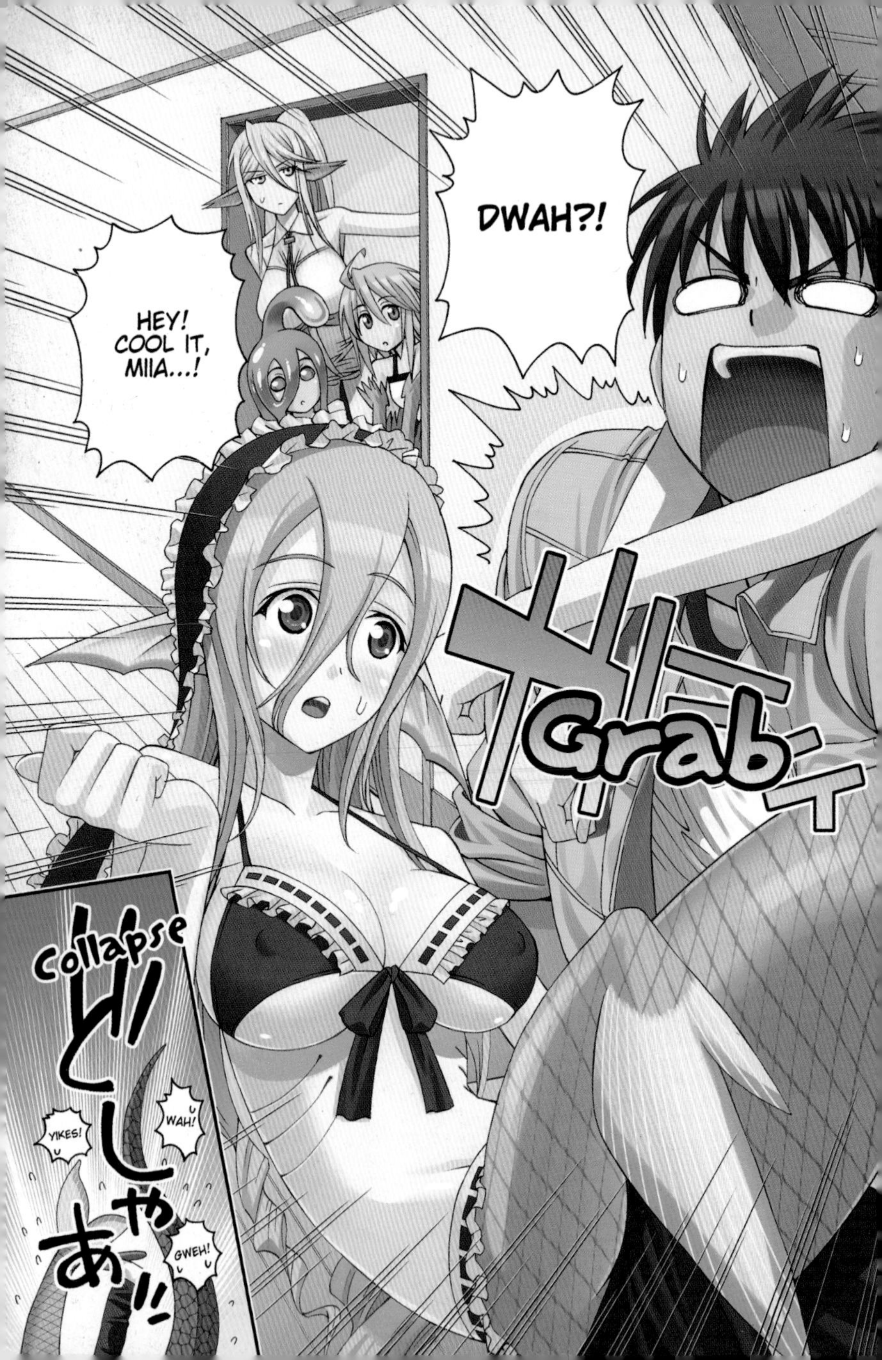
DWAH?!
HEY! COOL IT, MIIA...!
Grab
Collapse
どしゃあ!!
WAH!
YIKES!
GWEH!

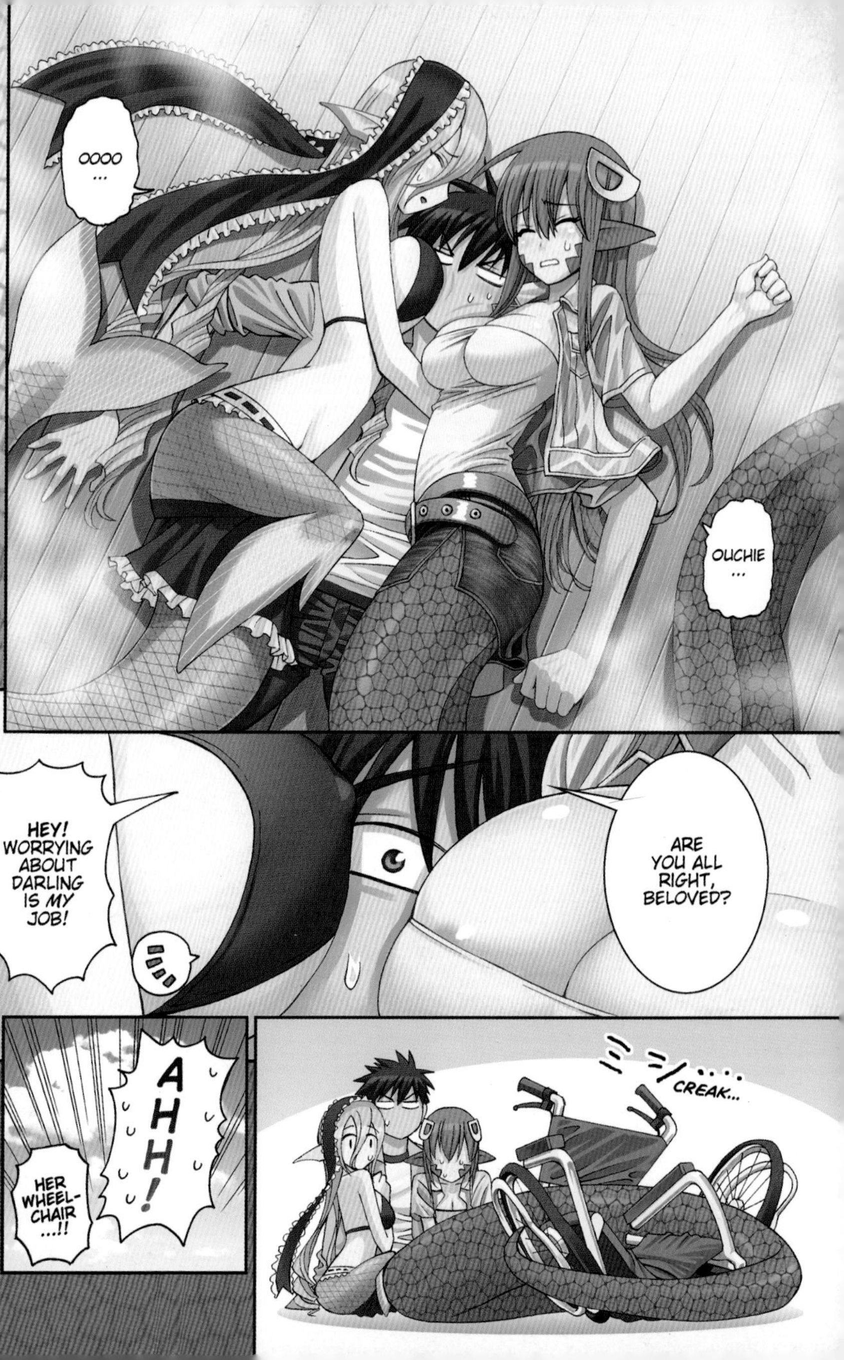
OUCHIE...
OOOO...
ARE YOU ALL RIGHT, BELOVED?
HEY! WORRYING ABOUT DARLING IS MY JOB!
ミシ...
CREAK...
AHH!
HER WHEELCHAIR...!!

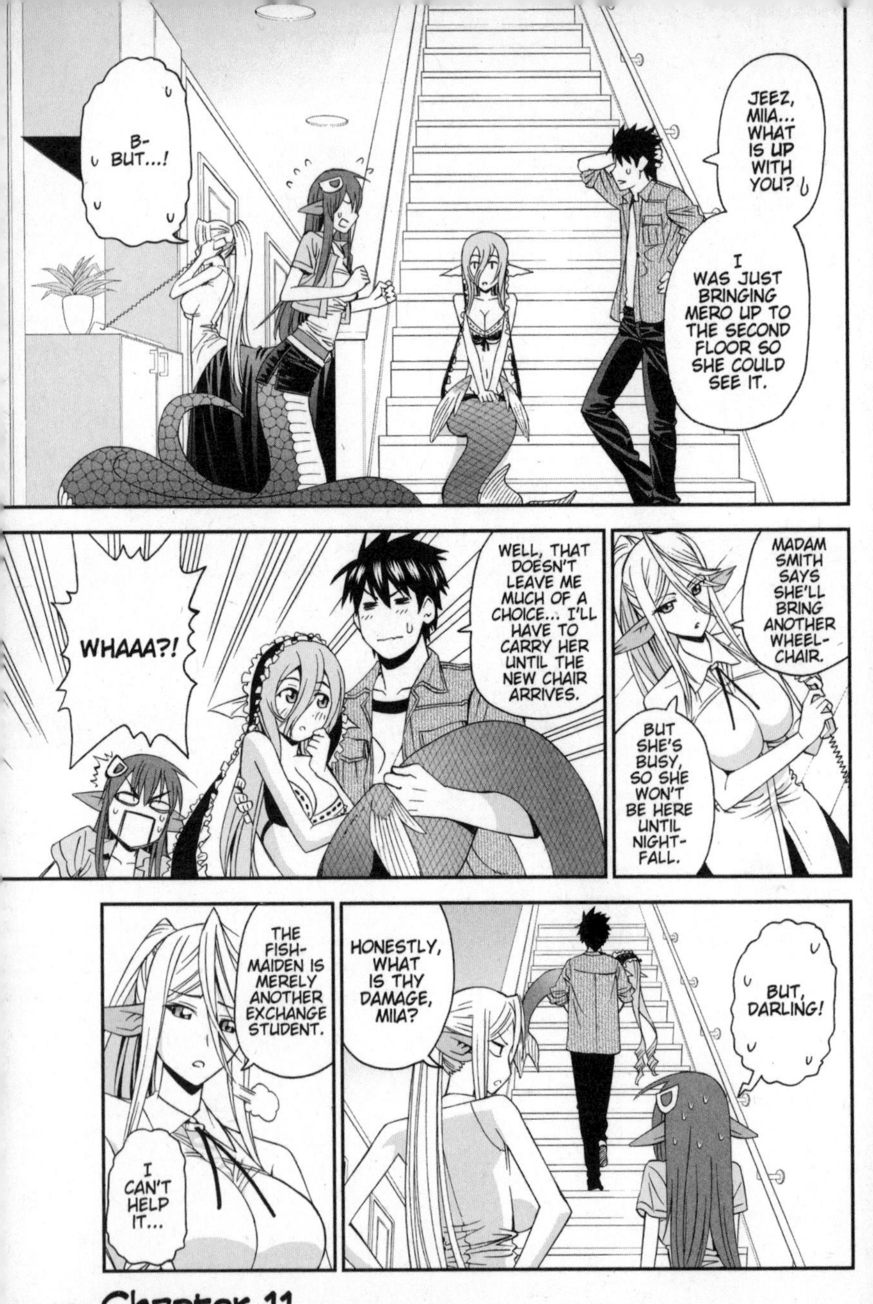
JEEZ, MIIA... WHAT IS UP WITH YOU?
I WAS JUST BRINGING MERO UP TO THE SECOND FLOOR SO SHE COULD SEE IT.
B- BUT...!
MADAM SMITH SAYS SHE'LL BRING ANOTHER WHEEL-CHAIR.
BUT SHE'S BUSY, SO SHE WON'T BE HERE UNTIL NIGHT-FALL.
WELL, THAT DOESN'T LEAVE ME MUCH OF A CHOICE... I'LL HAVE TO CARRY HER UNTIL THE NEW CHAIR ARRIVES.
WHAAA?!
BUT, DARLING!
HONESTLY, WHAT IS THY DAMAGE, MIIA?
THE FISH-MAIDEN IS MERELY ANOTHER EXCHANGE STUDENT.
I CAN'T HELP IT...

Chapter 11

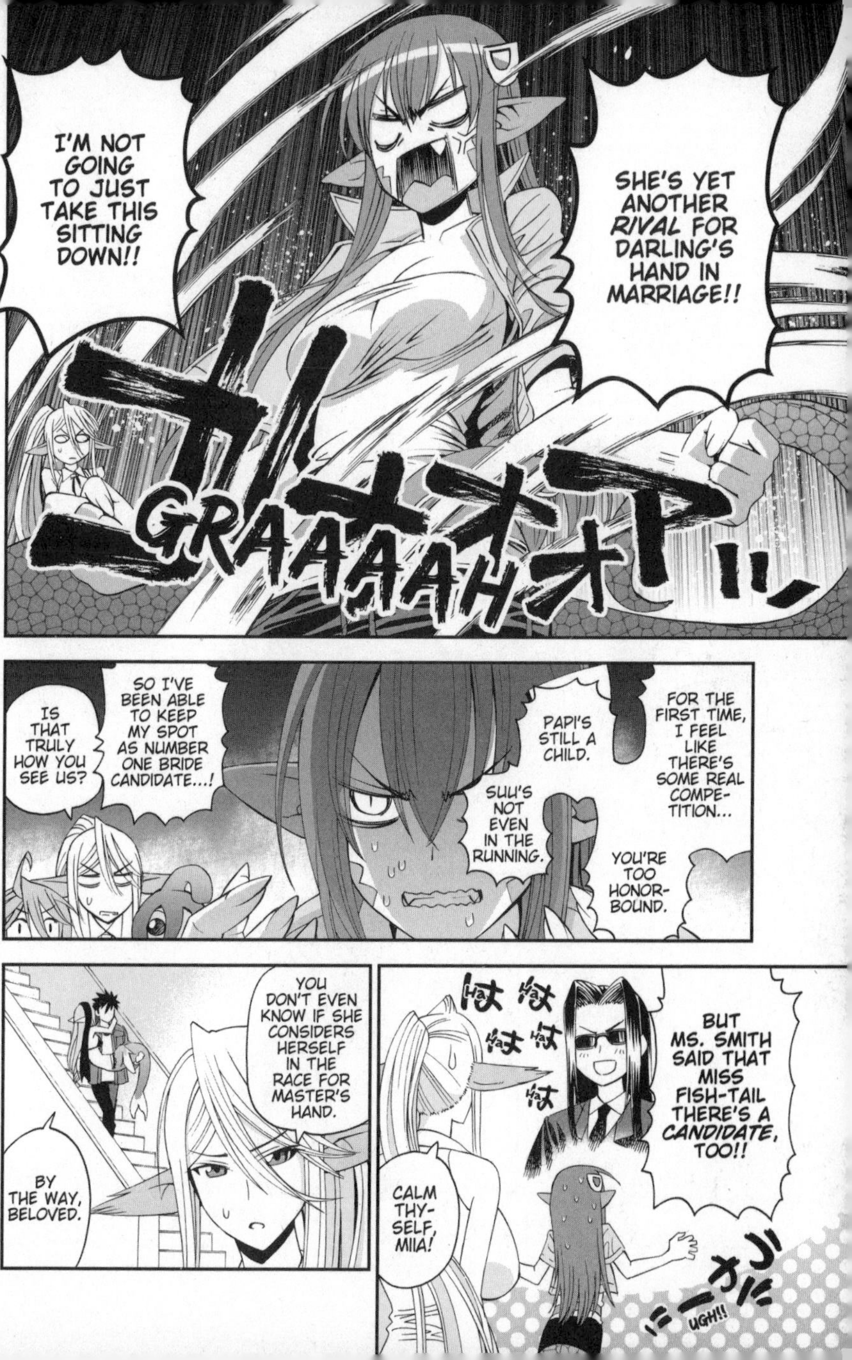
SHE'S YET ANOTHER RIVAL FOR DARLING'S HAND IN MARRIAGE!!
I'M NOT GOING TO JUST TAKE THIS SITTING DOWN!!
GRAAAAAH
FOR THE FIRST TIME, I FEEL LIKE THERE'S SOME REAL COMPETITION...
YOU'RE TOO HONOR-BOUND.
PAPI'S STILL A CHILD.
SUU'S NOT EVEN IN THE RUNNING.
SO I'VE BEEN ABLE TO KEEP MY SPOT AS NUMBER ONE BRIDE CANDIDATE...!
IS THAT TRULY HOW YOU SEE US?
BUT MS. SMITH SAID THAT MISS FISH-TAIL THERE'S A CANDIDATE, TOO!!
CALM THYSELF, MIIA!
UGH!!
YOU DON'T EVEN KNOW IF SHE CONSIDERS HERSELF IN THE RACE FOR MASTER'S HAND.
BY THE WAY, BELOVED.

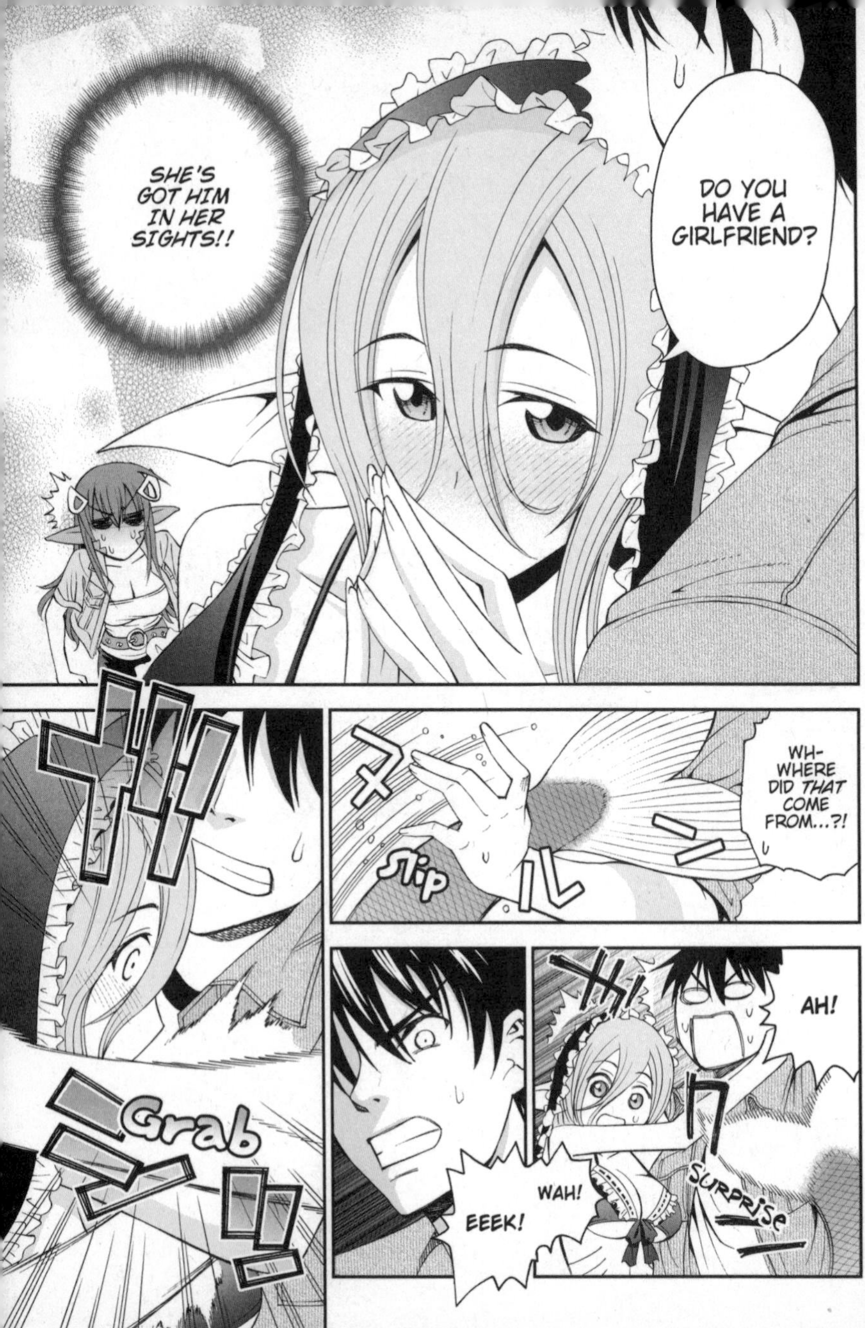
DO YOU HAVE A GIRLFRIEND?
SHE'S GOT HIM IN HER SIGHTS!!
WH-WHERE DID THAT COME FROM...?!
Slip
AH!
SURPRISE
WAH!
EEEK!
Grab

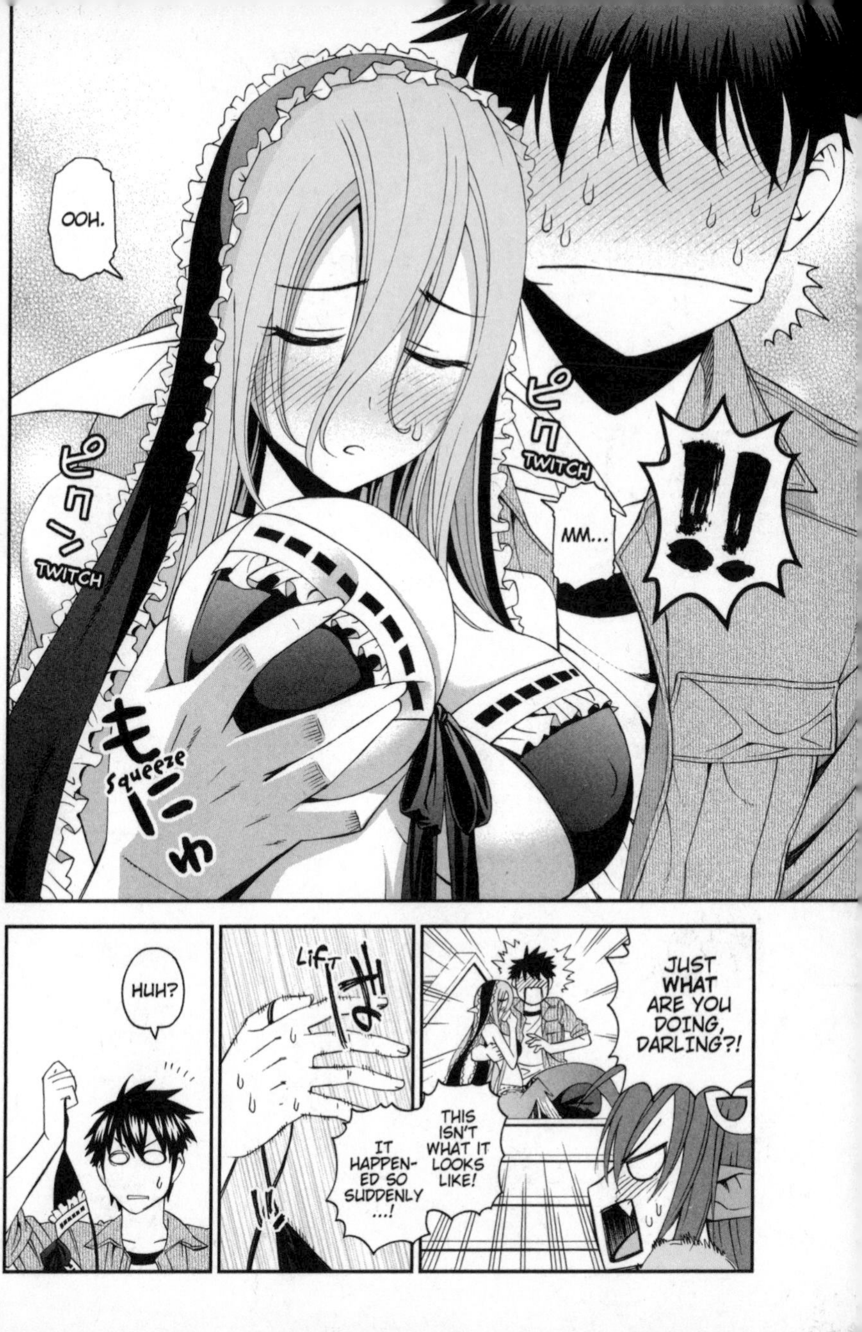

!!
ピク
TWITCH
MM...
OOH.
ピクン
TWITCH
もにゅ
squeeze
JUST WHAT ARE YOU DOING, DARLING?!
THIS ISN'T WHAT IT LOOKS LIKE!
IT HAPPEN-ED SO SUDDENLY ...!
ぱ
Lift
HUH?

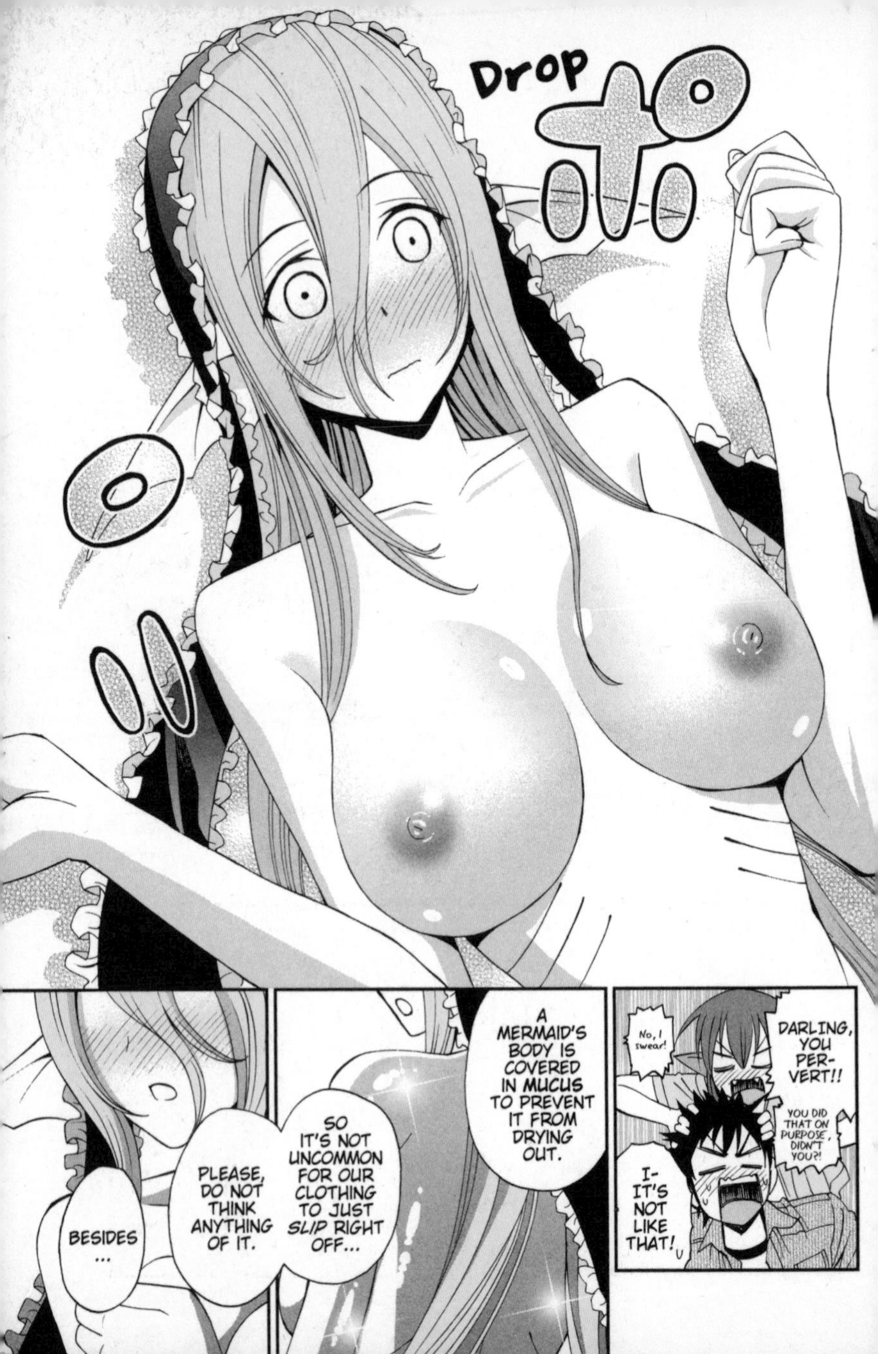
Drop
DARLING, YOU PER-VERT!!
No, I swear!
YOU DID THAT ON PURPOSE, DIDN'T YOU?!
I- IT'S NOT LIKE THAT!
A MERMAID'S BODY IS COVERED IN MUCUS TO PREVENT IT FROM DRYING OUT.
SO IT'S NOT UNCOMMON FOR OUR CLOTHING TO JUST *SLIP* RIGHT OFF...
PLEASE, DO NOT THINK ANYTHING OF IT.
BESIDES ...

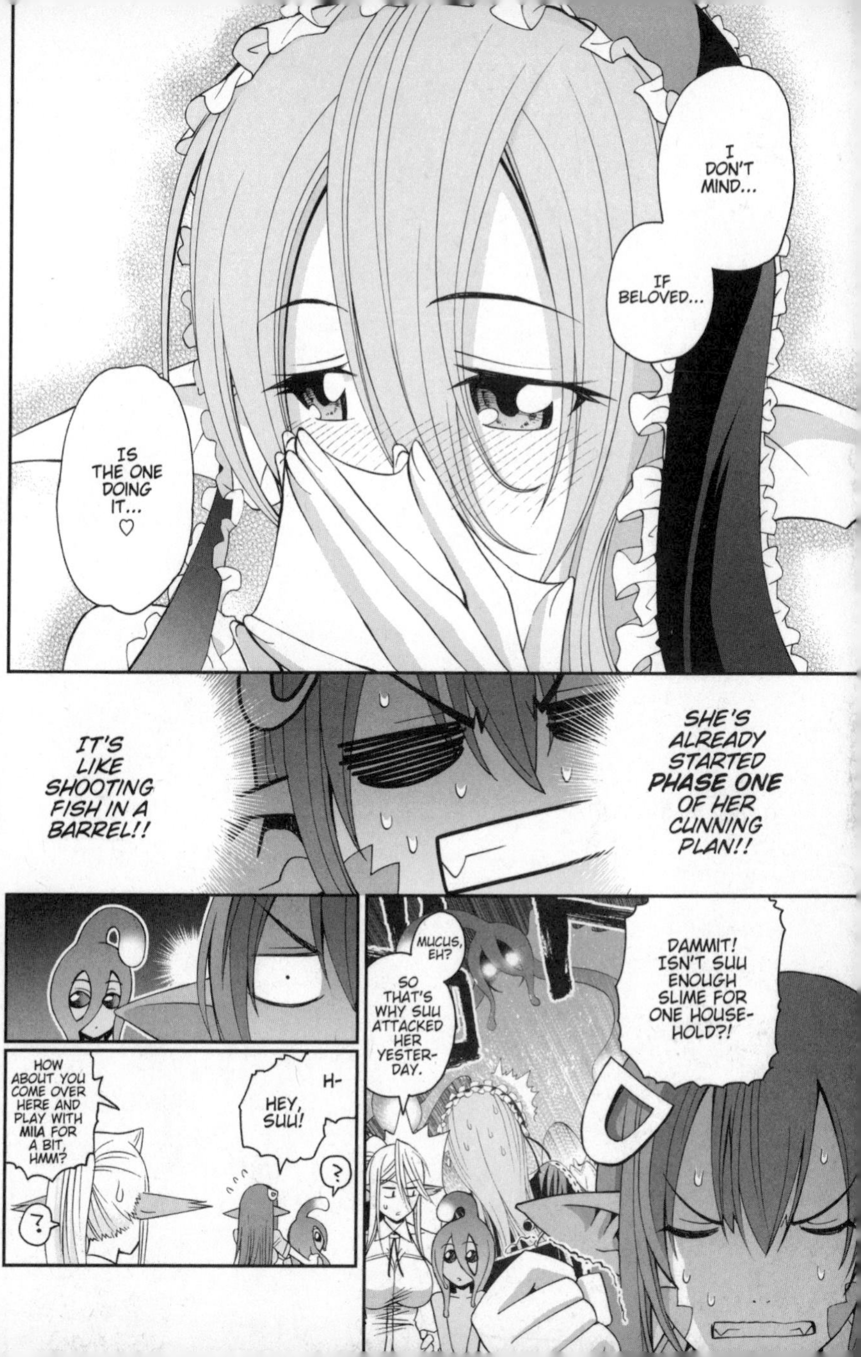

I DON'T MIND...
IF BELOVED...
IS THE ONE DOING IT... ♡
SHE'S ALREADY STARTED PHASE ONE OF HER CUNNING PLAN!!
IT'S LIKE SHOOTING FISH IN A BARREL!!
DAMMIT! ISN'T SUU ENOUGH SLIME FOR ONE HOUSE-HOLD?!
MUCUS, EH?
SO THAT'S WHY SUU ATTACKED HER YESTER-DAY.
H-
HEY, SUU!
?
HOW ABOUT YOU COME OVER HERE AND PLAY WITH MIIA FOR A BIT, HMM?
?

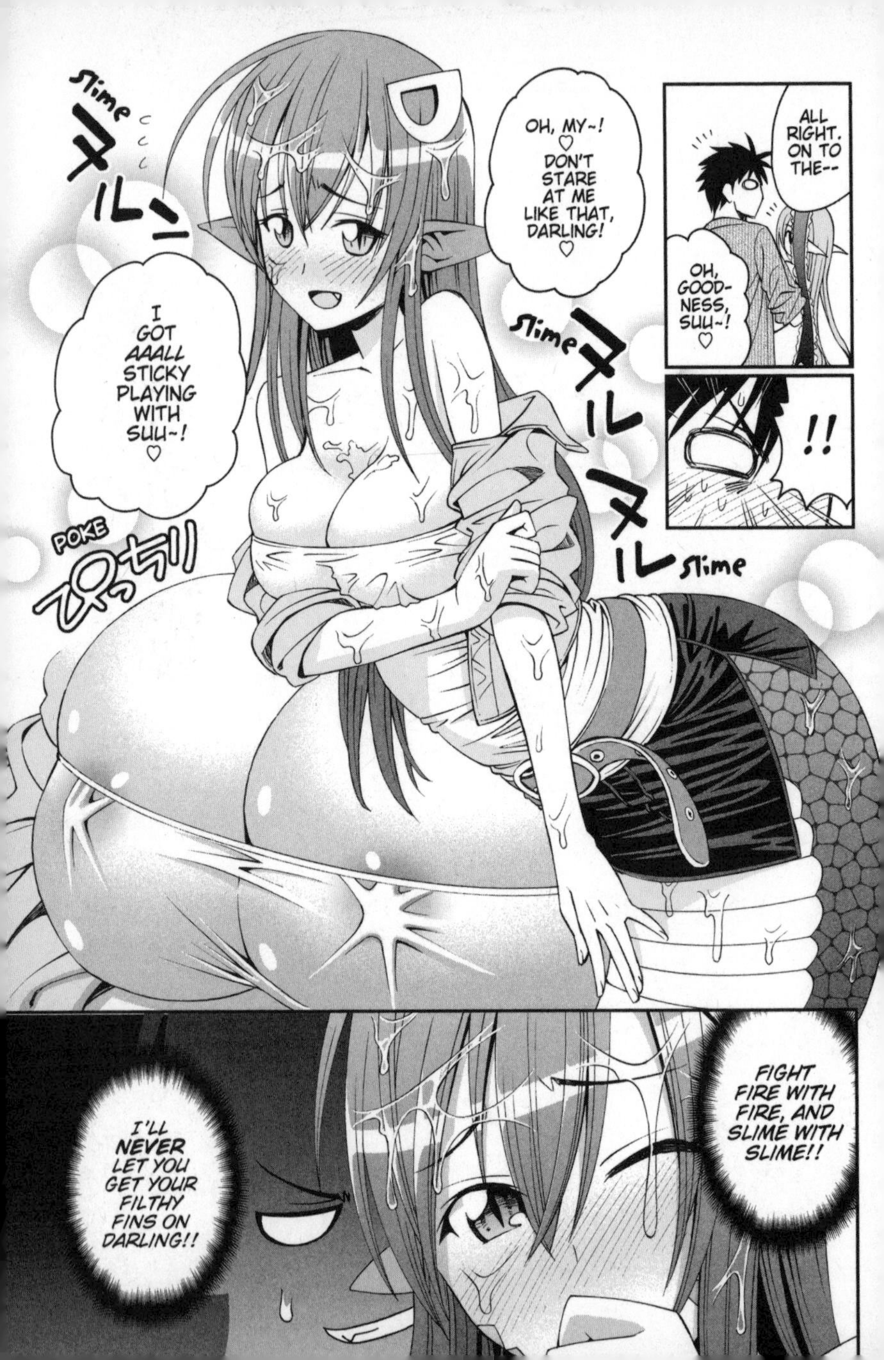
ALL RIGHT. ON TO THE--
OH, GOODNESS, SUU~! ♡
!!
Slime
OH, MY~! ♡ DON'T STARE AT ME LIKE THAT, DARLING! ♡
Slime
I GOT AAALL STICKY PLAYING WITH SUU~! ♡
Slime
POKE
FIGHT FIRE WITH FIRE, AND SLIME WITH SLIME!!
I'LL NEVER LET YOU GET YOUR FILTHY FINS ON DARLING!!

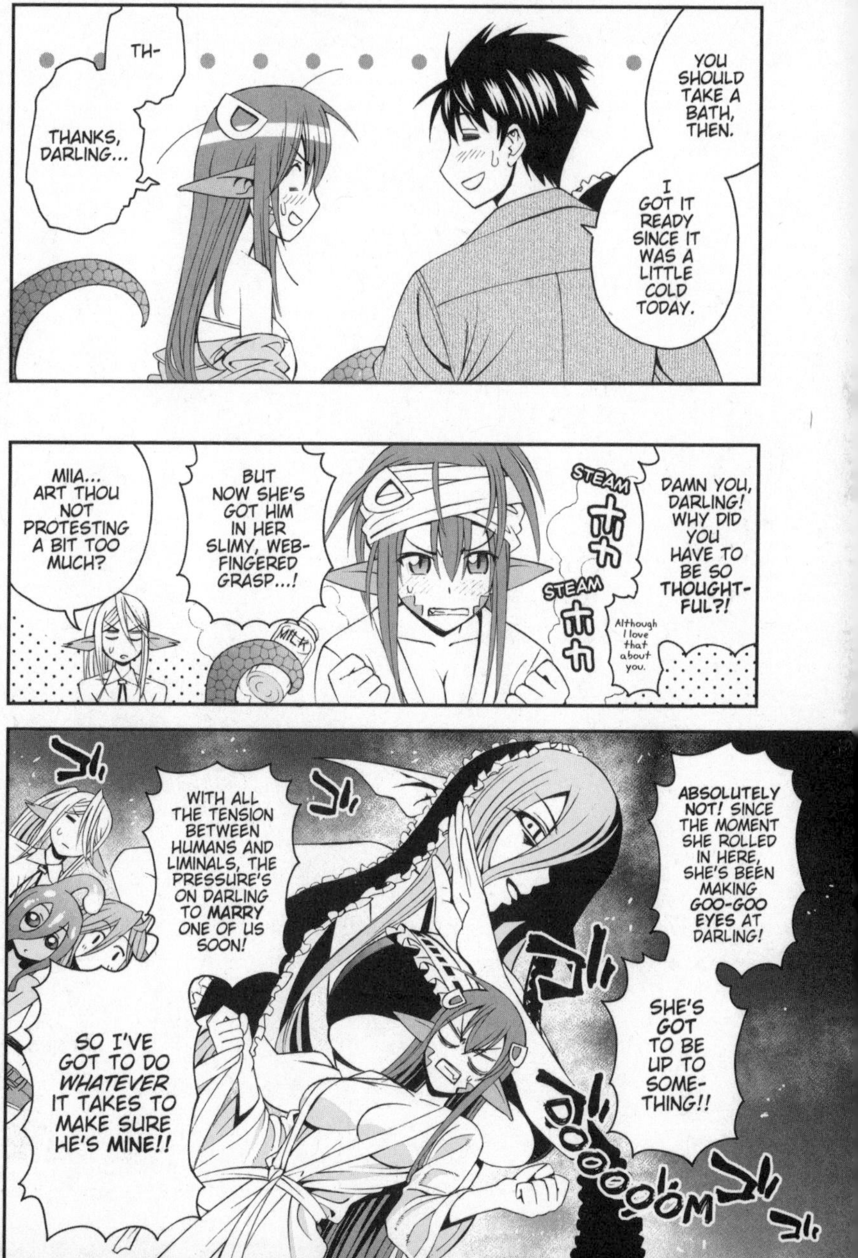
YOU SHOULD TAKE A BATH, THEN.
I GOT IT READY SINCE IT WAS A LITTLE COLD TODAY.
TH-
THANKS, DARLING...
DAMN YOU, DARLING! WHY DID YOU HAVE TO BE SO THOUGHTFUL?!
Although I love that about you.
STEAM
STEAM
BUT NOW SHE'S GOT HIM IN HER SLIMY, WEB-FINGERED GRASP...!
MILK
MIIA... ART THOU NOT PROTESTING A BIT TOO MUCH?
ABSOLUTELY NOT! SINCE THE MOMENT SHE ROLLED IN HERE, SHE'S BEEN MAKING GOO-GOO EYES AT DARLING!
SHE'S GOT TO BE UP TO SOMETHING!!
DOOOOOOOM
WITH ALL THE TENSION BETWEEN HUMANS AND LIMINALS, THE PRESSURE'S ON DARLING TO MARRY ONE OF US SOON!
SO I'VE GOT TO DO WHATEVER IT TAKES TO MAKE SURE HE'S MINE!!

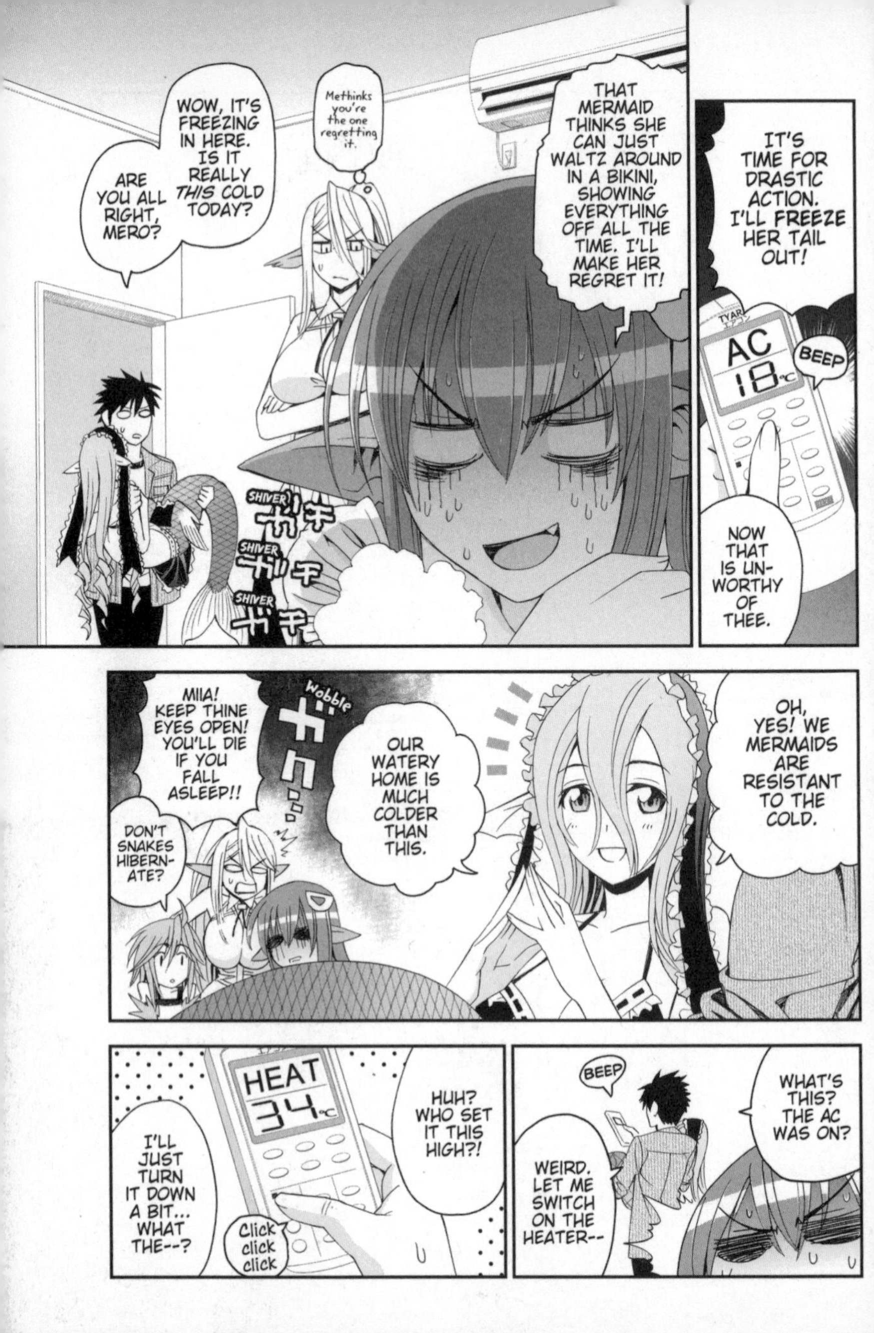
IT'S TIME FOR DRASTIC ACTION. I'LL FREEZE HER TAIL OUT!
TYAR
AC 18°C
BEEP
NOW THAT IS UN-WORTHY OF THEE.
THAT MERMAID THINKS SHE CAN JUST WALTZ AROUND IN A BIKINI, SHOWING EVERYTHING OFF ALL THE TIME. I'LL MAKE HER REGRET IT!
Methinks you're the one regretting it.
WOW, IT'S FREEZING IN HERE. IS IT REALLY *THIS* COLD TODAY?
ARE YOU ALL RIGHT, MERO?
SHIVER
SHIVER
SHIVER
OH, YES! WE MERMAIDS ARE RESISTANT TO THE COLD.
OUR WATERY HOME IS MUCH COLDER THAN THIS.
wobble
MIIA! KEEP THINE EYES OPEN! YOU'LL DIE IF YOU FALL ASLEEP!!
DON'T SNAKES HIBERN-ATE?
WHAT'S THIS? THE AC WAS ON?
BEEP
WEIRD. LET ME SWITCH ON THE HEATER--
HEAT 34°C
HUH? WHO SET IT THIS HIGH?!
I'LL JUST TURN IT DOWN A BIT... WHAT THE--?
Click click click

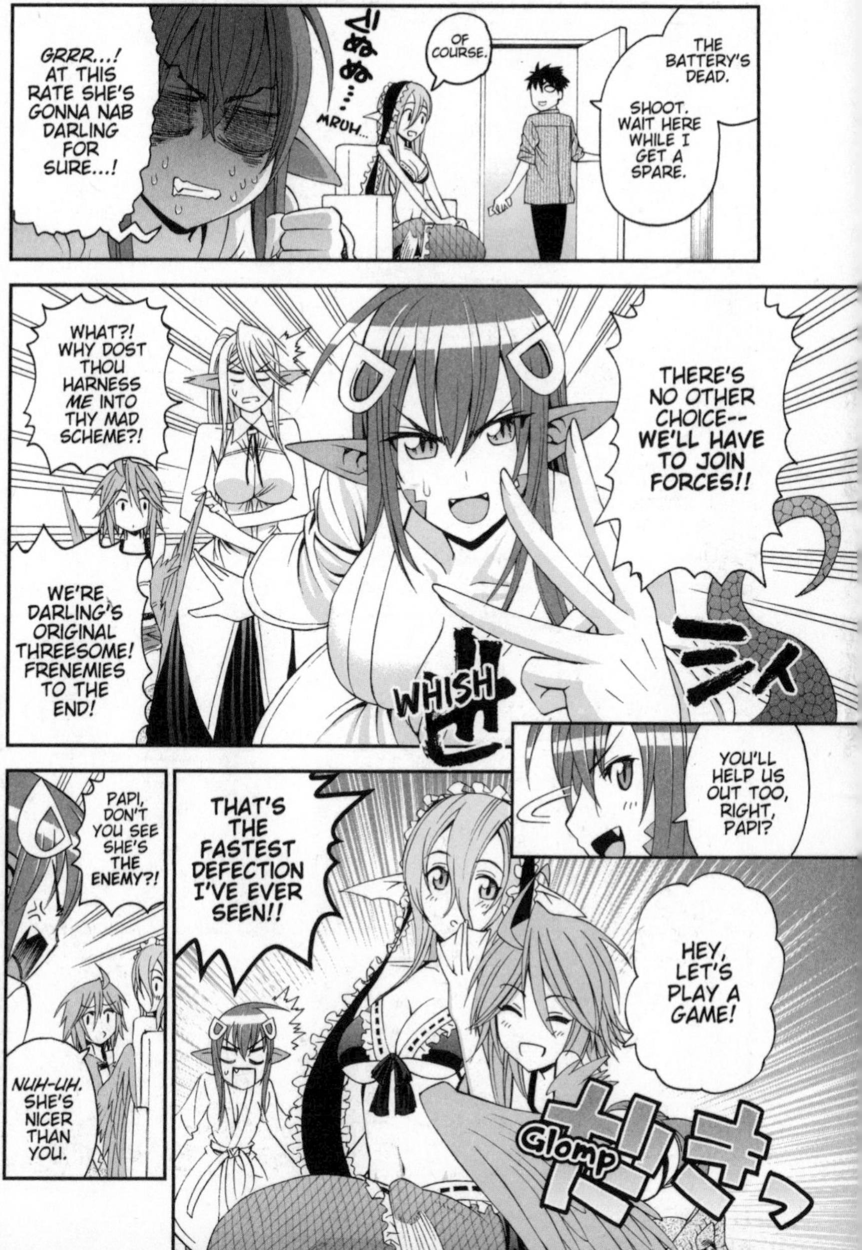
THE BATTERY'S DEAD.
SHOOT. WAIT HERE WHILE I GET A SPARE.
OF COURSE.
MRUH...
GRRR...! AT THIS RATE SHE'S GONNA NAB DARLING FOR SURE...!
THERE'S NO OTHER CHOICE-- WE'LL HAVE TO JOIN FORCES!!
WHAT?! WHY DOST THOU HARNESS *ME* INTO THY MAD SCHEME?!
WE'RE DARLING'S ORIGINAL THREESOME! FRENEMIES TO THE END!
WHISH
YOU'LL HELP US OUT TOO, RIGHT, PAPI?
HEY, LET'S PLAY A GAME!
Glomp
THAT'S THE FASTEST DEFECTION I'VE EVER SEEN!!
PAPI, DON'T YOU SEE SHE'S THE ENEMY?!
NUH-UH. SHE'S NICER THAN YOU.

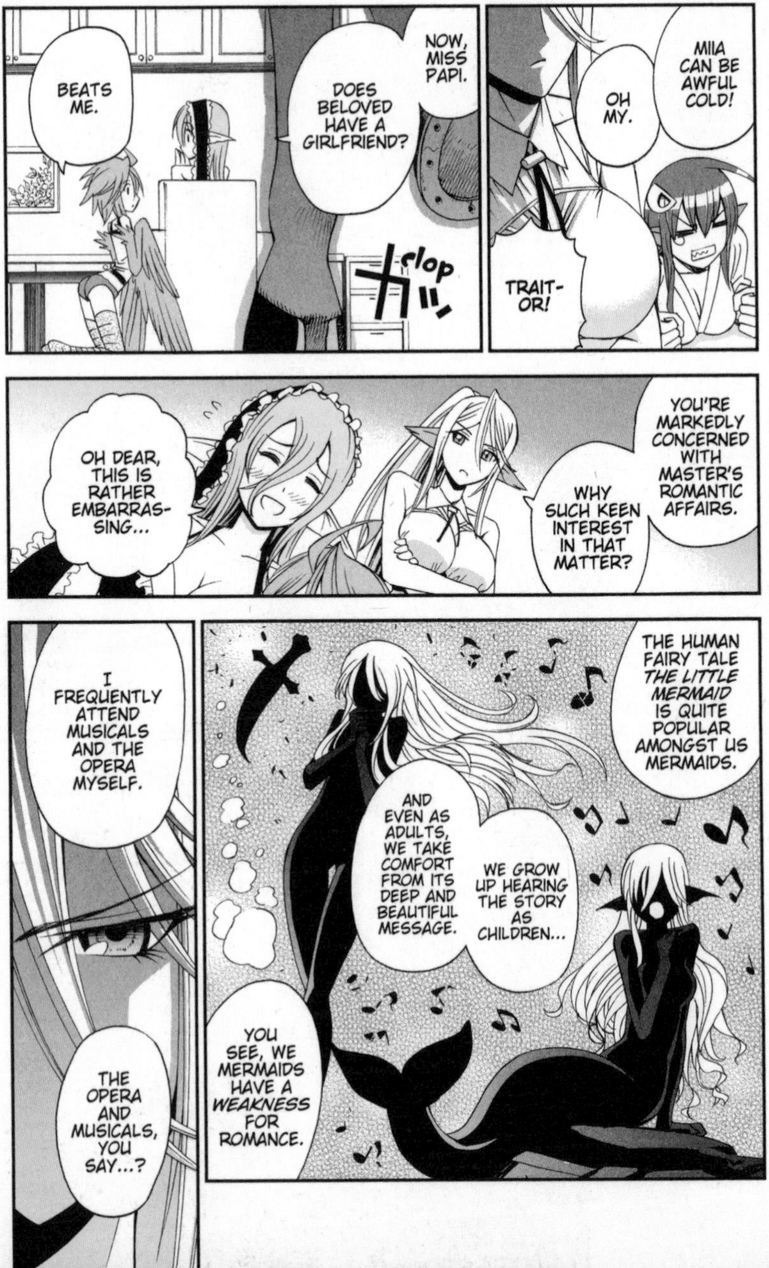
MIIA CAN BE AWFUL COLD!
OH MY.
TRAITOR!
NOW, MISS PAPI.
DOES BELOVED HAVE A GIRLFRIEND?
clop
BEATS ME.
YOU'RE MARKEDLY CONCERNED WITH MASTER'S ROMANTIC AFFAIRS.
WHY SUCH KEEN INTEREST IN THAT MATTER?
OH DEAR, THIS IS RATHER EMBARRAS-SING...
THE HUMAN FAIRY TALE *THE LITTLE MERMAID* IS QUITE POPULAR AMONGST US MERMAIDS.
WE GROW UP HEARING THE STORY AS CHILDREN...
AND EVEN AS ADULTS, WE TAKE COMFORT FROM ITS DEEP AND BEAUTIFUL MESSAGE.
YOU SEE, WE MERMAIDS HAVE A *WEAKNESS* FOR ROMANCE.
I FREQUENTLY ATTEND MUSICALS AND THE OPERA MYSELF.
THE OPERA AND MUSICALS, YOU SAY...?

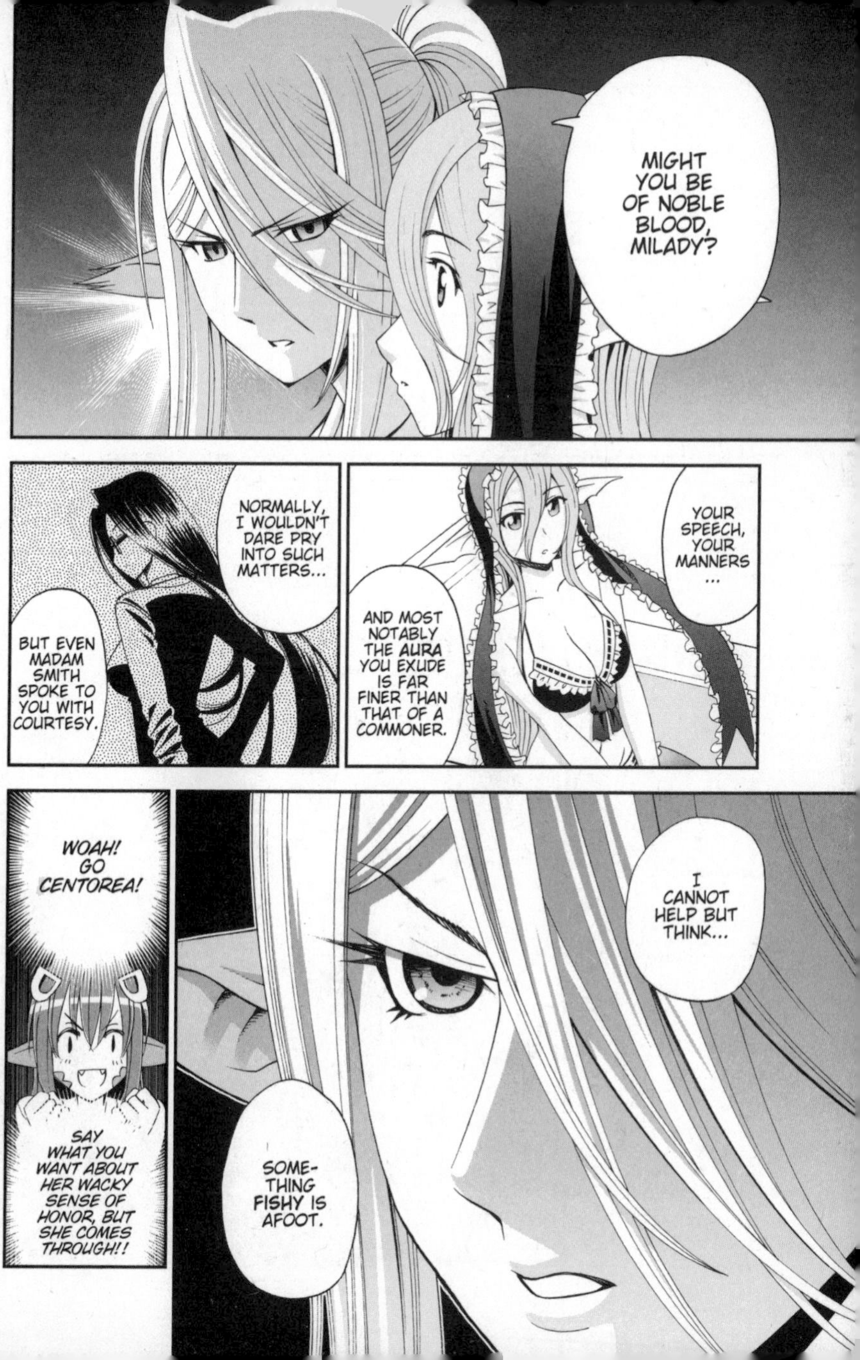
MIGHT YOU BE OF NOBLE BLOOD, MILADY?
YOUR SPEECH, YOUR MANNERS ...
AND MOST NOTABLY THE AURA YOU EXUDE IS FAR FINER THAN THAT OF A COMMONER.
NORMALLY, I WOULDN'T DARE PRY INTO SUCH MATTERS...
BUT EVEN MADAM SMITH SPOKE TO YOU WITH COURTESY.
I CANNOT HELP BUT THINK...
SOME-THING FISHY IS AFOOT.
WOAH! GO CENTOREA!
SAY WHAT YOU WANT ABOUT HER WACKY SENSE OF HONOR, BUT SHE COMES THROUGH!!

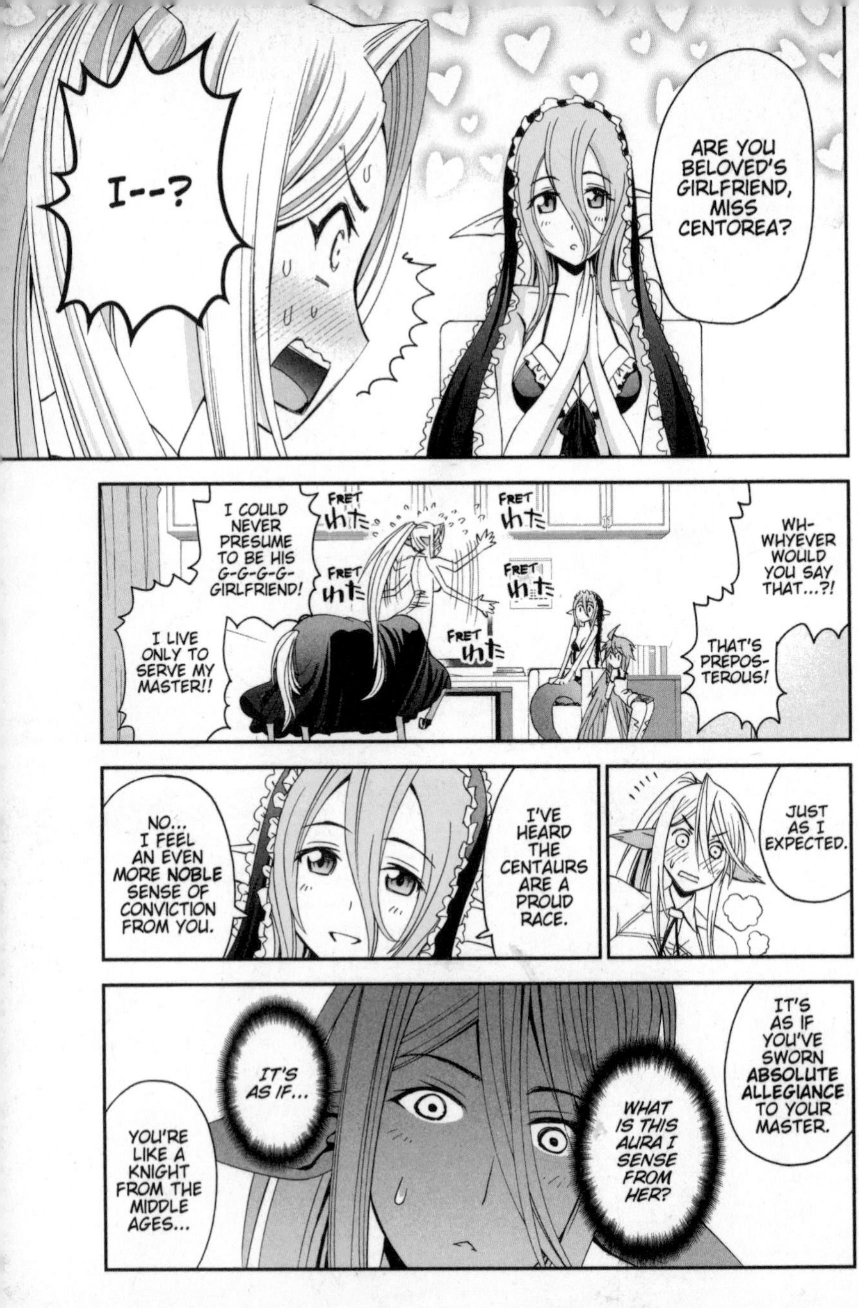
ARE YOU BELOVED'S GIRLFRIEND, MISS CENTOREA?
I--?
WH-WHYEVER WOULD YOU SAY THAT...?!
THAT'S PREPOSTEROUS!
FRET
FRET
FRET
FRET
I COULD NEVER PRESUME TO BE HIS G-G-G-G-GIRLFRIEND!
I LIVE ONLY TO SERVE MY MASTER!!
JUST AS I EXPECTED.
I'VE HEARD THE CENTAURS ARE A PROUD RACE.
NO... I FEEL AN EVEN MORE NOBLE SENSE OF CONVICTION FROM YOU.
IT'S AS IF YOU'VE SWORN ABSOLUTE ALLEGIANCE TO YOUR MASTER.
WHAT IS THIS AURA I SENSE FROM HER?
IT'S AS IF...
YOU'RE LIKE A KNIGHT FROM THE MIDDLE AGES...

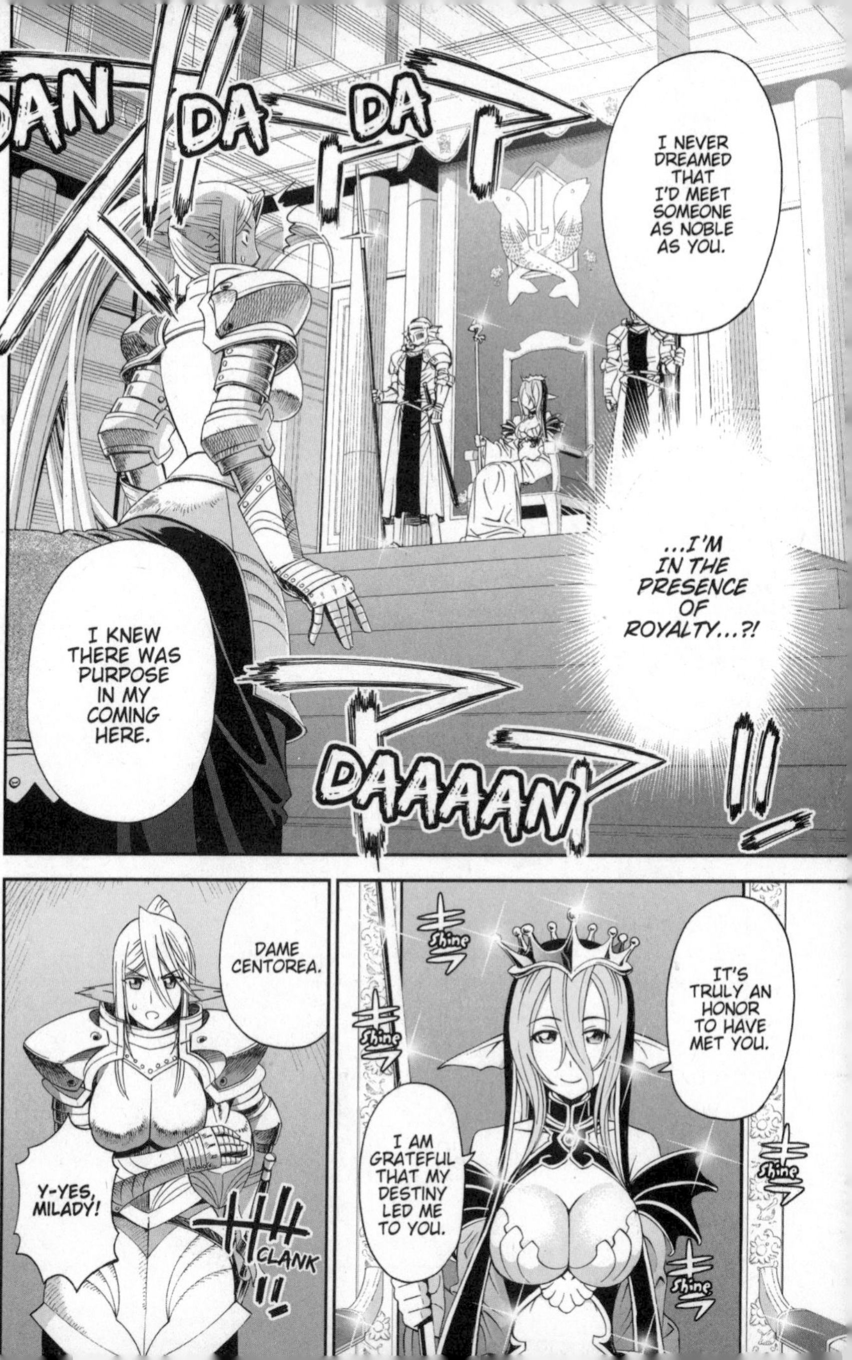
I NEVER DREAMED THAT I'D MEET SOMEONE AS NOBLE AS YOU.
DAN DA DA
...I'M IN THE PRESENCE OF ROYALTY...?!
I KNEW THERE WAS PURPOSE IN MY COMING HERE.
DAAAAN!!
IT'S TRULY AN HONOR TO HAVE MET YOU.
Shine
Shine
I AM GRATEFUL THAT MY DESTINY LED ME TO YOU.
Shine
Shine
DAME CENTOREA.
Y-YES, MILADY!
CLANK!!

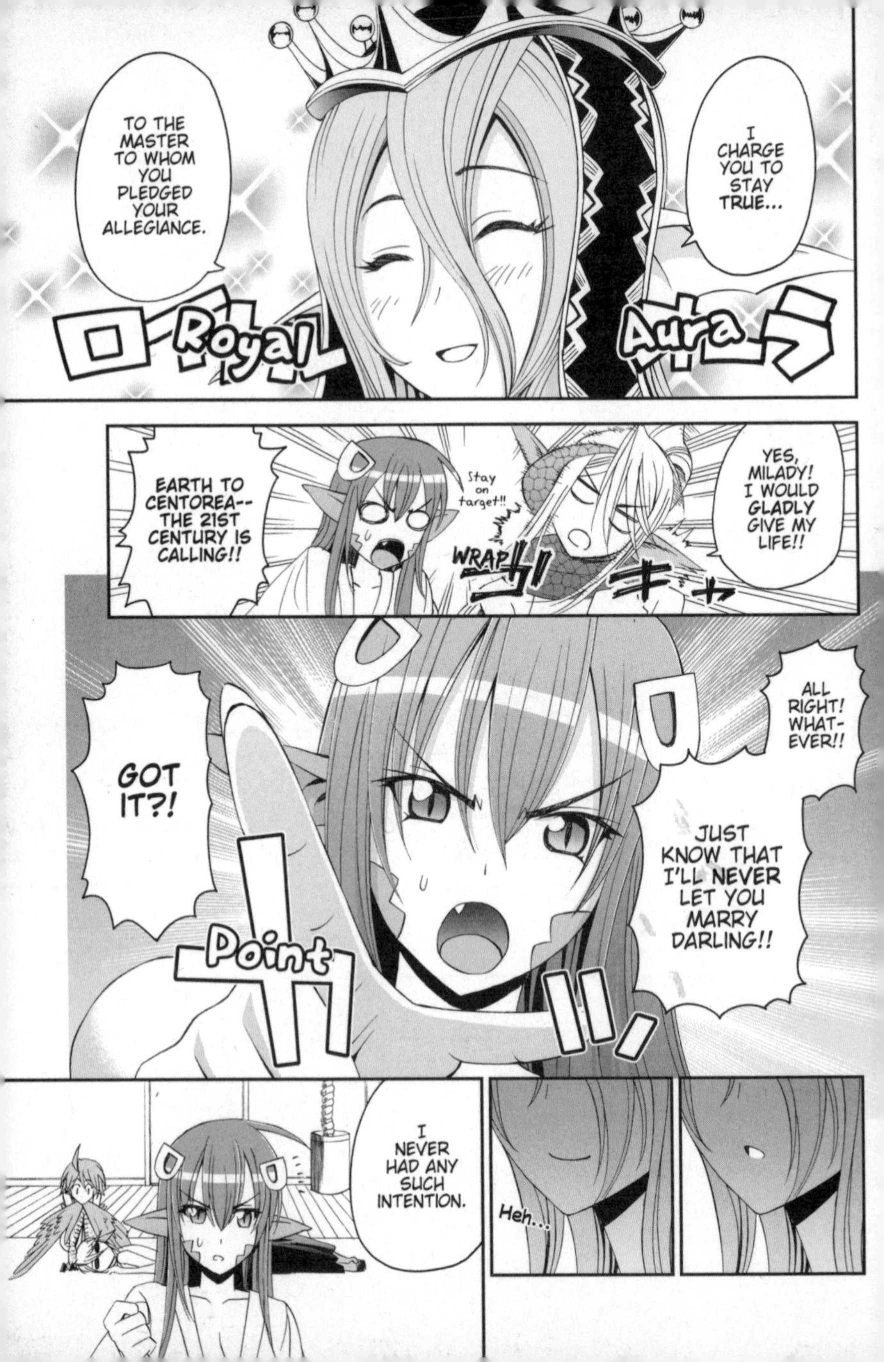
I CHARGE YOU TO STAY TRUE...
TO THE MASTER TO WHOM YOU PLEDGED YOUR ALLEGIANCE.
Royal Aura
YES, MILADY! I WOULD GLADLY GIVE MY LIFE!!
Stay on target!!
WRAP
EARTH TO CENTOREA-- THE 21ST CENTURY IS CALLING!!
ALL RIGHT! WHATEVER!!
JUST KNOW THAT I'LL NEVER LET YOU MARRY DARLING!!
GOT IT?!
Point
Heh...
I NEVER HAD ANY SUCH INTENTION.

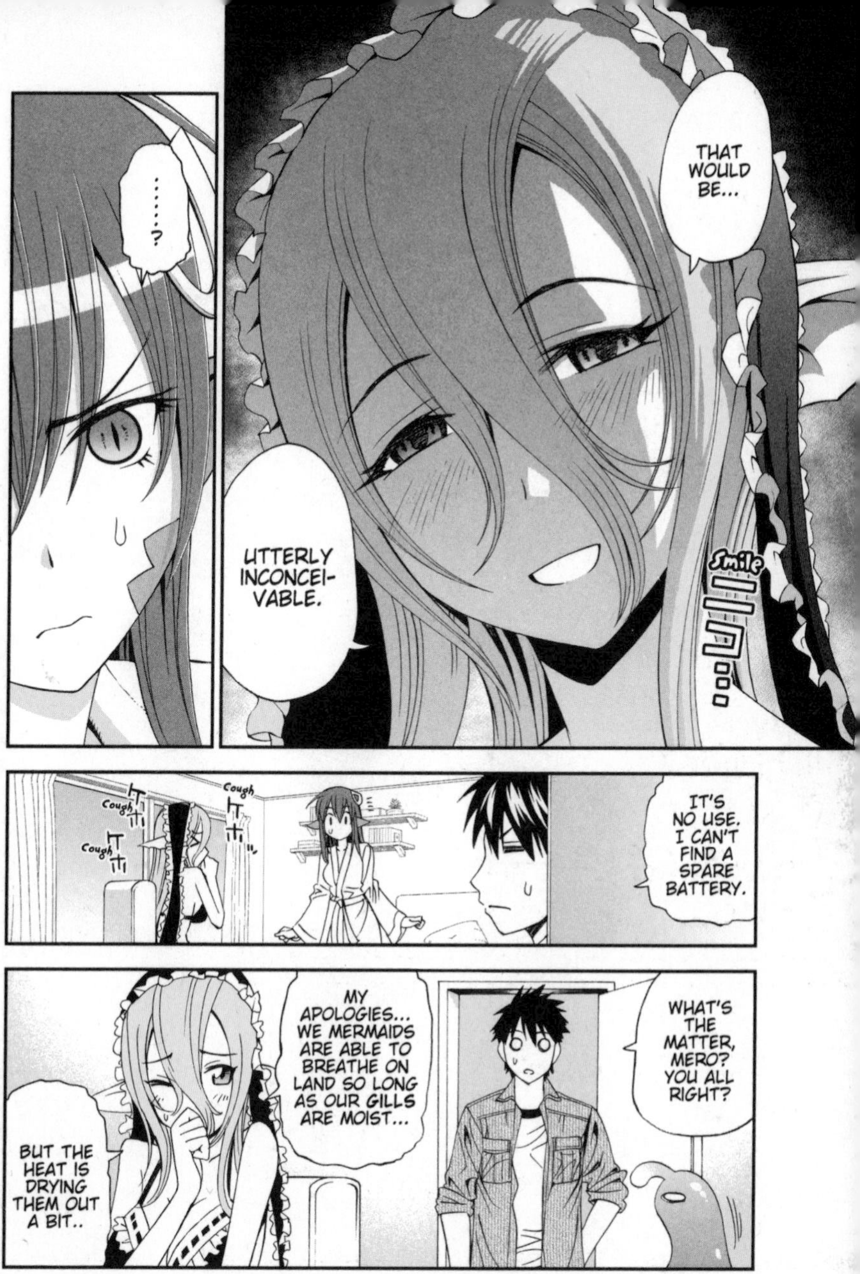
THAT WOULD BE...
UTTERLY INCONCEIVABLE.
Smile
ニコ...
......?
IT'S NO USE. I CAN'T FIND A SPARE BATTERY.
Cough
Cough
Cough
WHAT'S THE MATTER, MERO? YOU ALL RIGHT?
MY APOLOGIES... WE MERMAIDS ARE ABLE TO BREATHE ON LAND SO LONG AS OUR GILLS ARE MOIST...
BUT THE HEAT IS DRYING THEM OUT A BIT..

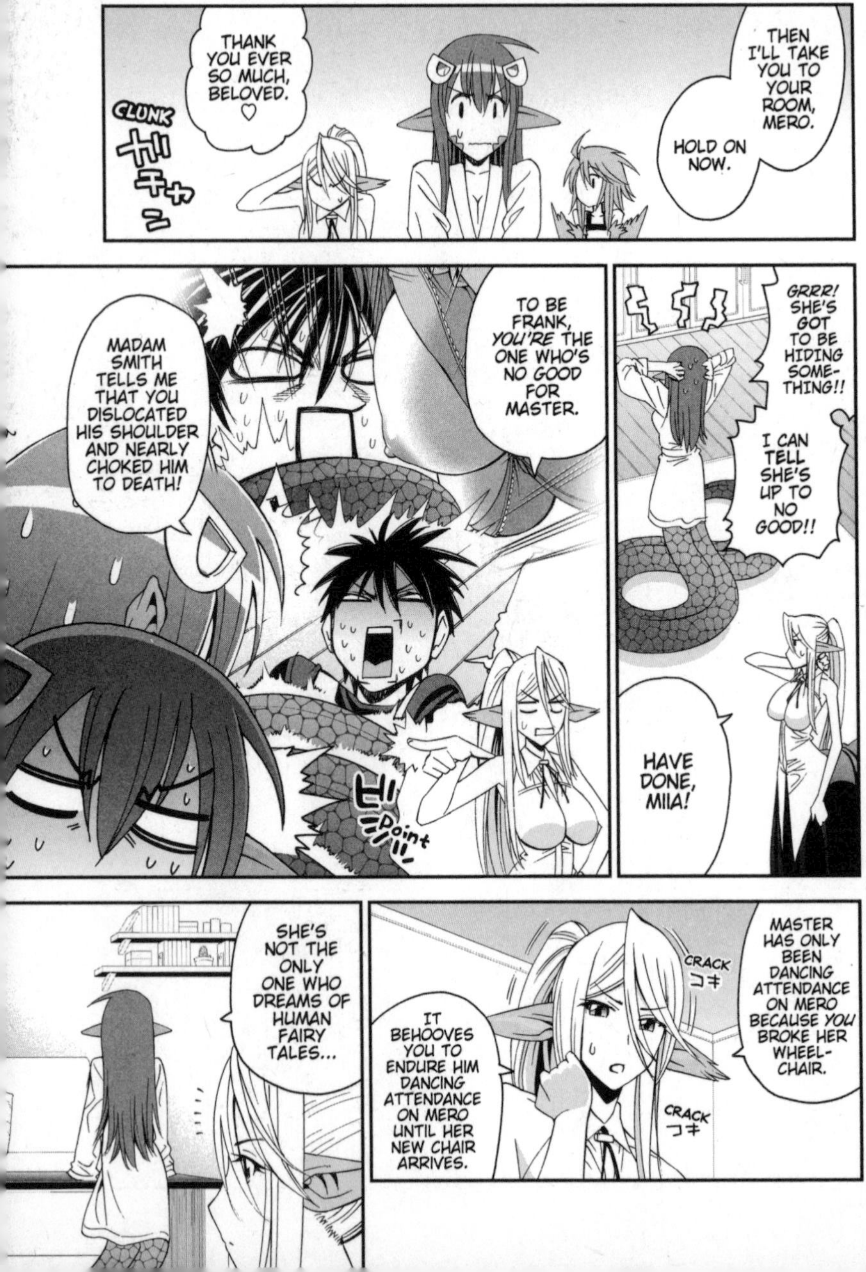
THEN I'LL TAKE YOU TO YOUR ROOM, MERO.
HOLD ON NOW.
THANK YOU EVER SO MUCH, BELOVED. ♡
CLUNK
GRRR! SHE'S GOT TO BE HIDING SOME-THING!!
I CAN TELL SHE'S UP TO NO GOOD!!
HAVE DONE, MIIA!
TO BE FRANK, YOU'RE THE ONE WHO'S NO GOOD FOR MASTER.
MADAM SMITH TELLS ME THAT YOU DISLOCATED HIS SHOULDER AND NEARLY CHOKED HIM TO DEATH!
Point
MASTER HAS ONLY BEEN DANCING ATTENDANCE ON MERO BECAUSE YOU BROKE HER WHEEL-CHAIR.
CRACK
IT BEHOOVES YOU TO ENDURE HIM DANCING ATTENDANCE ON MERO UNTIL HER NEW CHAIR ARRIVES.
CRACK
SHE'S NOT THE ONLY ONE WHO DREAMS OF HUMAN FAIRY TALES...

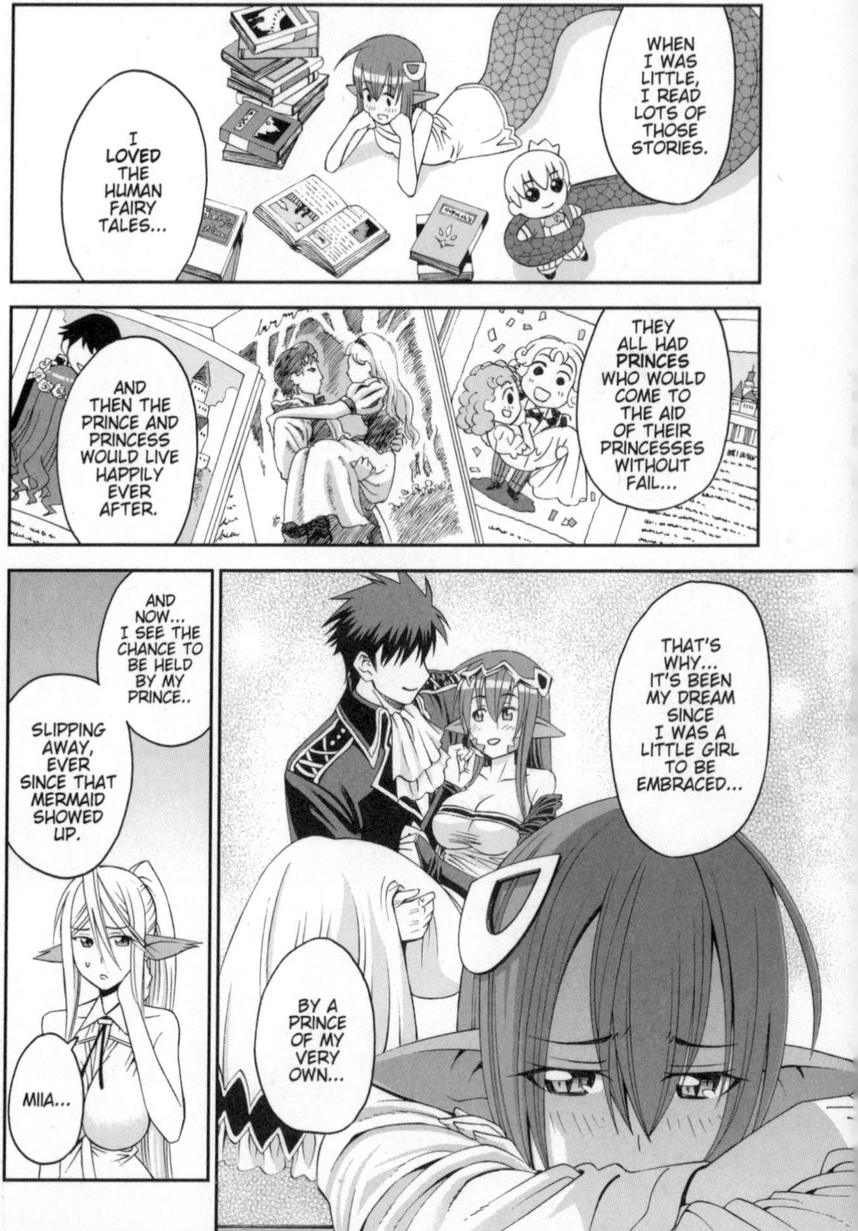

WHEN I WAS LITTLE, I READ LOTS OF THOSE STORIES.
I LOVED THE HUMAN FAIRY TALES...
THEY ALL HAD PRINCES WHO WOULD COME TO THE AID OF THEIR PRINCESSES WITHOUT FAIL...
AND THEN THE PRINCE AND PRINCESS WOULD LIVE HAPPILY EVER AFTER.
THAT'S WHY... IT'S BEEN MY DREAM SINCE I WAS A LITTLE GIRL TO BE EMBRACED...
BY A PRINCE OF MY VERY OWN...
AND NOW... I SEE THE CHANCE TO BE HELD BY MY PRINCE..
SLIPPING AWAY, EVER SINCE THAT MERMAID SHOWED UP.
MIIA...

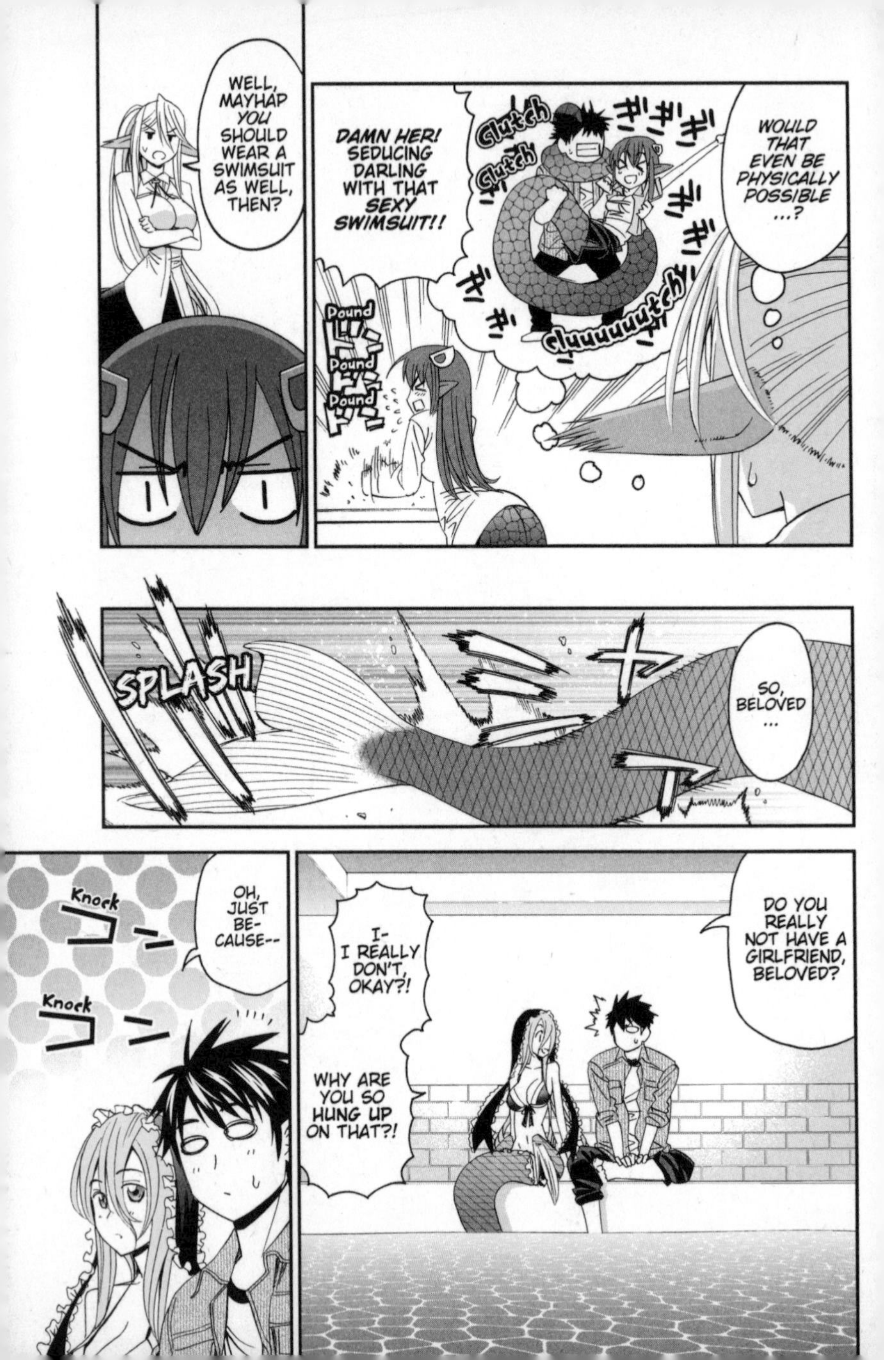
WOULD THAT EVEN BE PHYSICALLY POSSIBLE ...?
Clutch
Clutch
Cluuuuuutch
DAMN HER! SEDUCING DARLING WITH THAT SEXY SWIMSUIT!!
Pound
Pound
Pound
WELL, MAYHAP YOU SHOULD WEAR A SWIMSUIT AS WELL, THEN?
SPLASH
SO, BELOVED ...
DO YOU REALLY NOT HAVE A GIRLFRIEND, BELOVED?
I- I REALLY DON'T, OKAY?!
WHY ARE YOU SO HUNG UP ON THAT?!
OH, JUST BE-CAUSE--
Knock
Knock

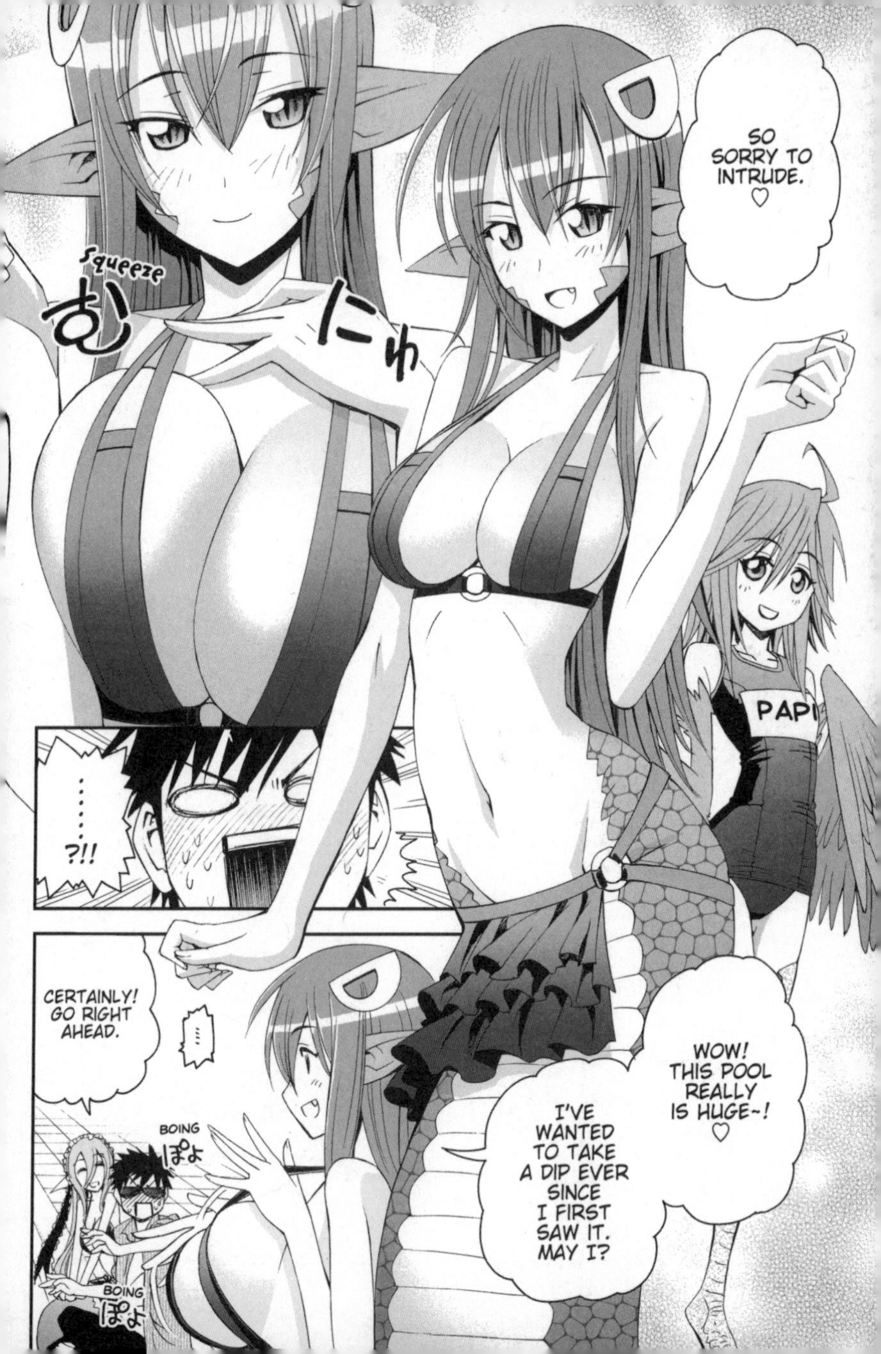

SO SORRY TO INTRUDE. ♡
SQUEEZE
むにゅ
......?!!
WOW! THIS POOL REALLY IS HUGE~! ♡
I'VE WANTED TO TAKE A DIP EVER SINCE I FIRST SAW IT. MAY I?
CERTAINLY! GO RIGHT AHEAD.
...
BOING
ぽよ
BOING
ぽよ

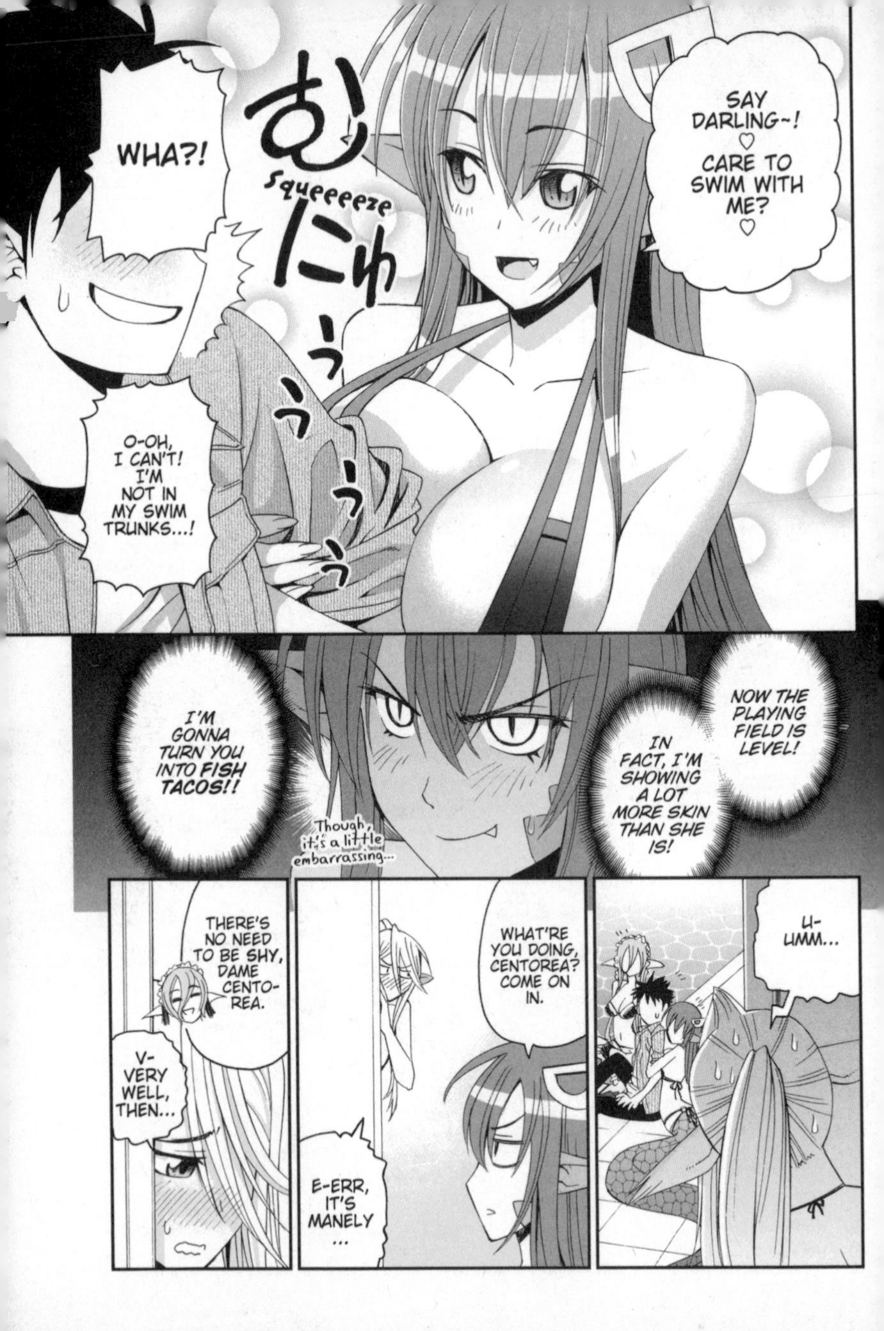
SAY DARLING~! ♡ CARE TO SWIM WITH ME? ♡
むにゅううう
Squeeeeeze
WHA?!
O-OH, I CAN'T! I'M NOT IN MY SWIM TRUNKS...!
NOW THE PLAYING FIELD IS LEVEL!
IN FACT, I'M SHOWING A LOT MORE SKIN THAN SHE IS!
I'M GONNA TURN YOU INTO FISH TACOS!!
Though, it's a little embarrassing...
U-UMM...
WHAT'RE YOU DOING, CENTOREA? COME ON IN.
E-ERR, IT'S MANELY ...
THERE'S NO NEED TO BE SHY, DAME CENTOREA.
V-VERY WELL, THEN...

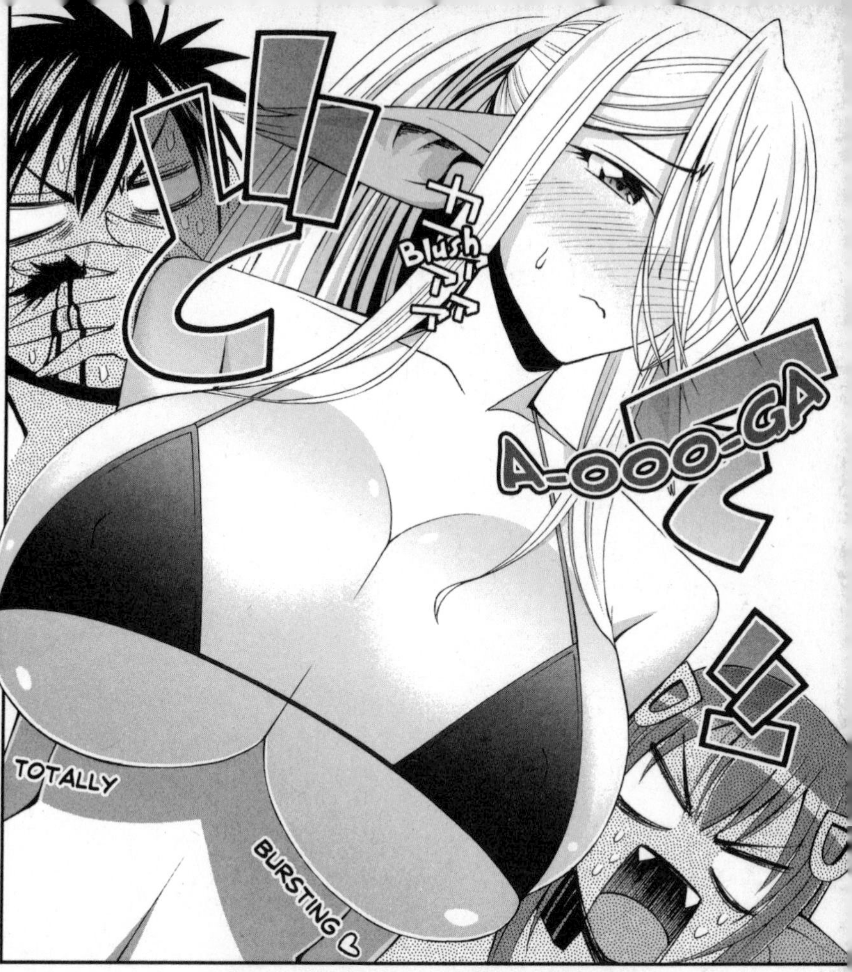
A-OOO-GA
Blush
TOTALLY
BURSTING ♡

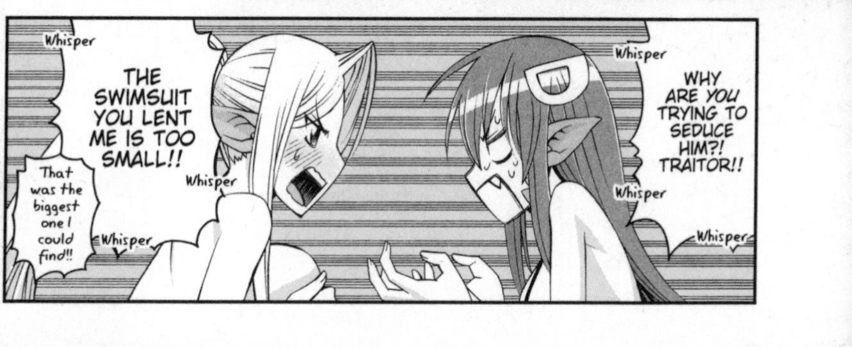
Whisper
WHY ARE YOU TRYING TO SEDUCE HIM?! TRAITOR!!
Whisper
Whisper
Whisper
THE SWIMSUIT YOU LENT ME IS TOO SMALL!!
Whisper
Whisper
That was the biggest one I could find!!

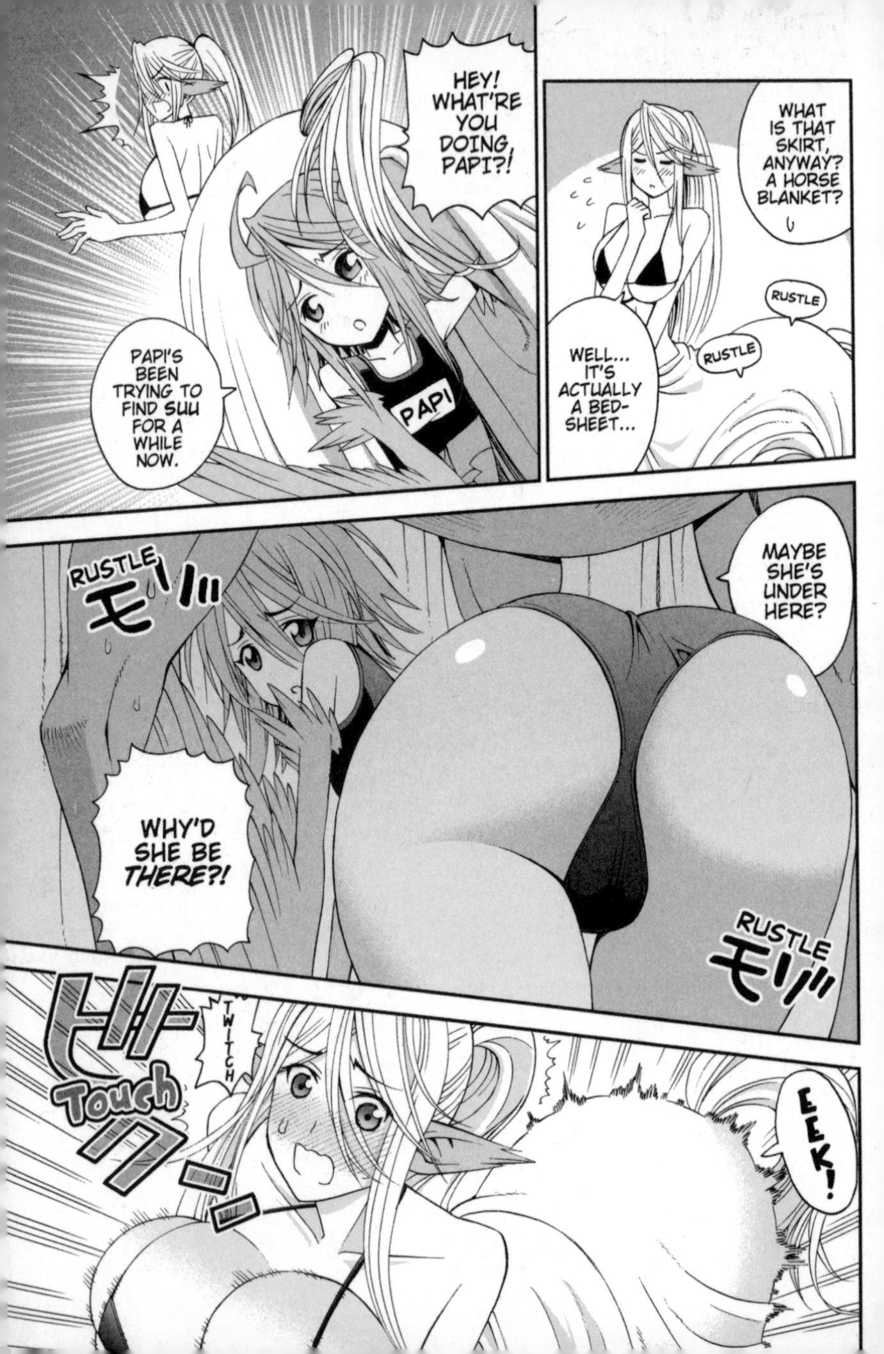
WHAT IS THAT SKIRT, ANYWAY? A HORSE BLANKET?
RUSTLE
RUSTLE
WELL... IT'S ACTUALLY A BED-SHEET...
HEY! WHAT'RE YOU DOING, PAPI?!
PAPI
PAPI'S BEEN TRYING TO FIND SUU FOR A WHILE NOW.
MAYBE SHE'S UNDER HERE?
RUSTLE
WHY'D SHE BE THERE?!
RUSTLE
EEK!
TWITCH
Touch

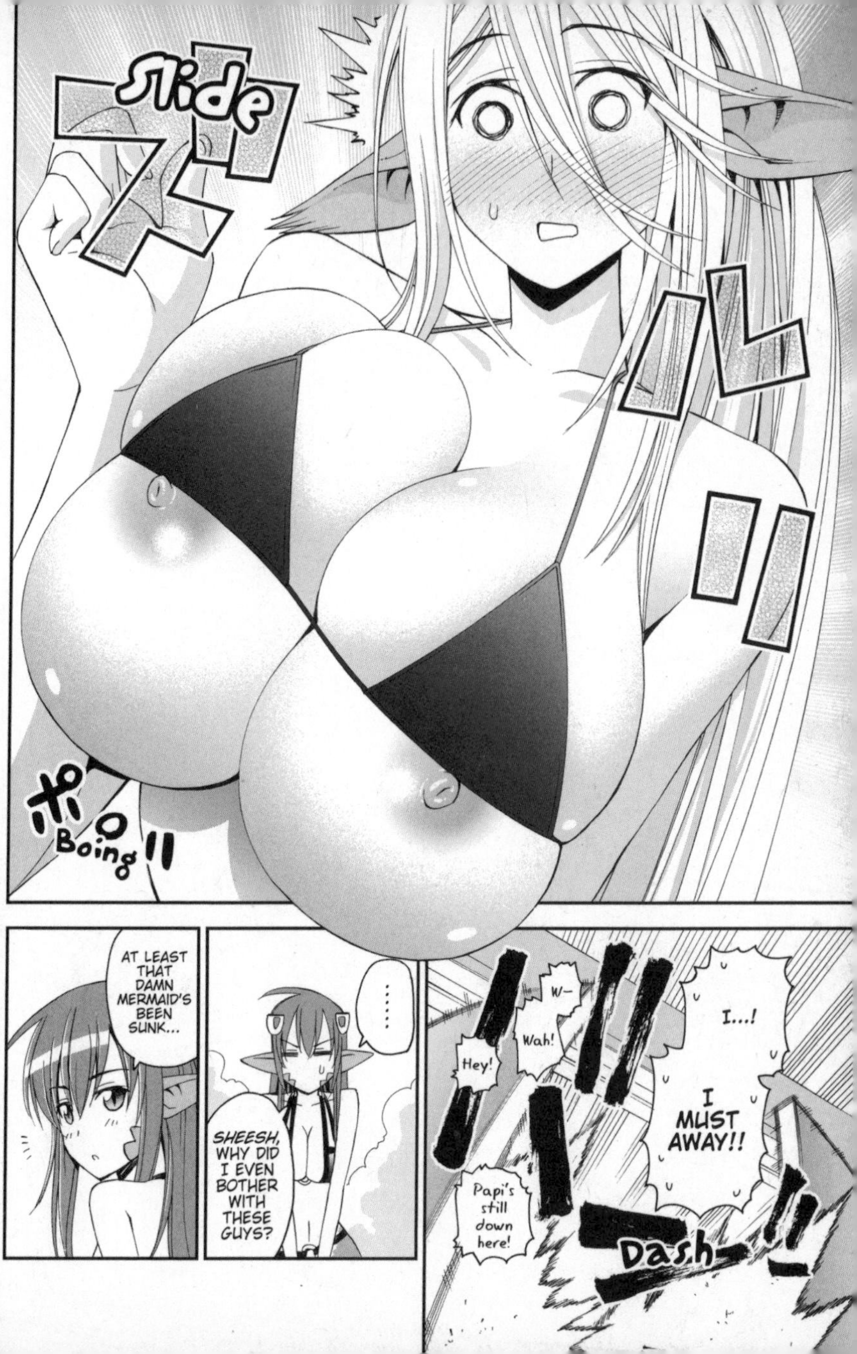
Slide
Boing!!
I...!
I MUST AWAY!!
W—
Wah!
Hey!
Papi's still down here!
Dash—!!
......
SHEESH, WHY DID I EVEN BOTHER WITH THESE GUYS?
AT LEAST THAT DAMN MERMAID'S BEEN SUNK...

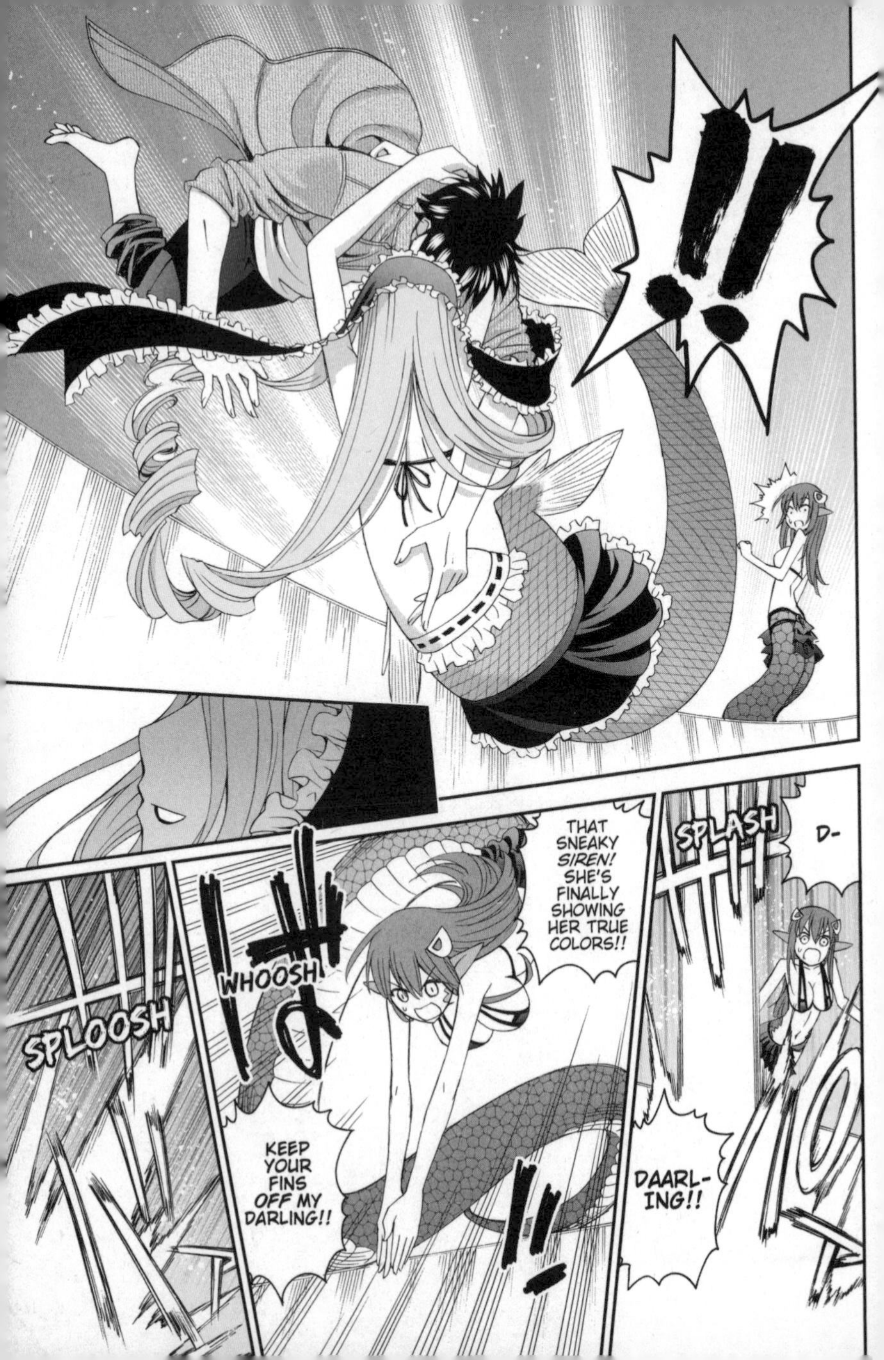
!!
SPLASH
D-
DAARLING!!
THAT SNEAKY SIREN! SHE'S FINALLY SHOWING HER TRUE COLORS!!
WHOOSH
KEEP YOUR FINS OFF MY DARLING!!
!!
SPLOOSH

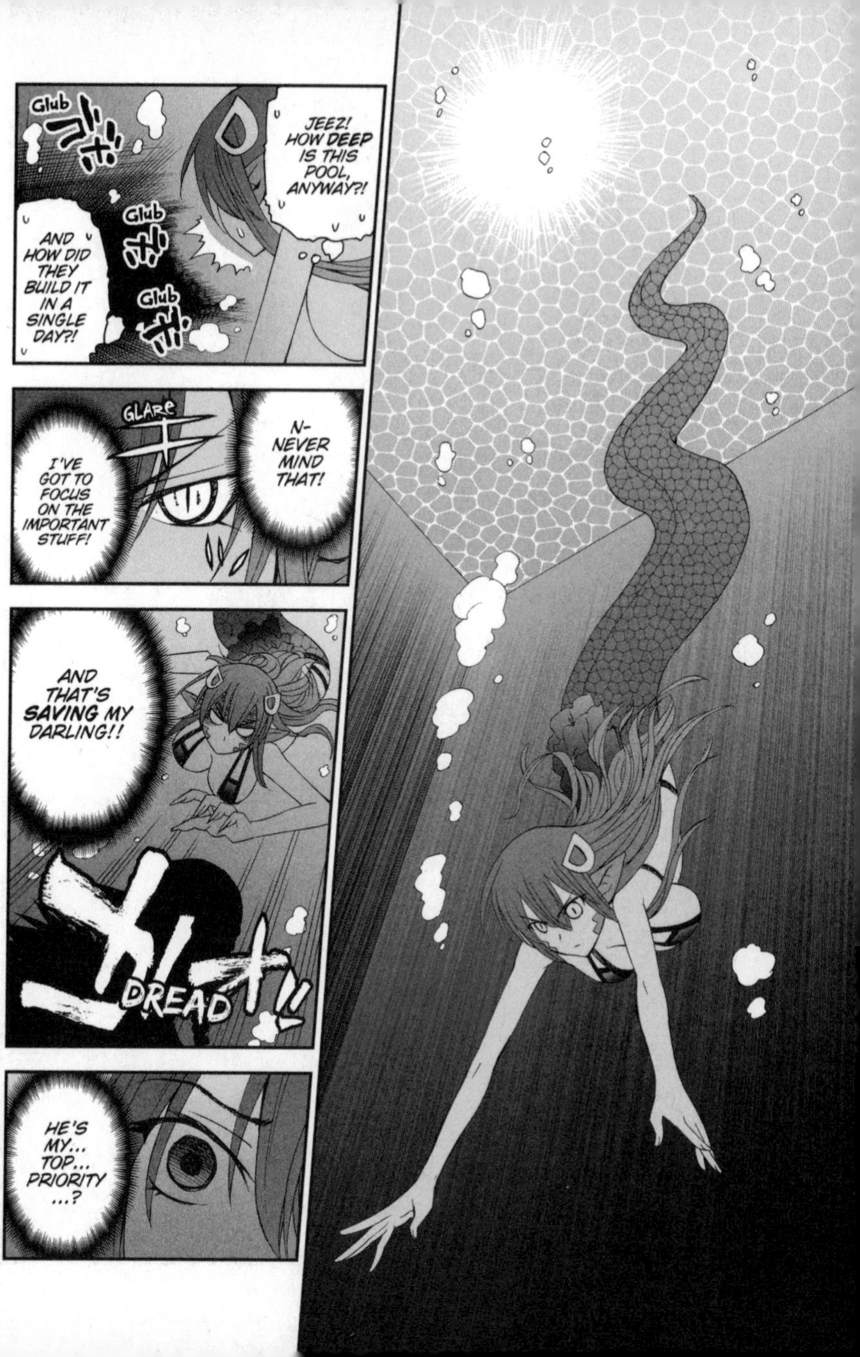
JEEZ! HOW DEEP IS THIS POOL, ANYWAY?!
Glub
Glub
Glub
AND HOW DID THEY BUILD IT IN A SINGLE DAY?!
N-NEVER MIND THAT!
GLARE
I'VE GOT TO FOCUS ON THE IMPORTANT STUFF!
AND THAT'S SAVING MY DARLING!!
DREAD
HE'S MY... TOP... PRIORITY ...?

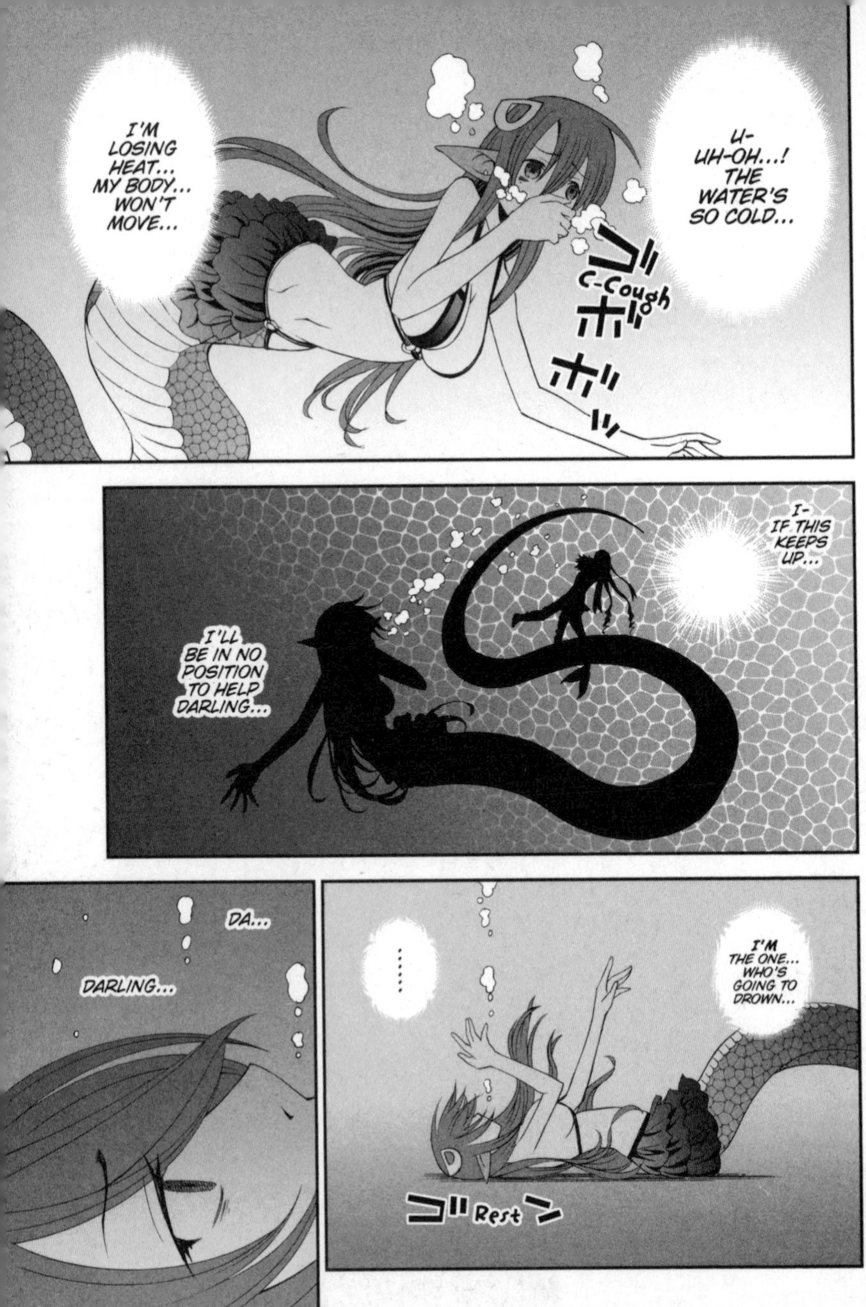
U-
UH-OH...! THE WATER'S SO COLD...
C-Cough
I'M LOSING HEAT... MY BODY... WON'T MOVE...
I- IF THIS KEEPS UP...
I'LL BE IN NO POSITION TO HELP DARLING...
I'M THE ONE... WHO'S GOING TO DROWN...
......
Rest
DA...
DARLING...

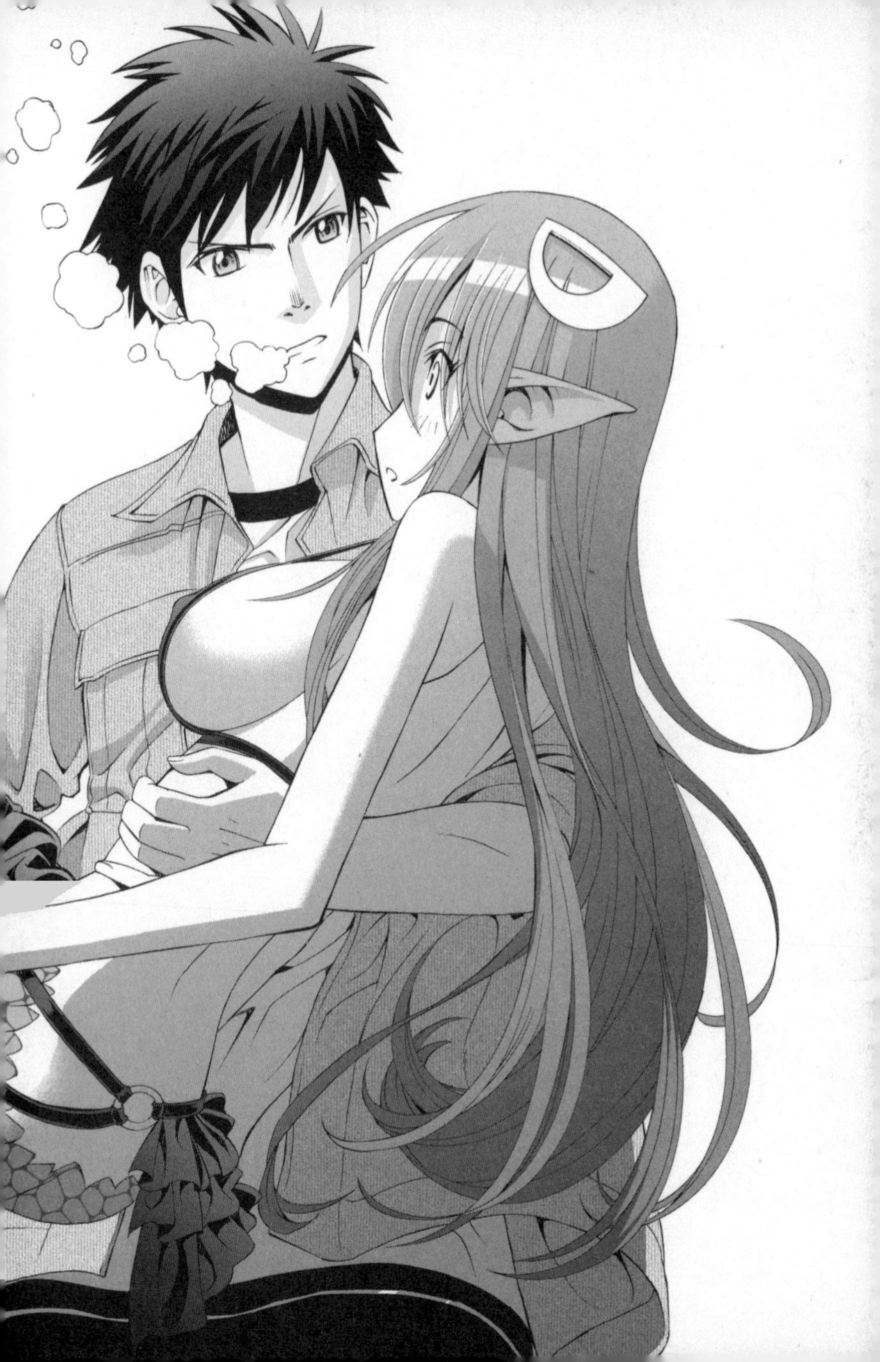

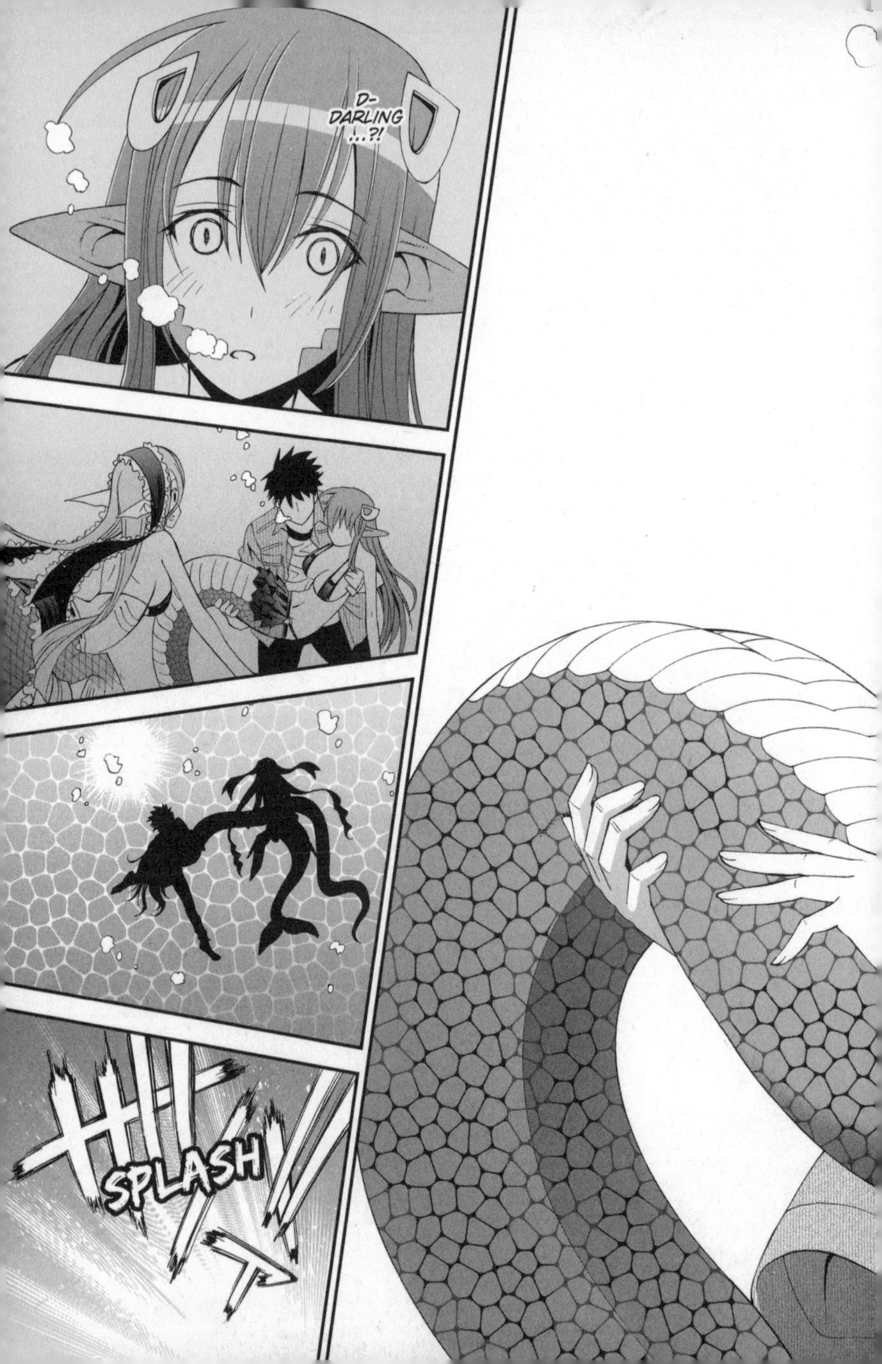
D-DARLING ...?!
SPLASH

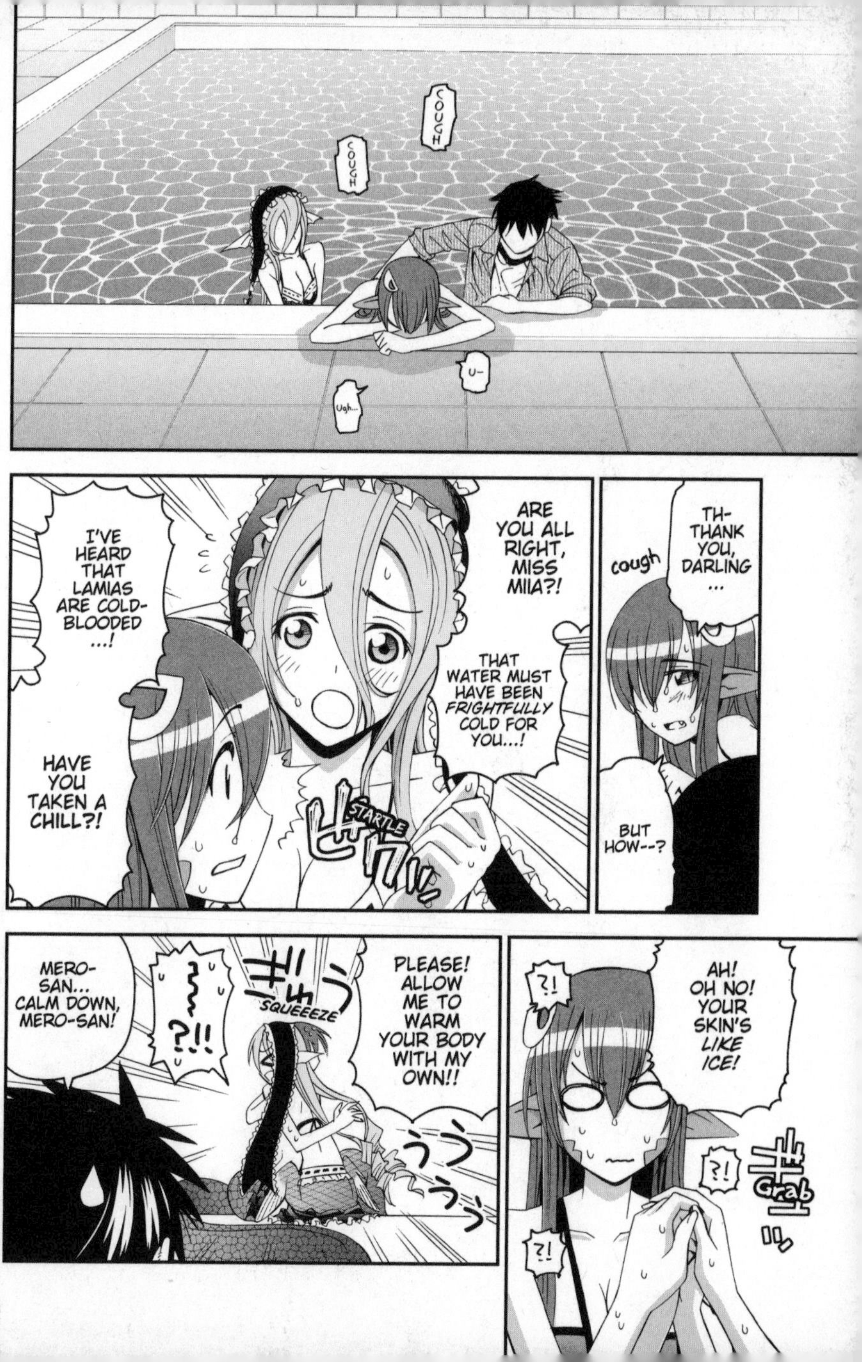
COUGH
COUGH
U-
Ugh...
TH-THANK YOU, DARLING...
cough
BUT HOW--?
ARE YOU ALL RIGHT, MISS MIIA?!
THAT WATER MUST HAVE BEEN *FRIGHTFULLY* COLD FOR YOU...!
I'VE HEARD THAT LAMIAS ARE COLD-BLOODED...!
STARTLE
HAVE YOU TAKEN A CHILL?!
?!
AH! OH NO! YOUR SKIN'S *LIKE* ICE!
?!
Grab
?!
PLEASE! ALLOW ME TO WARM YOUR BODY WITH MY OWN!!
SQUEEEEZE
~~?!!
MERO-SAN... CALM DOWN, MERO-SAN!

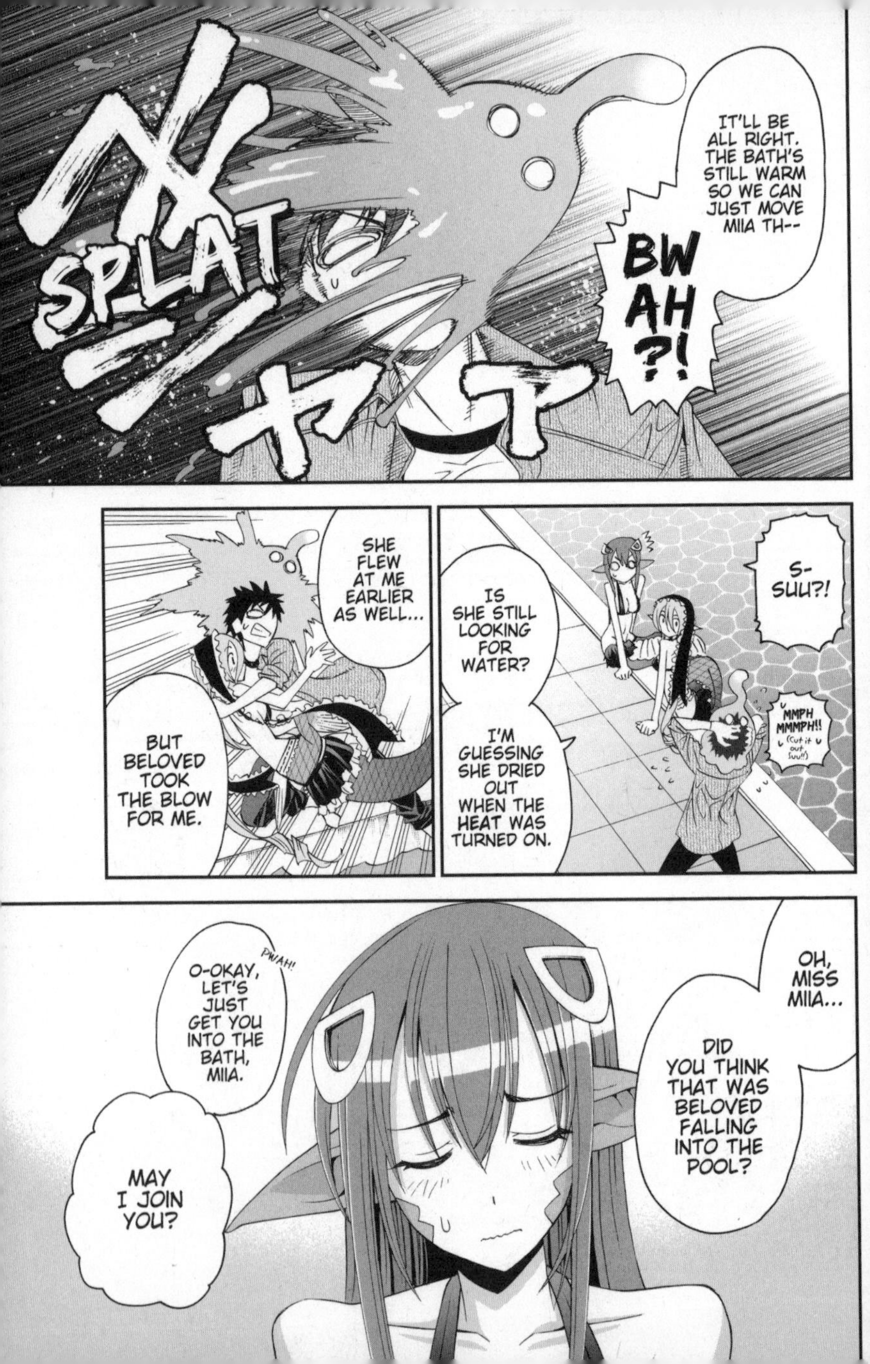
IT'LL BE ALL RIGHT. THE BATH'S STILL WARM SO WE CAN JUST MOVE MIIA TH--
BWAH?!
SPLAT
S-SUU?!
IS SHE STILL LOOKING FOR WATER?
I'M GUESSING SHE DRIED OUT WHEN THE HEAT WAS TURNED ON.
MMPH MMMPH!! (Cut it out, Suu!!)
SHE FLEW AT ME EARLIER AS WELL...
BUT BELOVED TOOK THE BLOW FOR ME.
OH, MISS MIIA...
DID YOU THINK THAT WAS BELOVED FALLING INTO THE POOL?
PWAH!
O-OKAY, LET'S JUST GET YOU INTO THE BATH, MIIA.
MAY I JOIN YOU?

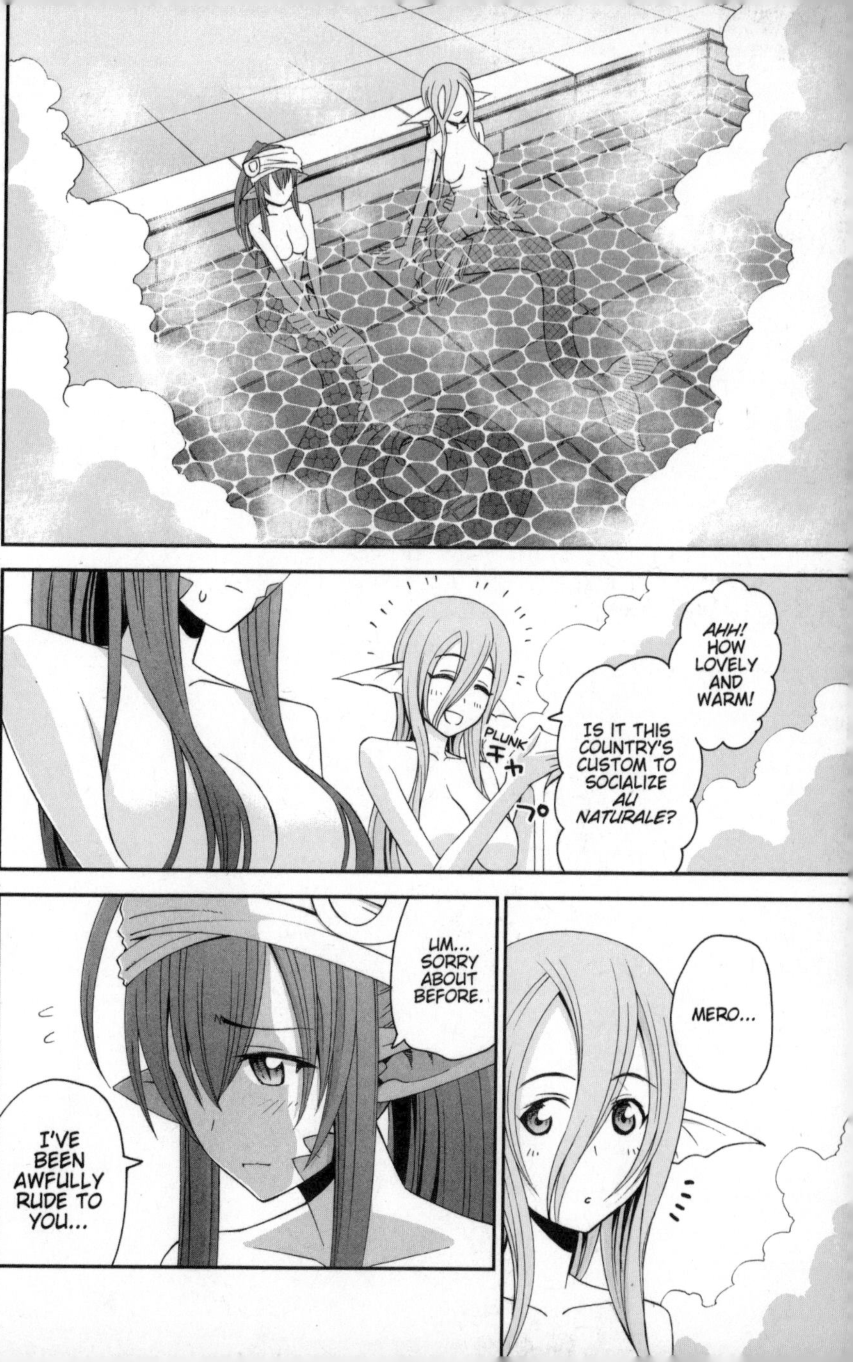
AHH! HOW LOVELY AND WARM!
IS IT THIS COUNTRY'S CUSTOM TO SOCIALIZE AU NATURALE?
PLUNK
MERO...
UM... SORRY ABOUT BEFORE.
I'VE BEEN AWFULLY RUDE TO YOU...

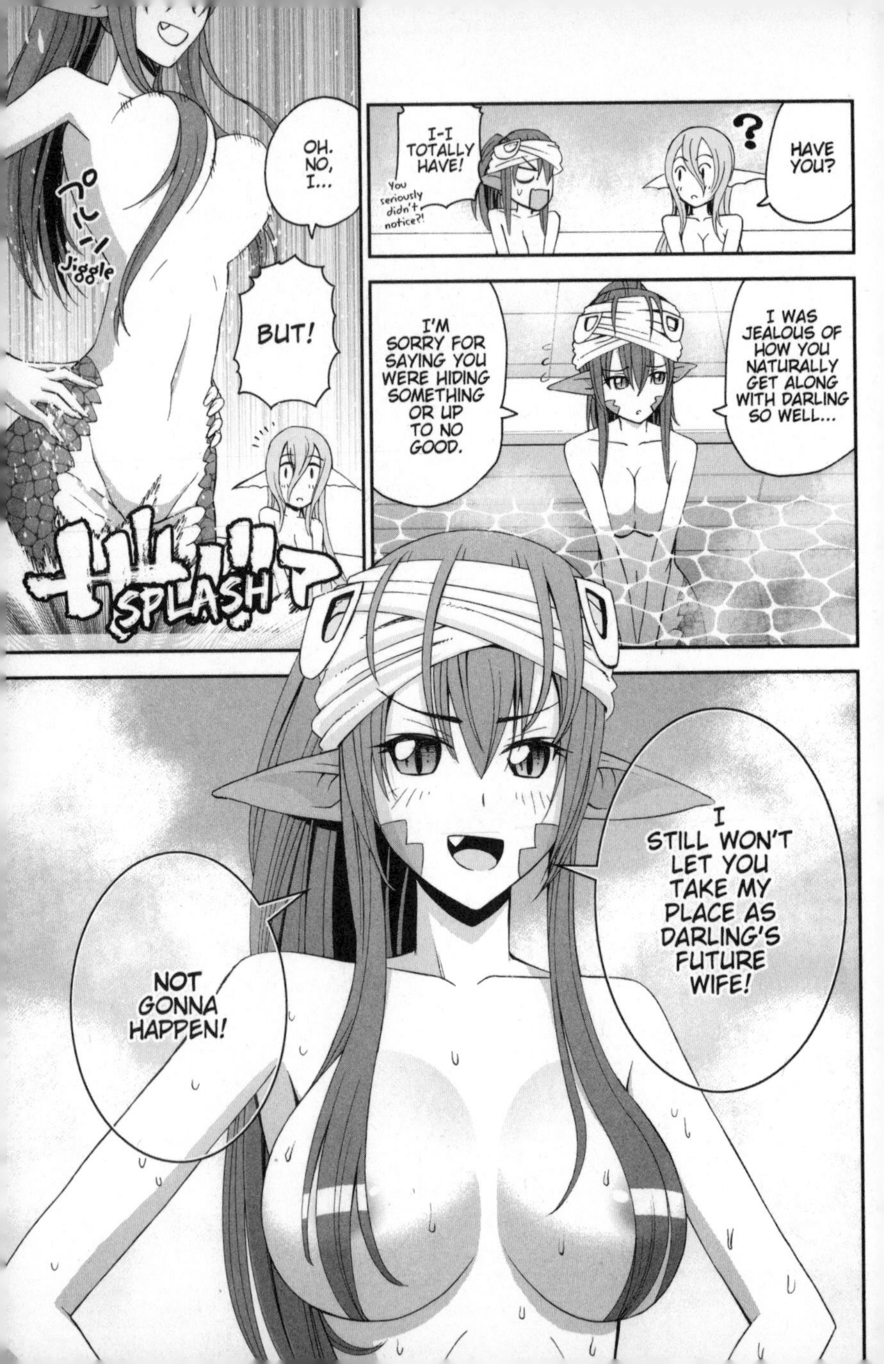
HAVE YOU?
I-I TOTALLY HAVE!
You seriously didn't notice?!
I WAS JEALOUS OF HOW YOU NATURALLY GET ALONG WITH DARLING SO WELL...
I'M SORRY FOR SAYING YOU WERE HIDING SOMETHING OR UP TO NO GOOD.
OH. NO, I...
jiggle
BUT!
SPLASH
I STILL WON'T LET YOU TAKE MY PLACE AS DARLING'S FUTURE WIFE!
NOT GONNA HAPPEN!

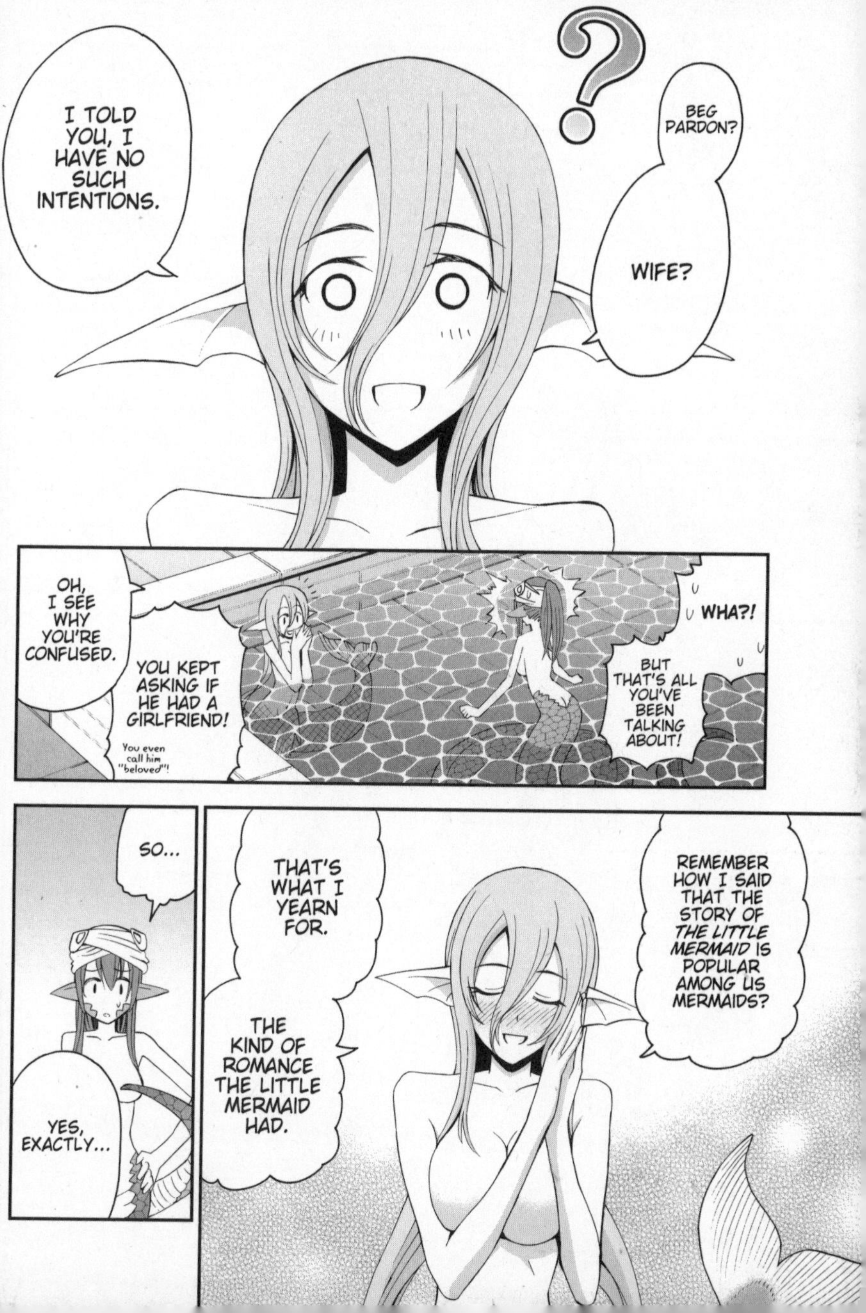
BEG PARDON?
WIFE?
I TOLD YOU, I HAVE NO SUCH INTENTIONS.
WHA?!
BUT THAT'S ALL YOU'VE BEEN TALKING ABOUT!
OH, I SEE WHY YOU'RE CONFUSED.
YOU KEPT ASKING IF HE HAD A GIRLFRIEND!
You even call him "beloved"!
REMEMBER HOW I SAID THAT THE STORY OF *THE LITTLE MERMAID* IS POPULAR AMONG US MERMAIDS?
THAT'S WHAT I YEARN FOR.
THE KIND OF ROMANCE THE LITTLE MERMAID HAD.
SO...
YES, EXACTLY...

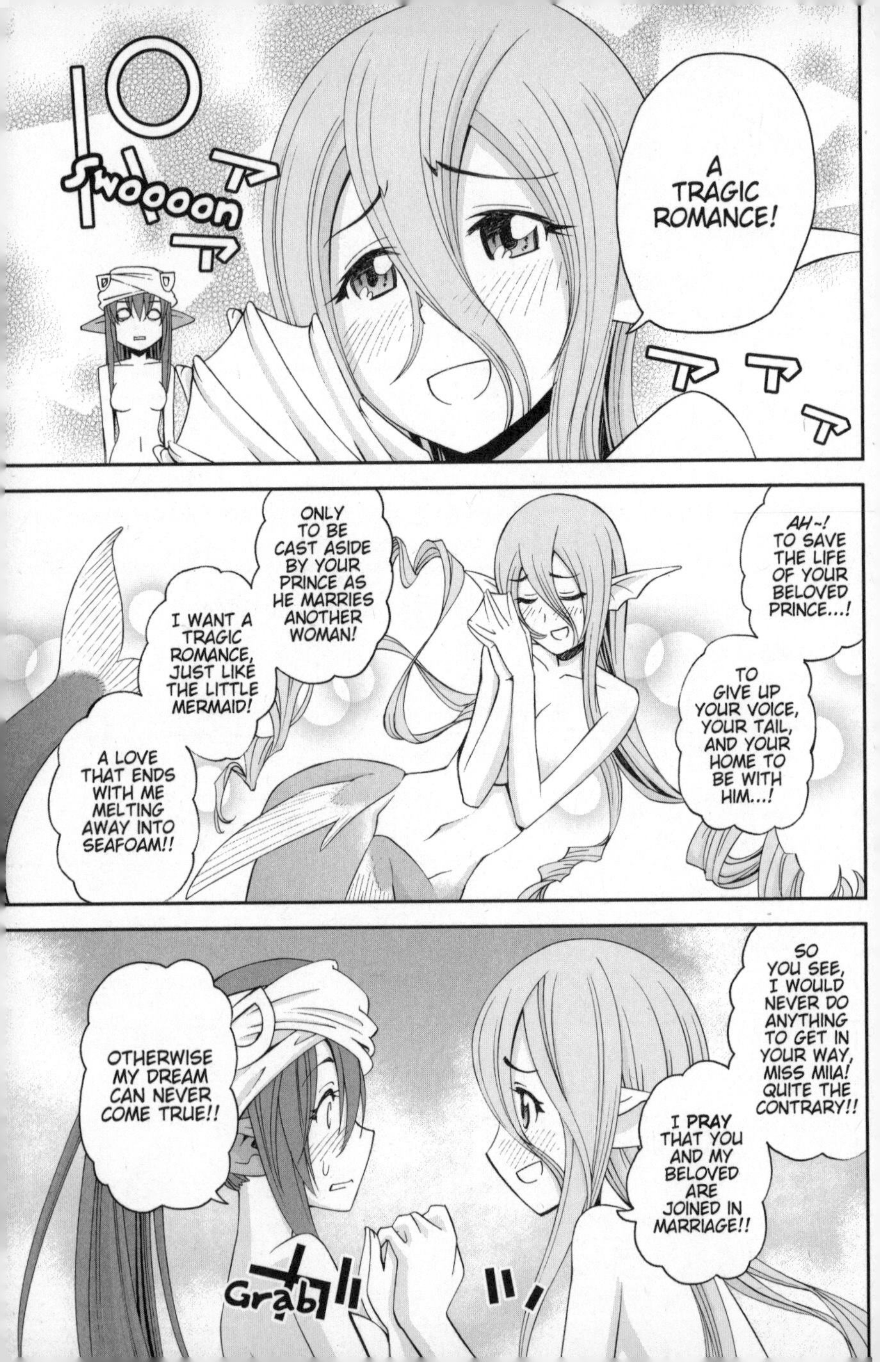
A TRAGIC ROMANCE!
swoooon
AH~! TO SAVE THE LIFE OF YOUR BELOVED PRINCE...!
TO GIVE UP YOUR VOICE, YOUR TAIL, AND YOUR HOME TO BE WITH HIM...!
ONLY TO BE CAST ASIDE BY YOUR PRINCE AS HE MARRIES ANOTHER WOMAN!
I WANT A TRAGIC ROMANCE, JUST LIKE THE LITTLE MERMAID!
A LOVE THAT ENDS WITH ME MELTING AWAY INTO SEAFOAM!!
SO YOU SEE, I WOULD NEVER DO ANYTHING TO GET IN YOUR WAY, MISS MIIA! QUITE THE CONTRARY!!
I PRAY THAT YOU AND MY BELOVED ARE JOINED IN MARRIAGE!!
OTHERWISE MY DREAM CAN NEVER COME TRUE!!
Grab

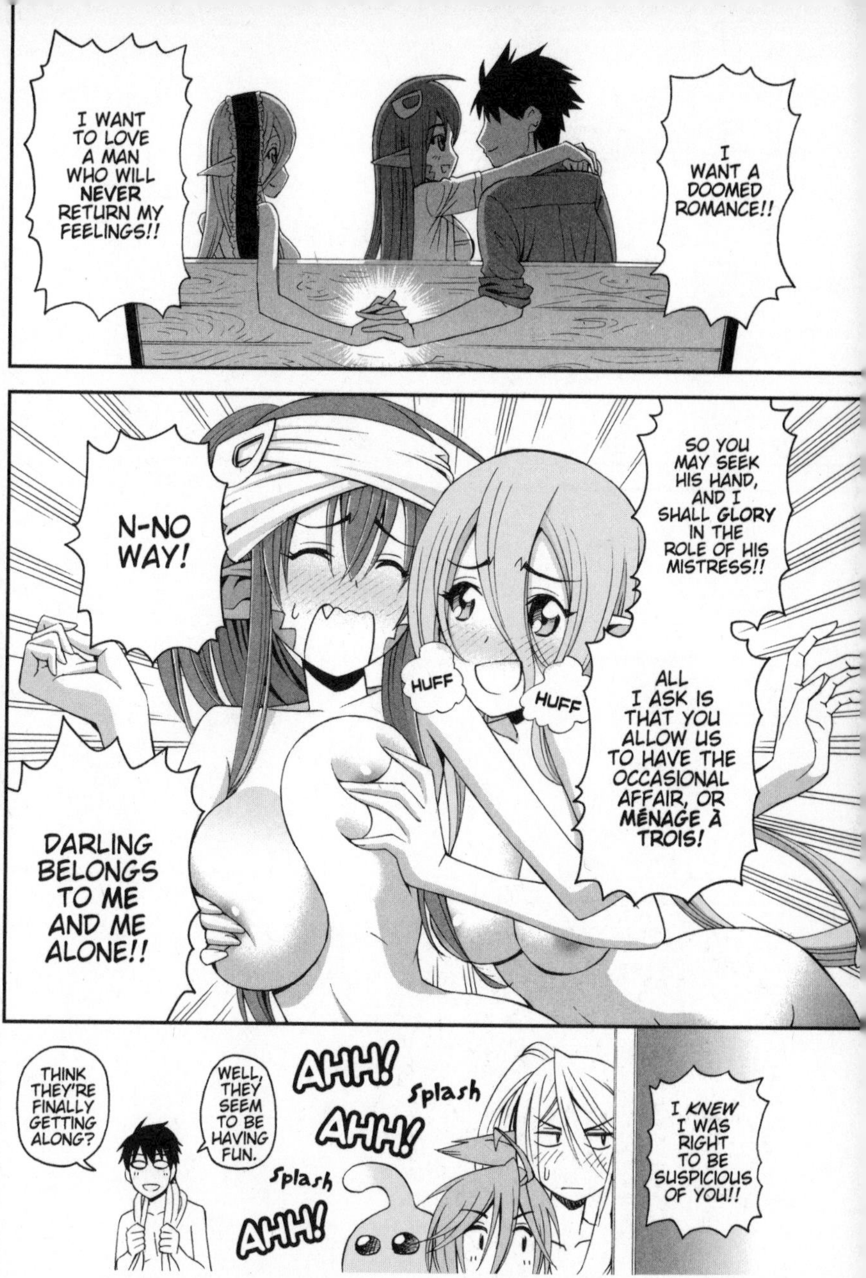
I WANT A DOOMED ROMANCE!!
I WANT TO LOVE A MAN WHO WILL NEVER RETURN MY FEELINGS!!
SO YOU MAY SEEK HIS HAND, AND I SHALL GLORY IN THE ROLE OF HIS MISTRESS!!
HUFF
HUFF
ALL I ASK IS THAT YOU ALLOW US TO HAVE THE OCCASIONAL AFFAIR, OR MÉNAGE À TROIS!
N-NO WAY!
DARLING BELONGS TO ME AND ME ALONE!!
I KNEW I WAS RIGHT TO BE SUSPICIOUS OF YOU!!
AHH!
Splash
AHH!
Splash
AHH!
THINK THEY'RE FINALLY GETTING ALONG?
WELL, THEY SEEM TO BE HAVING FUN.

Monster Musume

Everyday Life with Monster Girls

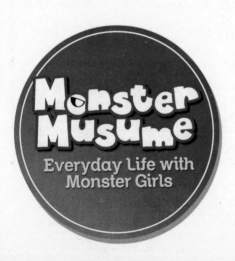

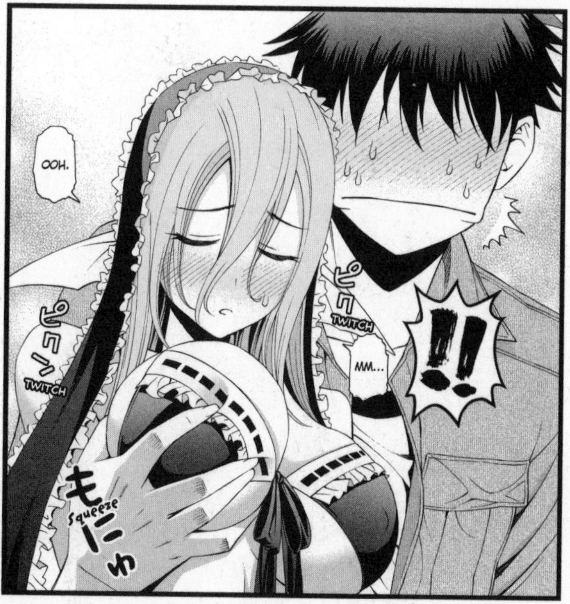
OOH.
!!
TWITCH
MM...
TWITCH
Squeeze

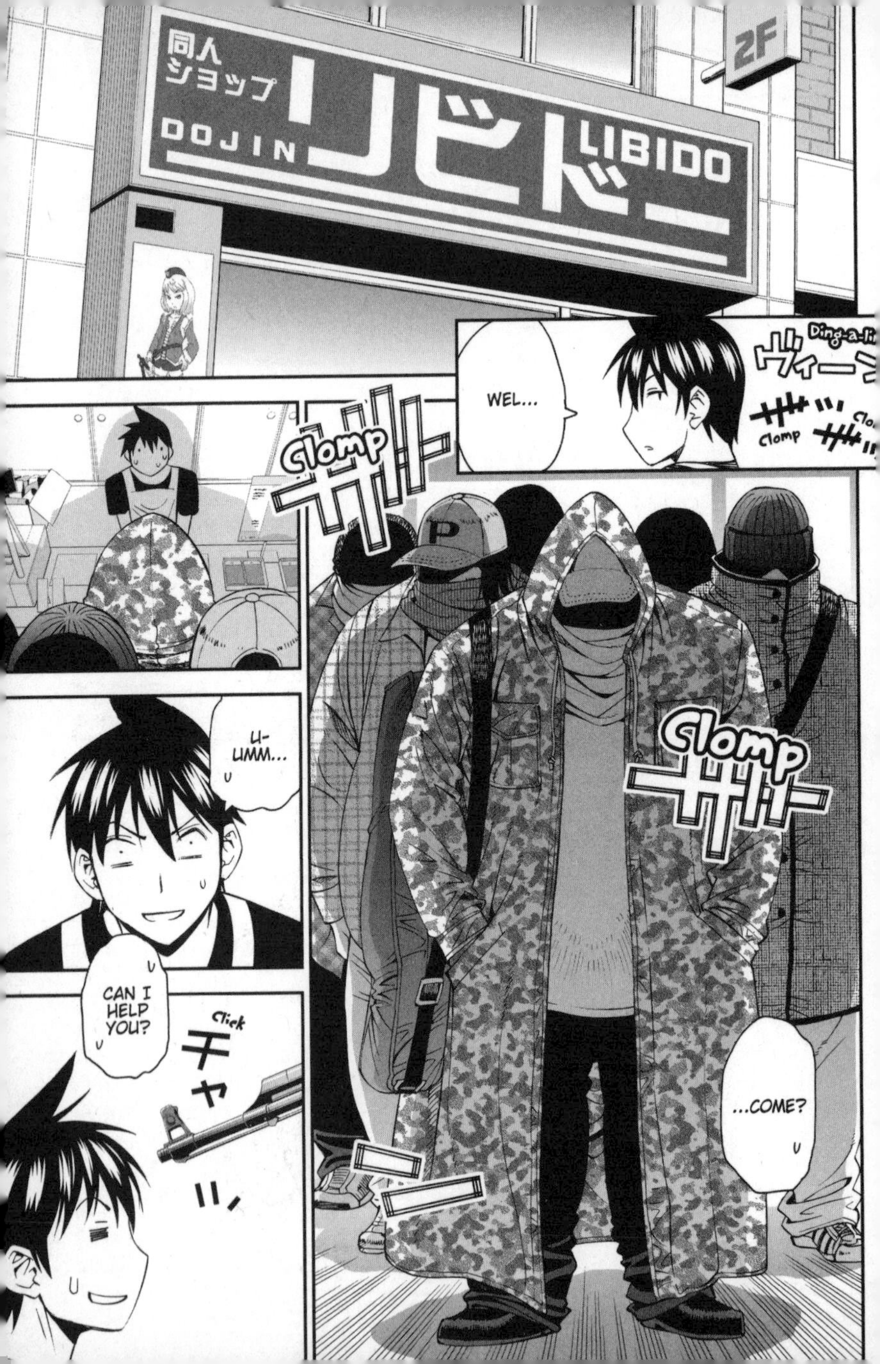
同人ショップ
DOJIN
リビドー
LIBIDO
2F
WEL...
Ding-a-li
ヴィーン
ザッ
Clomp
ザッ
Clo
Clomp
ザッ
Clomp
ザッ
...COME?
U-UMM...
CAN I HELP YOU?
Click
チャ

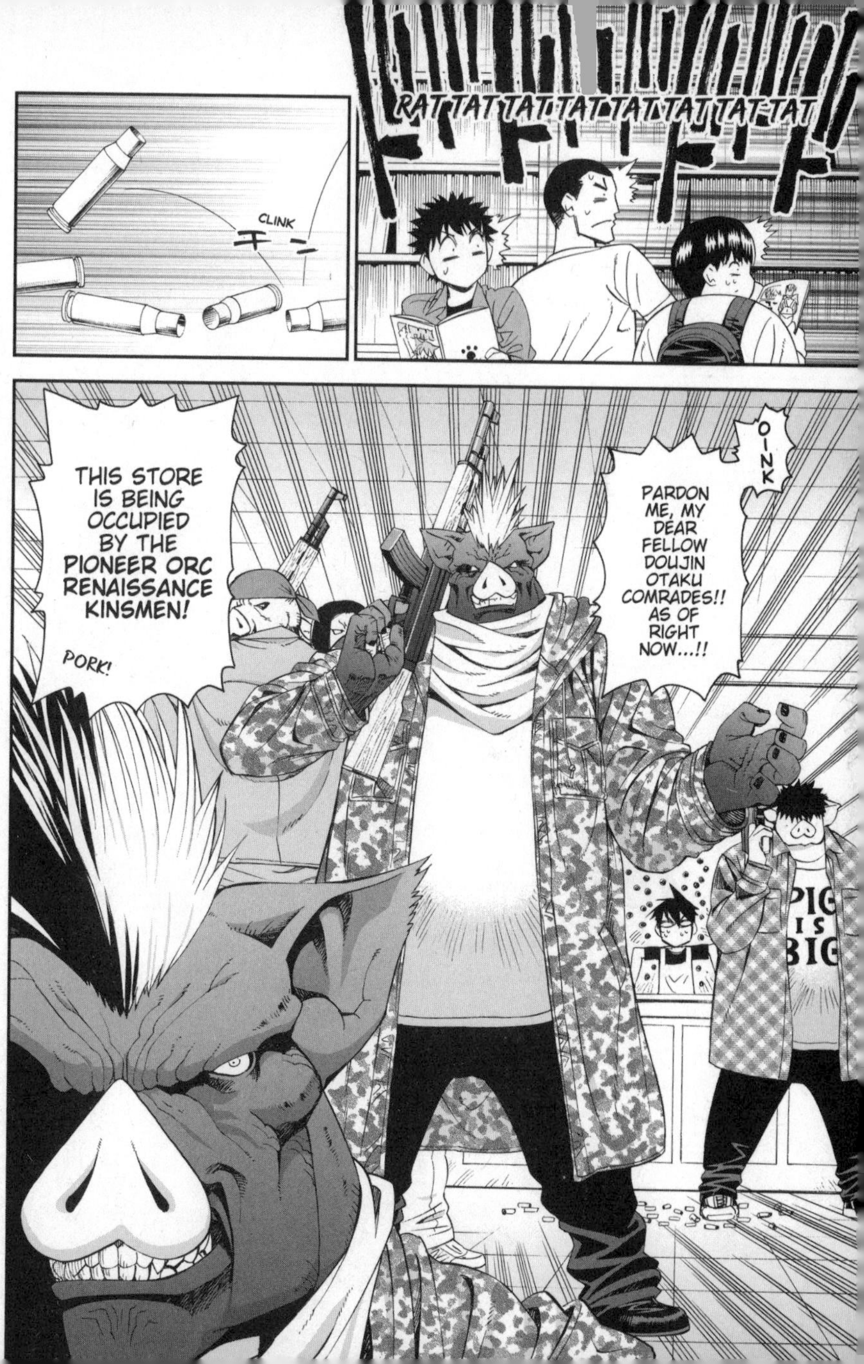
RAT TAT TAT TAT TAT TAT TAT TAT
CLINK
O-I-N-K
PARDON ME, MY DEAR FELLOW DOUJIN OTAKU COMRADES!! AS OF RIGHT NOW...!!
THIS STORE IS BEING OCCUPIED BY THE PIONEER ORC RENAISSANCE KINSMEN!
PORK!
PIG IS BIG

Chapter 12

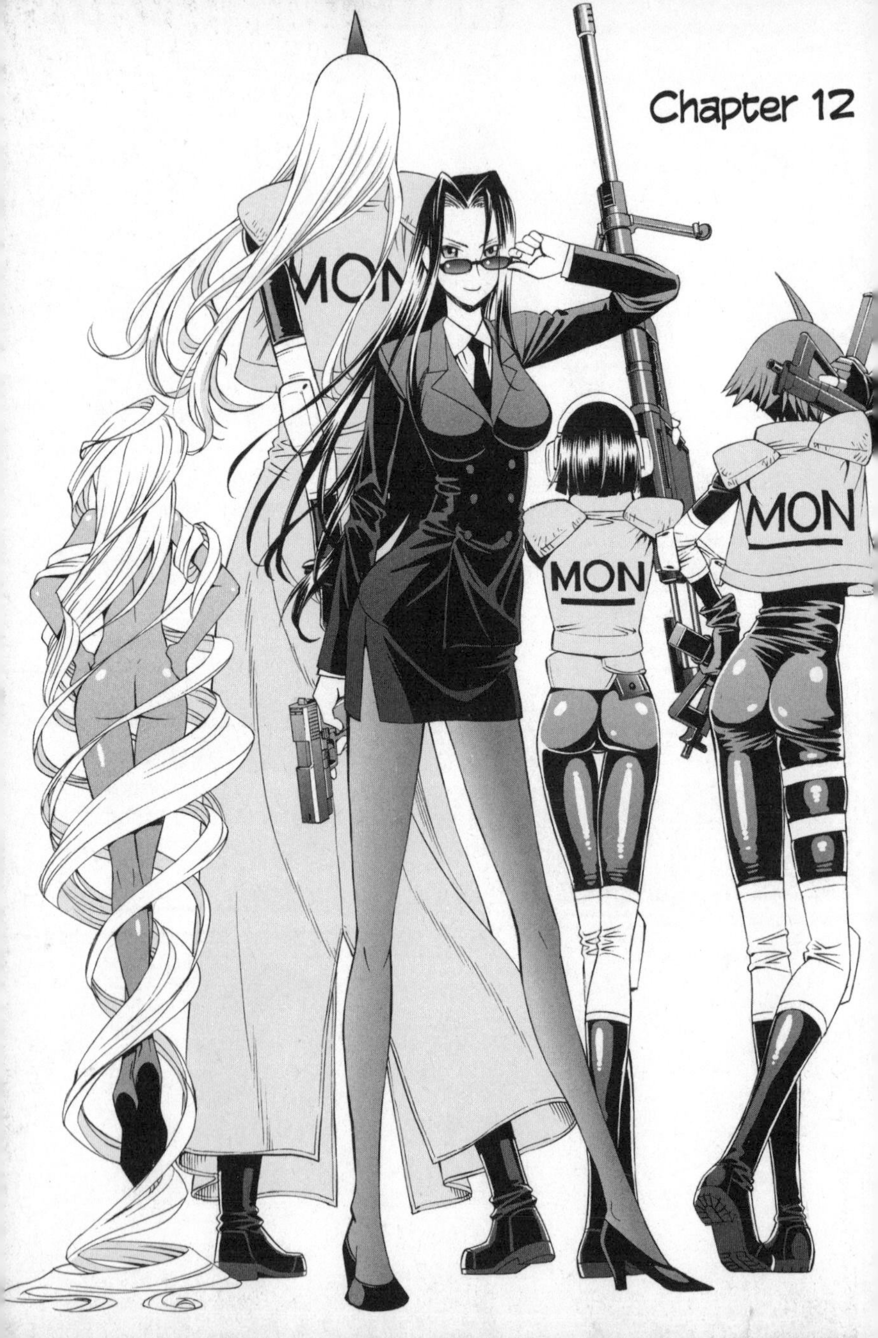
MON
MON
MON
MON

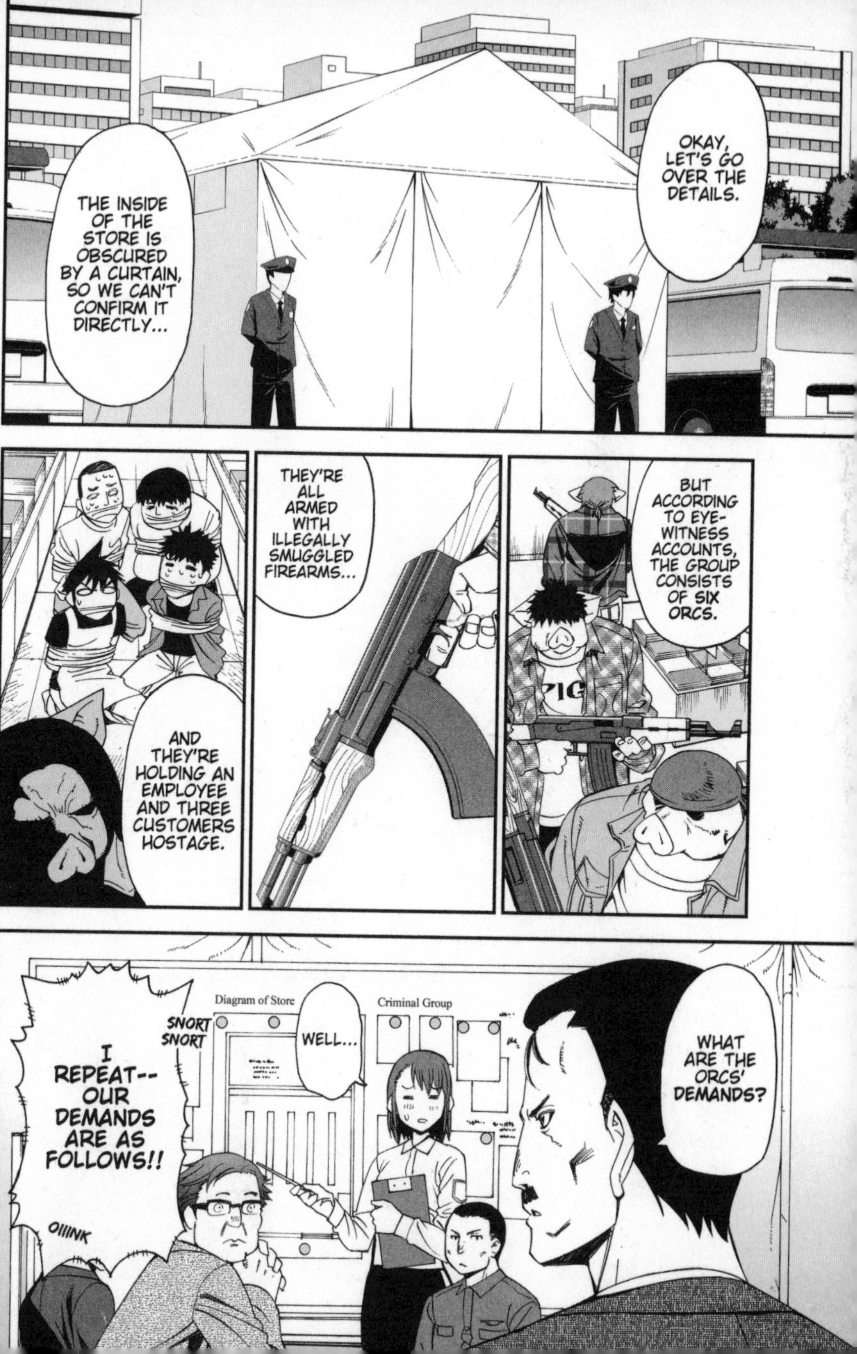
OKAY, LET'S GO OVER THE DETAILS.
THE INSIDE OF THE STORE IS OBSCURED BY A CURTAIN, SO WE CAN'T CONFIRM IT DIRECTLY...
BUT ACCORDING TO EYE-WITNESS ACCOUNTS, THE GROUP CONSISTS OF SIX ORCS.
PIG
THEY'RE ALL ARMED WITH ILLEGALLY SMUGGLED FIREARMS...
AND THEY'RE HOLDING AN EMPLOYEE AND THREE CUSTOMERS HOSTAGE.
WHAT ARE THE ORCS' DEMANDS?
Criminal Group
WELL...
Diagram of Store
SNORT SNORT
I REPEAT--OUR DEMANDS ARE AS FOLLOWS!!
OIIINK

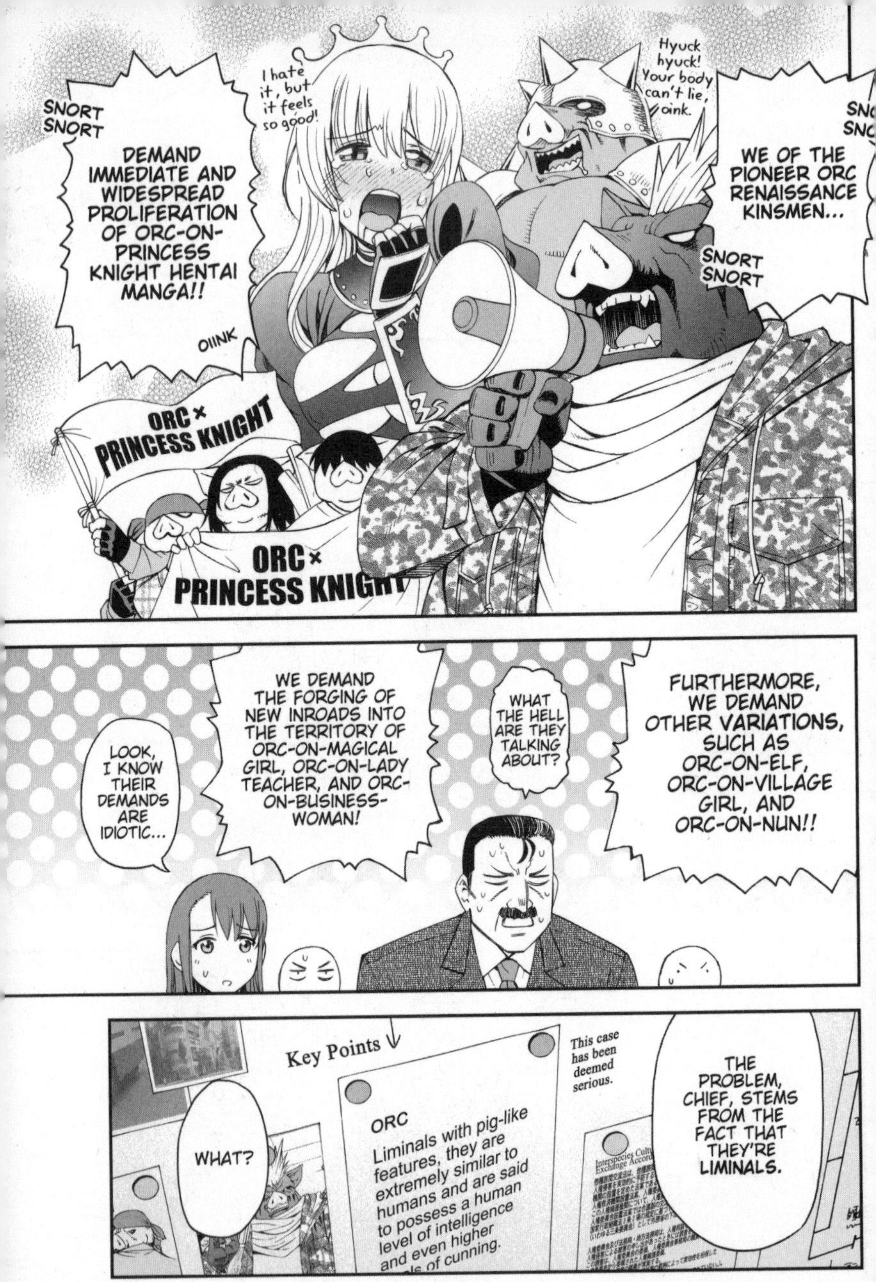

WE OF THE PIONEER ORC RENAISSANCE KINSMEN...
SNORT SNORT
Hyuck hyuck! Your body can't lie, oink.
I hate it, but it feels so good!
SNORT SNORT
DEMAND IMMEDIATE AND WIDESPREAD PROLIFERATION OF ORC-ON-PRINCESS KNIGHT HENTAI MANGA!!
OIINK
ORC × PRINCESS KNIGHT
ORC × PRINCESS KNIGHT
FURTHERMORE, WE DEMAND OTHER VARIATIONS, SUCH AS ORC-ON-ELF, ORC-ON-VILLAGE GIRL, AND ORC-ON-NUN!!
WHAT THE HELL ARE THEY TALKING ABOUT?
WE DEMAND THE FORGING OF NEW INROADS INTO THE TERRITORY OF ORC-ON-MAGICAL GIRL, ORC-ON-LADY TEACHER, AND ORC-ON-BUSINESS-WOMAN!
LOOK, I KNOW THEIR DEMANDS ARE IDIOTIC...
THE PROBLEM, CHIEF, STEMS FROM THE FACT THAT THEY'RE LIMINALS.
This case has been deemed serious.
Key Points
ORC
Liminals with pig-like features, they are extremely similar to humans and are said to possess a human level of intelligence and even higher
WHAT?

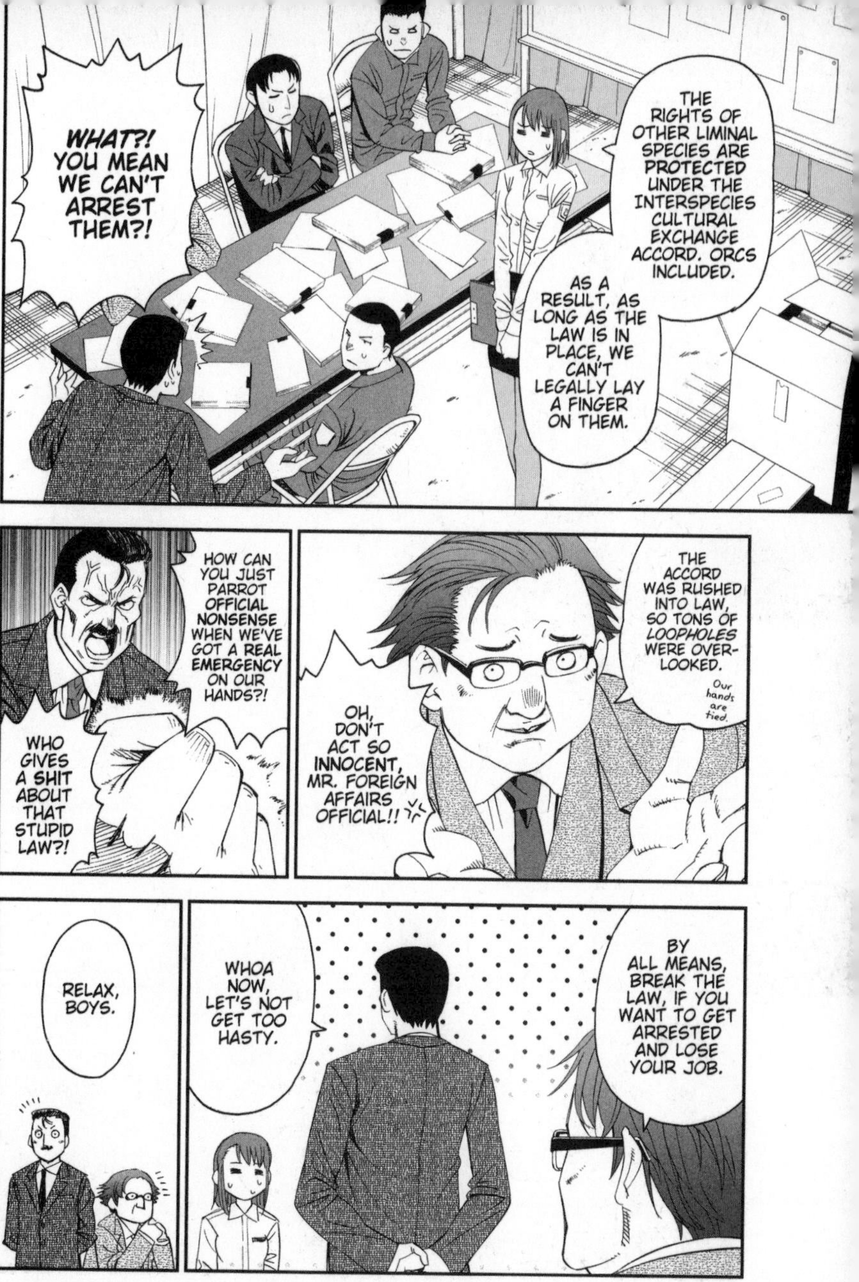
THE RIGHTS OF OTHER LIMINAL SPECIES ARE PROTECTED UNDER THE INTERSPECIES CULTURAL EXCHANGE ACCORD. ORCS INCLUDED.
AS A RESULT, AS LONG AS THE LAW IS IN PLACE, WE CAN'T LEGALLY LAY A FINGER ON THEM.
WHAT?! YOU MEAN WE CAN'T ARREST THEM?!
THE ACCORD WAS RUSHED INTO LAW, SO TONS OF LOOPHOLES WERE OVER-LOOKED.
Our hands are tied.
OH, DON'T ACT SO INNOCENT, MR. FOREIGN AFFAIRS OFFICIAL!!
HOW CAN YOU JUST PARROT OFFICIAL NONSENSE WHEN WE'VE GOT A REAL EMERGENCY ON OUR HANDS?!
WHO GIVES A SHIT ABOUT THAT STUPID LAW?!
BY ALL MEANS, BREAK THE LAW, IF YOU WANT TO GET ARRESTED AND LOSE YOUR JOB.
WHOA NOW, LET'S NOT GET TOO HASTY.
RELAX, BOYS.

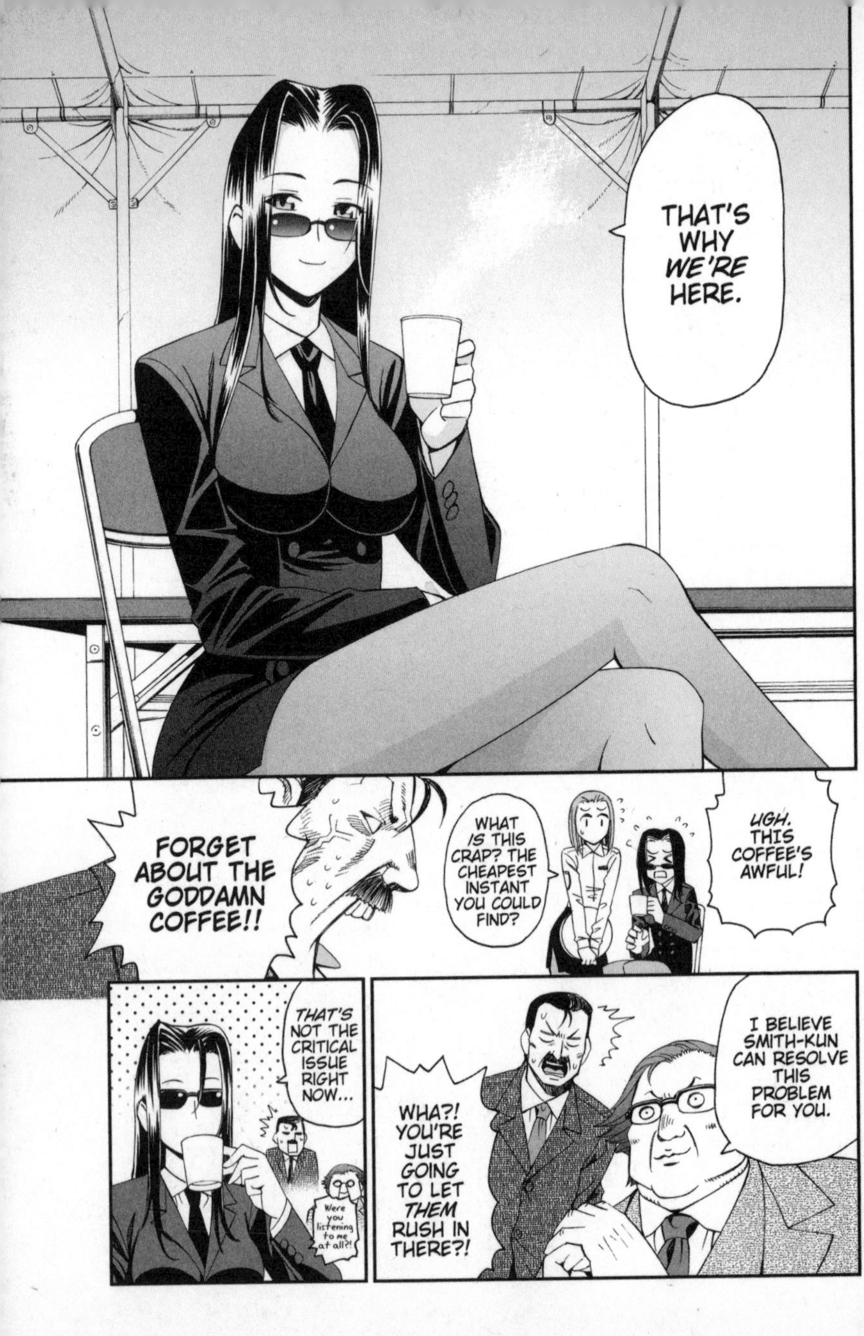
THAT'S WHY WE'RE HERE.
UGH. THIS COFFEE'S AWFUL!
WHAT IS THIS CRAP? THE CHEAPEST INSTANT YOU COULD FIND?
FORGET ABOUT THE GODDAMN COFFEE!!
I BELIEVE SMITH-KUN CAN RESOLVE THIS PROBLEM FOR YOU.
WHA?! YOU'RE JUST GOING TO LET THEM RUSH IN THERE?!
THAT'S NOT THE CRITICAL ISSUE RIGHT NOW...
Were you listening to me at all?!

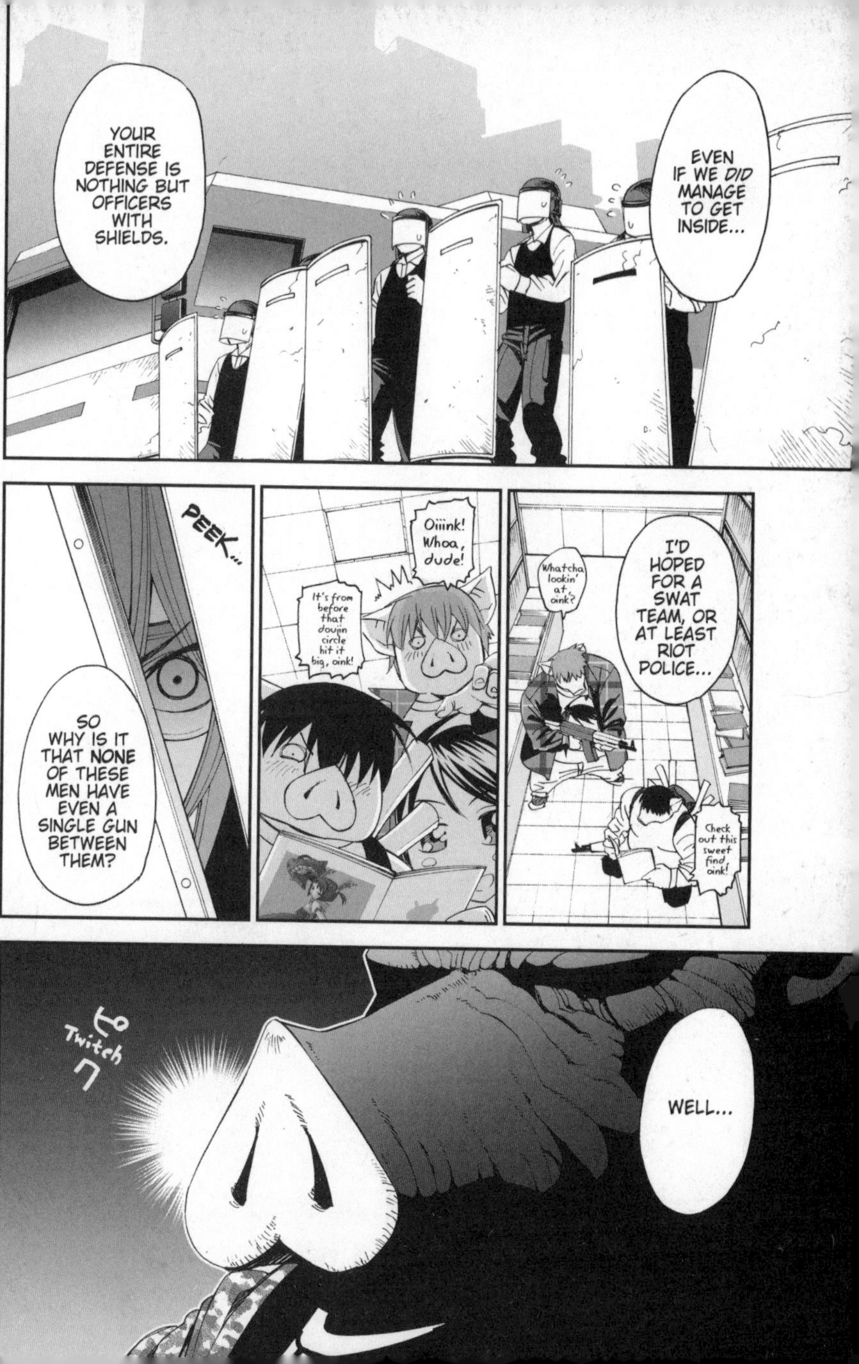
EVEN IF WE DID MANAGE TO GET INSIDE...
YOUR ENTIRE DEFENSE IS NOTHING BUT OFFICERS WITH SHIELDS.
I'D HOPED FOR A SWAT TEAM, OR AT LEAST RIOT POLICE...
Whatcha lookin' at, oink?
Check out this sweet find oink!
Oiiink! Whoa, dude!
It's from before that doujin circle hit it big, oink!
PEEK...
SO WHY IS IT THAT NONE OF THESE MEN HAVE EVEN A SINGLE GUN BETWEEN THEM?
WELL...
ピク
Twitch

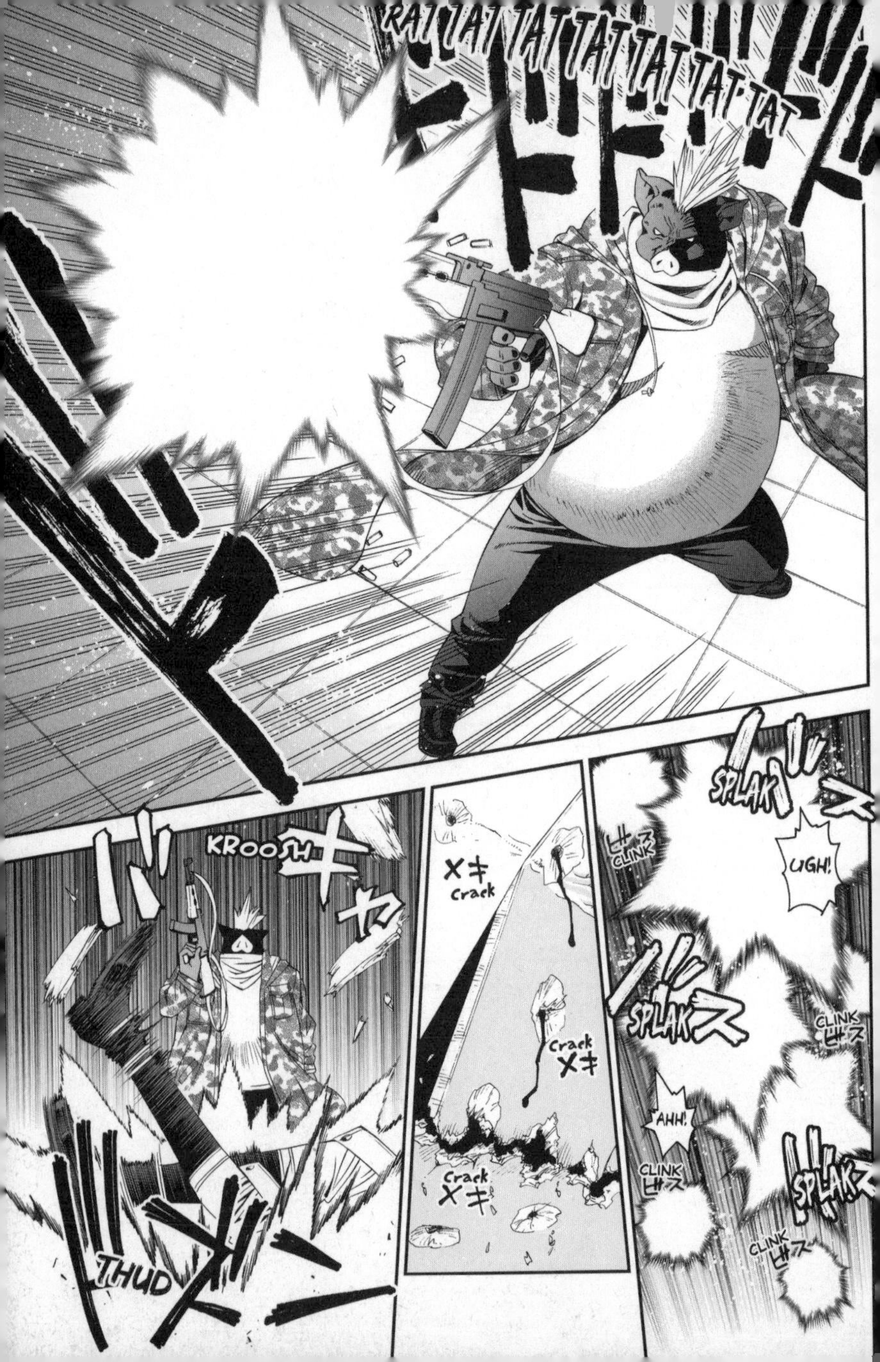

RAT TAT TAT TAT TAT TAT TAT·TAT TAT
SPLAK
ビス CLINK
UGH!
SPLAK
CLINK ビス
AHH!
CLINK ビス
SPLAK
CLINK ビス
メキ Crack
Crack メキ
Crack メキ
KROOSH
THUD

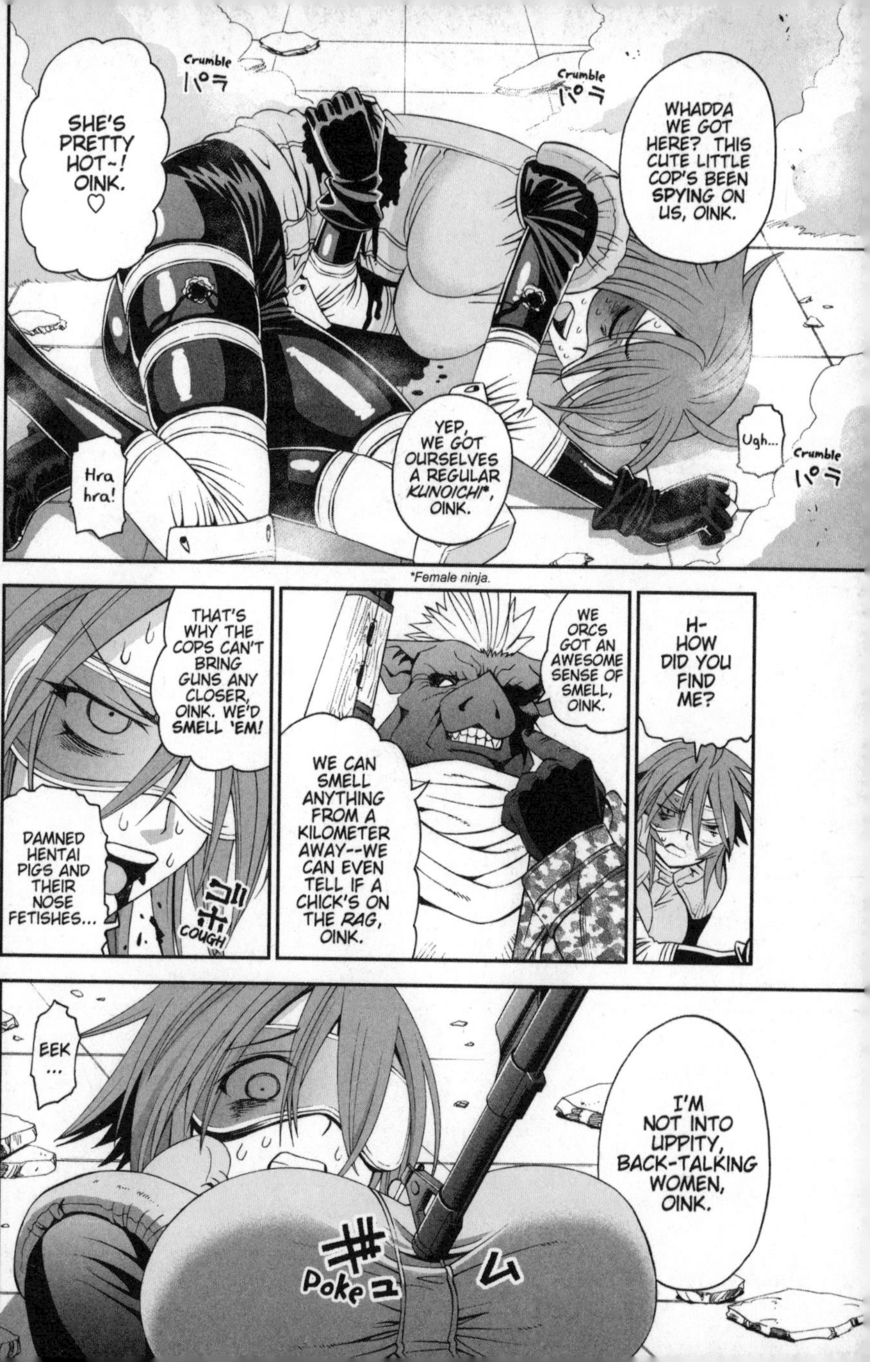
Crumble パラ
WHADDA WE GOT HERE? THIS CUTE LITTLE COP'S BEEN SPYING ON US, OINK.
Crumble パラ
SHE'S PRETTY HOT~! OINK. ♡
Crumble パラ
Ugh...
YEP, WE GOT OURSELVES A REGULAR *KUNOICHI**, OINK.
Hra hra!
H-HOW DID YOU FIND ME?
WE ORCS GOT AN AWESOME SENSE OF SMELL, OINK.
WE CAN SMELL ANYTHING FROM A KILOMETER AWAY--WE CAN EVEN TELL IF A CHICK'S ON THE *RAG*, OINK.
THAT'S WHY THE COPS CAN'T BRING GUNS ANY CLOSER, OINK. WE'D SMELL 'EM!
ゴホ COUGH
DAMNED HENTAI PIGS AND THEIR NOSE FETISHES...
I'M NOT INTO UPPITY, BACK-TALKING WOMEN, OINK.
EEK ...
Poke ギュム

Female ninja.

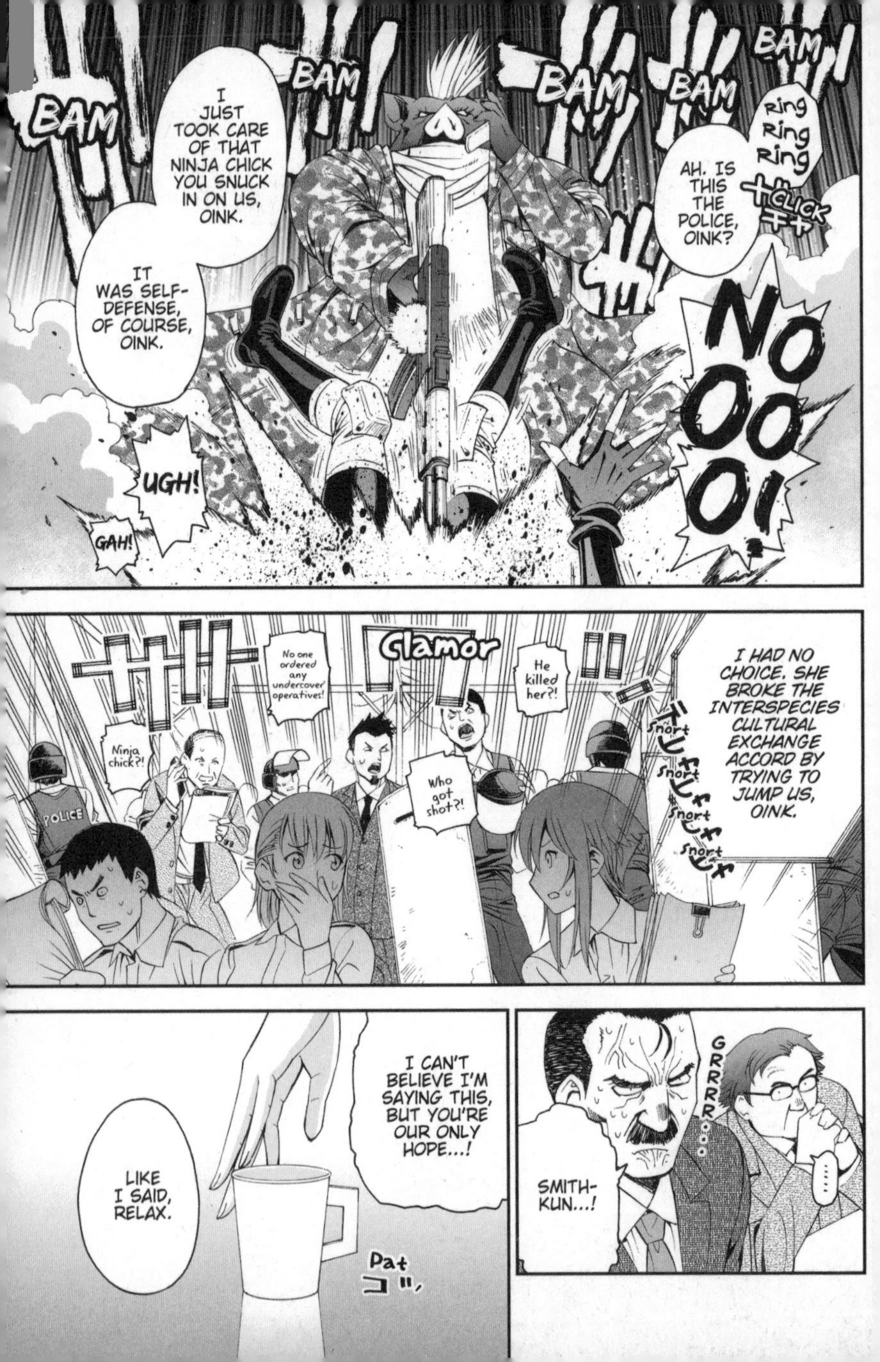
BAM
BAM
BAM
Ring Ring Ring
AH. IS THIS THE POLICE, OINK?
CLICK
BAM
I JUST TOOK CARE OF THAT NINJA CHICK YOU SNUCK IN ON US, OINK.
BAM
IT WAS SELF-DEFENSE, OF COURSE, OINK.
NOOOOOO!
UGH!
GAH!
I HAD NO CHOICE. SHE BROKE THE INTERSPECIES CULTURAL EXCHANGE ACCORD BY TRYING TO JUMP US, OINK.
Snort
Snort
Snort
Snort
He killed her?!
Clamor
Who got shot?!
No one ordered any undercover operatives!
Ninja chick?!
GRRRR...
......
SMITH-KUN...!
I CAN'T BELIEVE I'M SAYING THIS, BUT YOU'RE OUR ONLY HOPE...!
LIKE I SAID, RELAX.
Pat

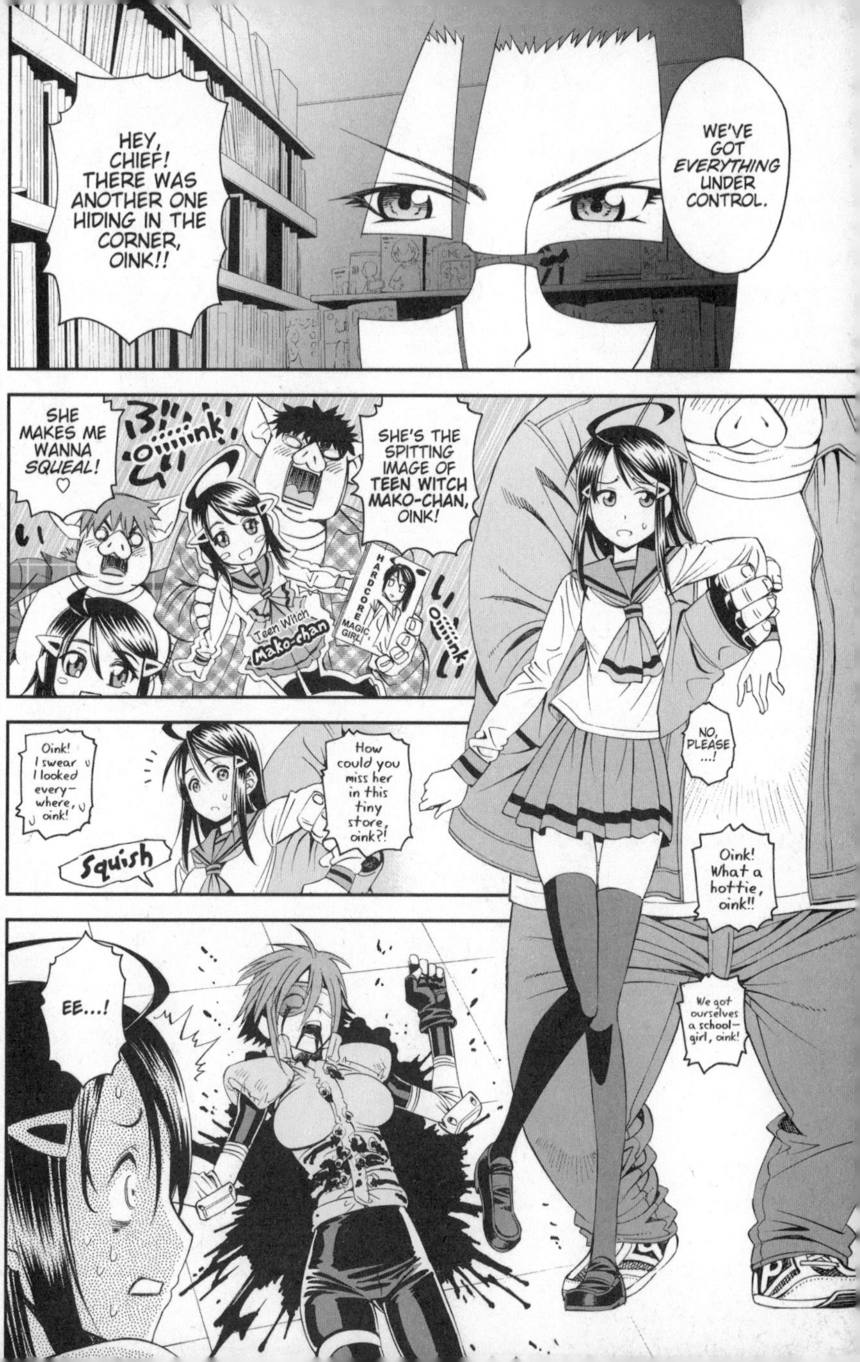
WE'VE GOT EVERYTHING UNDER CONTROL.
HEY, CHIEF! THERE WAS ANOTHER ONE HIDING IN THE CORNER, OINK!!
NO, PLEASE ...!
Oink! What a hottie, oink!!
We got ourselves a school-girl, oink!
SHE'S THE SPITTING IMAGE OF TEEN WITCH MAKO-CHAN, OINK!
Oiiiiink!
SHE MAKES ME WANNA SQUEAL! ♡
HARDCORE MAGIC GIRL
Teen Witch Mako-chan
Oiiiiink
How could you miss her in this tiny store, oink?!
Oink! I swear I looked every-where, oink!
Squish
EE...!

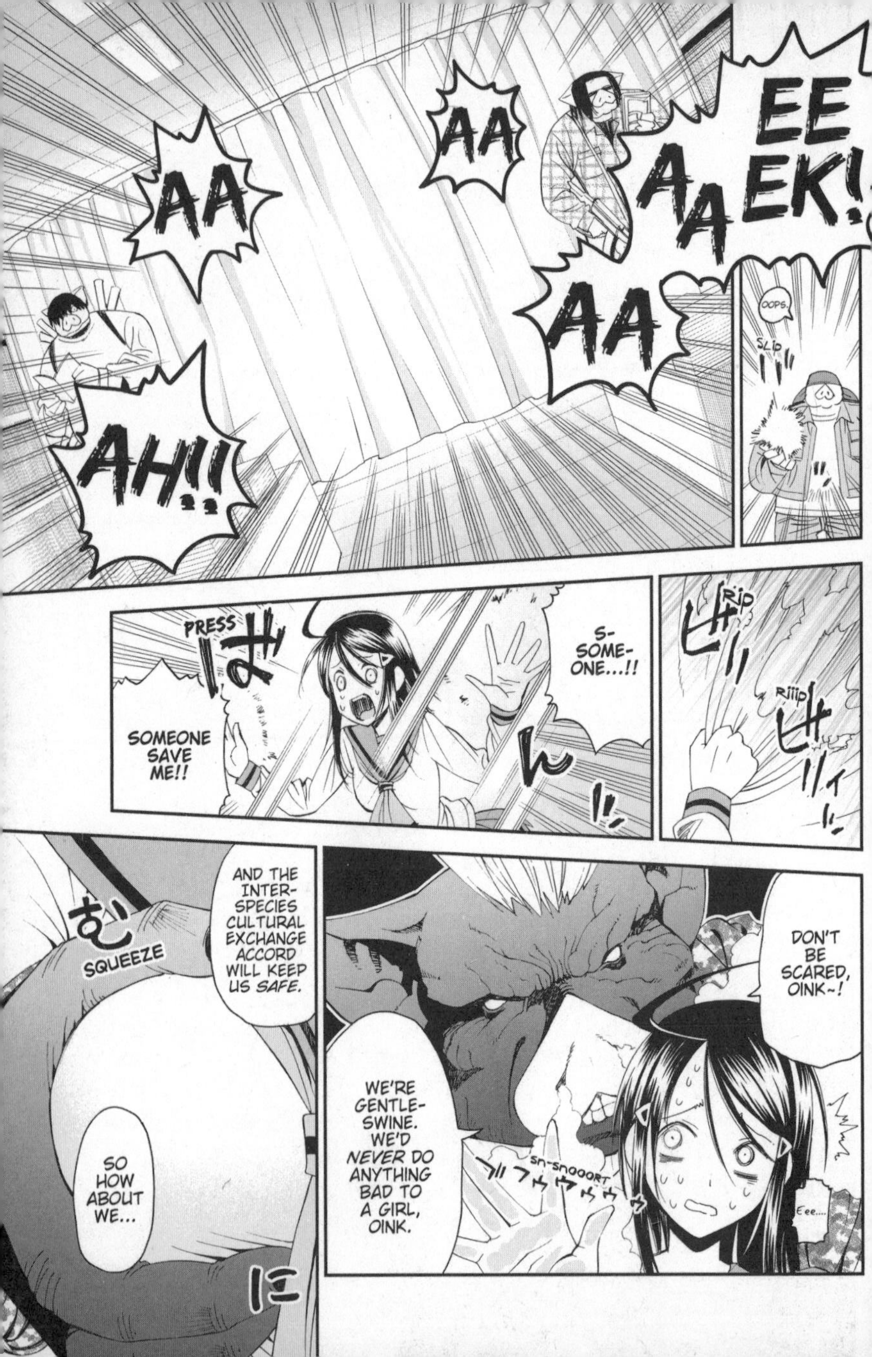

OOPS.
SLIP
EE
AAEK!
AA
AA
AA
AH!!
Rip
Riiip
S-SOME-ONE...!!
PRESS
SOMEONE SAVE ME!!
DON'T BE SCARED, OINK~!
Eee....
sn-snooort
WE'RE GENTLE-SWINE. WE'D *NEVER* DO ANYTHING BAD TO A GIRL, OINK.
AND THE INTER-SPECIES CULTURAL EXCHANGE ACCORD WILL KEEP US *SAFE*.
SQUEEZE
SO HOW ABOUT WE...

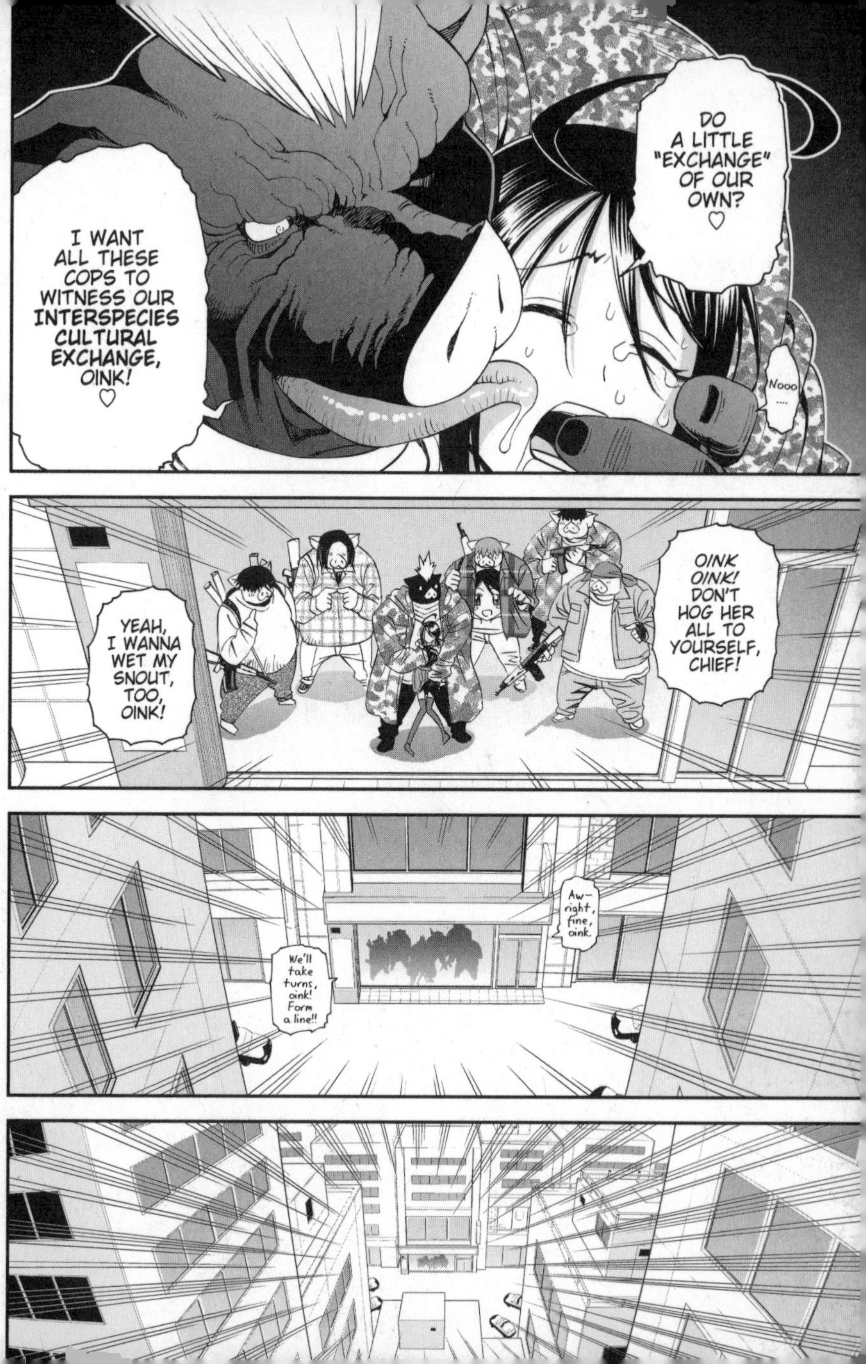
DO A LITTLE "EXCHANGE" OF OUR OWN? ♡
I WANT ALL THESE COPS TO WITNESS OUR INTERSPECIES CULTURAL EXCHANGE, OINK! ♡
Nooo ....
OINK OINK! DON'T HOG HER ALL TO YOURSELF, CHIEF!
YEAH, I WANNA WET MY SNOUT, TOO, OINK!
Aw-right, fine, oink.
We'll take turns, oink! Form a line!!

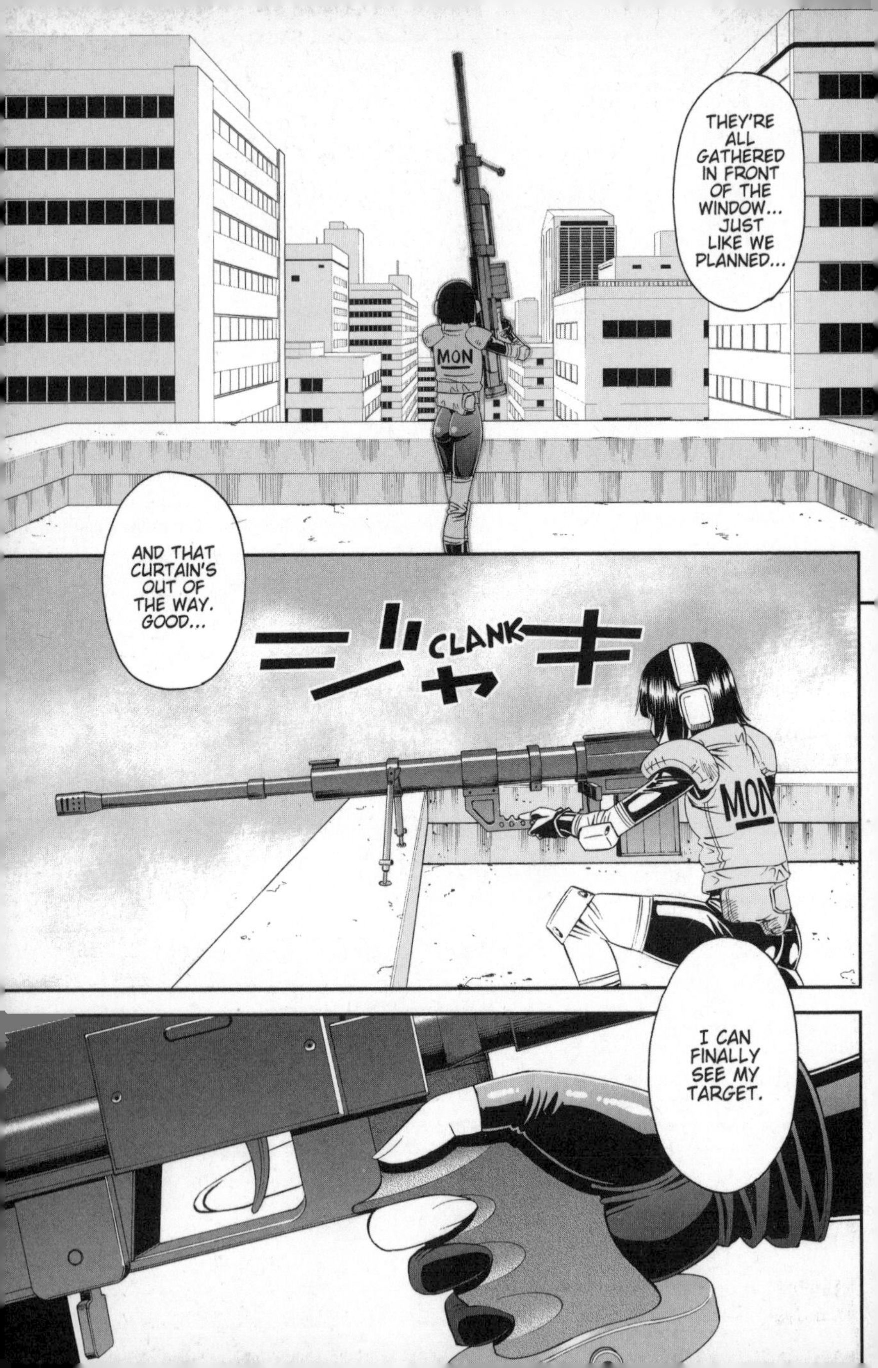
THEY'RE ALL GATHERED IN FRONT OF THE WINDOW... JUST LIKE WE PLANNED...
MON
AND THAT CURTAIN'S OUT OF THE WAY. GOOD...
CLANK
MON
I CAN FINALLY SEE MY TARGET.

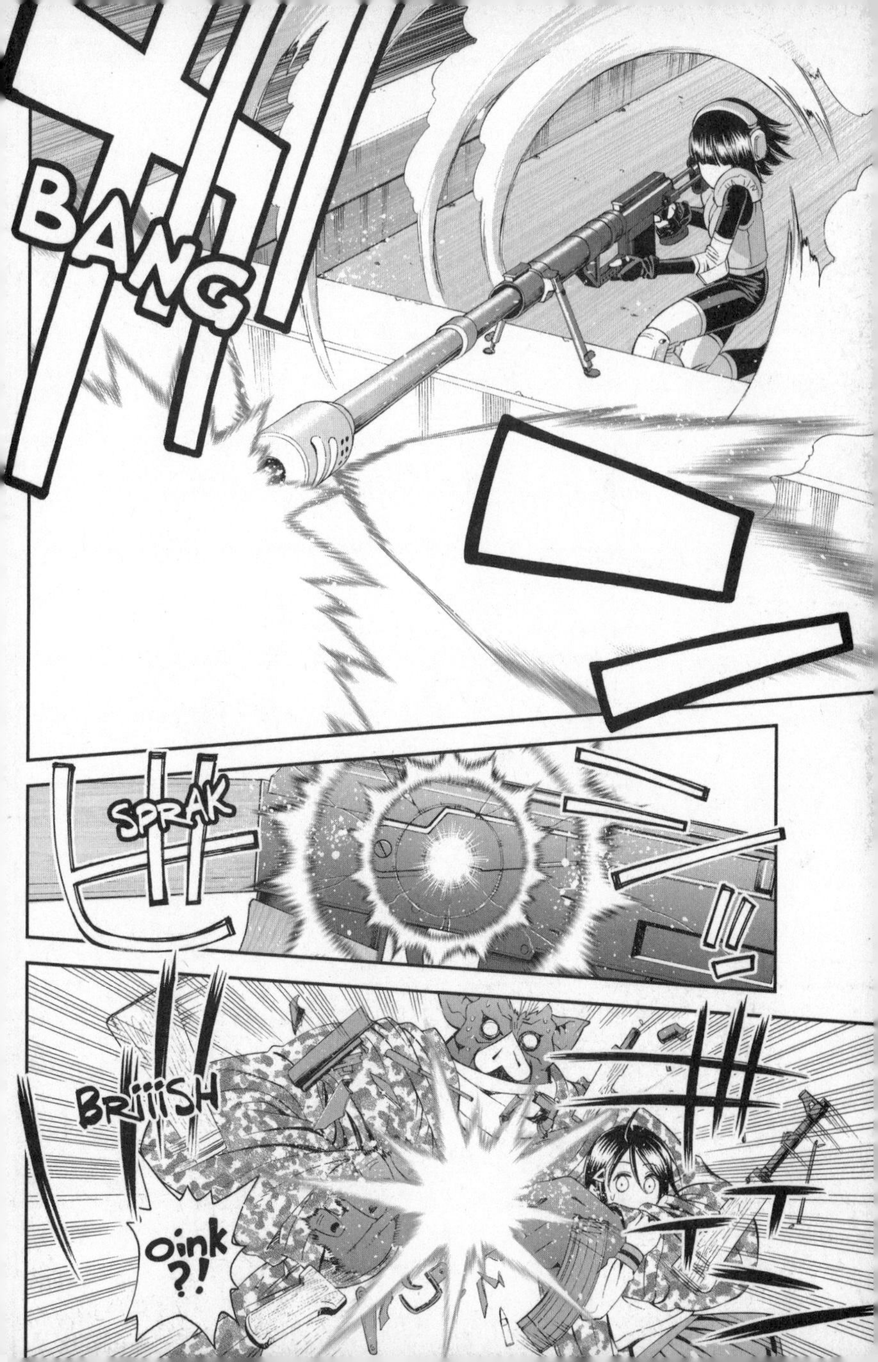
BANG
SPRAK
BRiiiSH
Oink ?!

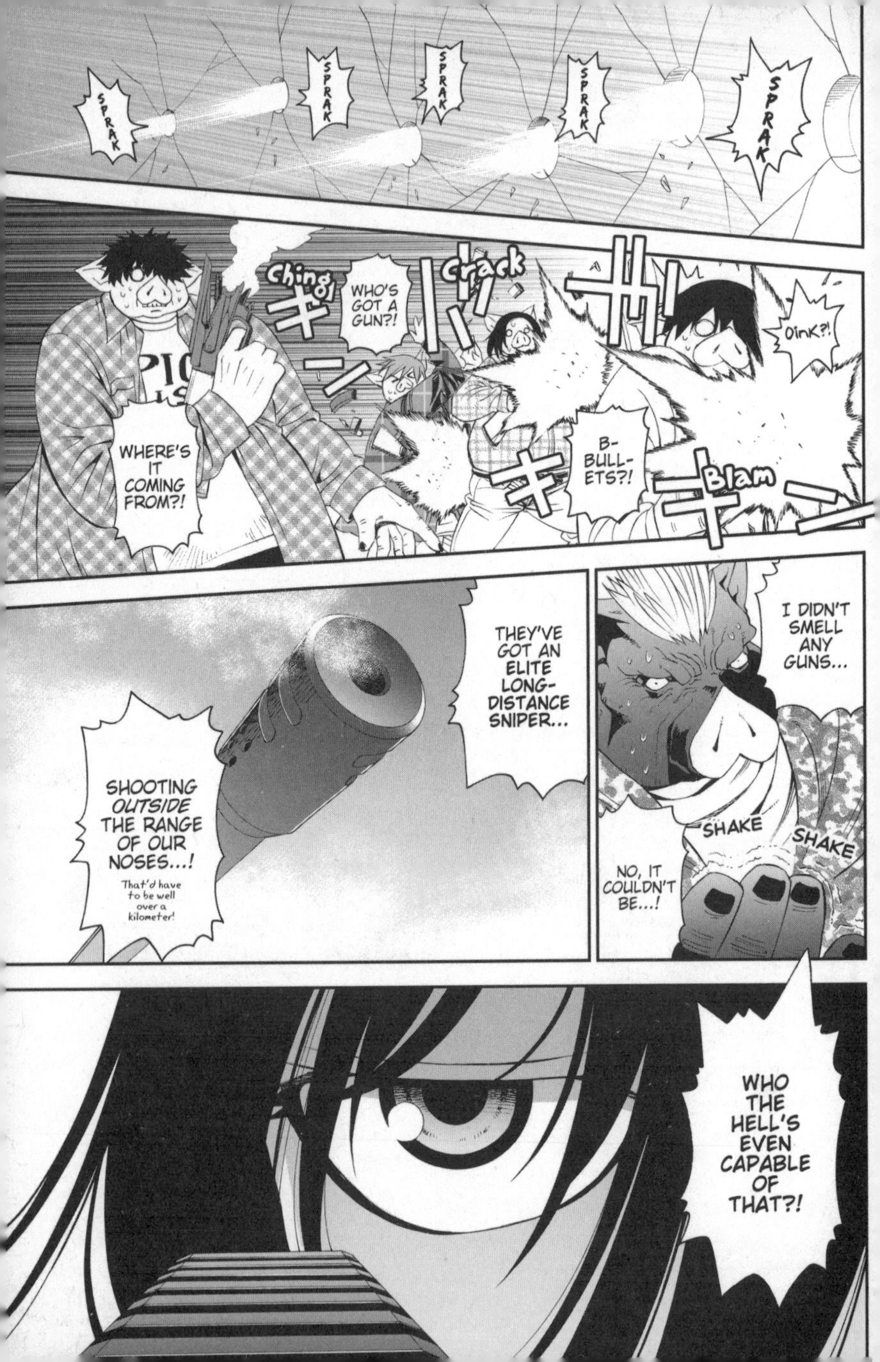
SPRAK
SPRAK
SPRAK
SPRAK
SPRAK
Oink?!
Blam
B-BULLETS?!
Crack
WHO'S GOT A GUN?!
Ching
WHERE'S IT COMING FROM?!
I DIDN'T SMELL ANY GUNS...
SHAKE
SHAKE
NO, IT COULDN'T BE...!
THEY'VE GOT AN ELITE LONG-DISTANCE SNIPER...
SHOOTING *OUTSIDE* THE RANGE OF OUR NOSES...!
That'd have to be well over a kilometer!
WHO THE HELL'S EVEN CAPABLE OF THAT?!

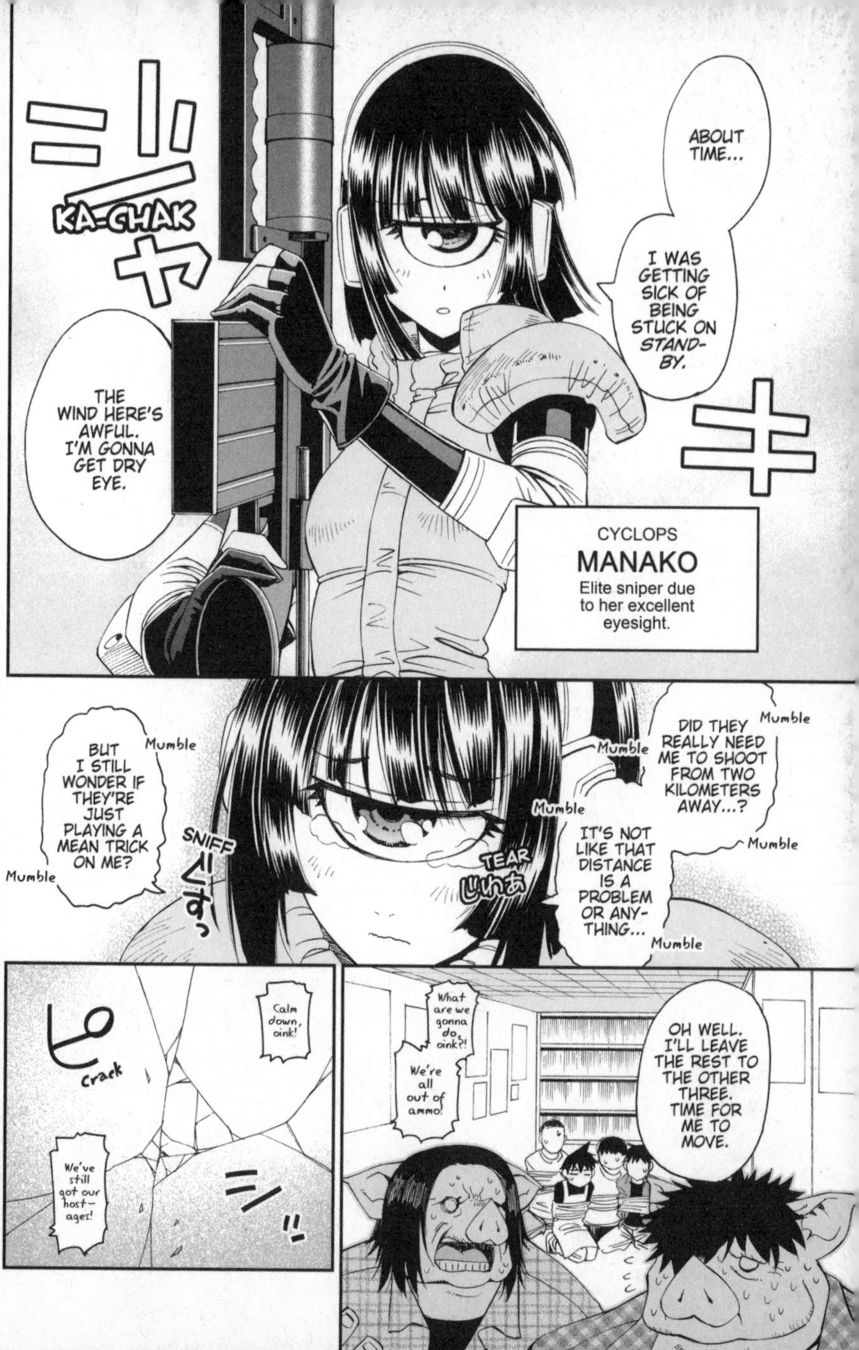

ABOUT TIME...
I WAS GETTING SICK OF BEING STUCK ON STAND-BY.
KA-CHAK
THE WIND HERE'S AWFUL. I'M GONNA GET DRY EYE.
CYCLOPS
MANAKO
Elite sniper due to her excellent eyesight.
Mumble
DID THEY REALLY NEED ME TO SHOOT FROM TWO KILOMETERS AWAY...?
Mumble
Mumble
IT'S NOT LIKE THAT DISTANCE IS A PROBLEM OR ANYTHING...
Mumble
Mumble
TEAR
SNIFF
Mumble
BUT I STILL WONDER IF THEY'RE JUST PLAYING A MEAN TRICK ON ME?
Mumble
OH WELL. I'LL LEAVE THE REST TO THE OTHER THREE. TIME FOR ME TO MOVE.
What are we gonna do, oink?!
We're all out of ammo!
Calm down, oink!
We've still got our host-ages!
Crack

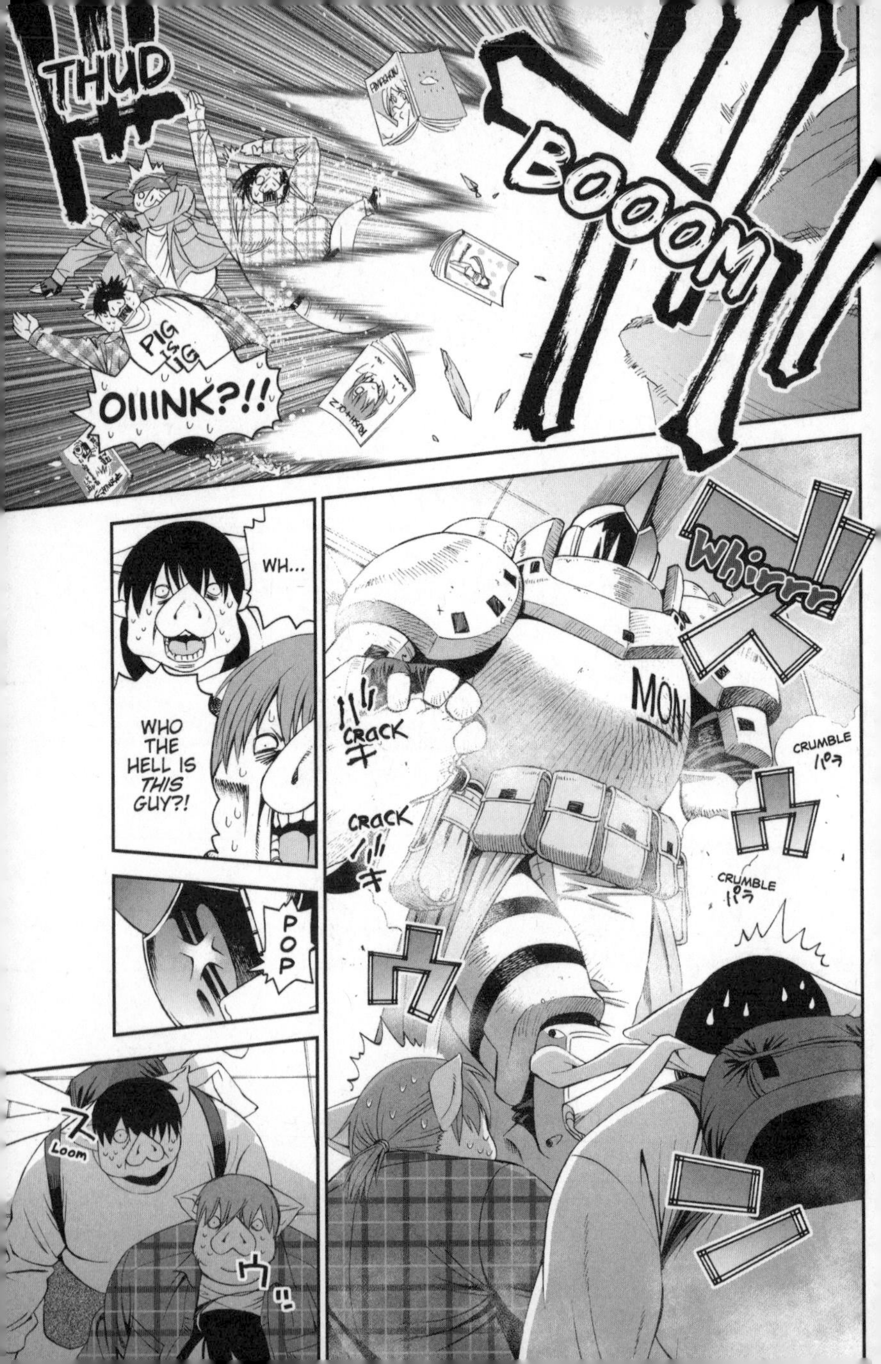
BOOOM
THUD
PIG IS UG
OIIINK?!!
Whirrr
MON
CRACK
CRACK
CRUMBLE
CRUMBLE
WH...
WHO THE HELL IS THIS GUY?!
POP
Loom

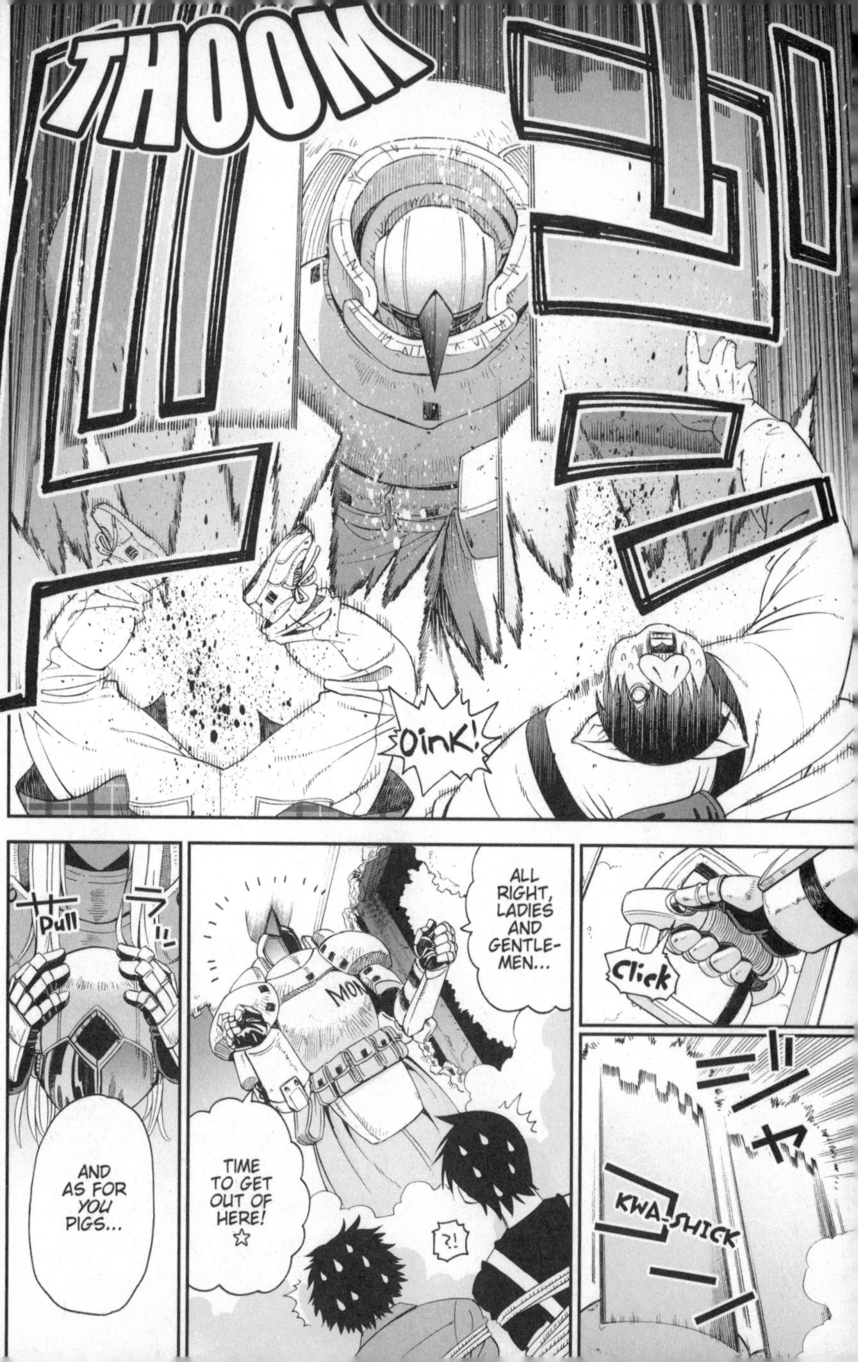
THOOM
Oink!
Click
KWA-SHICK
ALL RIGHT, LADIES AND GENTLEMEN...
TIME TO GET OUT OF HERE! ☆
?!
Pull
AND AS FOR *YOU* PIGS...

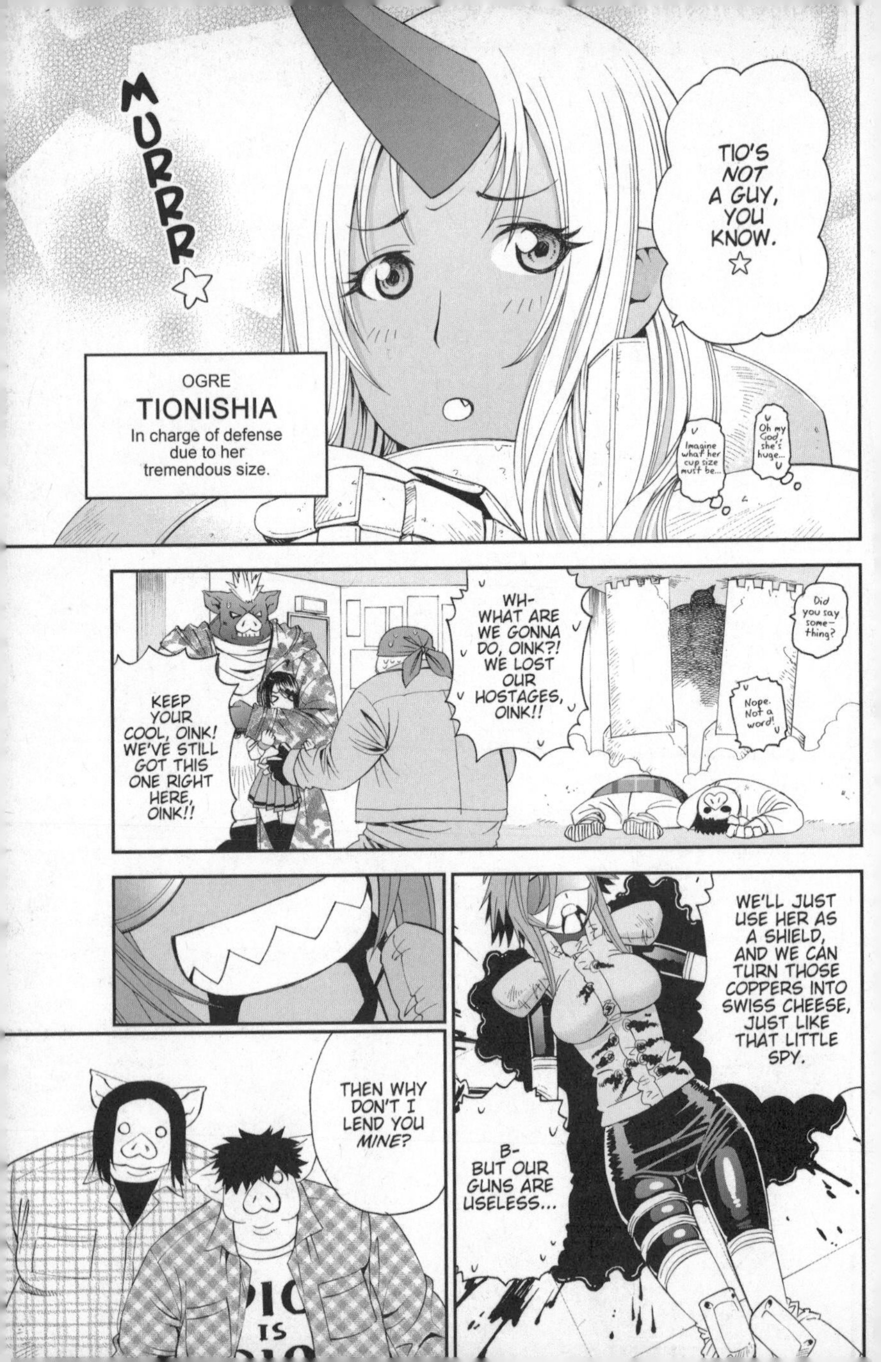
TIO'S *NOT* A GUY, YOU KNOW. ☆
MURRR ☆
Oh my God, she's huge...
Imagine what her cup size must be...
OGRE
TIONISHIA
In charge of defense due to her tremendous size.
Did you say some-thing?
Nope. Not a word!
WH- WHAT ARE WE GONNA DO, OINK?! WE LOST OUR HOSTAGES, OINK!!
KEEP YOUR COOL, OINK! WE'VE STILL GOT THIS ONE RIGHT HERE, OINK!!
WE'LL JUST USE HER AS A SHIELD, AND WE CAN TURN THOSE COPPERS INTO SWISS CHEESE, JUST LIKE THAT LITTLE SPY.
B- BUT OUR GUNS ARE USELESS...
THEN WHY DON'T I LEND YOU *MINE*?

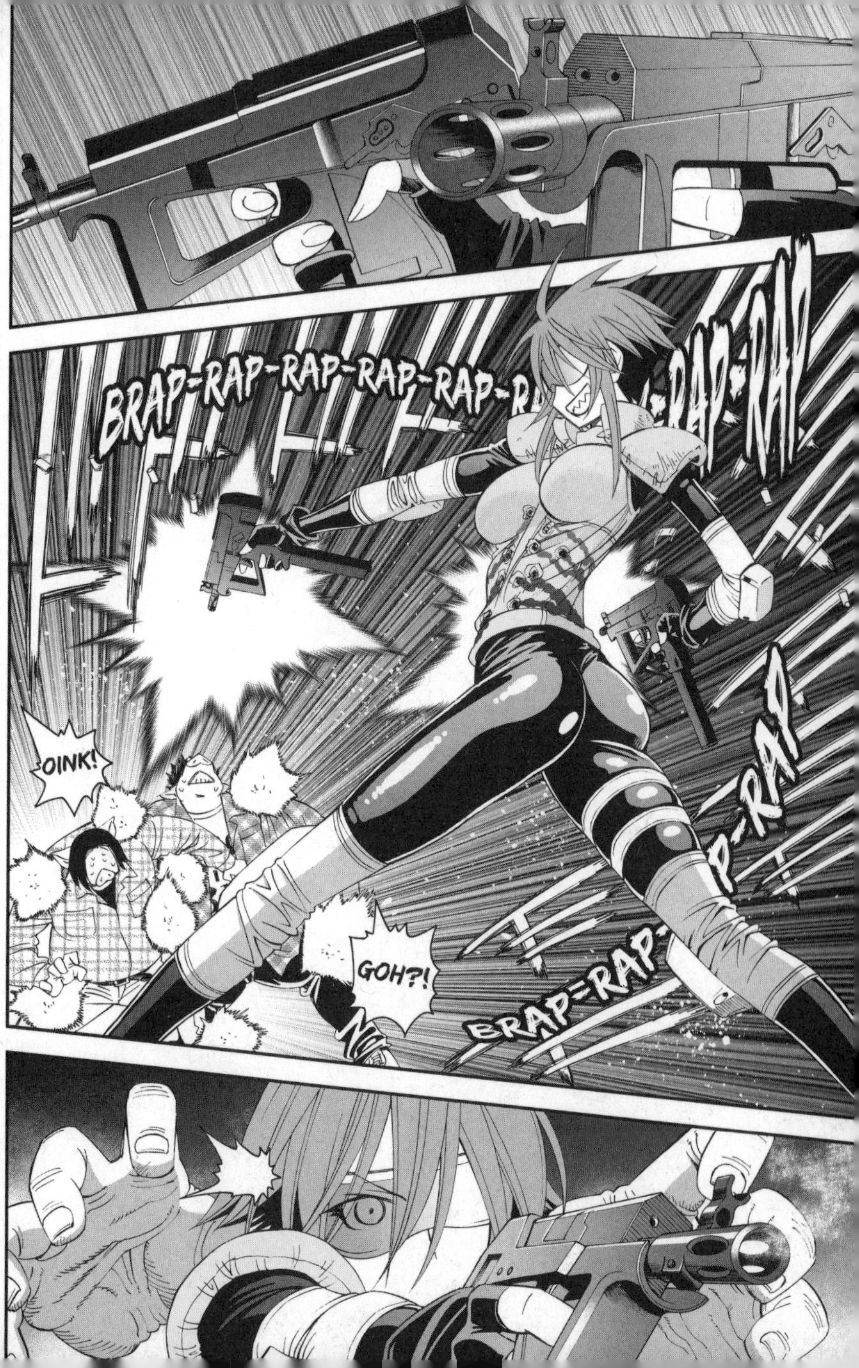
BRAP-RAP-RAP-RAP-RAP-RA
RAP-RAP
OINK!
GOH?!
BRAP-RAP-RAP-RAP
BRAP=RAP-

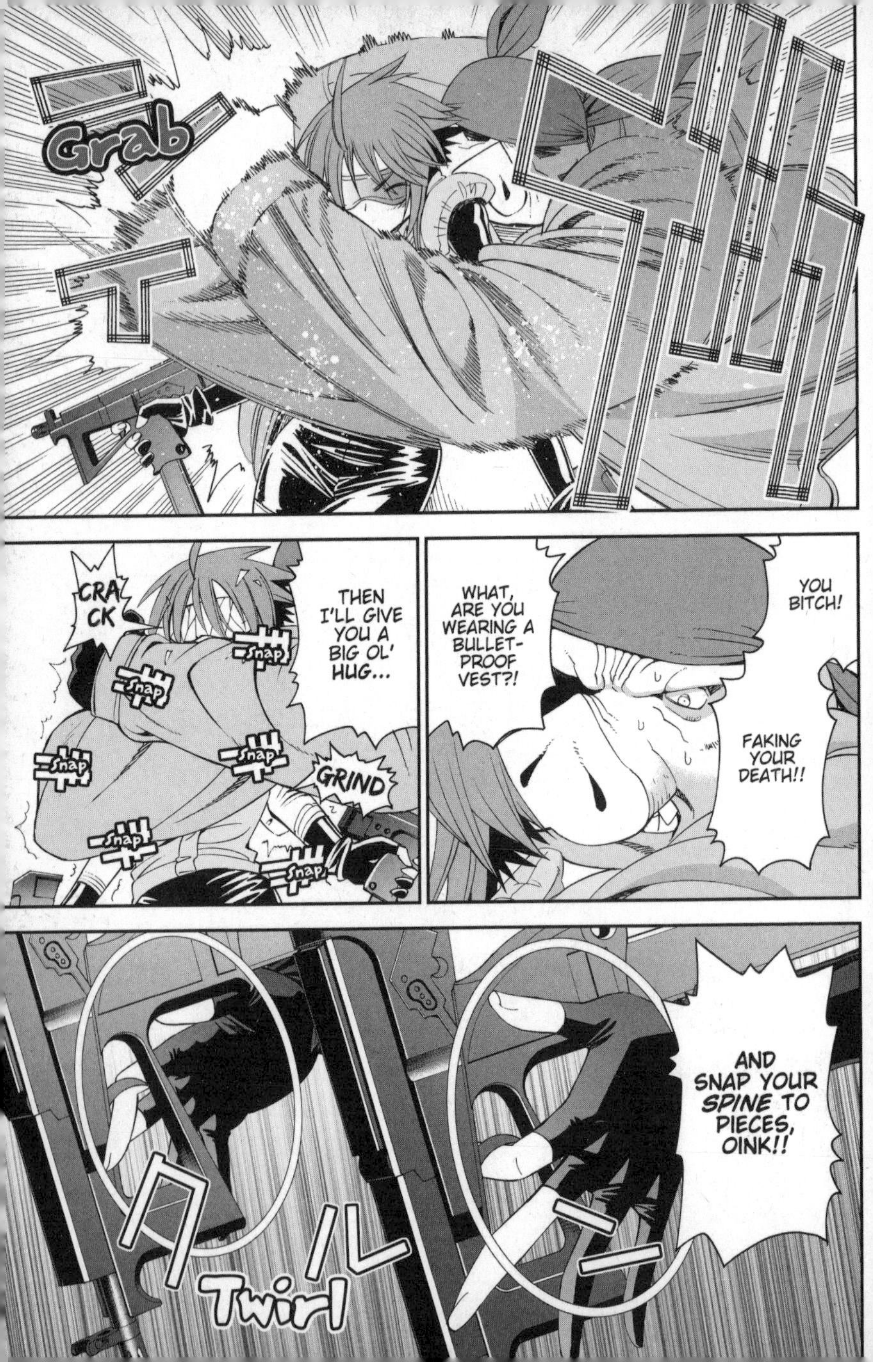
Grab
YOU BITCH!
FAKING YOUR DEATH!!
WHAT, ARE YOU WEARING A BULLET-PROOF VEST?!
THEN I'LL GIVE YOU A BIG OL' HUG...
CRACK
Snap
Snap
Snap
Snap
GRIND
Snap
Snap
AND SNAP YOUR SPINE TO PIECES, OINK!!
Twirl

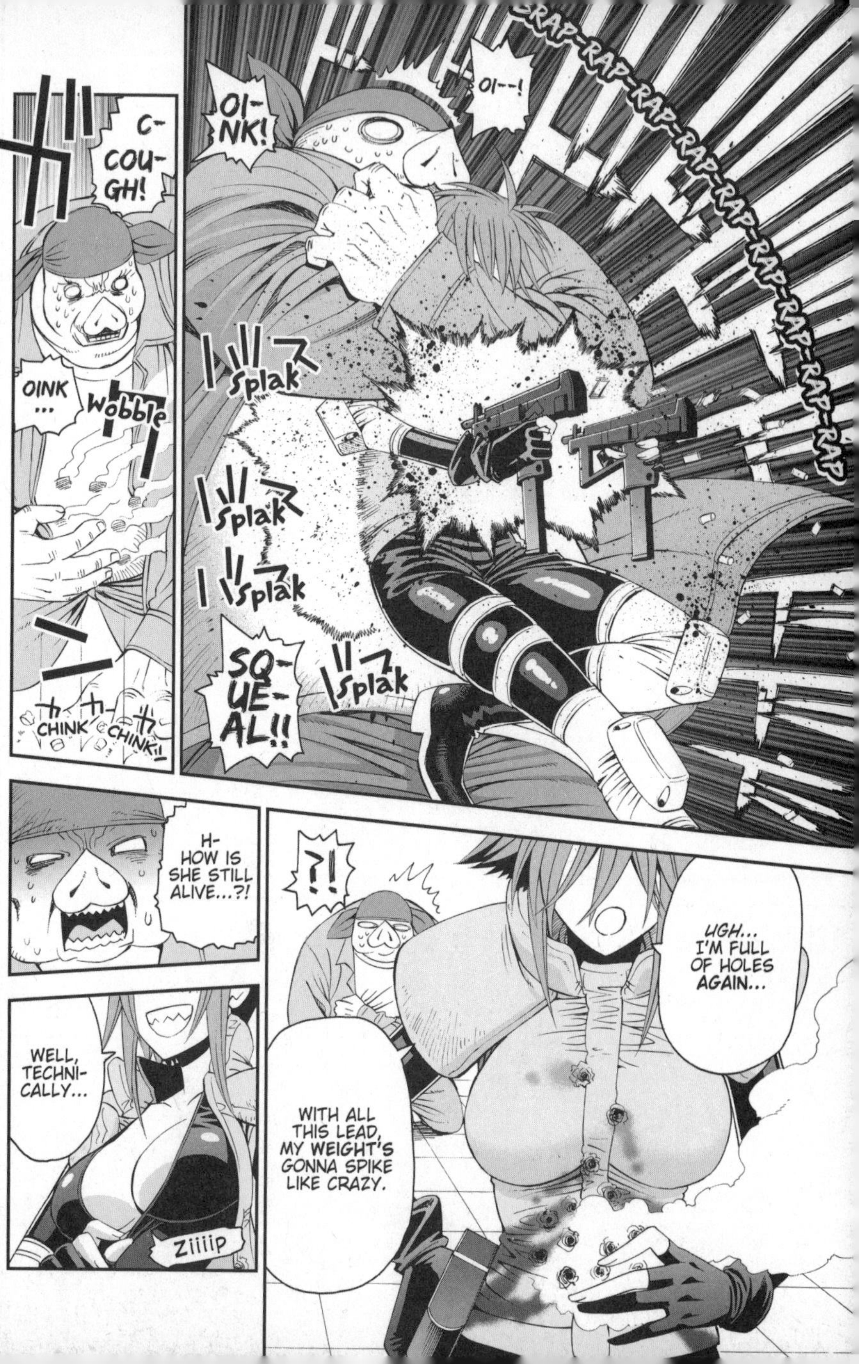
RAP-RAP-RAP-RAP-RAP-RAP-RAP-RAP-RAP-RAP-RAP
OI--!
OI-NK!
Splak
Splak
Splak
Splak
SQ-UE-AL!!
C-COUGH!
OINK...
wobble
CHINK
CHINK!!
?!
UGH... I'M FULL OF HOLES AGAIN...
WITH ALL THIS LEAD, MY WEIGHT'S GONNA SPIKE LIKE CRAZY.
H-HOW IS SHE STILL ALIVE...?!
WELL, TECHNICALLY...
Ziiiip

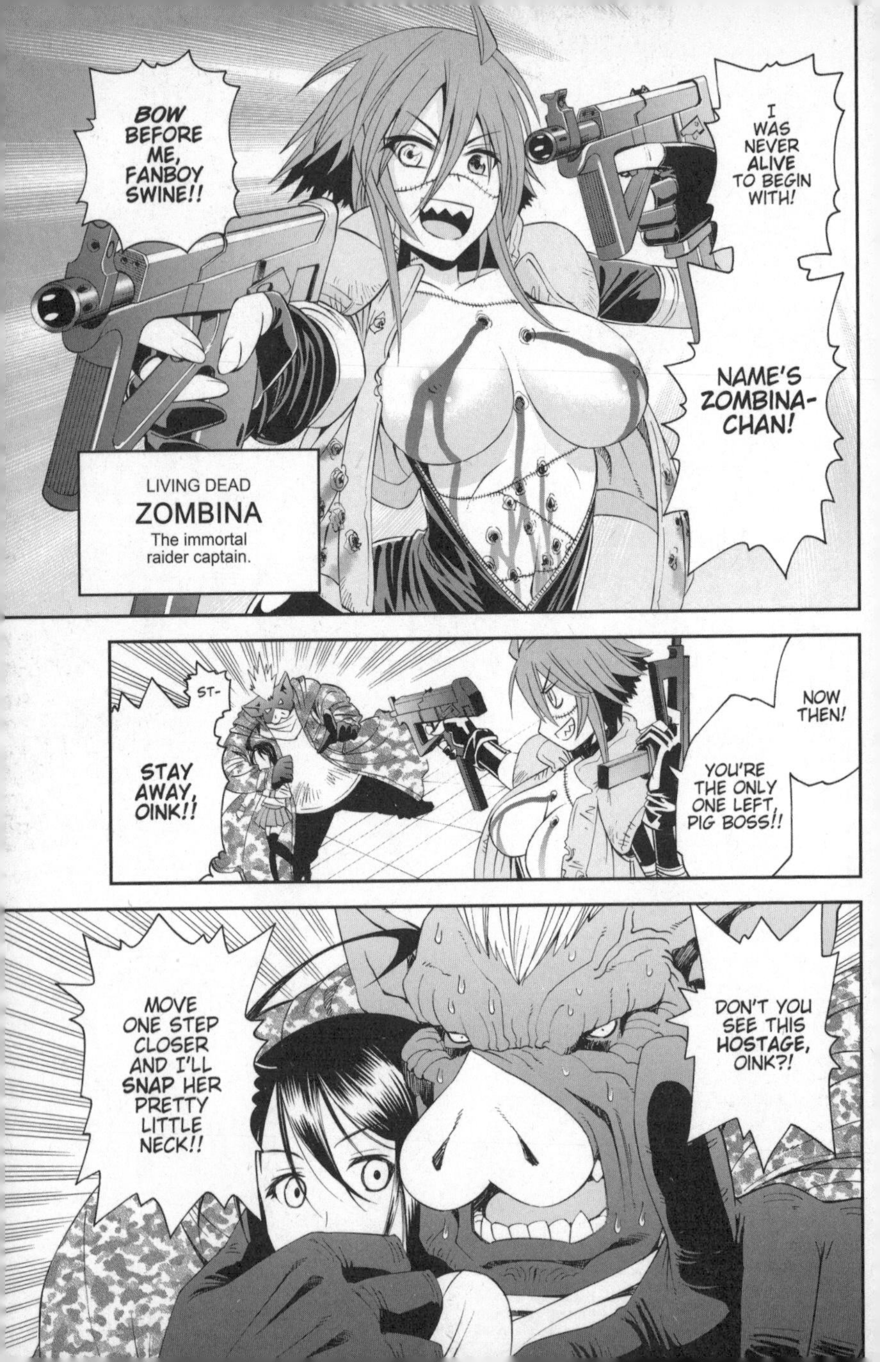
I WAS NEVER ALIVE TO BEGIN WITH!
NAME'S ZOMBINA-CHAN!
BOW BEFORE ME, FANBOY SWINE!!
LIVING DEAD
ZOMBINA
The immortal raider captain.
NOW THEN!
YOU'RE THE ONLY ONE LEFT, PIG BOSS!!
ST-
STAY AWAY, OINK!!
DON'T YOU SEE THIS HOSTAGE, OINK?!
MOVE ONE STEP CLOSER AND I'LL SNAP HER PRETTY LITTLE NECK!!

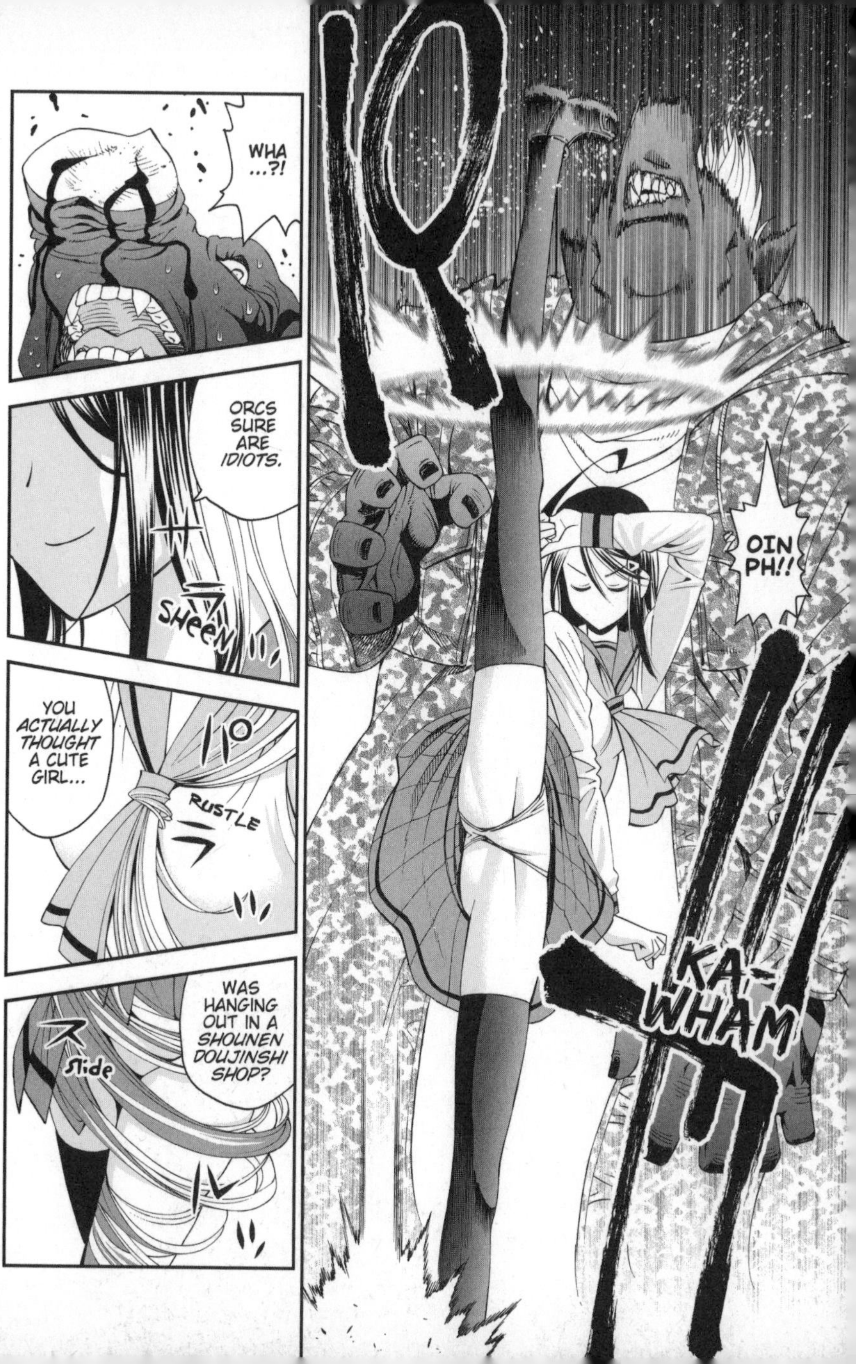
OINPH!!
KA-WHAM
WHA ...?!
ORCS SURE ARE IDIOTS.
SHEEN
YOU ACTUALLY THOUGHT A CUTE GIRL...
RUSTLE
WAS HANGING OUT IN A SHOUNEN DOUJINSHI SHOP?
slide

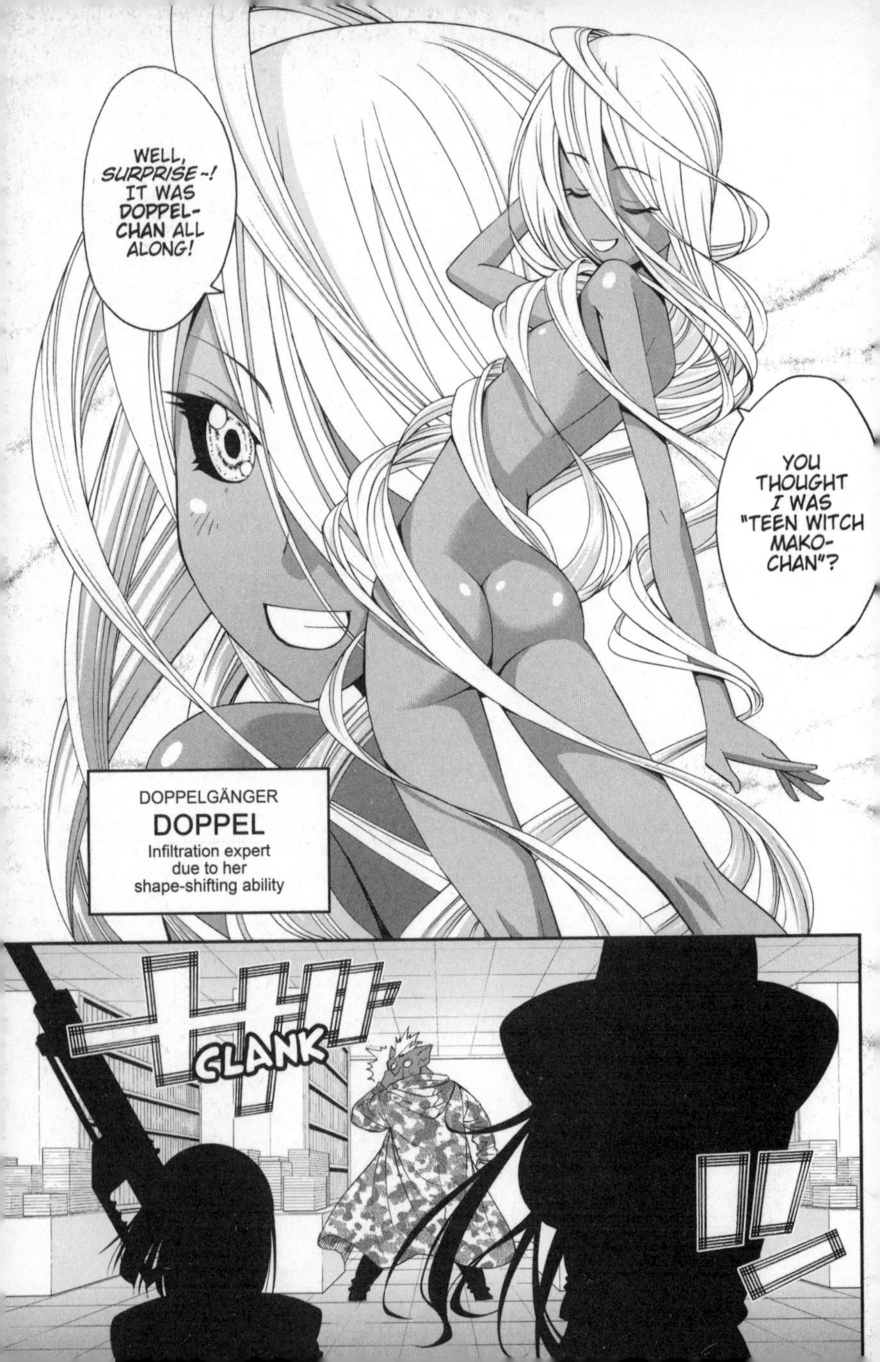
YOU THOUGHT I WAS "TEEN WITCH MAKO-CHAN"?
WELL, SURPRISE~! IT WAS DOPPEL-CHAN ALL ALONG!
DOPPELGÄNGER
DOPPEL
Infiltration expert due to her shape-shifting ability
CLANK

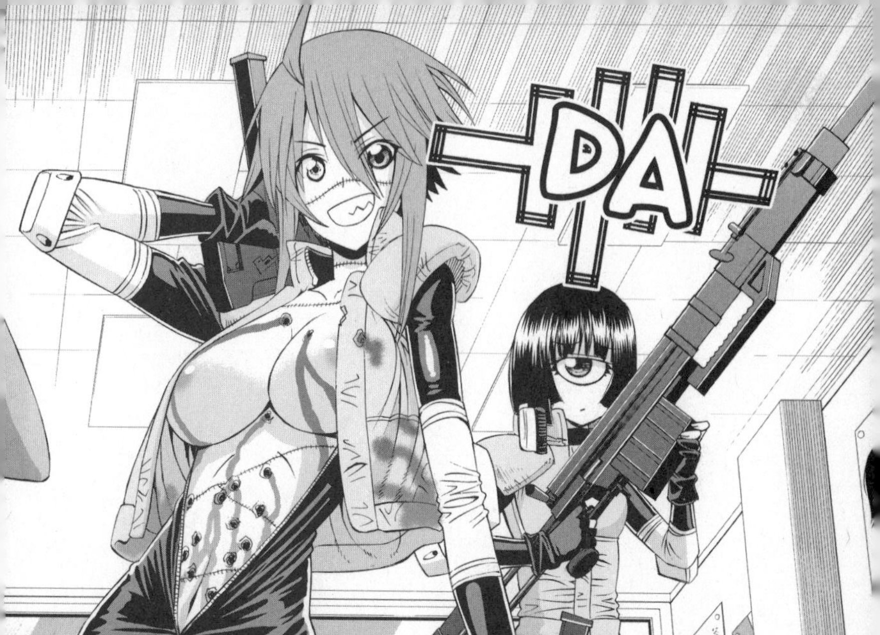
DA

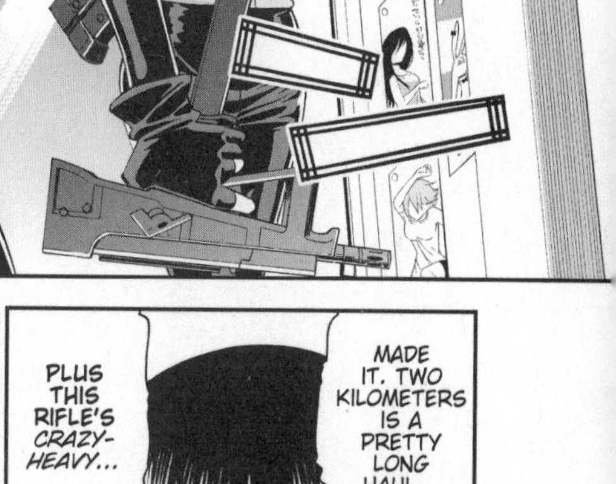
MADE IT. TWO KILOMETERS IS A PRETTY LONG HAUL...
PLUS THIS RIFLE'S *CRAZY-HEAVY*...
Great job, Mana-chan!

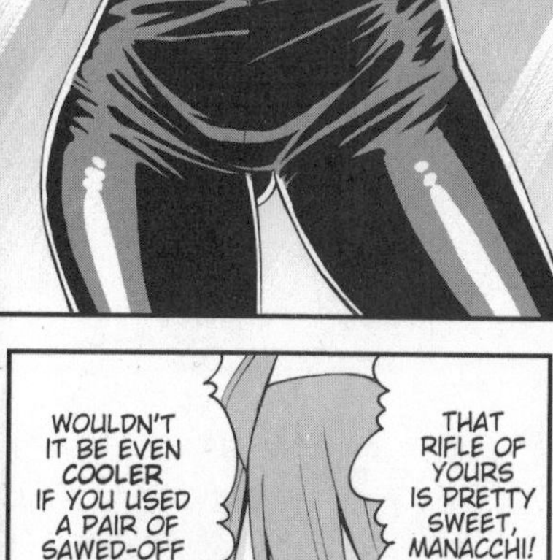
THAT RIFLE OF YOURS IS PRETTY SWEET, MANACCHI!
WOULDN'T IT BE EVEN COOLER IF YOU USED A PAIR OF SAWED-OFF SHOTGUNS?!
My arms would fall off.

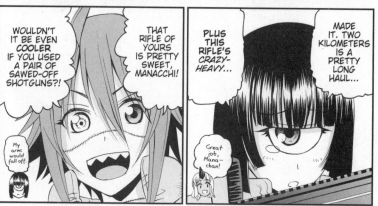

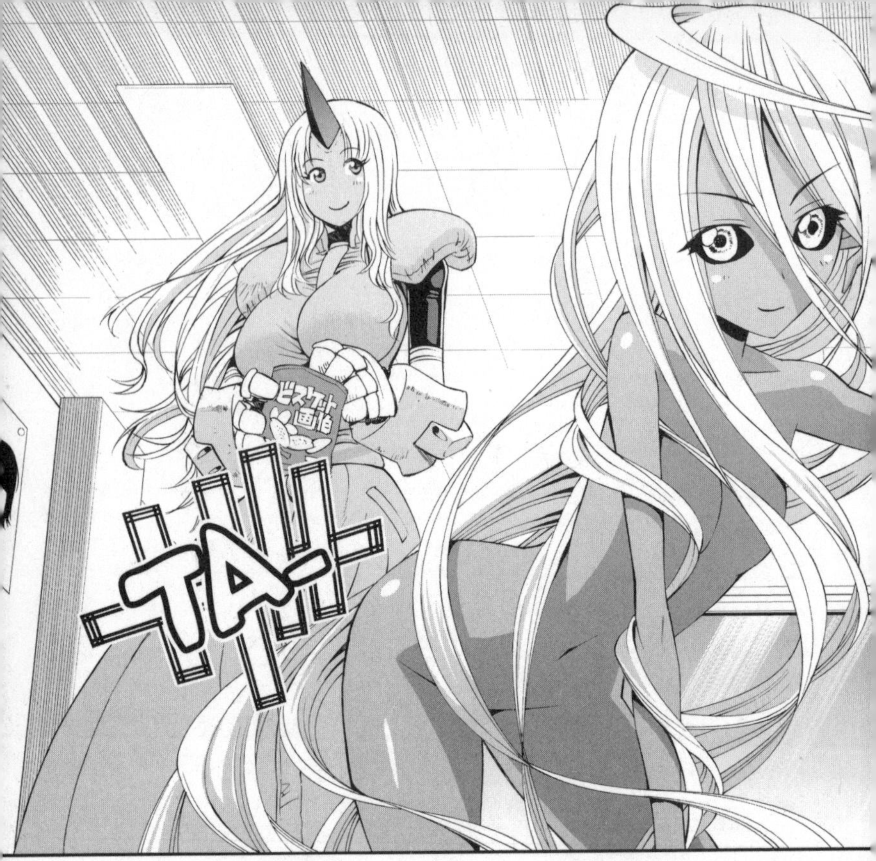
ビスケット画伯
-TA-

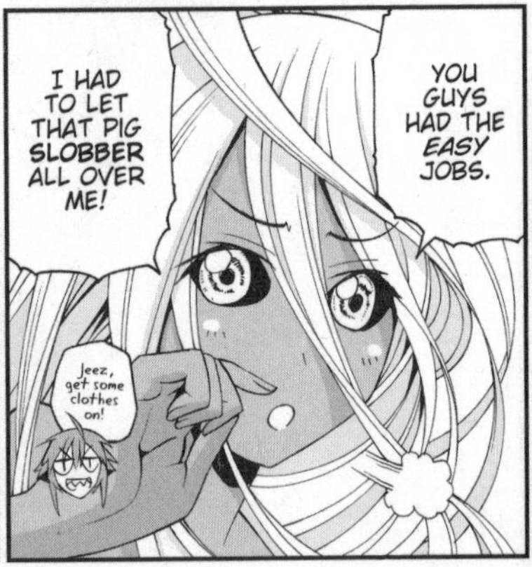
YOU GUYS HAD THE EASY JOBS.
I HAD TO LET THAT PIG SLOBBER ALL OVER ME!
Jeez, get some clothes on!

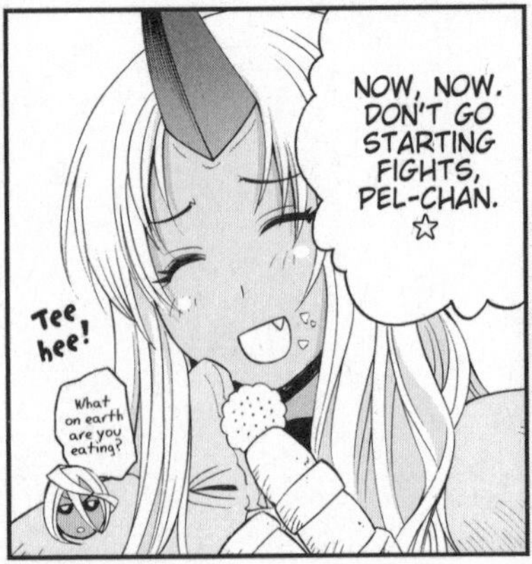
NOW, NOW. DON'T GO STARTING FIGHTS, PEL-CHAN. ☆
Tee hee!
What on earth are you eating?

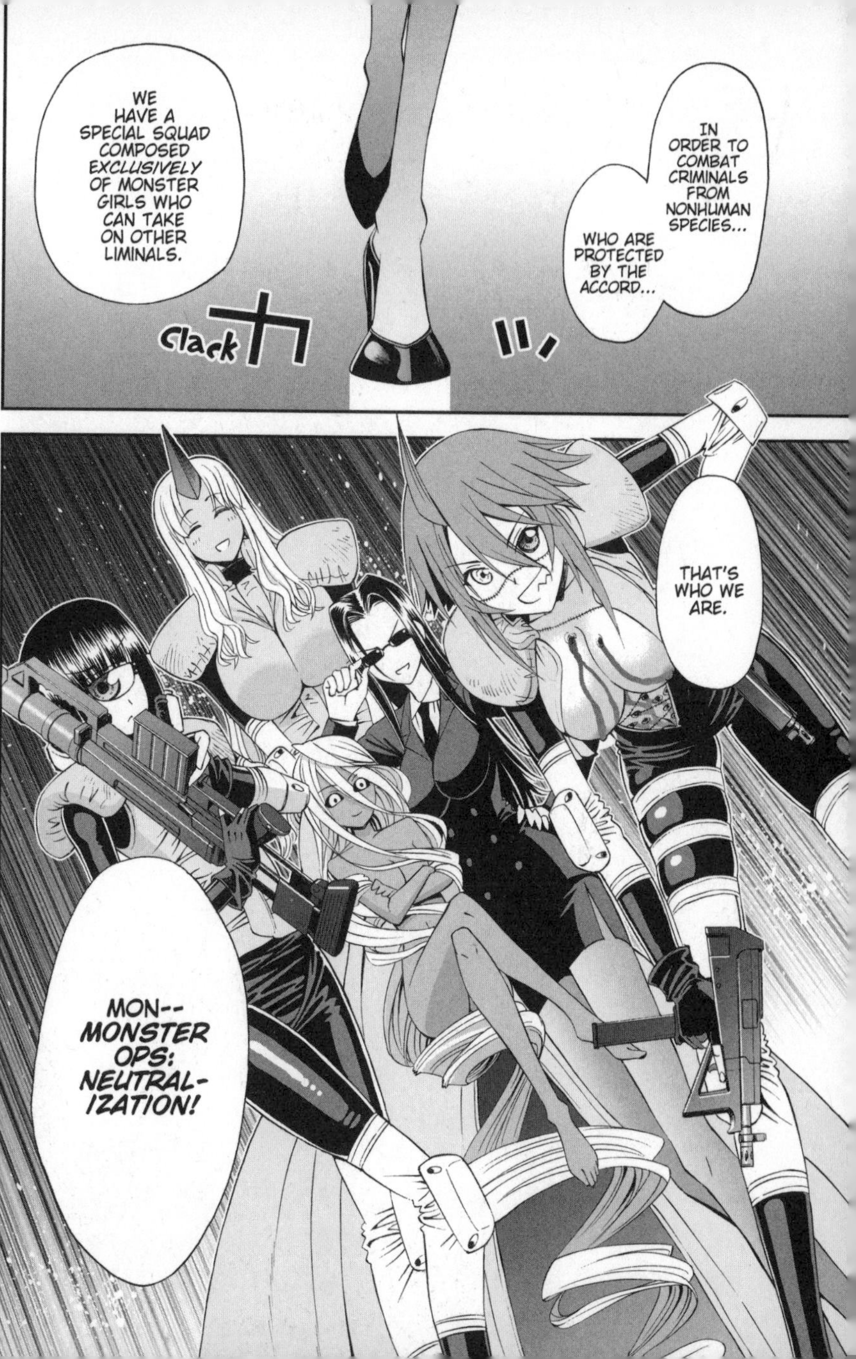
IN ORDER TO COMBAT CRIMINALS FROM NONHUMAN SPECIES...
WHO ARE PROTECTED BY THE ACCORD...
WE HAVE A SPECIAL SQUAD COMPOSED *EXCLUSIVELY* OF MONSTER GIRLS WHO CAN TAKE ON OTHER LIMINALS.
Clack
THAT'S WHO WE ARE.
MON-- MONSTER OPS: NEUTRALIZATION!

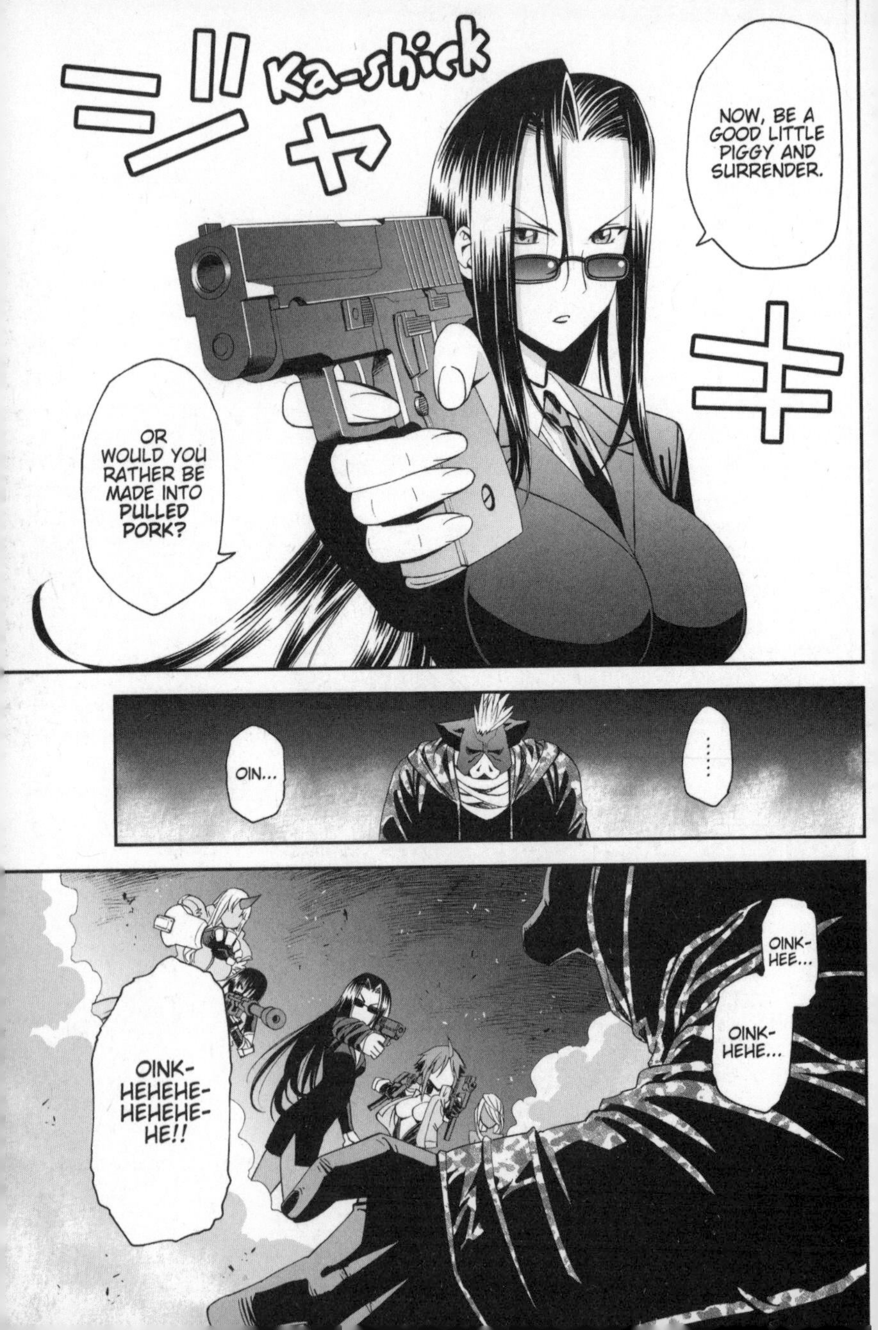
Ka-shick
NOW, BE A GOOD LITTLE PIGGY AND SURRENDER.
OR WOULD YOU RATHER BE MADE INTO PULLED PORK?
......
OIN...
OINK-HEE...
OINK-HEHE...
OINK-HEHEHE-HEHEHE-HE!!

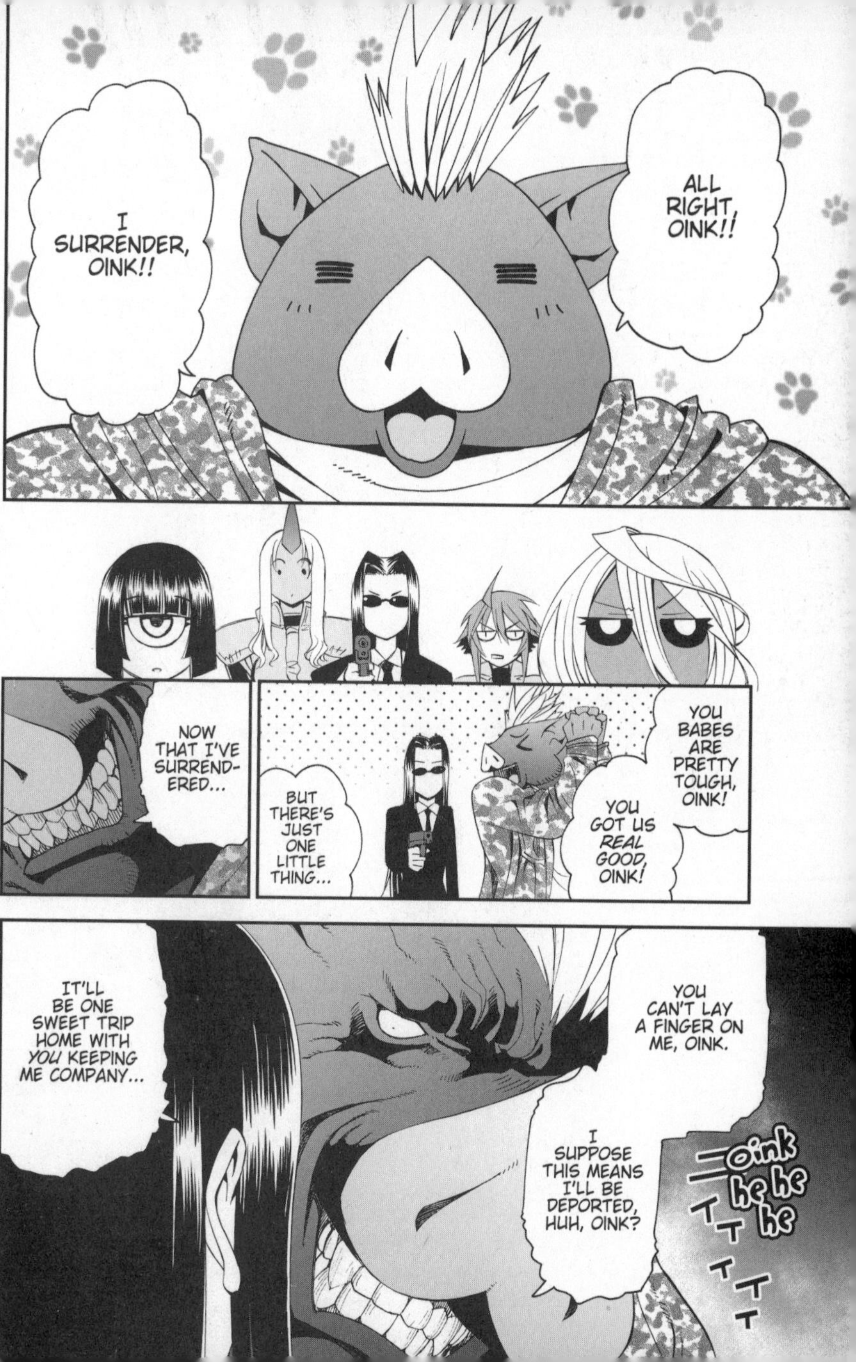
ALL RIGHT, OINK!!
I SURRENDER, OINK!!
YOU BABES ARE PRETTY TOUGH, OINK!
YOU GOT US *REAL* GOOD, OINK!
BUT THERE'S JUST ONE LITTLE THING...
NOW THAT I'VE SURRENDERED...
YOU CAN'T LAY A FINGER ON ME, OINK.
I SUPPOSE THIS MEANS I'LL BE DEPORTED, HUH, OINK?
oink he he he
IT'LL BE ONE SWEET TRIP HOME WITH *YOU* KEEPING ME COMPANY...

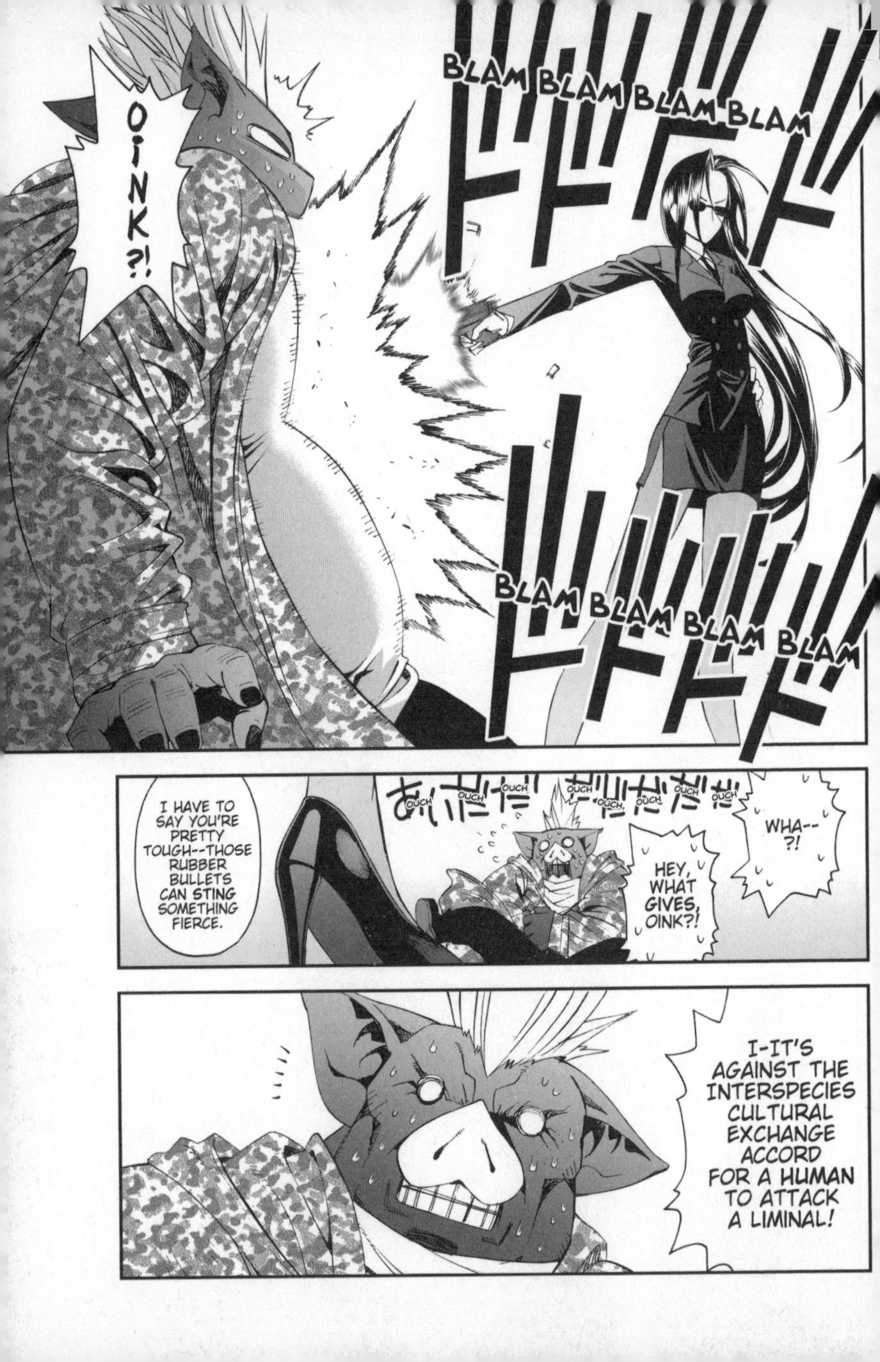
BLAM BLAM BLAM BLAM
OINK?!
BLAM BLAM BLAM BLAM
WHA--?!
OUCH OUCH OUCH OUCH OUCH OUCH OUCH OUCH
HEY, WHAT GIVES, OINK?!
I HAVE TO SAY YOU'RE PRETTY TOUGH--THOSE RUBBER BULLETS CAN STING SOMETHING FIERCE.
I-IT'S AGAINST THE INTERSPECIES CULTURAL EXCHANGE ACCORD FOR A HUMAN TO ATTACK A LIMINAL!

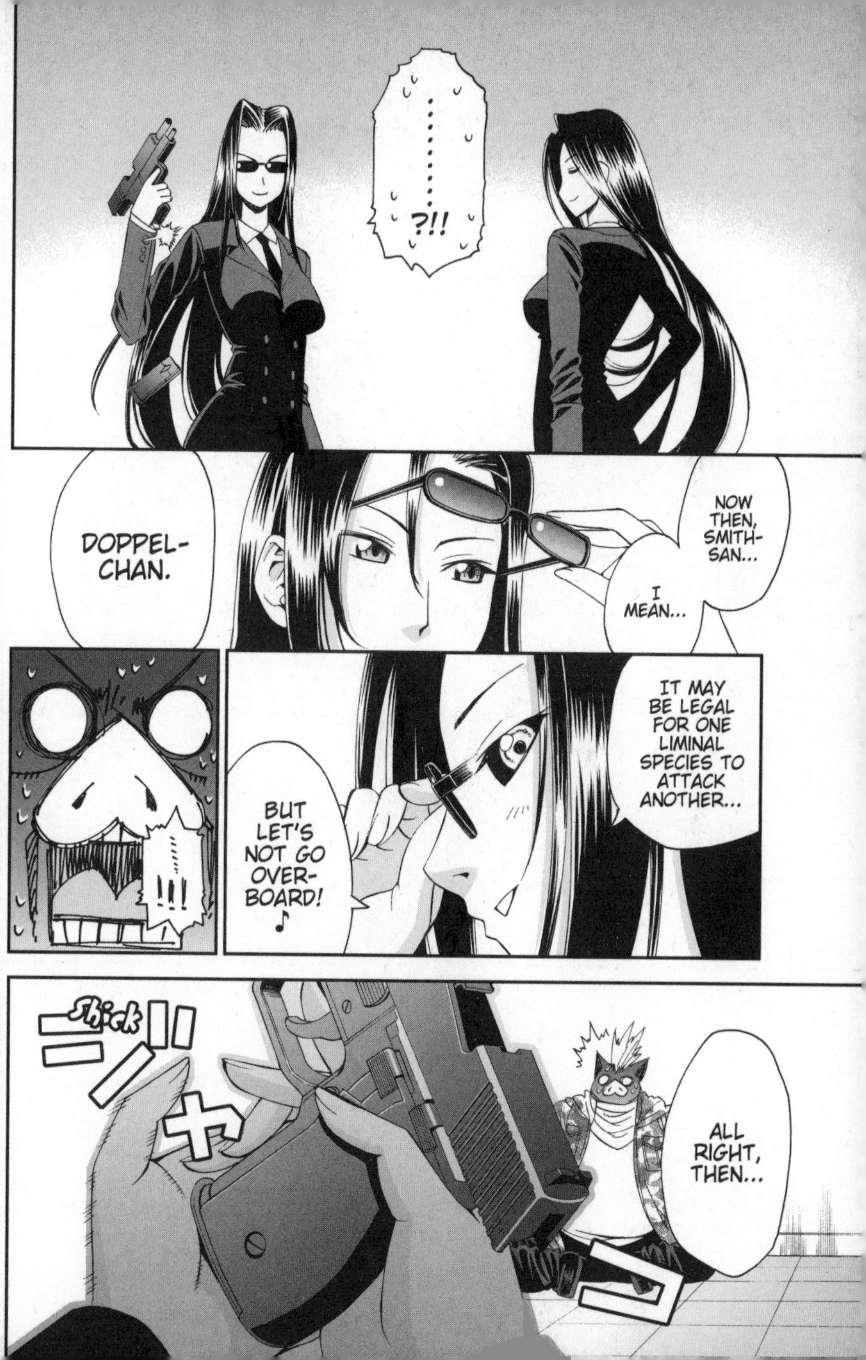
......?!!
NOW THEN, SMITH-SAN...
I MEAN...
DOPPEL-CHAN.
IT MAY BE LEGAL FOR ONE LIMINAL SPECIES TO ATTACK ANOTHER...
BUT LET'S NOT GO OVER-BOARD! ♪
......!!!
ALL RIGHT, THEN...
Shick

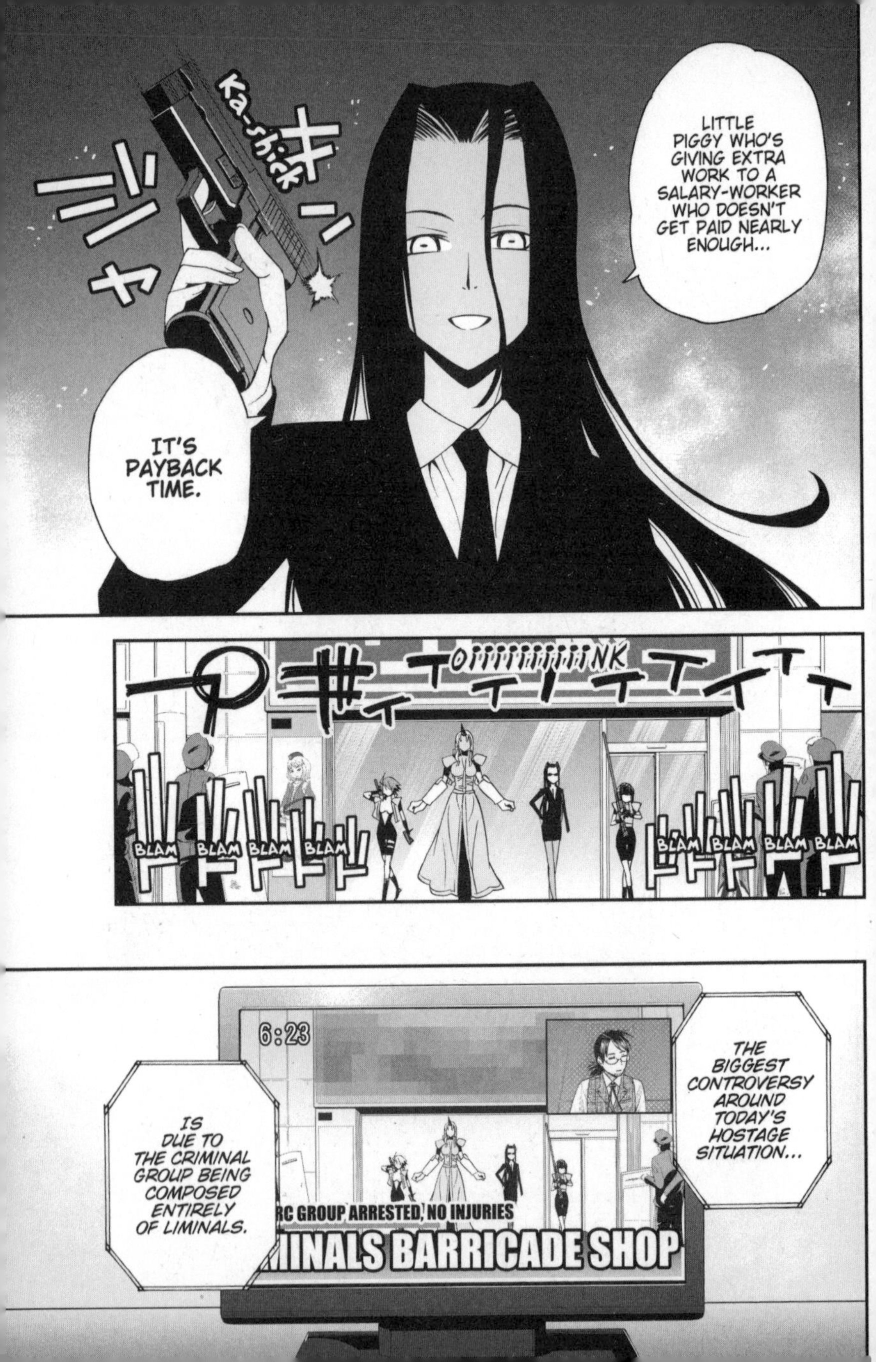

LITTLE PIGGY WHO'S GIVING EXTRA WORK TO A SALARY-WORKER WHO DOESN'T GET PAID NEARLY ENOUGH...
Ka-shick
IT'S PAYBACK TIME.
TOiiiiiiiiiiNK
BLAM BLAM BLAM BLAM
BLAM BLAM BLAM BLAM
6:23
THE BIGGEST CONTROVERSY AROUND TODAY'S HOSTAGE SITUATION...
IS DUE TO THE CRIMINAL GROUP BEING COMPOSED ENTIRELY OF LIMINALS.
RC GROUP ARRESTED, NO INJURIES
IINALS BARRICADE SHOP

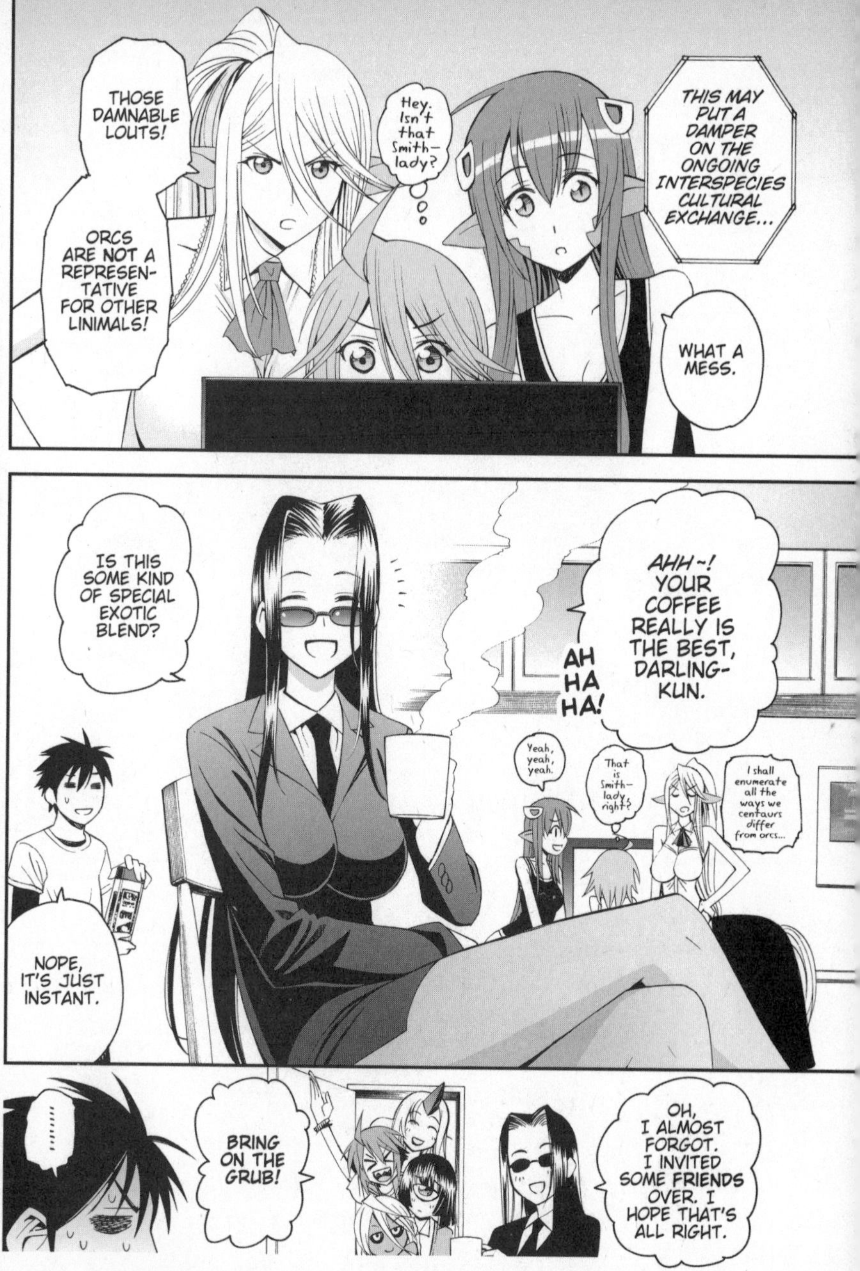
THIS MAY PUT A DAMPER ON THE ONGOING INTERSPECIES CULTURAL EXCHANGE...
WHAT A MESS.
Hey. Isn't that Smith-lady?
THOSE DAMNABLE LOUTS!
ORCS ARE NOT A REPRESENTATIVE FOR OTHER LINIMALS!
AHH~! YOUR COFFEE REALLY IS THE BEST, DARLING-KUN.
AH HA HA!
I shall enumerate all the ways we centaurs differ from orcs...
That is Smith-lady, right?
Yeah, yeah, yeah.
IS THIS SOME KIND OF SPECIAL EXOTIC BLEND?
NOPE, IT'S JUST INSTANT.
OH, I ALMOST FORGOT. I INVITED SOME FRIENDS OVER. I HOPE THAT'S ALL RIGHT.
BRING ON THE GRUB!
......

Monster Musume

Everyday Life with Monster Girls

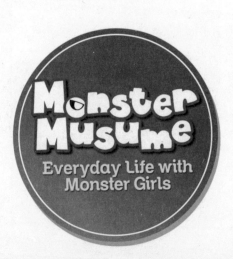

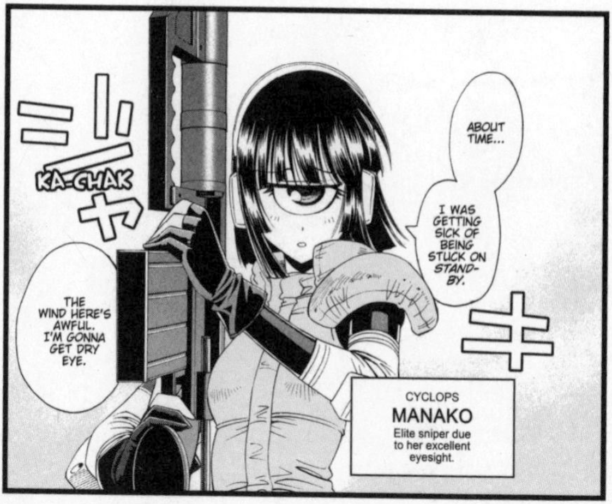
ABOUT TIME...
I WAS GETTING SICK OF BEING STUCK ON STAND-BY.
KA-CHAK
THE WIND HERE'S AWFUL. I'M GONNA GET DRY EYE.
CYCLOPS
MANAKO
Elite sniper due to her excellent eyesight.

Chapter 13

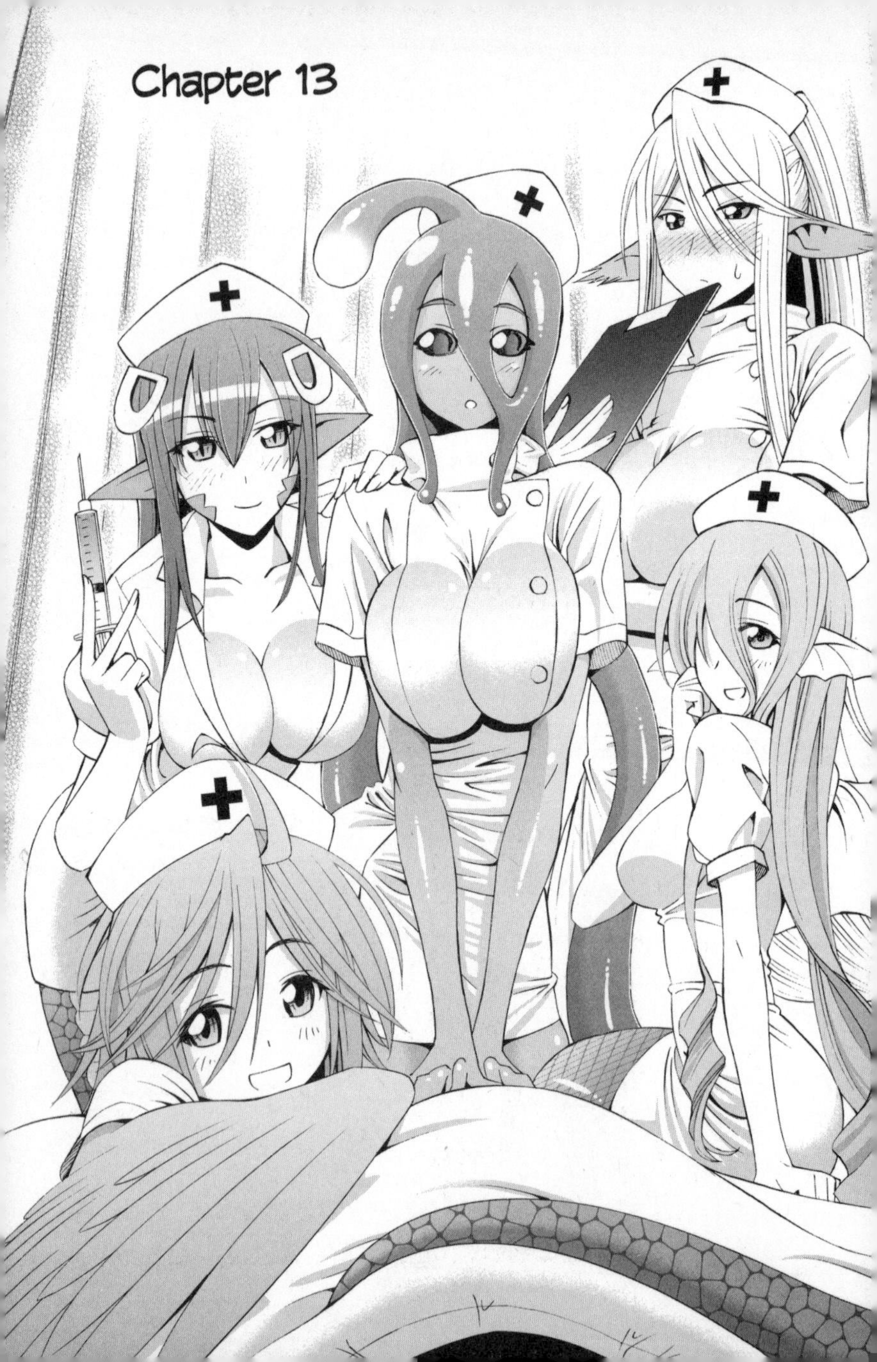

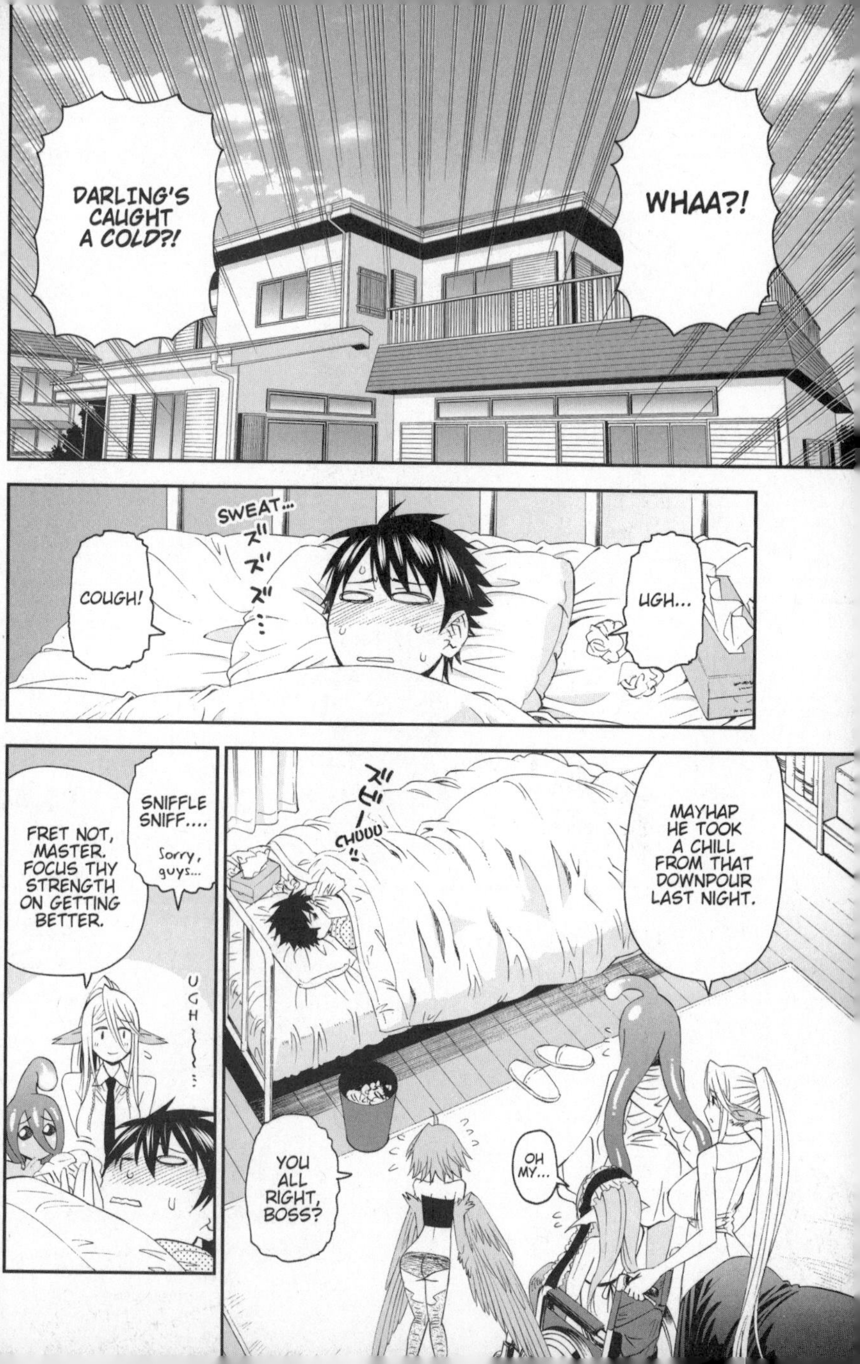
WHAA?!
DARLING'S CAUGHT A COLD?!
UGH...
SWEAT...
ズズズ...
COUGH!
MAYHAP HE TOOK A CHILL FROM THAT DOWNPOUR LAST NIGHT.
ズビー
CHUUU
OH MY...
YOU ALL RIGHT, BOSS?
SNIFFLE SNIFF....
Sorry, guys...
FRET NOT, MASTER. FOCUS THY STRENGTH ON GETTING BETTER.
UGH~~...

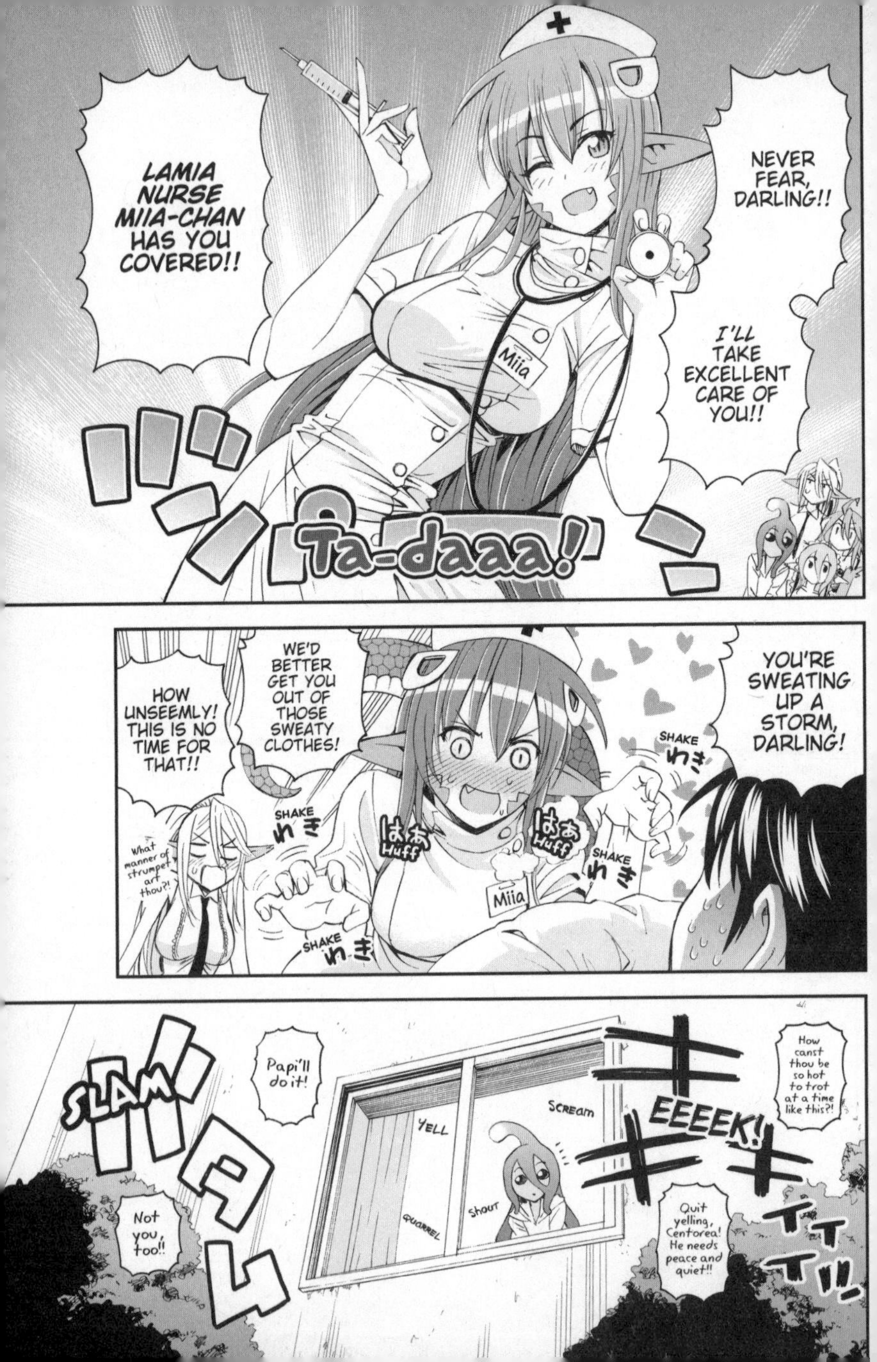
NEVER FEAR, DARLING!!
I'LL TAKE EXCELLENT CARE OF YOU!!
LAMIA NURSE MIIA-CHAN HAS YOU COVERED!!
Miia
Ta-daaa!
YOU'RE SWEATING UP A STORM, DARLING!
SHAKE わき
WE'D BETTER GET YOU OUT OF THOSE SWEATY CLOTHES!
はあ Huff
はあ Huff
SHAKE わき
Miia
SHAKE わき
SHAKE わき
HOW UNSEEMLY! THIS IS NO TIME FOR THAT!!
What manner of strumpet art thou?!
How canst thou be so hot to trot at a time like this?!
EEEEK!
Quit yelling, Centorea! He needs peace and quiet!!
SCREAM
YELL
Shout
QUARREL
Papi'll do it!
Not you, too!!
SLAM

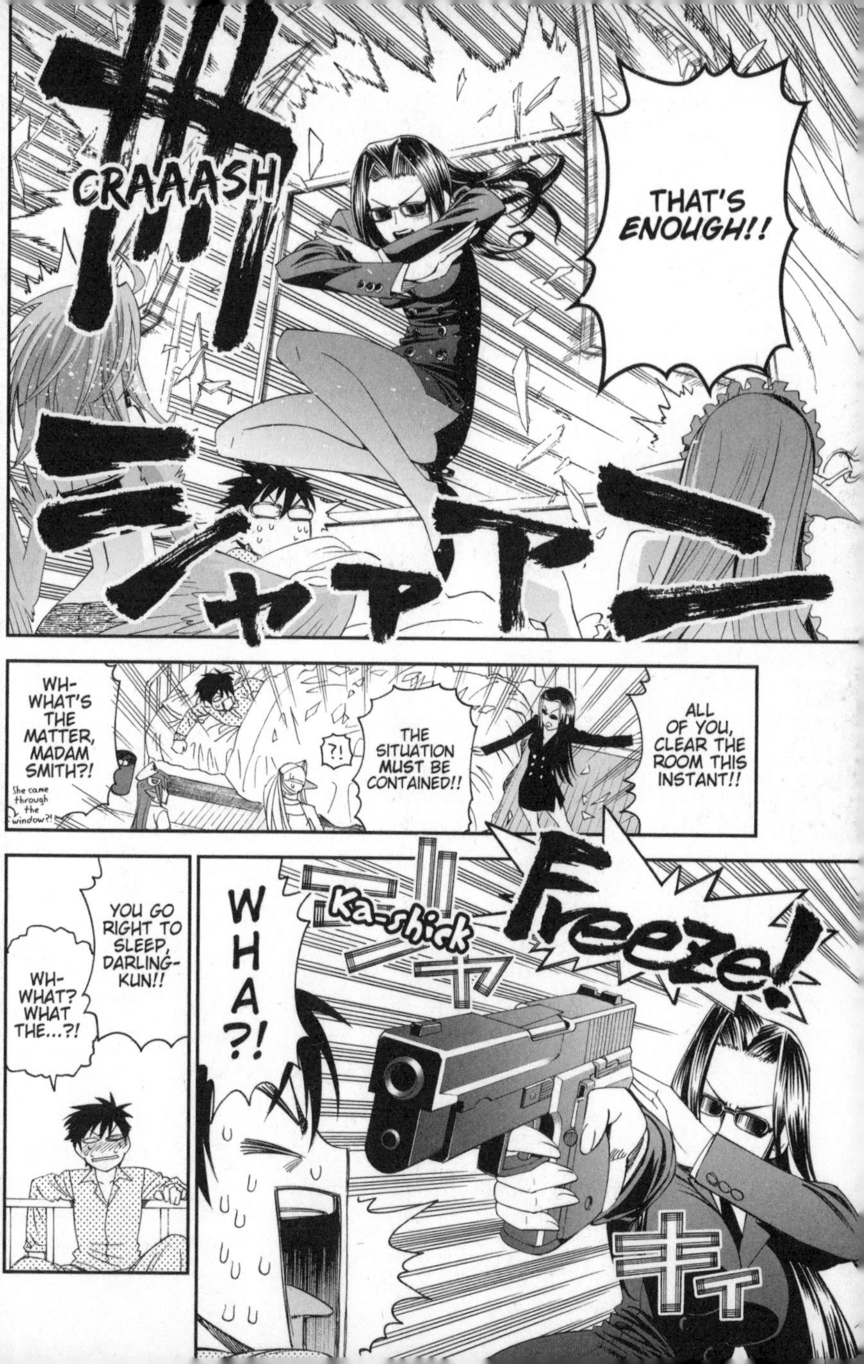
THAT'S ENOUGH!!
CRAAASH
ALL OF YOU, CLEAR THE ROOM THIS INSTANT!!
THE SITUATION MUST BE CONTAINED!!
?!
WH-WHAT'S THE MATTER, MADAM SMITH?!
She came through the window?!
Freeze!
Ka-shick
WHA?!
YOU GO RIGHT TO SLEEP, DARLING-KUN!!
WH-WHAT? WHAT THE...?!

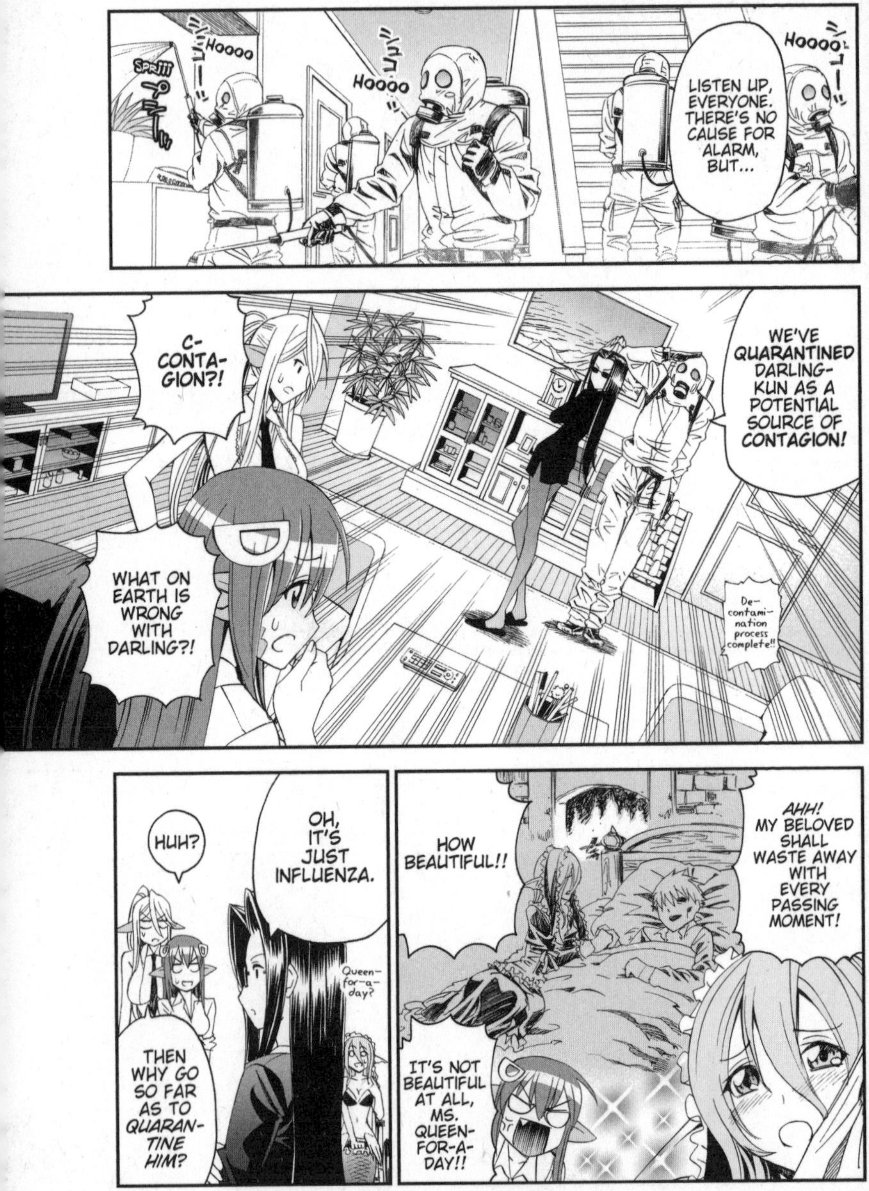
Hoooo
LISTEN UP, EVERYONE. THERE'S NO CAUSE FOR ALARM, BUT...
Hoooo
Hoooo
Spriiii
WE'VE QUARANTINED DARLING-KUN AS A POTENTIAL SOURCE OF CONTAGION!
De-contamination process complete!!
C-CONTAGION?!
WHAT ON EARTH IS WRONG WITH DARLING?!
AHH! MY BELOVED SHALL WASTE AWAY WITH EVERY PASSING MOMENT!
HOW BEAUTIFUL!!
IT'S NOT BEAUTIFUL AT ALL, MS. QUEEN-FOR-A-DAY!!
OH, IT'S JUST INFLUENZA.
HUH?
Queen-for-a-day?
THEN WHY GO SO FAR AS TO QUARANTINE HIM?

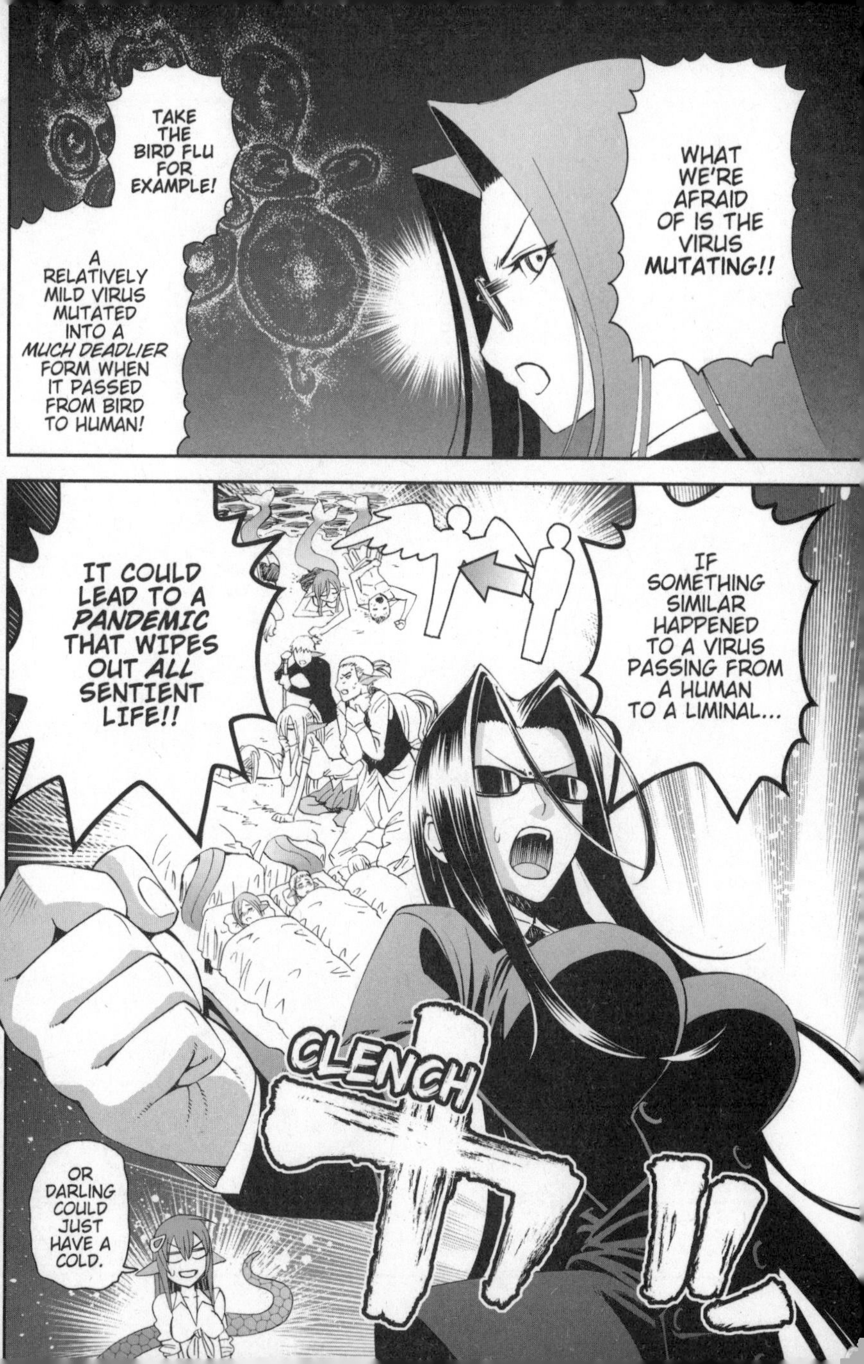
WHAT WE'RE AFRAID OF IS THE VIRUS MUTATING!!
TAKE THE BIRD FLU FOR EXAMPLE!
A RELATIVELY MILD VIRUS MUTATED INTO A *MUCH DEADLIER* FORM WHEN IT PASSED FROM BIRD TO HUMAN!
IF SOMETHING SIMILAR HAPPENED TO A VIRUS PASSING FROM A HUMAN TO A LIMINAL...
IT COULD LEAD TO A *PANDEMIC* THAT WIPES OUT *ALL* SENTIENT LIFE!!
CLENCH
OR DARLING COULD JUST HAVE A COLD.

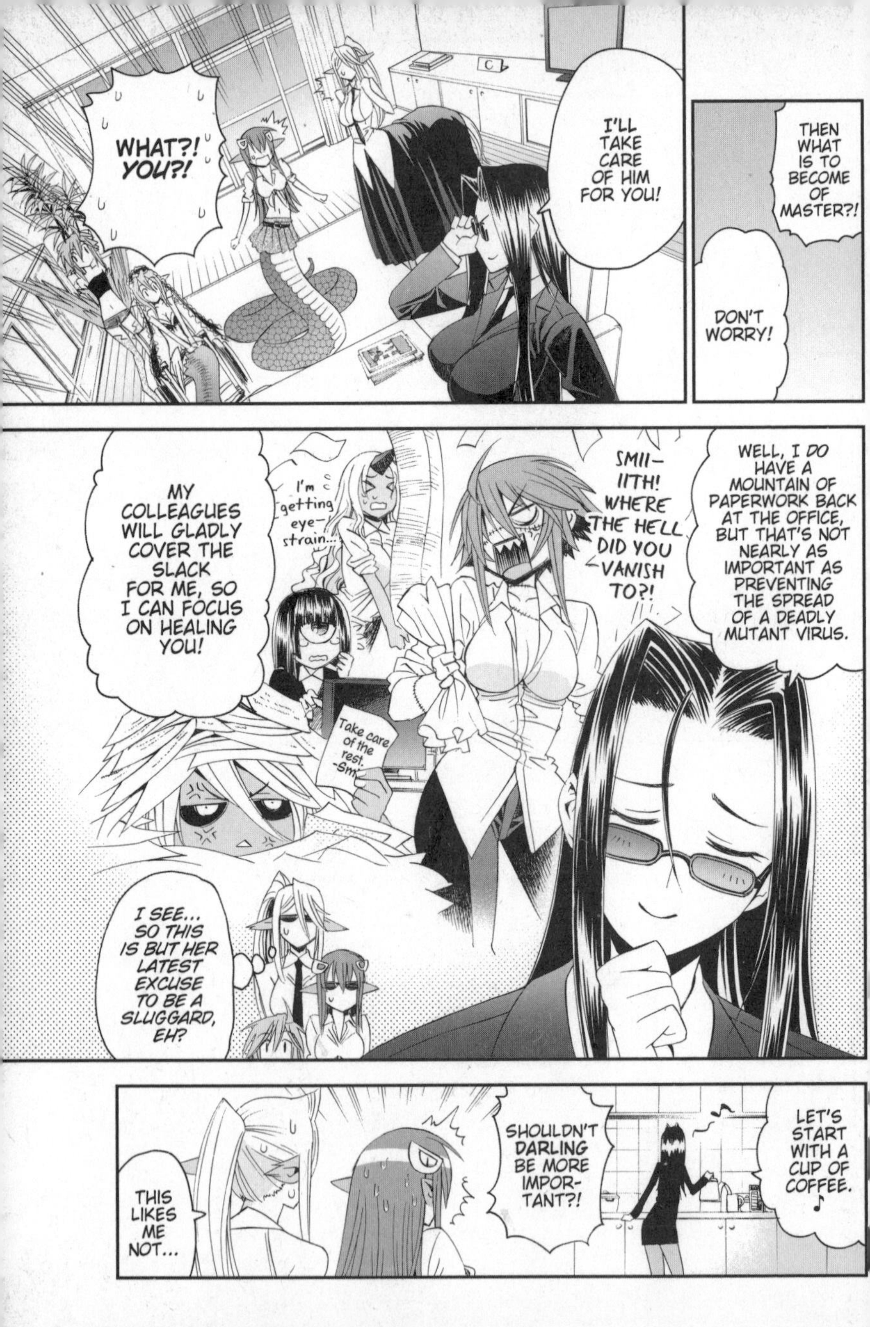
THEN WHAT IS TO BECOME OF MASTER?!
DON'T WORRY!
I'LL TAKE CARE OF HIM FOR YOU!
WHAT?! YOU?!
WELL, I DO HAVE A MOUNTAIN OF PAPERWORK BACK AT THE OFFICE, BUT THAT'S NOT NEARLY AS IMPORTANT AS PREVENTING THE SPREAD OF A DEADLY MUTANT VIRUS.
SMII-IITH! WHERE THE HELL DID YOU VANISH TO?!
I'm getting eye-strain...
Take care of the rest. -Smi
MY COLLEAGUES WILL GLADLY COVER THE SLACK FOR ME, SO I CAN FOCUS ON HEALING YOU!
I SEE... SO THIS IS BUT HER LATEST EXCUSE TO BE A SLUGGARD, EH?
LET'S START WITH A CUP OF COFFEE. ♪
SHOULDN'T DARLING BE MORE IMPOR-TANT?!
THIS LIKES ME NOT...

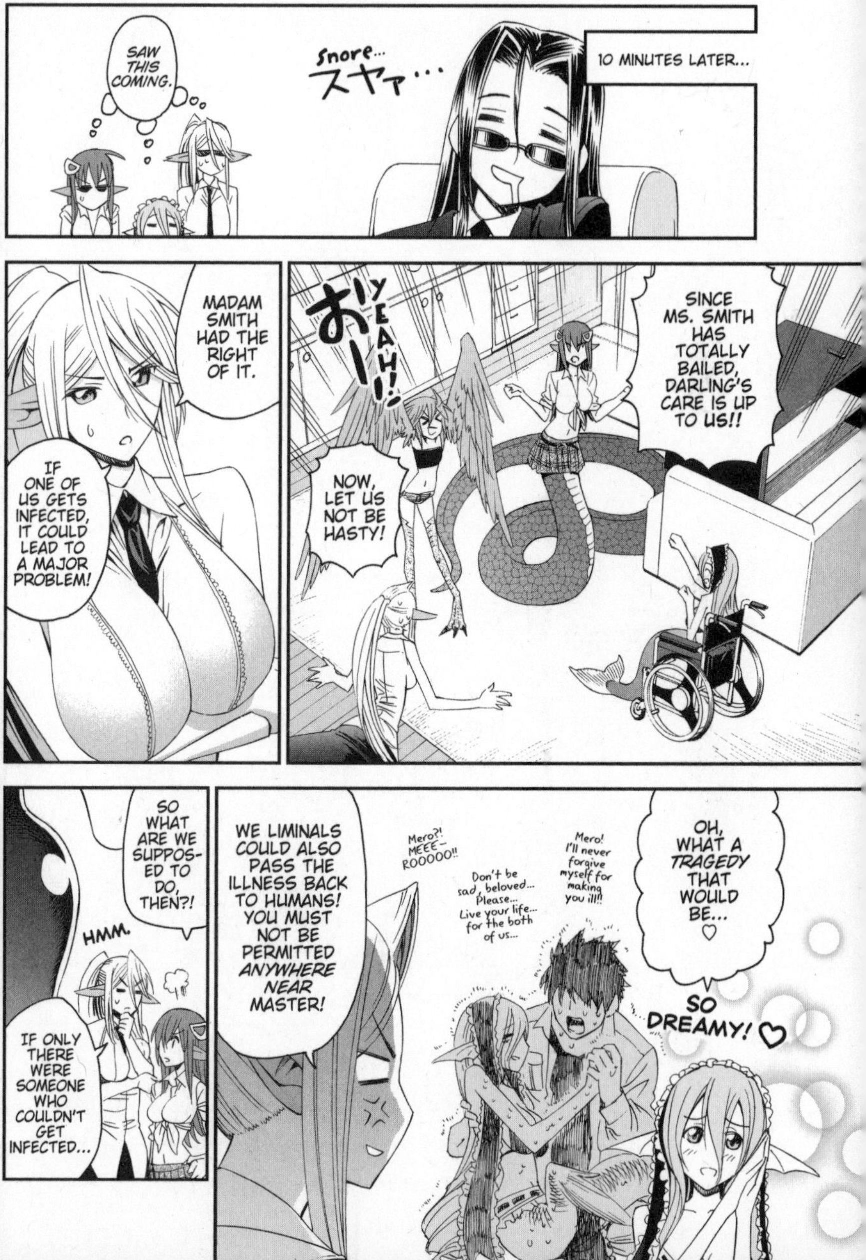
10 MINUTES LATER...
Snore... スヤァ...
SAW THIS COMING.
SINCE MS. SMITH HAS TOTALLY BAILED, DARLING'S CARE IS UP TO US!!
YEAH!! おー!!
NOW, LET US NOT BE HASTY!
MADAM SMITH HAD THE RIGHT OF IT.
IF ONE OF US GETS INFECTED, IT COULD LEAD TO A MAJOR PROBLEM!
OH, WHAT A TRAGEDY THAT WOULD BE... ♡
Mero! I'll never forgive myself for making you ill!!
Don't be sad, beloved... Please... Live your life... for the both of us...
Mero?! MEEE-ROOOOO!!
SO DREAMY! ♡
WE LIMINALS COULD ALSO PASS THE ILLNESS BACK TO HUMANS! YOU MUST NOT BE PERMITTED ANYWHERE NEAR MASTER!
SO WHAT ARE WE SUPPOS-ED TO DO, THEN?!
HMM.
IF ONLY THERE WERE SOMEONE WHO COULDN'T GET INFECTED...

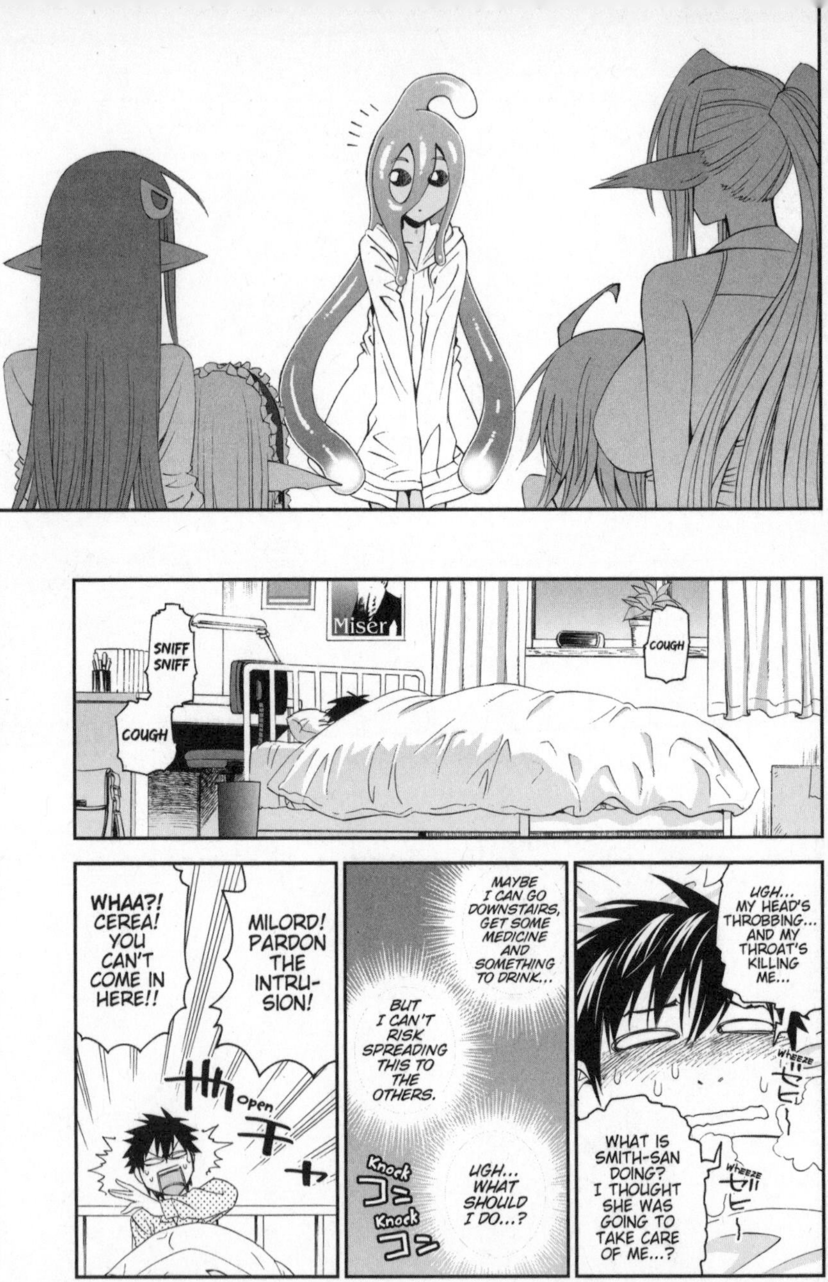
Miser
COUGH
SNIFF SNIFF
COUGH
UGH... MY HEAD'S THROBBING... AND MY THROAT'S KILLING ME...
WHEEZE
WHAT IS SMITH-SAN DOING? I THOUGHT SHE WAS GOING TO TAKE CARE OF ME...?
WHEEZE
MAYBE I CAN GO DOWNSTAIRS, GET SOME MEDICINE AND SOMETHING TO DRINK...
BUT I CAN'T RISK SPREADING THIS TO THE OTHERS.
UGH... WHAT SHOULD I DO...?
Knock
Knock
MILORD! PARDON THE INTRUSION!
WHAA?! CEREA! YOU CAN'T COME IN HERE!!
open

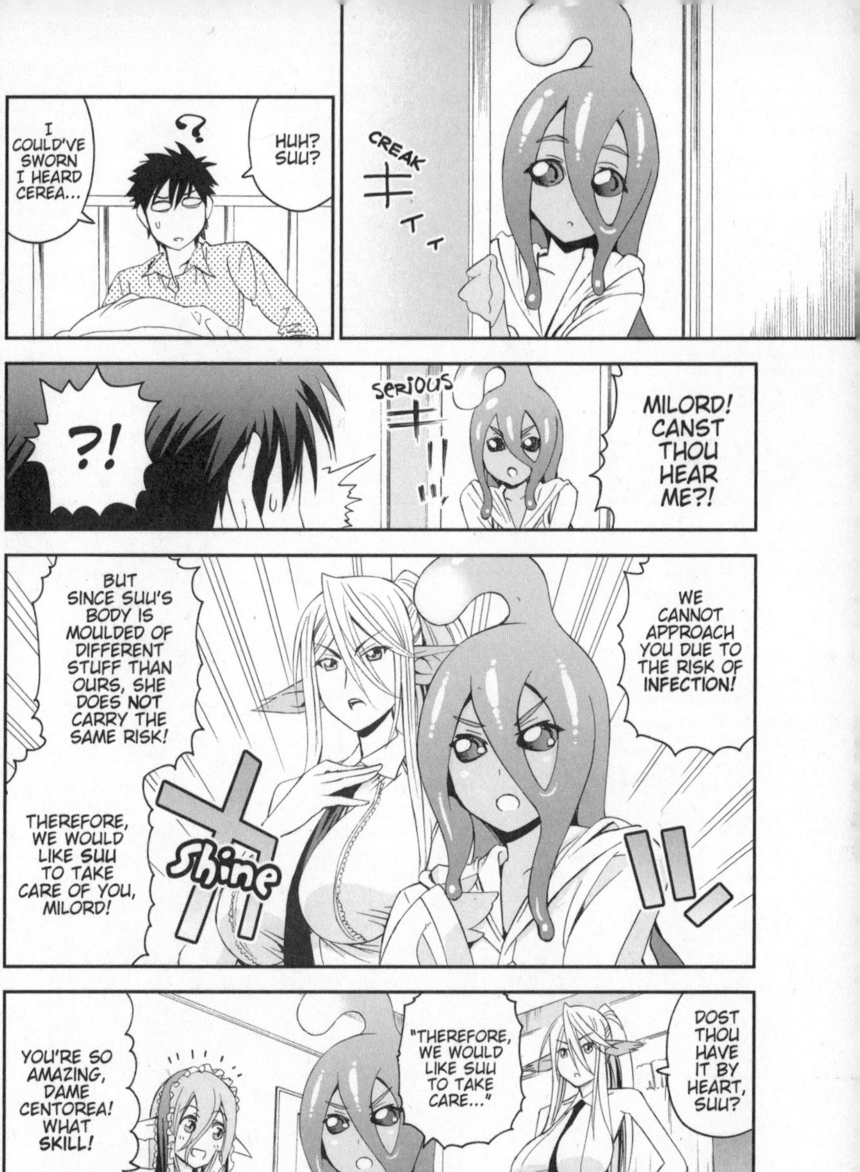
CREAK
HUH? SUU?
I COULD'VE SWORN I HEARD CEREA...
MILORD! CANST THOU HEAR ME?!
serious
?!
WE CANNOT APPROACH YOU DUE TO THE RISK OF INFECTION!
BUT SINCE SUU'S BODY IS MOULDED OF DIFFERENT STUFF THAN OURS, SHE DOES NOT CARRY THE SAME RISK!
THEREFORE, WE WOULD LIKE SUU TO TAKE CARE OF YOU, MILORD!
Shine
DOST THOU HAVE IT BY HEART, SUU?
"THEREFORE, WE WOULD LIKE SUU TO TAKE CARE..."
YOU'RE SO AMAZING, DAME CENTOREA! WHAT SKILL!

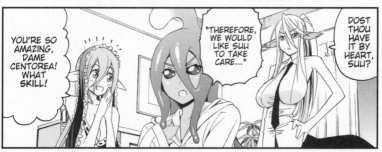

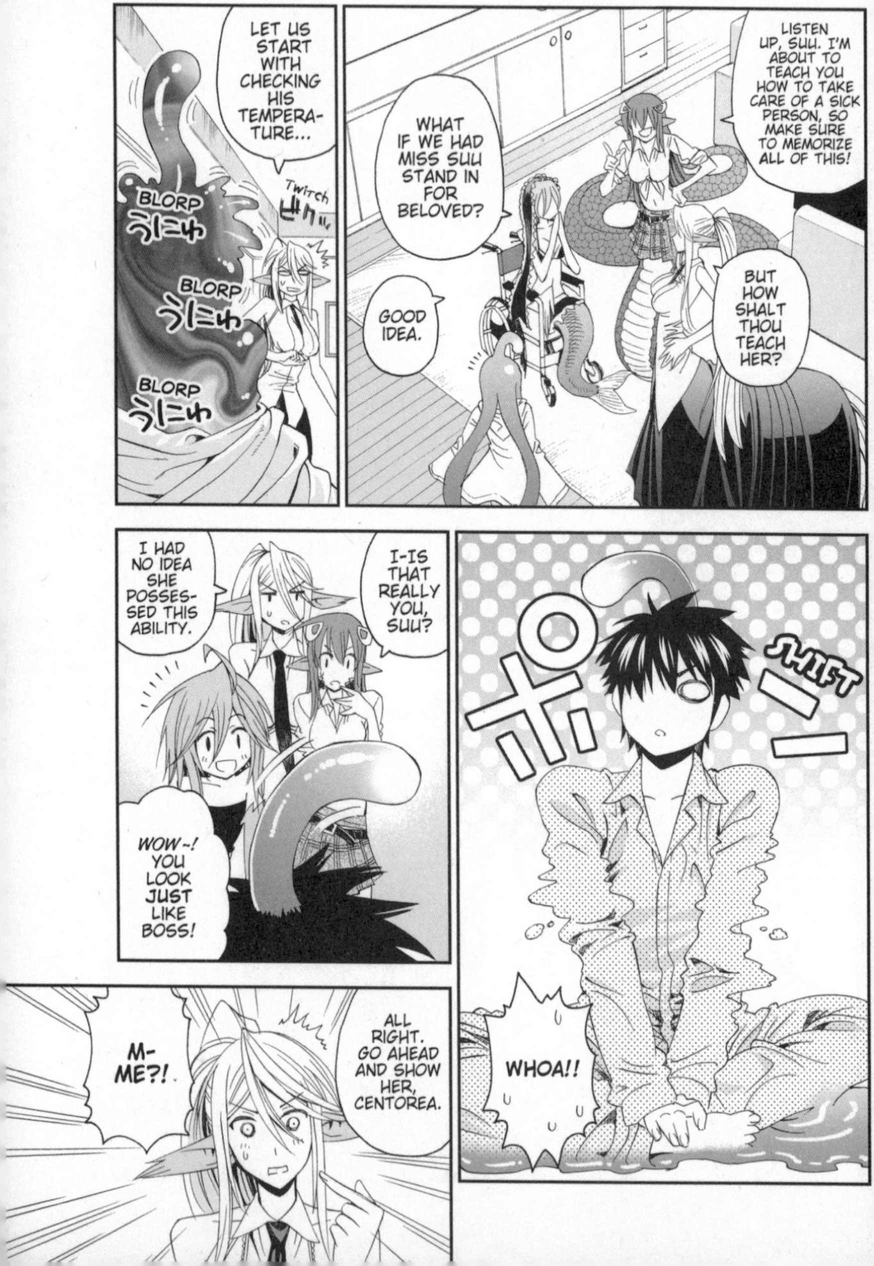
LISTEN UP, SUU. I'M ABOUT TO TEACH YOU HOW TO TAKE CARE OF A SICK PERSON, SO MAKE SURE TO MEMORIZE ALL OF THIS!
BUT HOW SHALT THOU TEACH HER?
WHAT IF WE HAD MISS SUU STAND IN FOR BELOVED?
GOOD IDEA.
LET US START WITH CHECKING HIS TEMPERATURE...
Twitch
ビクッ
BLORP
うにゅ
BLORP
うにゅ
BLORP
うにゅ
SHIFT
ポー
WHOA!!
I-IS THAT REALLY YOU, SUU?
I HAD NO IDEA SHE POSSESSED THIS ABILITY.
WOW-! YOU LOOK JUST LIKE BOSS!
ALL RIGHT. GO AHEAD AND SHOW HER, CENTOREA.
M-ME?!

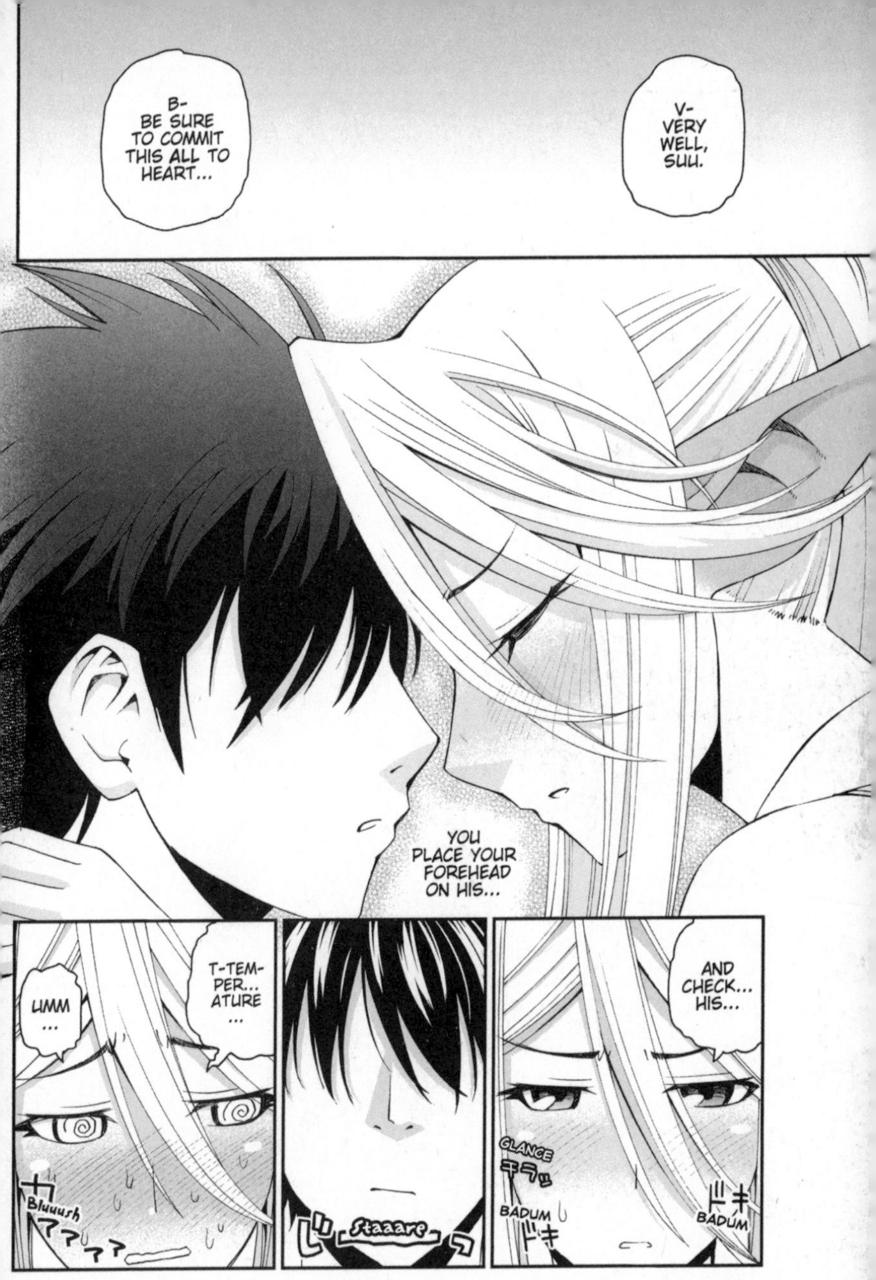
V- VERY WELL, SUU.
B- BE SURE TO COMMIT THIS ALL TO HEART...
YOU PLACE YOUR FOREHEAD ON HIS...
AND CHECK... HIS...
GLANCE
キラッ
ドキ
BADUM
BADUM
ドキ
Staaare
T-TEMPER... ATURE ...
UMM ...
Bluuush

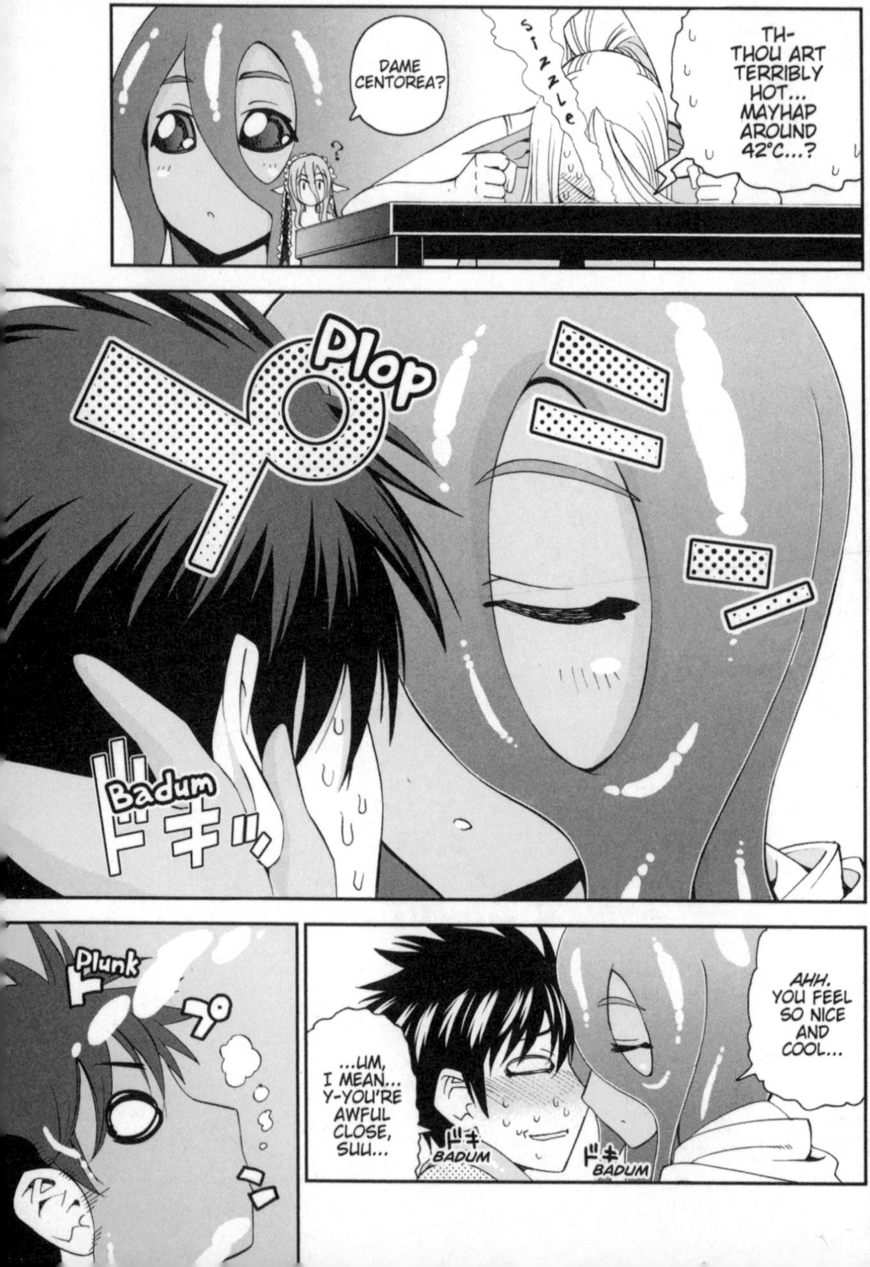
TH-THOU ART TERRIBLY HOT... MAYHAP AROUND 42°C...?
sizzle
DAME CENTOREA?
Plop
Badum
ドキッ
AHH. YOU FEEL SO NICE AND COOL...
ドキ
BADUM
...UM, I MEAN... Y-YOU'RE AWFUL CLOSE, SUU...
ドキ
BADUM
Plunk

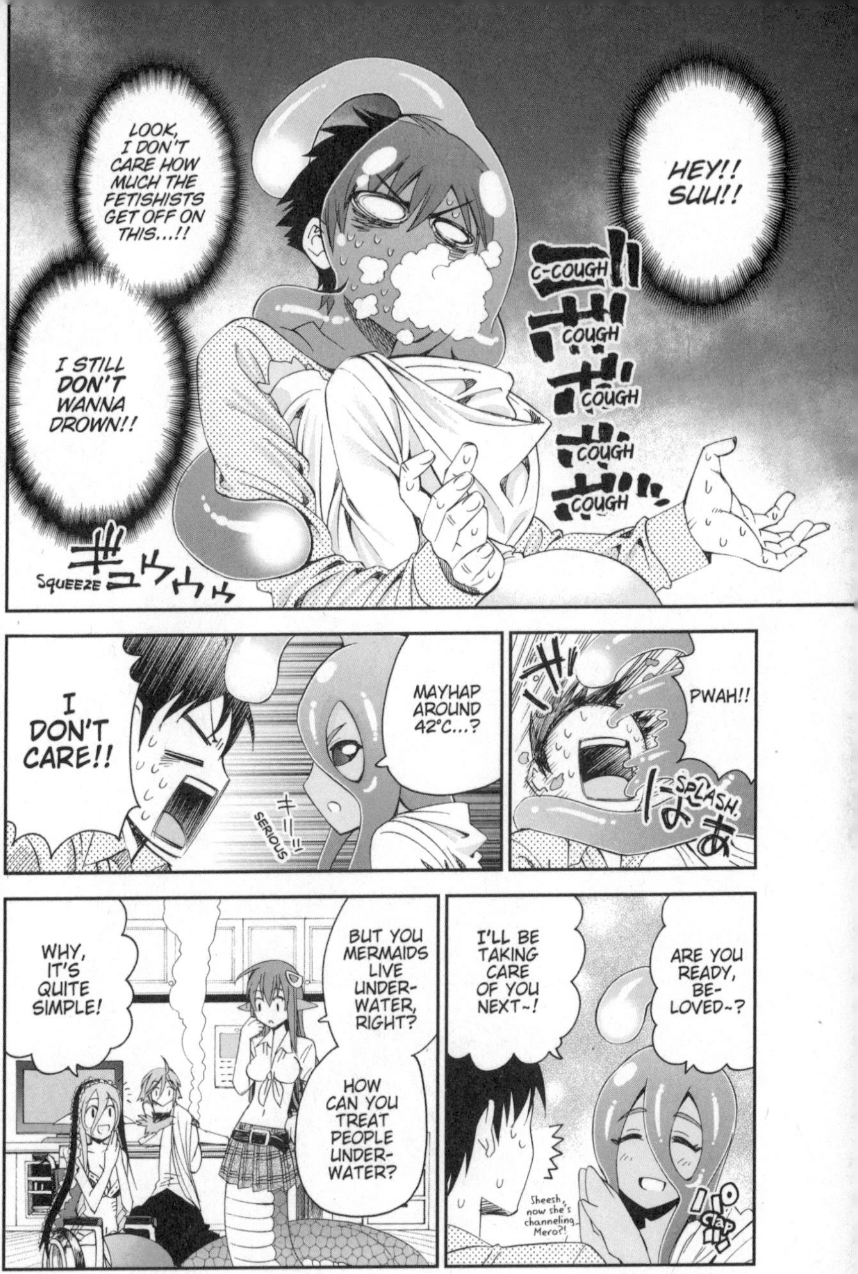
HEY!! SUU!!
C-COUGH
COUGH
COUGH
COUGH
COUGH
LOOK, I DON'T CARE HOW MUCH THE FETISHISTS GET OFF ON THIS...!!
I STILL DON'T WANNA DROWN!!
Squeeze
PWAH!!
SPLASH.
MAYHAP AROUND 42°C...?
SERIOUS
I DON'T CARE!!
ARE YOU READY, BE-LOVED~?
I'LL BE TAKING CARE OF YOU NEXT~!
Sheesh, now she's channeling Mero?!
Clap
BUT YOU MERMAIDS LIVE UNDER-WATER, RIGHT?
HOW CAN YOU TREAT PEOPLE UNDER-WATER?
WHY, IT'S QUITE SIMPLE!

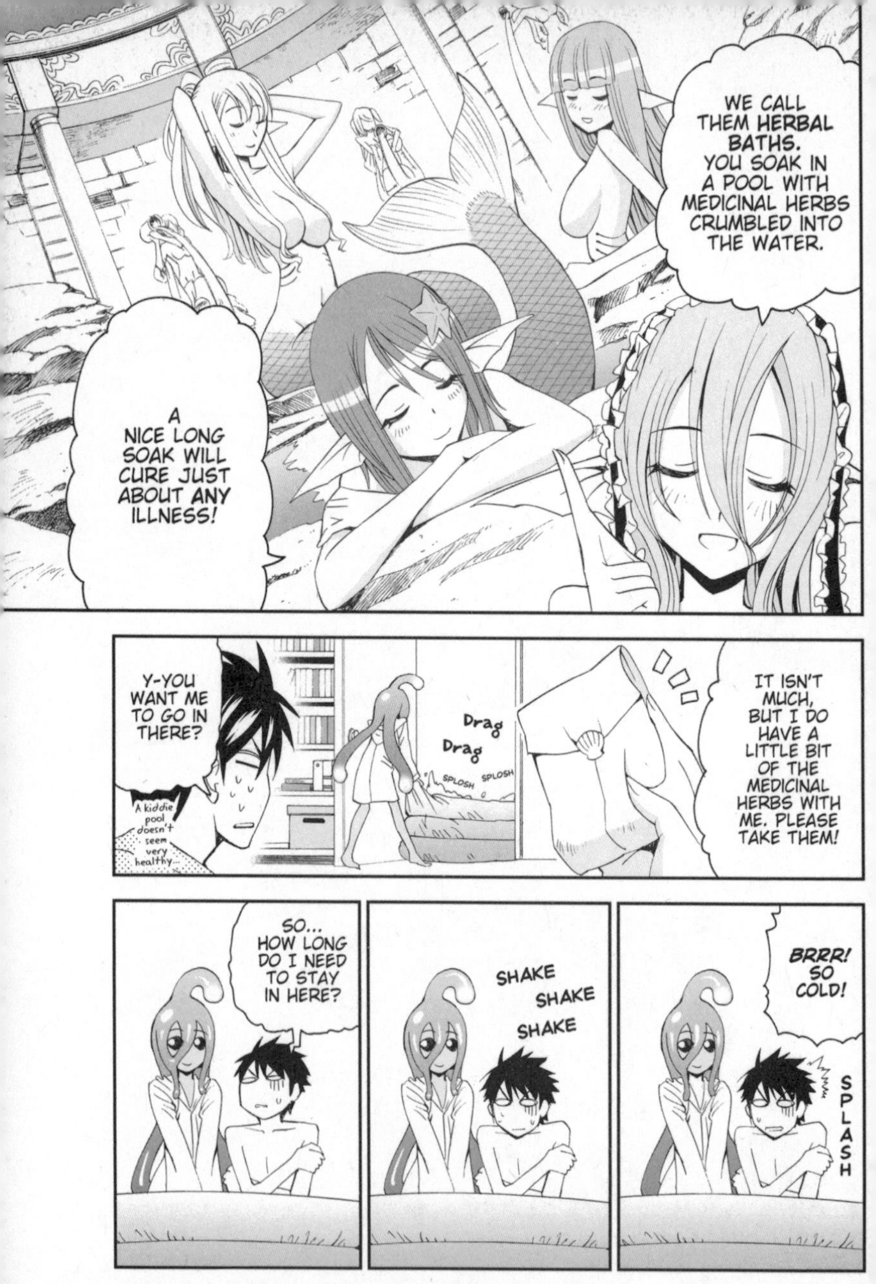
WE CALL THEM HERBAL BATHS. YOU SOAK IN A POOL WITH MEDICINAL HERBS CRUMBLED INTO THE WATER.
A NICE LONG SOAK WILL CURE JUST ABOUT ANY ILLNESS!
IT ISN'T MUCH, BUT I DO HAVE A LITTLE BIT OF THE MEDICINAL HERBS WITH ME. PLEASE TAKE THEM!
Drag
Drag
SPLOSH
SPLOSH
Y-YOU WANT ME TO GO IN THERE?
A kiddie pool doesn't seem very healthy...
BRRR! SO COLD!
SPLASH
SHAKE
SHAKE
SHAKE
SO... HOW LONG DO I NEED TO STAY IN HERE?

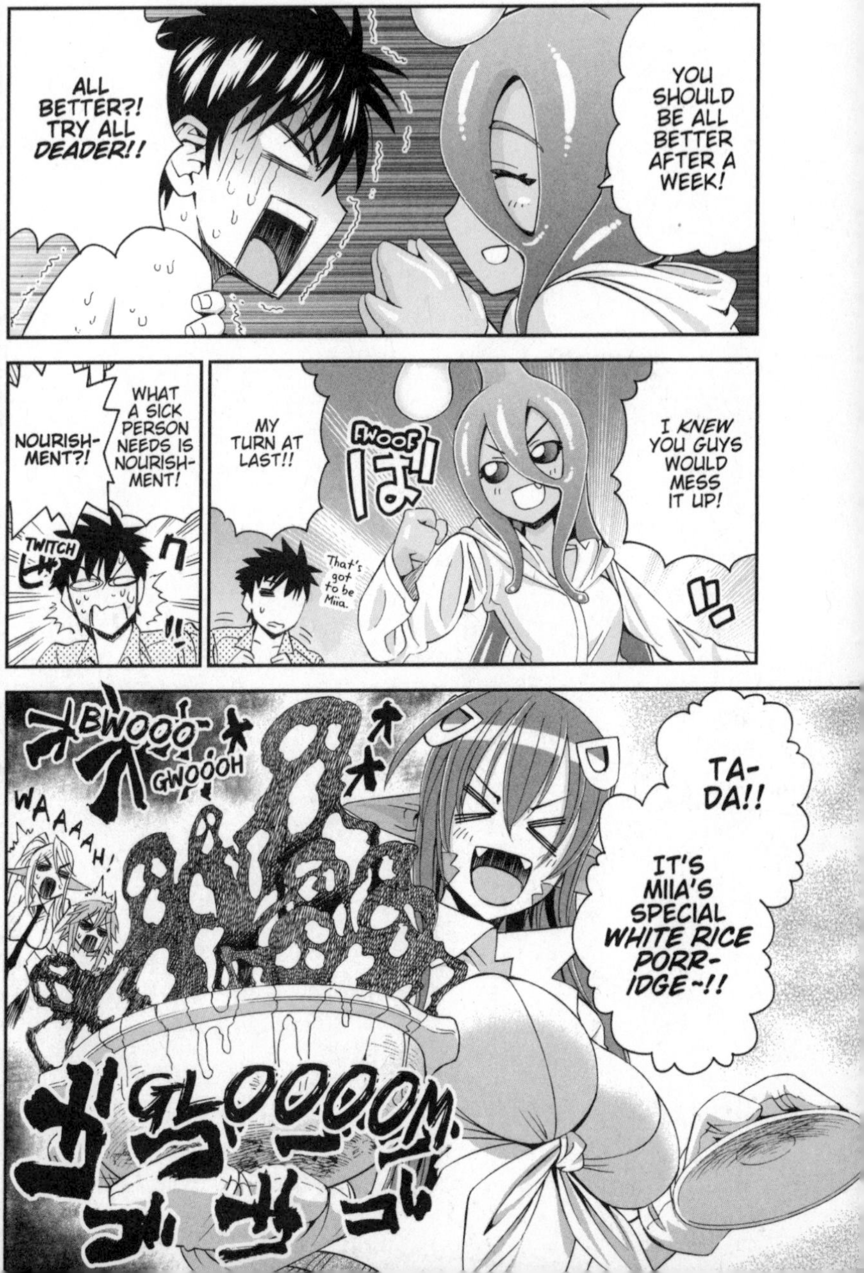
YOU SHOULD BE ALL BETTER AFTER A WEEK!
ALL BETTER?! TRY ALL DEADER!!
I KNEW YOU GUYS WOULD MESS IT UP!
BWOOF
MY TURN AT LAST!!
That's got to be Miia.
WHAT A SICK PERSON NEEDS IS NOURISH-MENT!
NOURISH-MENT?!
TWITCH
TA-DA!!
IT'S MIIA'S SPECIAL WHITE RICE PORR-IDGE~!!
BWOOO
GWOOOH
WAAAAAH!
GLOOOOM

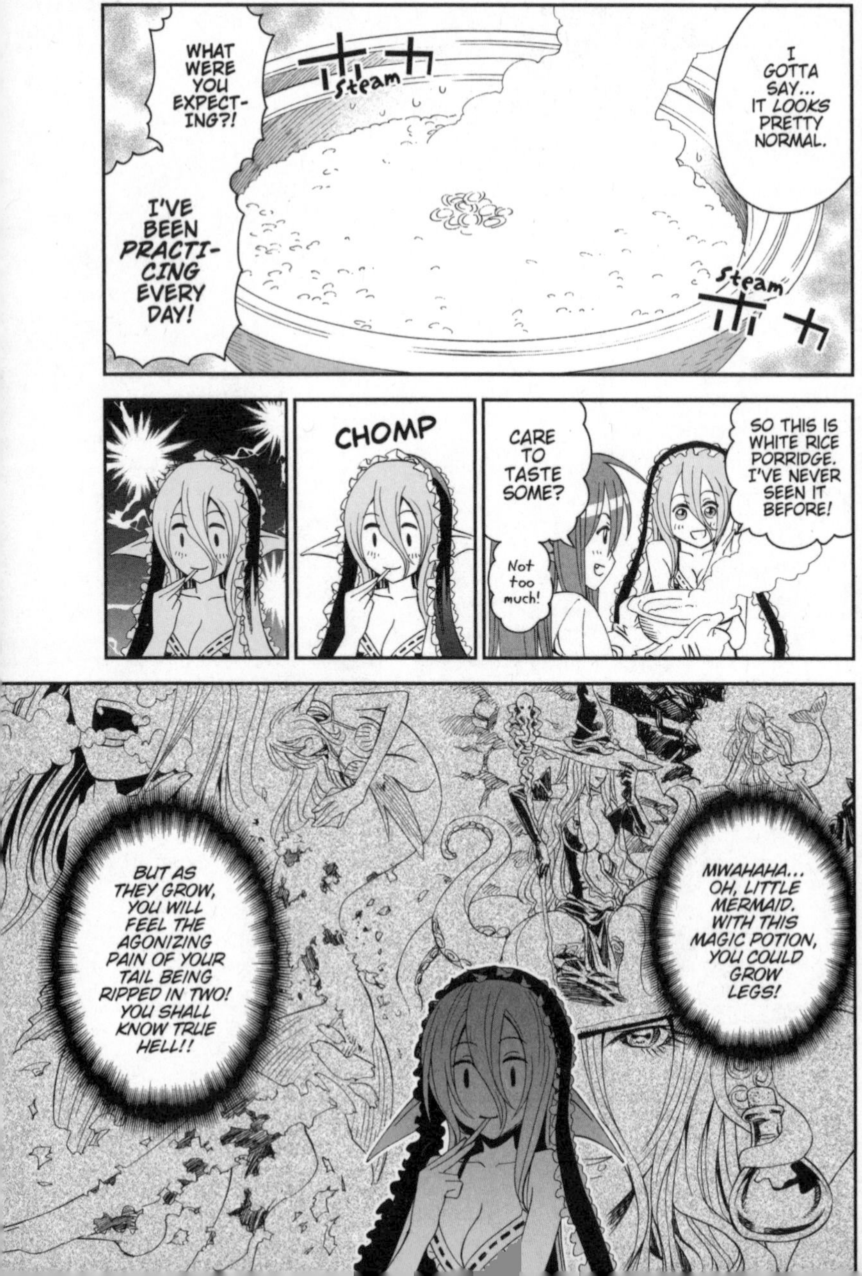
I GOTTA SAY... IT LOOKS PRETTY NORMAL.
Steam
WHAT WERE YOU EXPECTING?!
I'VE BEEN PRACTICING EVERY DAY!
Steam
SO THIS IS WHITE RICE PORRIDGE. I'VE NEVER SEEN IT BEFORE!
CARE TO TASTE SOME?
Not too much!
CHOMP
MWAHAHA... OH, LITTLE MERMAID. WITH THIS MAGIC POTION, YOU COULD GROW LEGS!
BUT AS THEY GROW, YOU WILL FEEL THE AGONIZING PAIN OF YOUR TAIL BEING RIPPED IN TWO! YOU SHALL KNOW TRUE HELL!!

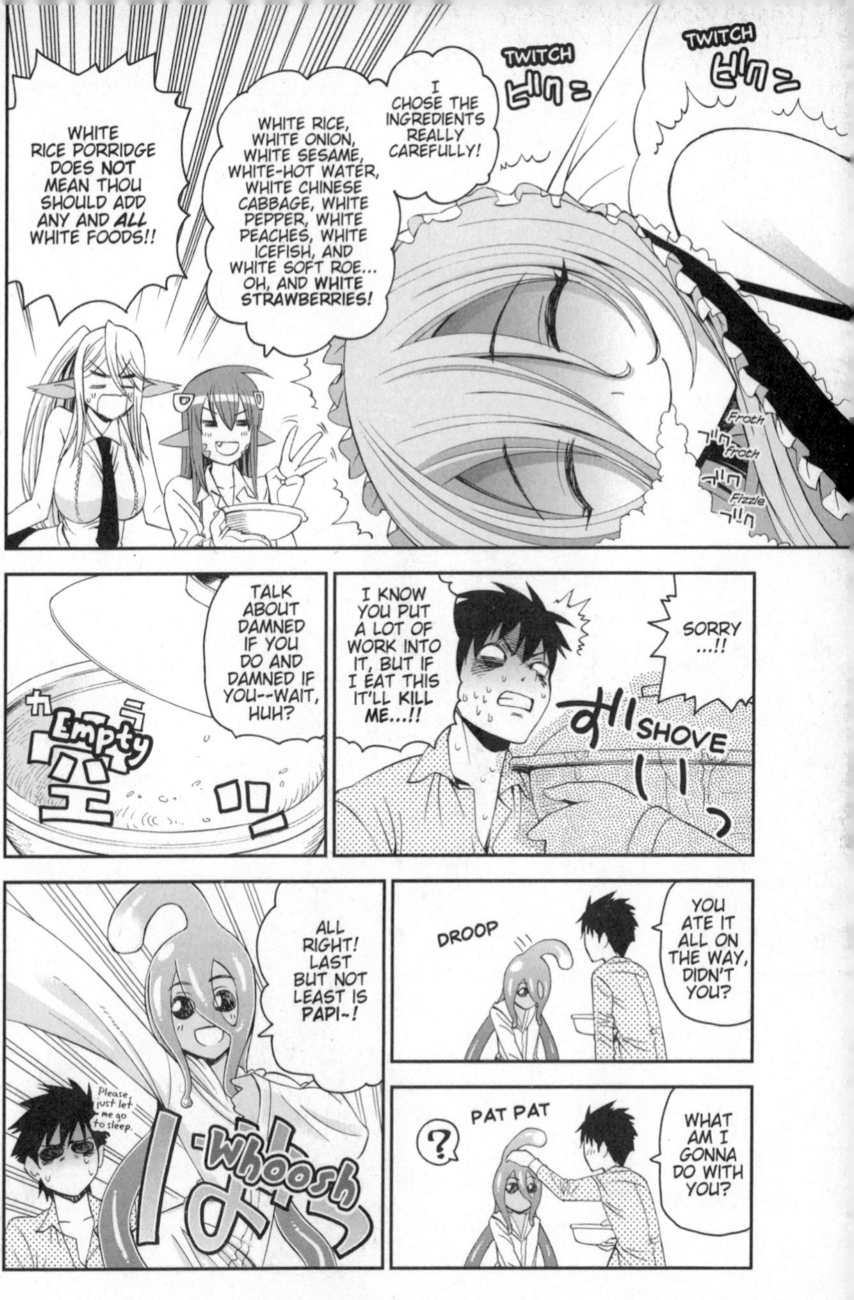
TWITCH
TWITCH
I CHOSE THE INGREDIENTS REALLY CAREFULLY!
WHITE RICE, WHITE ONION, WHITE SESAME, WHITE-HOT WATER, WHITE CHINESE CABBAGE, WHITE PEPPER, WHITE PEACHES, WHITE ICEFISH, AND WHITE SOFT ROE... OH, AND WHITE STRAWBERRIES!
WHITE RICE PORRIDGE DOES NOT MEAN THOU SHOULD ADD ANY AND *ALL* WHITE FOODS!!
Froth
froth
Fizzle
SORRY ...!!
I KNOW YOU PUT A LOT OF WORK INTO IT, BUT IF I EAT THIS IT'LL KILL ME...!!
SHOVE
TALK ABOUT DAMNED IF YOU DO AND DAMNED IF YOU--WAIT, HUH?
Empty
YOU ATE IT ALL ON THE WAY, DIDN'T YOU?
DROOP
WHAT AM I GONNA DO WITH YOU?
PAT PAT
?
ALL RIGHT! LAST BUT NOT LEAST IS PAPI~!
Please, just let me go to sleep.
Whoosh

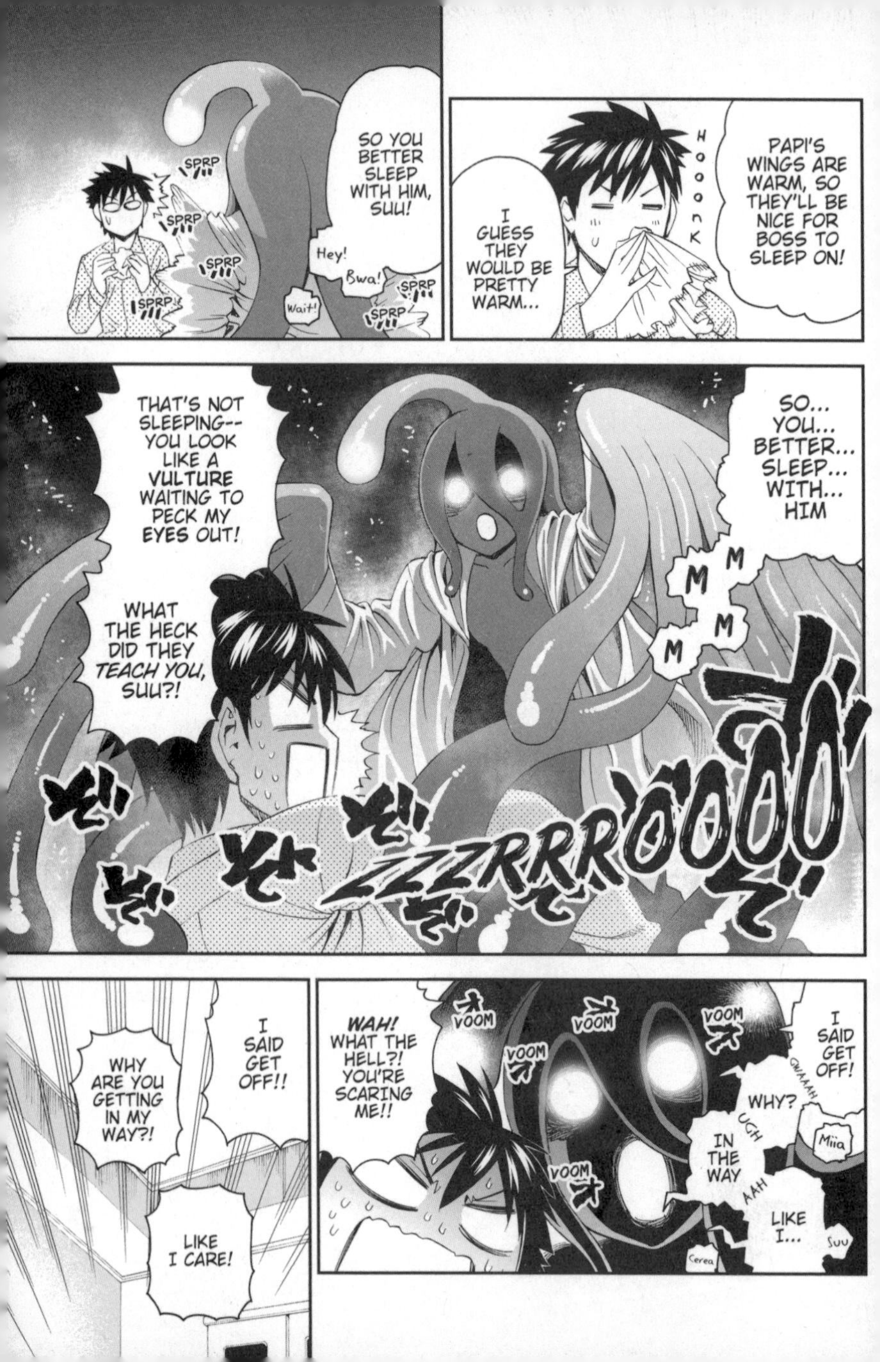
PAPI'S WINGS ARE WARM, SO THEY'LL BE NICE FOR BOSS TO SLEEP ON!
HOOONK
I GUESS THEY WOULD BE PRETTY WARM...
SO YOU BETTER SLEEP WITH HIM, SUU!
SPRP
SPRP
SPRP
SPRP
Hey!
Bwa!
Wait!
SPRP
SPRP
SO... YOU... BETTER... SLEEP... WITH... HIM
MMMMM
THAT'S NOT SLEEPING-- YOU LOOK LIKE A VULTURE WAITING TO PECK MY EYES OUT!
WHAT THE HECK DID THEY *TEACH YOU,* SUU?!
ZZZRRROOOO
I SAID GET OFF!
GWAAAH
WHY?
Miia
UGH
IN THE WAY
AAH
LIKE I...
Suu
Cerea
VOOM
VOOM
VOOM
VOOM
VOOM
WAH! WHAT THE HELL?! YOU'RE SCARING ME!!
I SAID GET OFF!!
WHY ARE YOU GETTING IN MY WAY?!
LIKE I CARE!

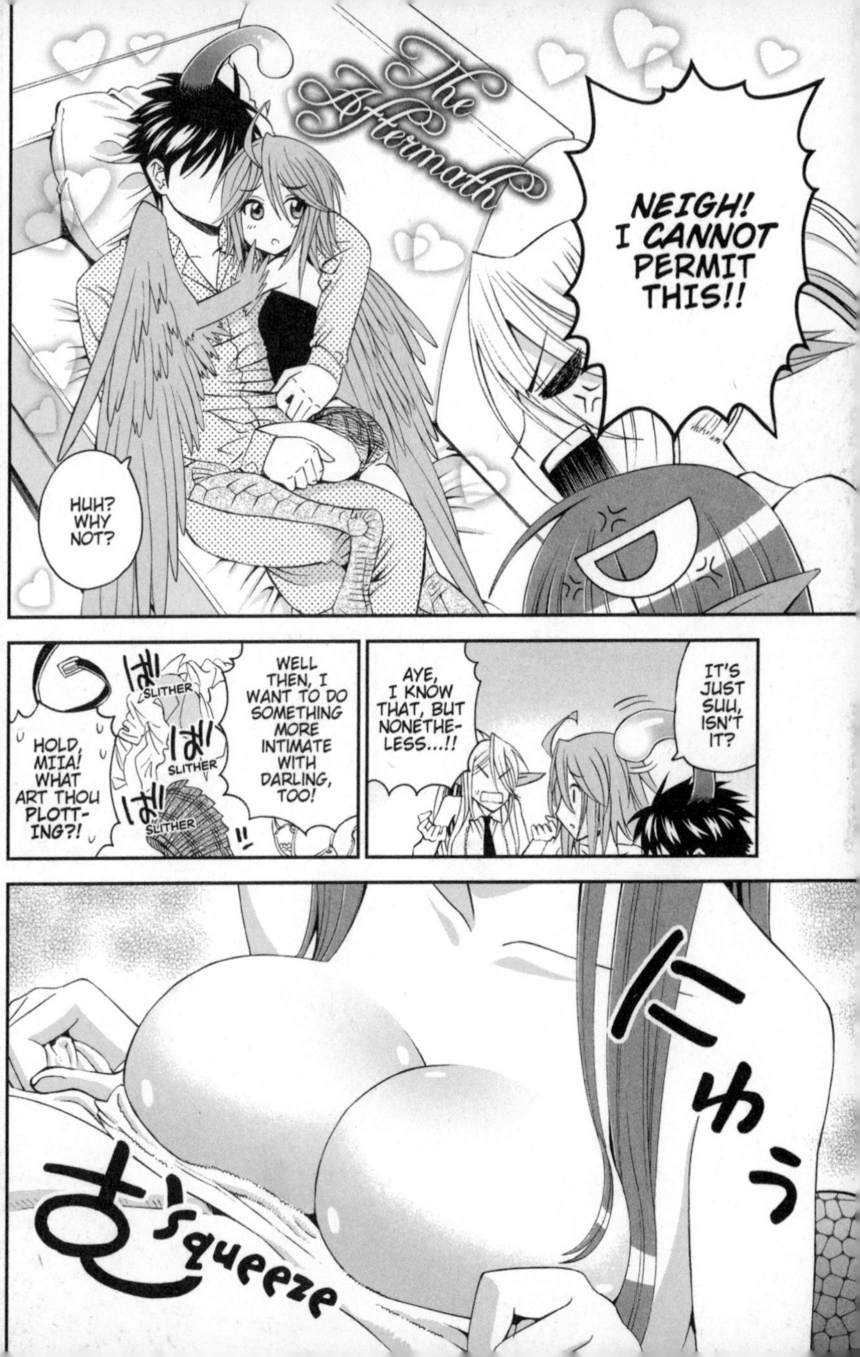
The Aftermath
NEIGH! I CANNOT PERMIT THIS!!
HUH? WHY NOT?
IT'S JUST SUU, ISN'T IT?
AYE, I KNOW THAT, BUT NONETHE-LESS...!!
WELL THEN, I WANT TO DO SOMETHING MORE INTIMATE WITH DARLING, TOO!
SLITHER
SLITHER
SLITHER
HOLD, MIIA! WHAT ART THOU PLOTT-ING?!
にゅう
む
squeeze

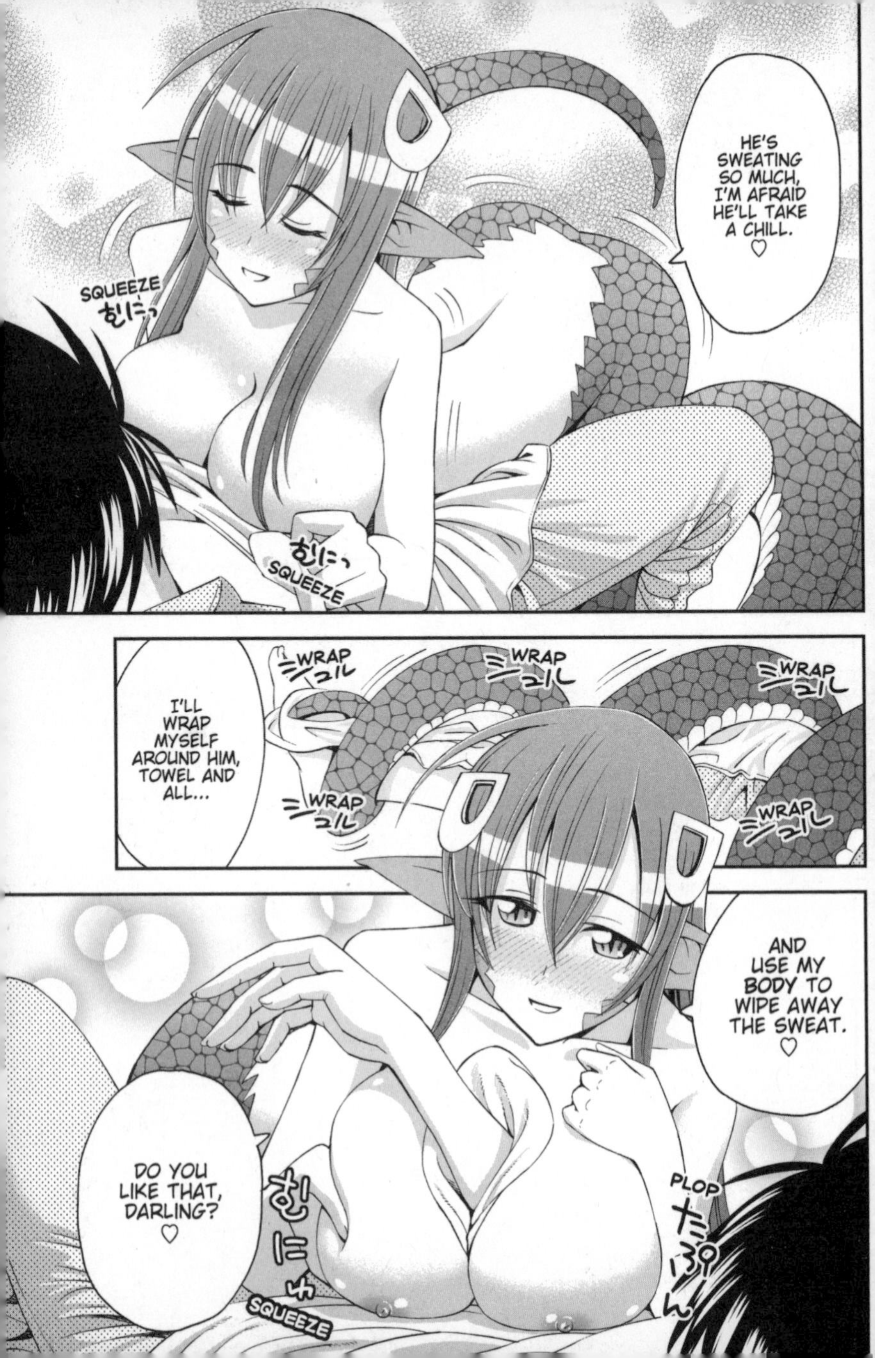
HE'S SWEATING SO MUCH, I'M AFRAID HE'LL TAKE A CHILL. ♡
SQUEEZE むにっ
むにっ SQUEEZE
WRAP シュル
WRAP シュル
WRAP シュル
WRAP シュル
I'LL WRAP MYSELF AROUND HIM, TOWEL AND ALL...
WRAP シュル
AND USE MY BODY TO WIPE AWAY THE SWEAT. ♡
PLOP たぷん
むにゅ SQUEEZE
DO YOU LIKE THAT, DARLING? ♡

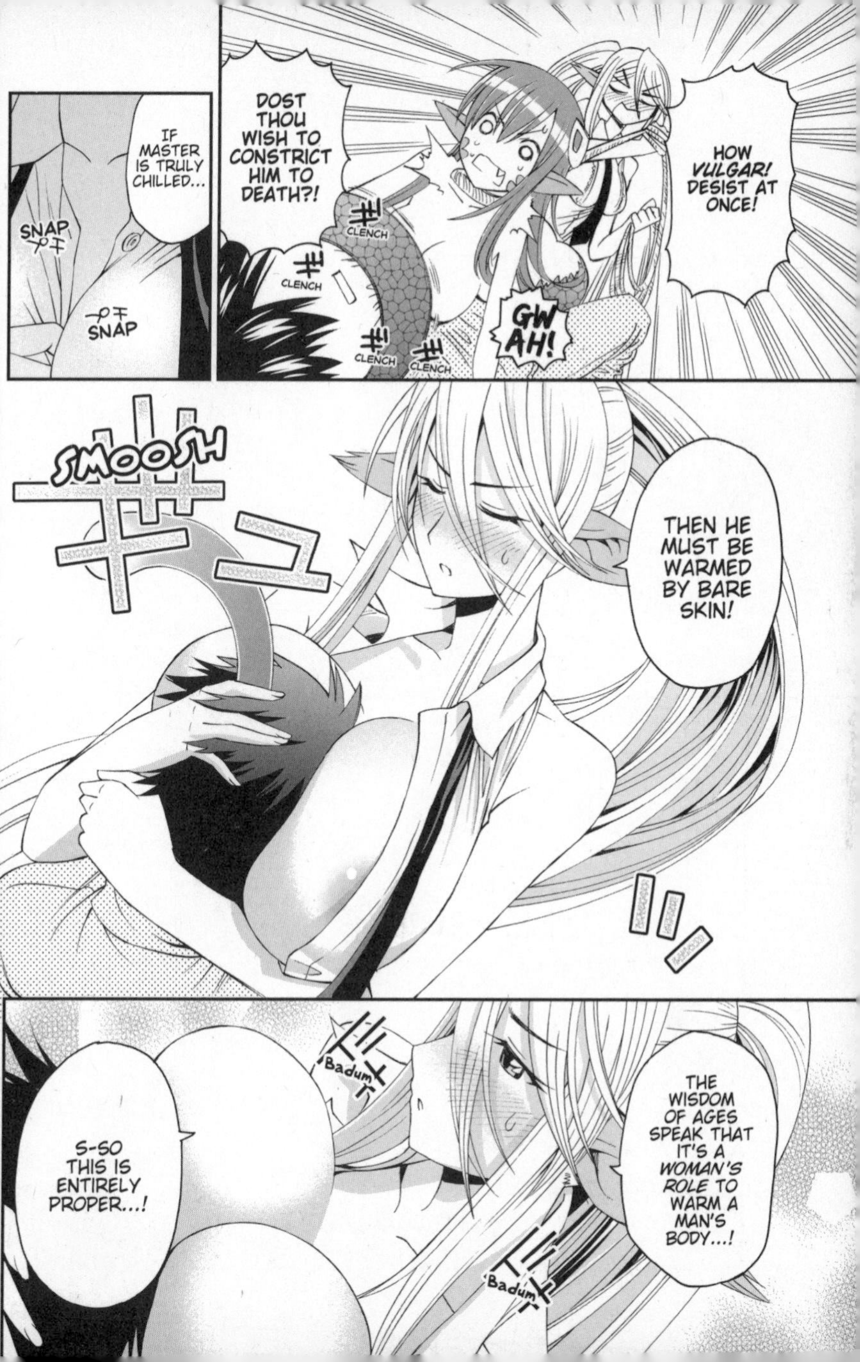
HOW VULGAR! DESIST AT ONCE!
DOST THOU WISH TO CONSTRICT HIM TO DEATH?!
GWAH!
CLENCH
CLENCH
CLENCH
CLENCH
IF MASTER IS TRULY CHILLED...
SNAP
SNAP
THEN HE MUST BE WARMED BY BARE SKIN!
SMOOSH
THE WISDOM OF AGES SPEAK THAT IT'S A WOMAN'S ROLE TO WARM A MAN'S BODY...!
Badum
Badum
S-SO THIS IS ENTIRELY PROPER...!

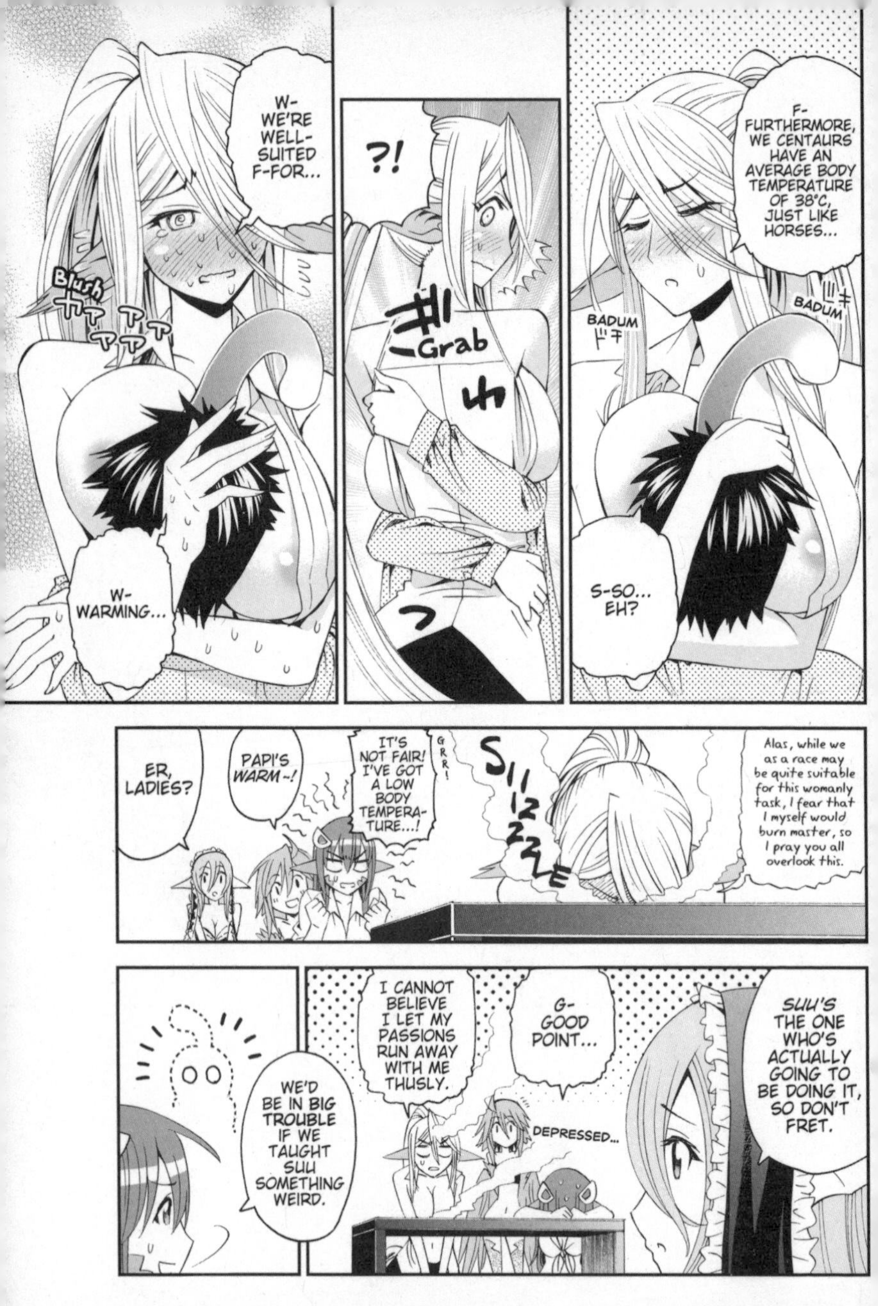
F-FURTHERMORE, WE CENTAURS HAVE AN AVERAGE BODY TEMPERATURE OF 38°C, JUST LIKE HORSES...
BADUM
BADUM
S-SO... EH?
?!
Grab
W-WE'RE WELL-SUITED F-FOR...
Blush
W-WARMING...
Alas, while we as a race may be quite suitable for this womanly task, I fear that I myself would burn master, so I pray you all overlook this.
SIZZZZLE
GRR!
IT'S NOT FAIR! I'VE GOT A LOW BODY TEMPERATURE...!
PAPI'S WARM~!
ER, LADIES?
SUU'S THE ONE WHO'S ACTUALLY GOING TO BE DOING IT, SO DON'T FRET.
G-GOOD POINT...
I CANNOT BELIEVE I LET MY PASSIONS RUN AWAY WITH ME THUSLY.
DEPRESSED...
WE'D BE IN BIG TROUBLE IF WE TAUGHT SUU SOMETHING WEIRD.

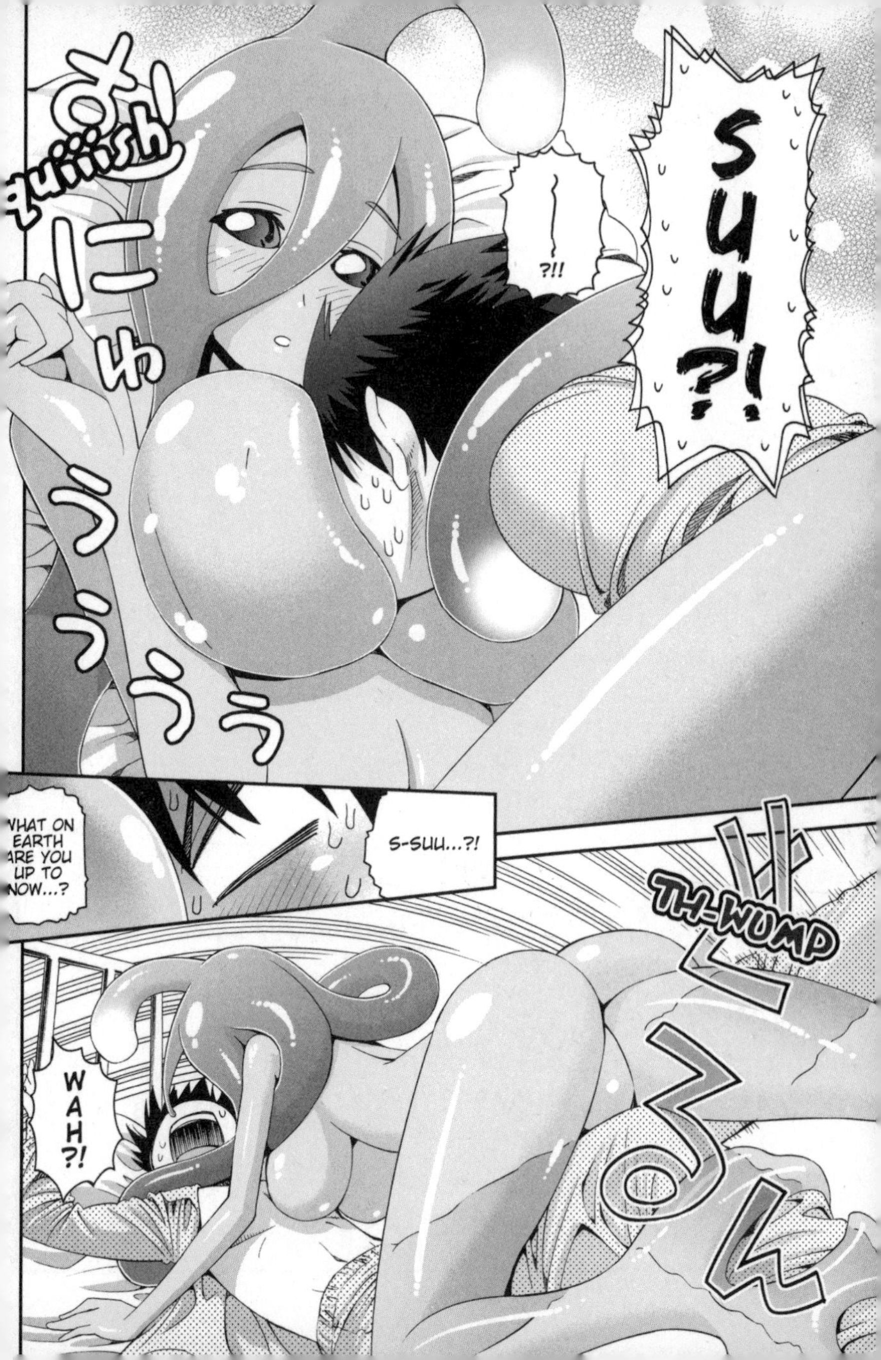
SUU?!
—?!!
squiiish!
S-SUU...?!
WHAT ON EARTH ARE YOU UP TO NOW...?
TH-WUMP
WAH?!

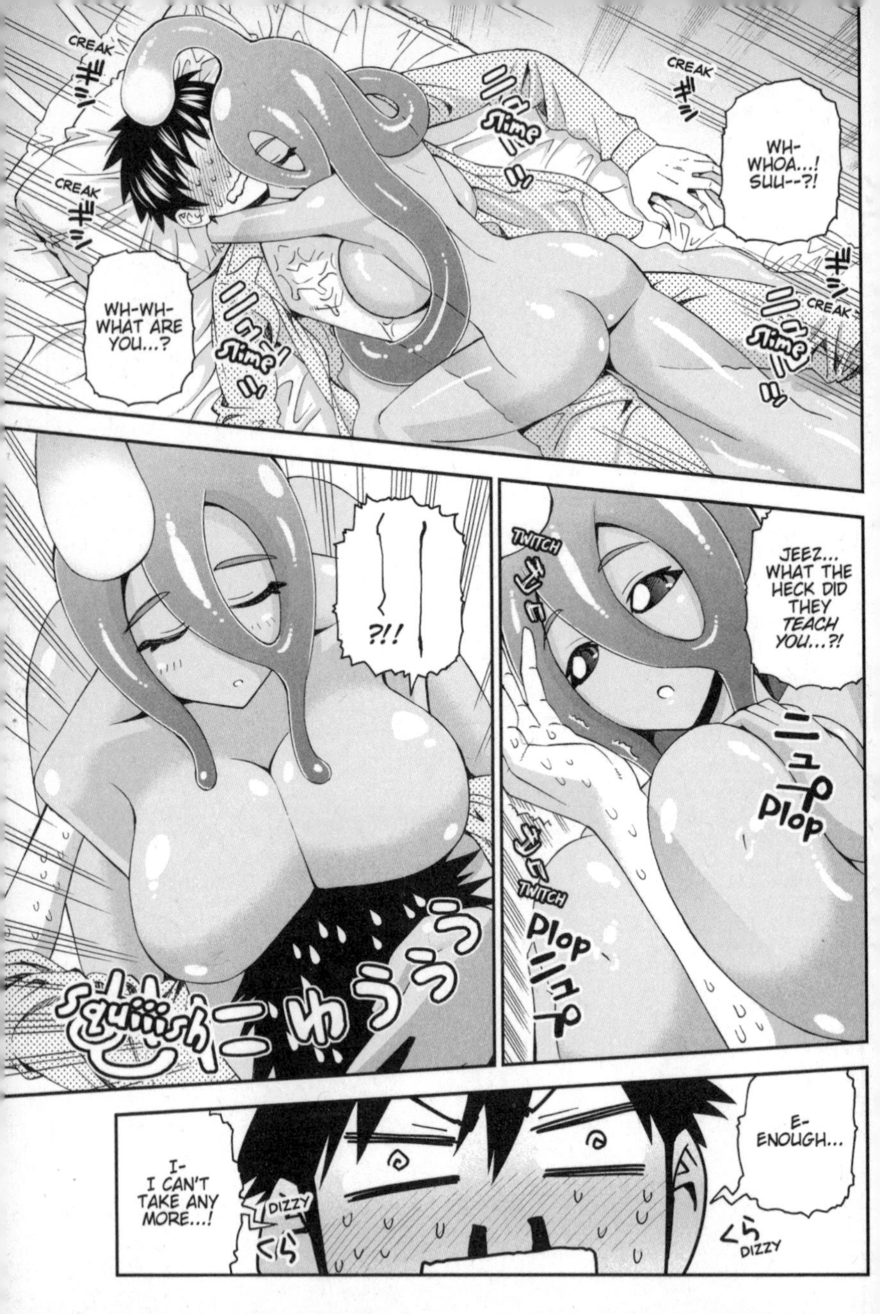
CREAK
WH-WHOA...! SUU--?!
CREAK
SLIME
CREAK
SLIME
CREAK
WH-WH-WHAT ARE YOU...?
SLIME
TWITCH
JEEZ... WHAT THE HECK DID THEY TEACH YOU...?!
PLOP
TWITCH
PLOP
?!!
SQUIIIISH
E-ENOUGH...
I- I CAN'T TAKE ANY MORE...!
DIZZY
くら
くら
DIZZY

Wheeze
ゼ~
ゼ~
Wheeze
?
ス su
ス su
ス su
Stop
ピ
CAN'T BREATHE
PAIN
LUST
DIZZY
CHILLS
SLIMY
FEVER
THIRSTY
SLUGGISH
HEAD-ACHE
SHAKING
JOINT PAIN
BOOBS
SWEAT

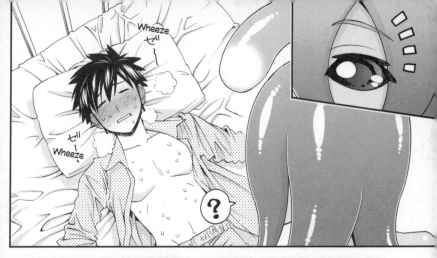

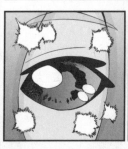

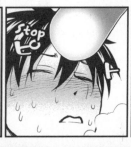

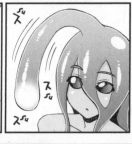

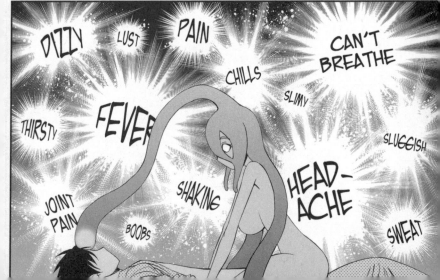

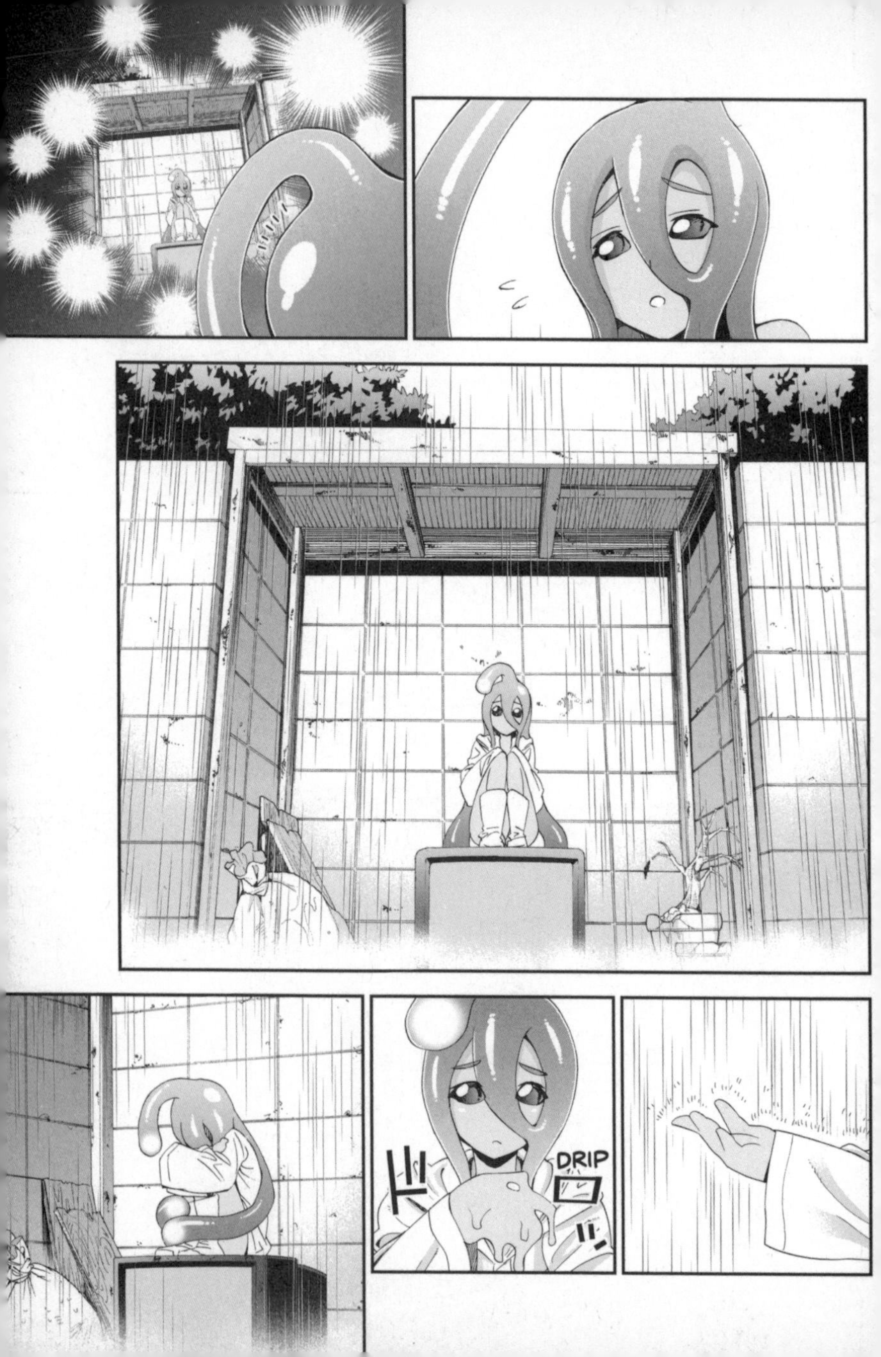
DRIP

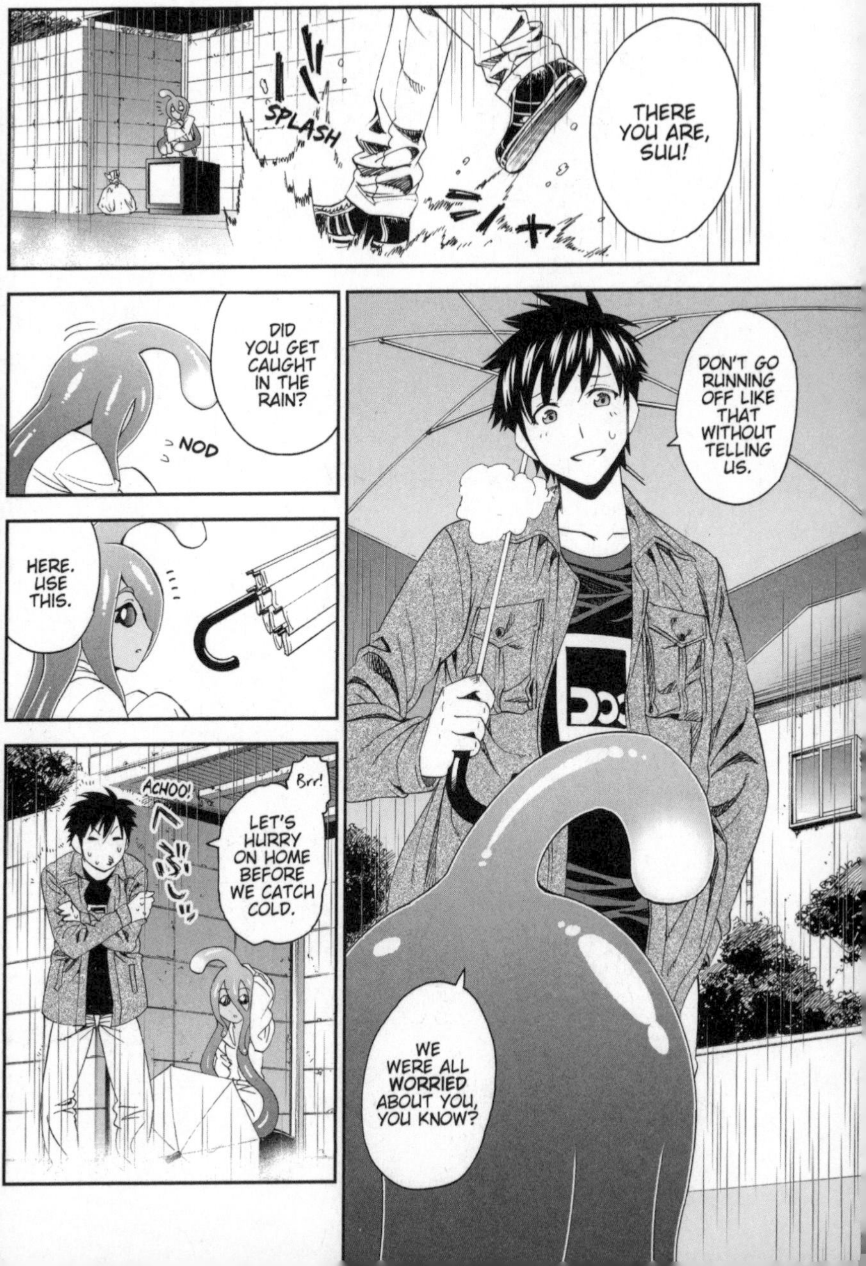
SPLASH
THERE YOU ARE, SUU!
DON'T GO RUNNING OFF LIKE THAT WITHOUT TELLING US.
WE WERE ALL WORRIED ABOUT YOU, YOU KNOW?
DID YOU GET CAUGHT IN THE RAIN?
NOD
HERE. USE THIS.
Brr!
LET'S HURRY ON HOME BEFORE WE CATCH COLD.
ACHOO!

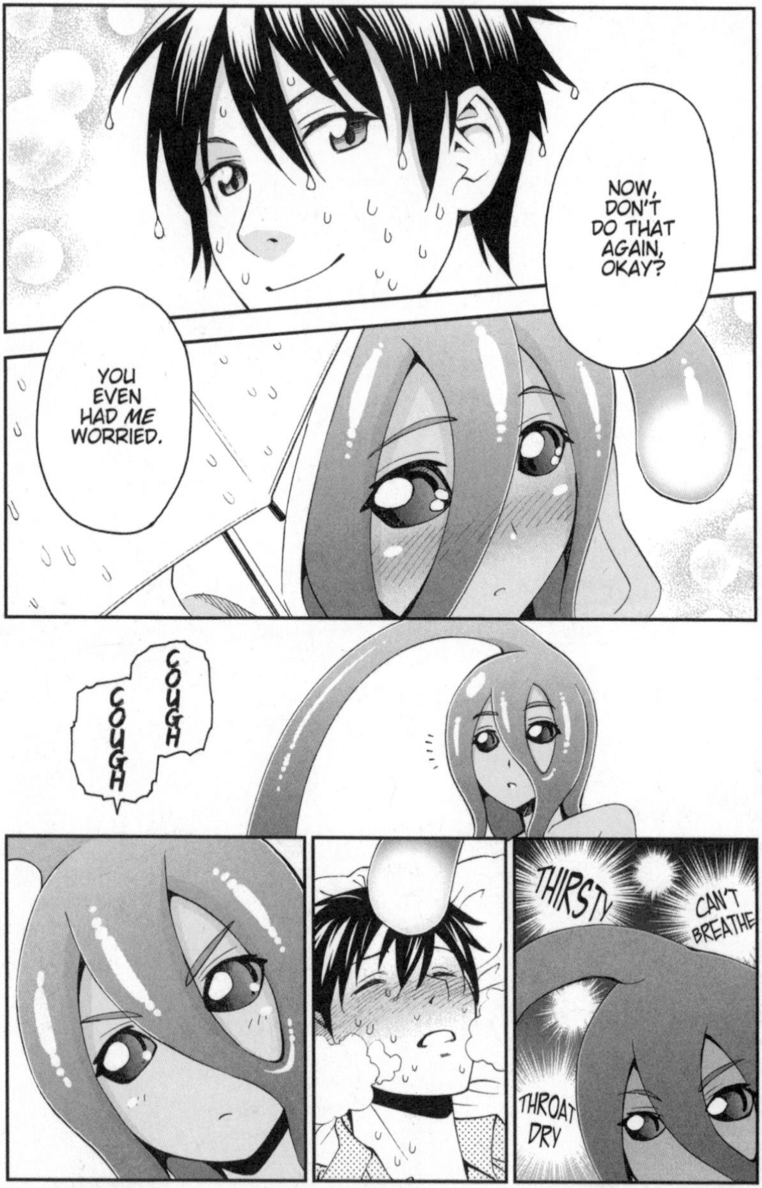
NOW, DON'T DO THAT AGAIN, OKAY?
YOU EVEN HAD ME WORRIED.
COUGH COUGH
COUGH
THIRSTY
CAN'T BREATHE
THROAT DRY

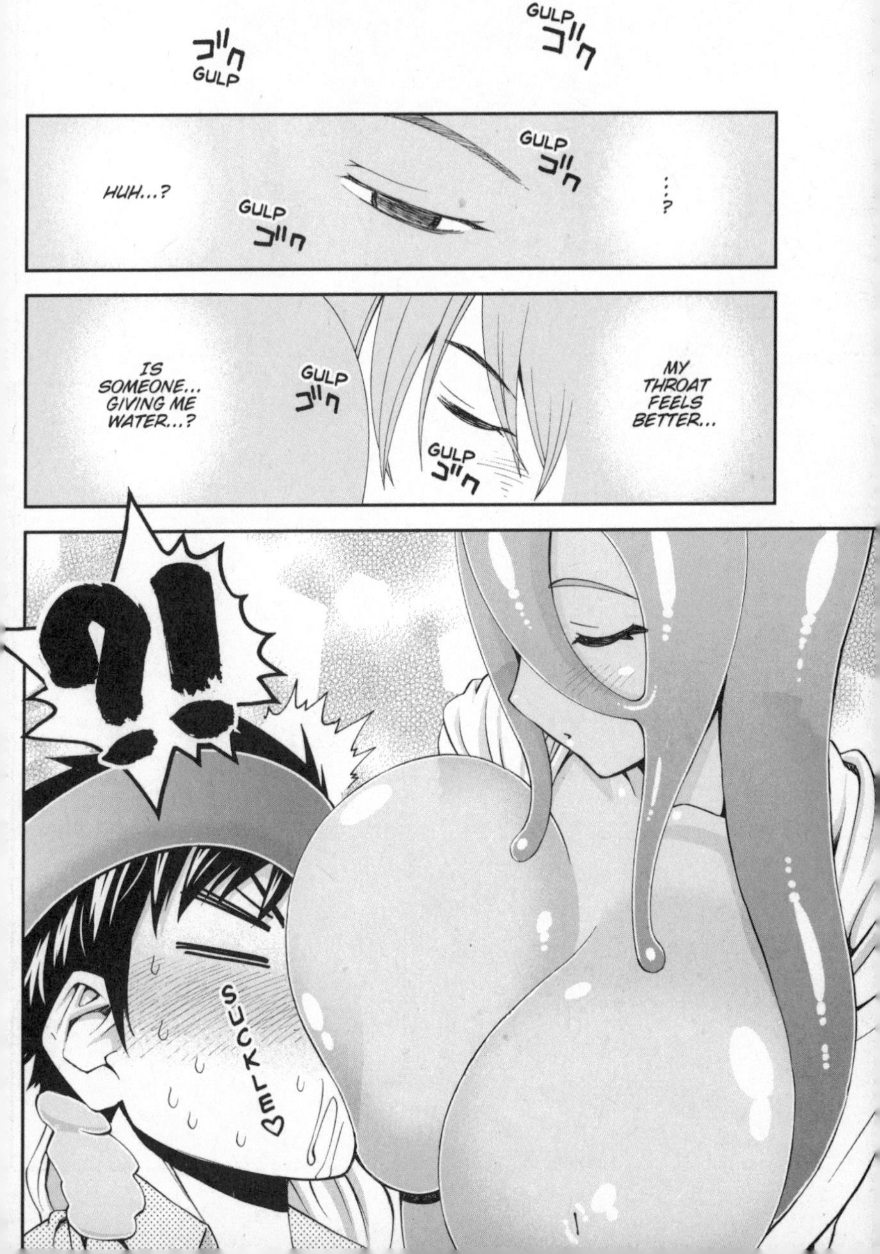

GULP
ゴク
ゴク
GULP
...?
GULP
ゴク
GULP
ゴク
HUH...?
MY THROAT FEELS BETTER...
GULP
ゴク
GULP
ゴク
IS SOMEONE... GIVING ME WATER...?
?!
SUCKLE

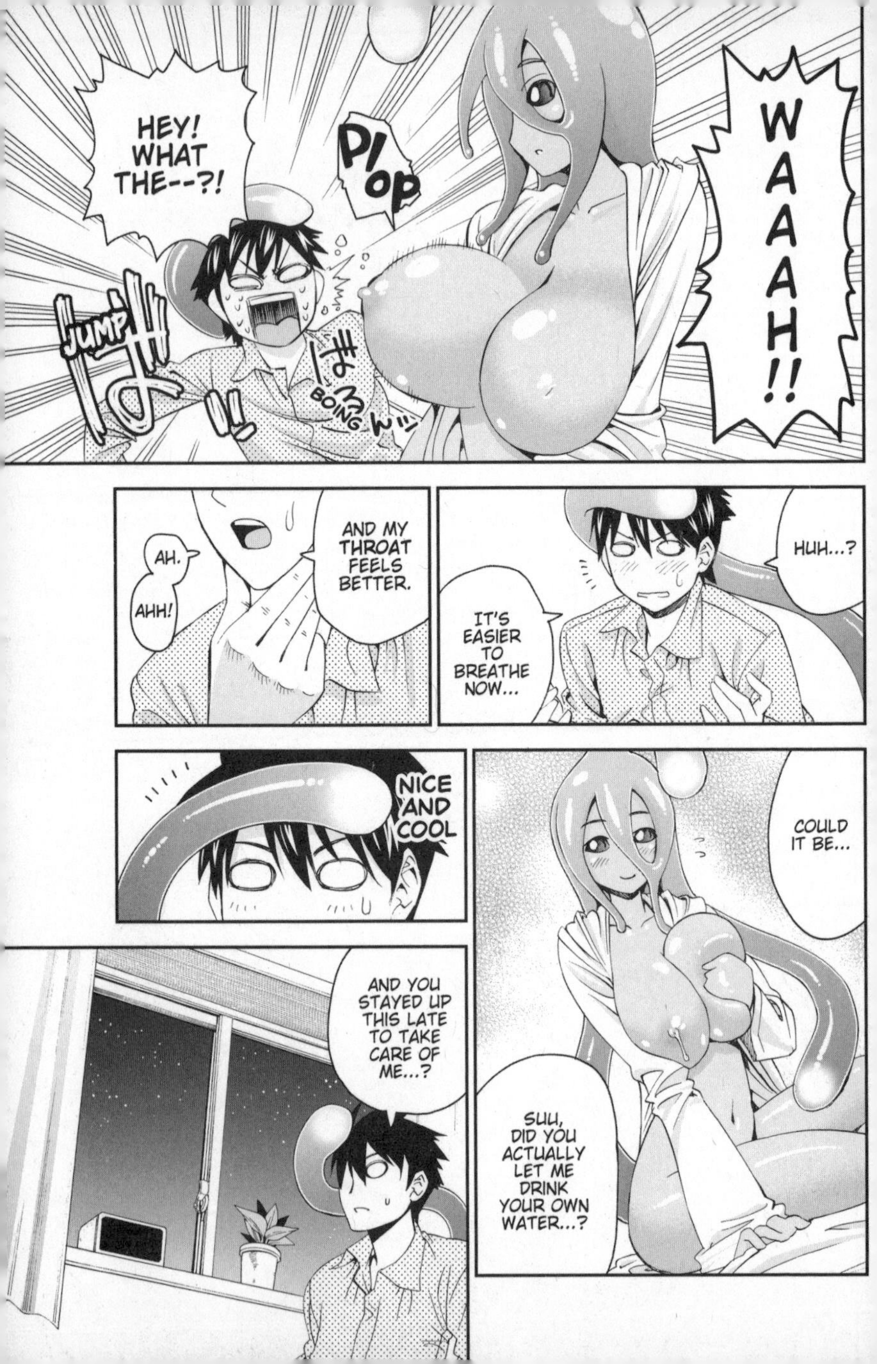
WAAAAH!!
PLOP
HEY! WHAT THE--?!
JUMP
BOING
HUH...?
IT'S EASIER TO BREATHE NOW...
AND MY THROAT FEELS BETTER.
AH.
AHH!
COULD IT BE...
SUU, DID YOU ACTUALLY LET ME DRINK YOUR OWN WATER...?
NICE AND COOL
AND YOU STAYED UP THIS LATE TO TAKE CARE OF ME...?

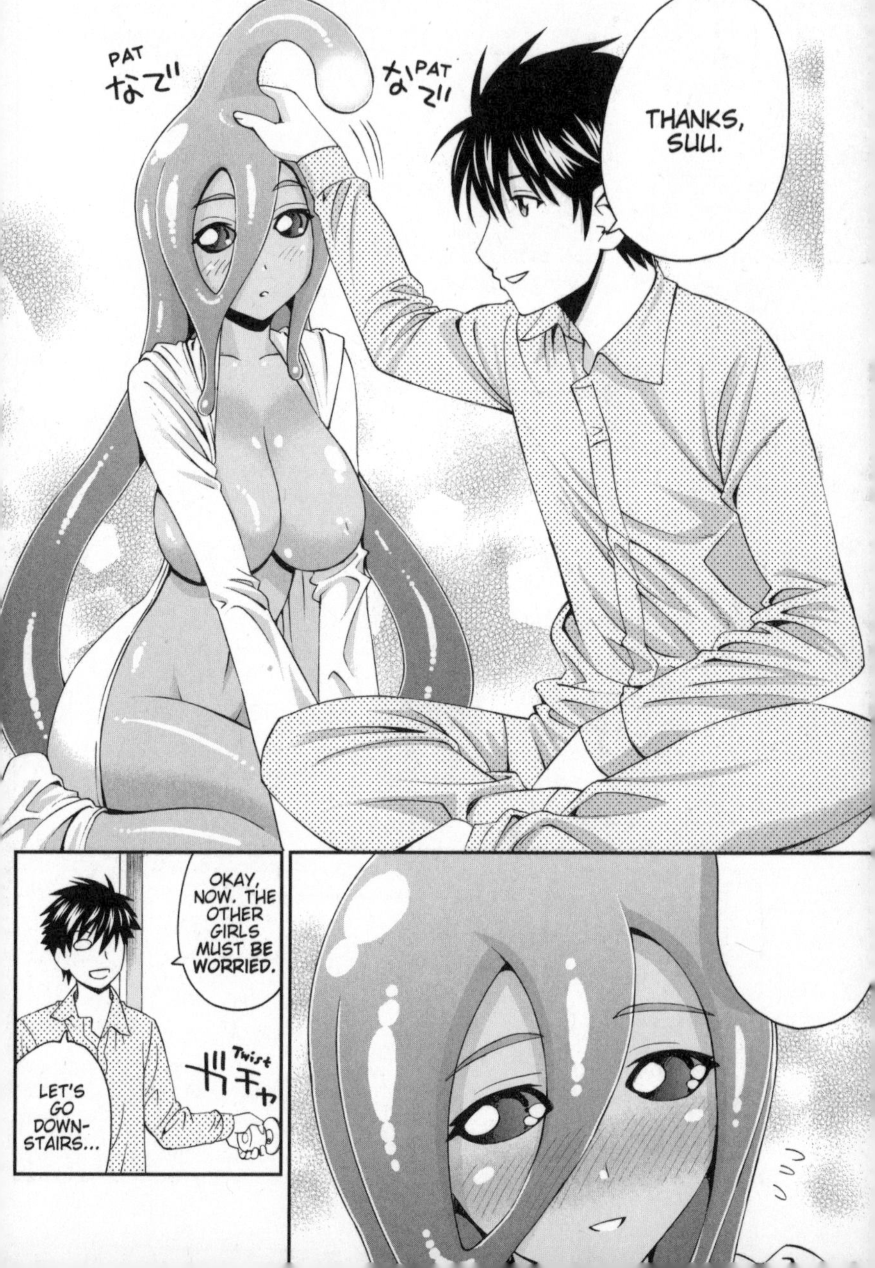
THANKS, SUU.
PAT なで
PAT なで
OKAY, NOW. THE OTHER GIRLS MUST BE WORRIED.
Twist ガチャ
LET'S GO DOWN-STAIRS...

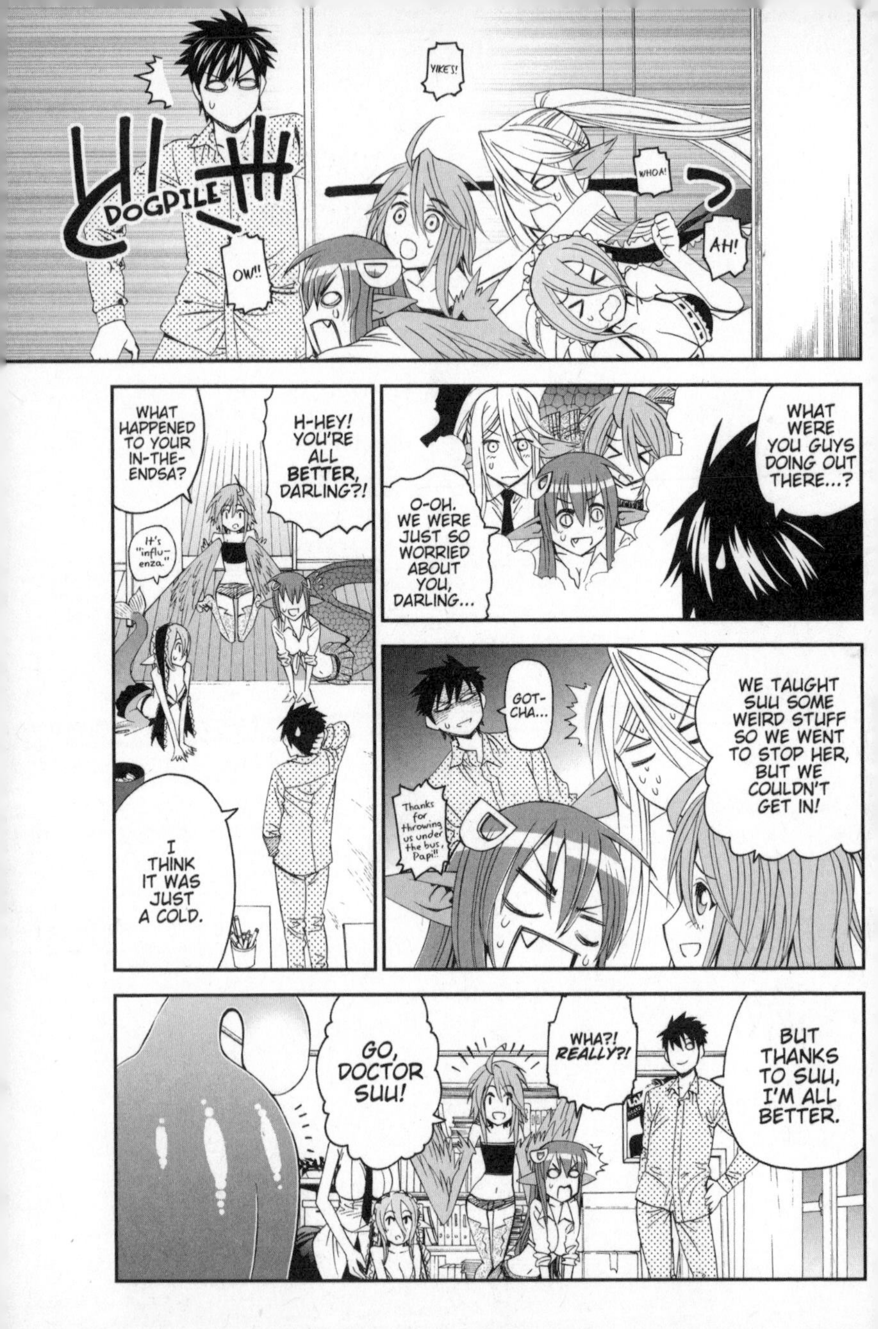
YIKES!
WHOA!
AH!
DOGPILE
OW!!
WHAT WERE YOU GUYS DOING OUT THERE...?
O-OH. WE WERE JUST SO WORRIED ABOUT YOU, DARLING...
WE TAUGHT SUU SOME WEIRD STUFF SO WE WENT TO STOP HER, BUT WE COULDN'T GET IN!
GOT-CHA...
Thanks for throwing us under the bus, Papi!!
H-HEY! YOU'RE ALL BETTER, DARLING?!
WHAT HAPPENED TO YOUR IN-THE-ENDSA?
It's "influenza."
I THINK IT WAS JUST A COLD.
BUT THANKS TO SUU, I'M ALL BETTER.
WHA?! *REALLY?!*
GO, DOCTOR SUU!

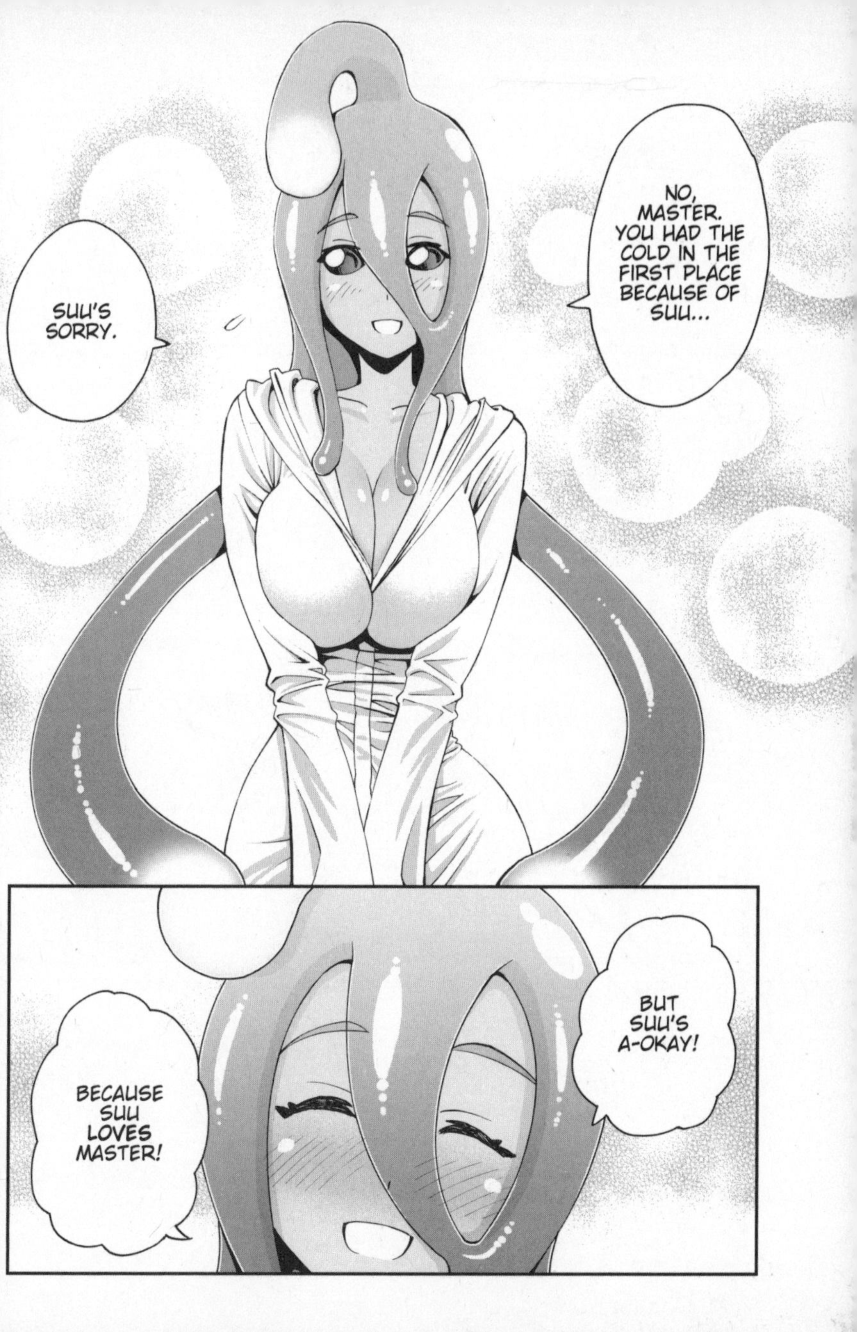
NO, MASTER. YOU HAD THE COLD IN THE FIRST PLACE BECAUSE OF SUU...
SUU'S SORRY.
BUT SUU'S A-OKAY!
BECAUSE SUU LOVES MASTER!

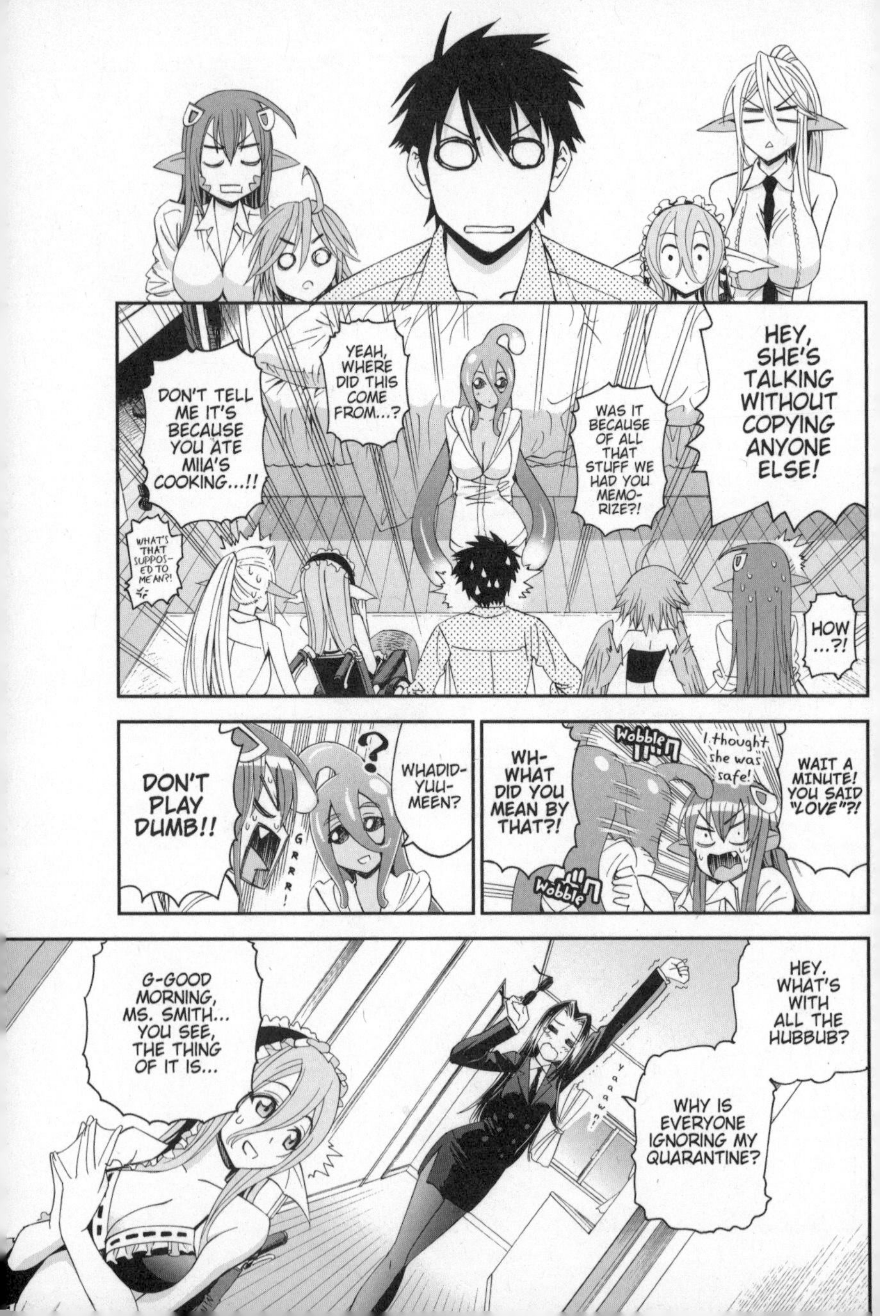
HEY, SHE'S TALKING WITHOUT COPYING ANYONE ELSE!
WAS IT BECAUSE OF ALL THAT STUFF WE HAD YOU MEMO-RIZE?!
YEAH, WHERE DID THIS COME FROM...?
DON'T TELL ME IT'S BECAUSE YOU ATE MIIA'S COOKING...!!
HOW...?!
WHAT'S THAT SUPPOS-ED TO MEAN?!
WAIT A MINUTE! YOU SAID "LOVE"?!
I thought she was safe!
Wobble
WH-WHAT DID YOU MEAN BY THAT?!
Wobble
WHADID-YUU-MEEN?
?
DON'T PLAY DUMB!!
HEY. WHAT'S WITH ALL THE HUBBUB?
WHY IS EVERYONE IGNORING MY QUARANTINE?
G-GOOD MORNING, MS. SMITH... YOU SEE, THE THING OF IT IS...

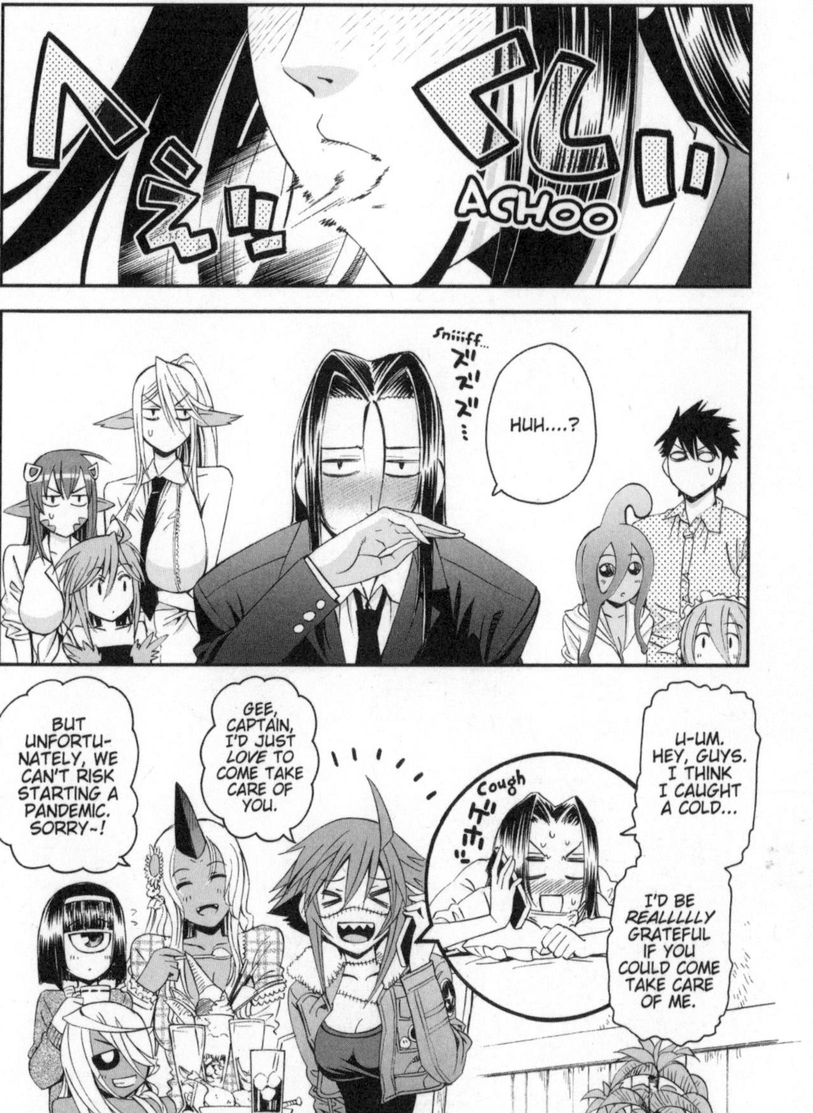
ACHOO
Sniiiff...
ズズズ…
HUH....?
U-UM. HEY, GUYS. I THINK I CAUGHT A COLD...
Cough
ゲホ
I'D BE *REALLLLLY* GRATEFUL IF YOU COULD COME TAKE CARE OF ME.
GEE, CAPTAIN, I'D JUST *LOVE* TO COME TAKE CARE OF YOU.
BUT UNFORTU-NATELY, WE CAN'T RISK STARTING A PANDEMIC. SORRY~!

Monster Musume

Everyday Life with Monster Girls

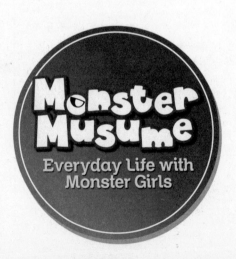

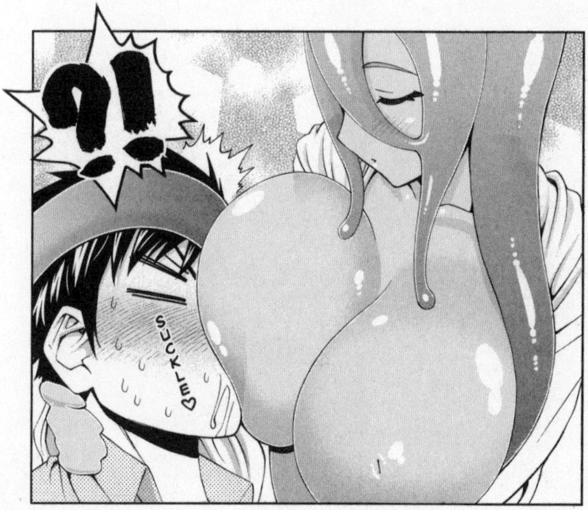
?!
SUCKLE♡

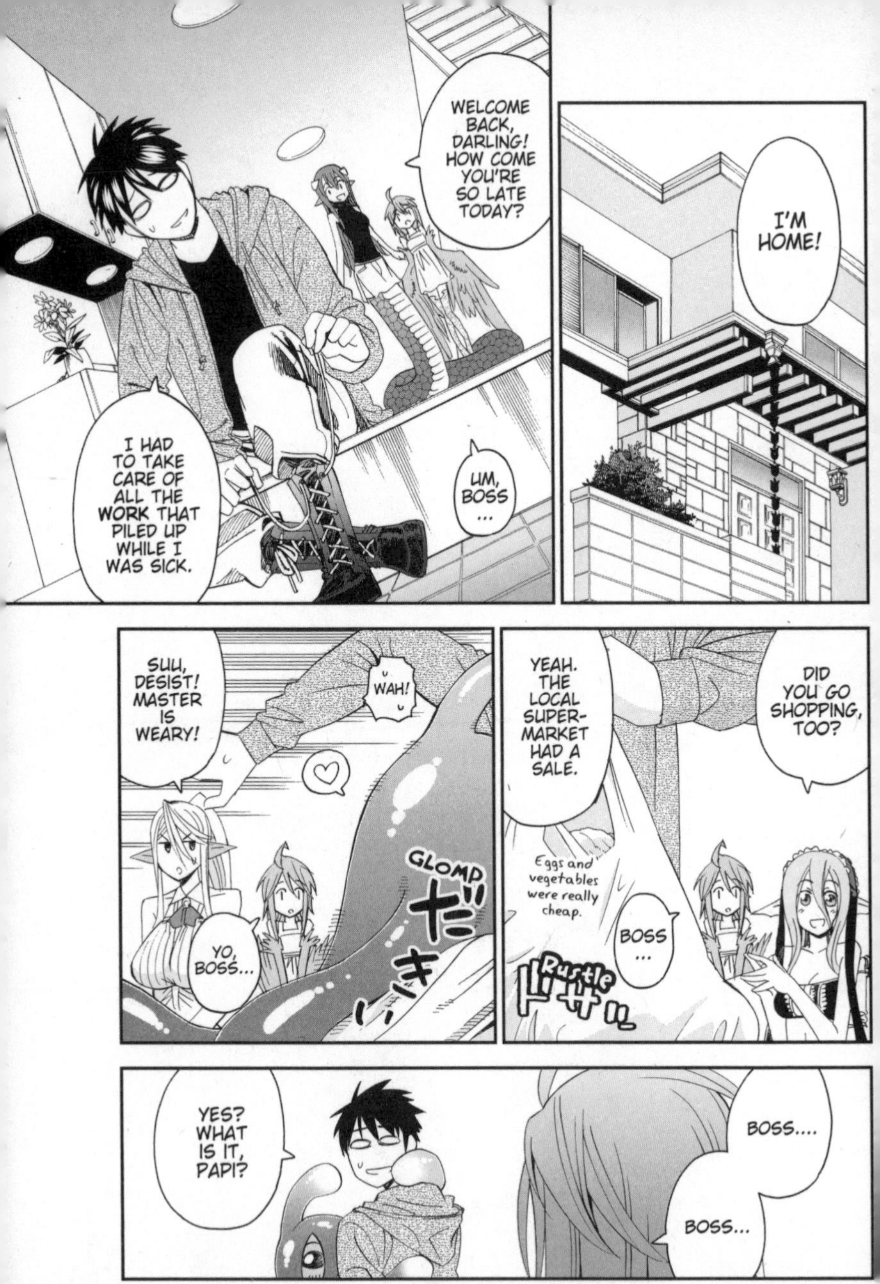
I'M HOME!
WELCOME BACK, DARLING! HOW COME YOU'RE SO LATE TODAY?
UM, BOSS ...
I HAD TO TAKE CARE OF ALL THE WORK THAT PILED UP WHILE I WAS SICK.
DID YOU GO SHOPPING, TOO?
YEAH. THE LOCAL SUPER-MARKET HAD A SALE.
Eggs and vegetables were really cheap.
BOSS ...
Rustle
WAH!
SUU, DESIST! MASTER IS WEARY!
GLOMP
YO, BOSS...
BOSS....
BOSS...
YES? WHAT IS IT, PAPI?

Chapter 14

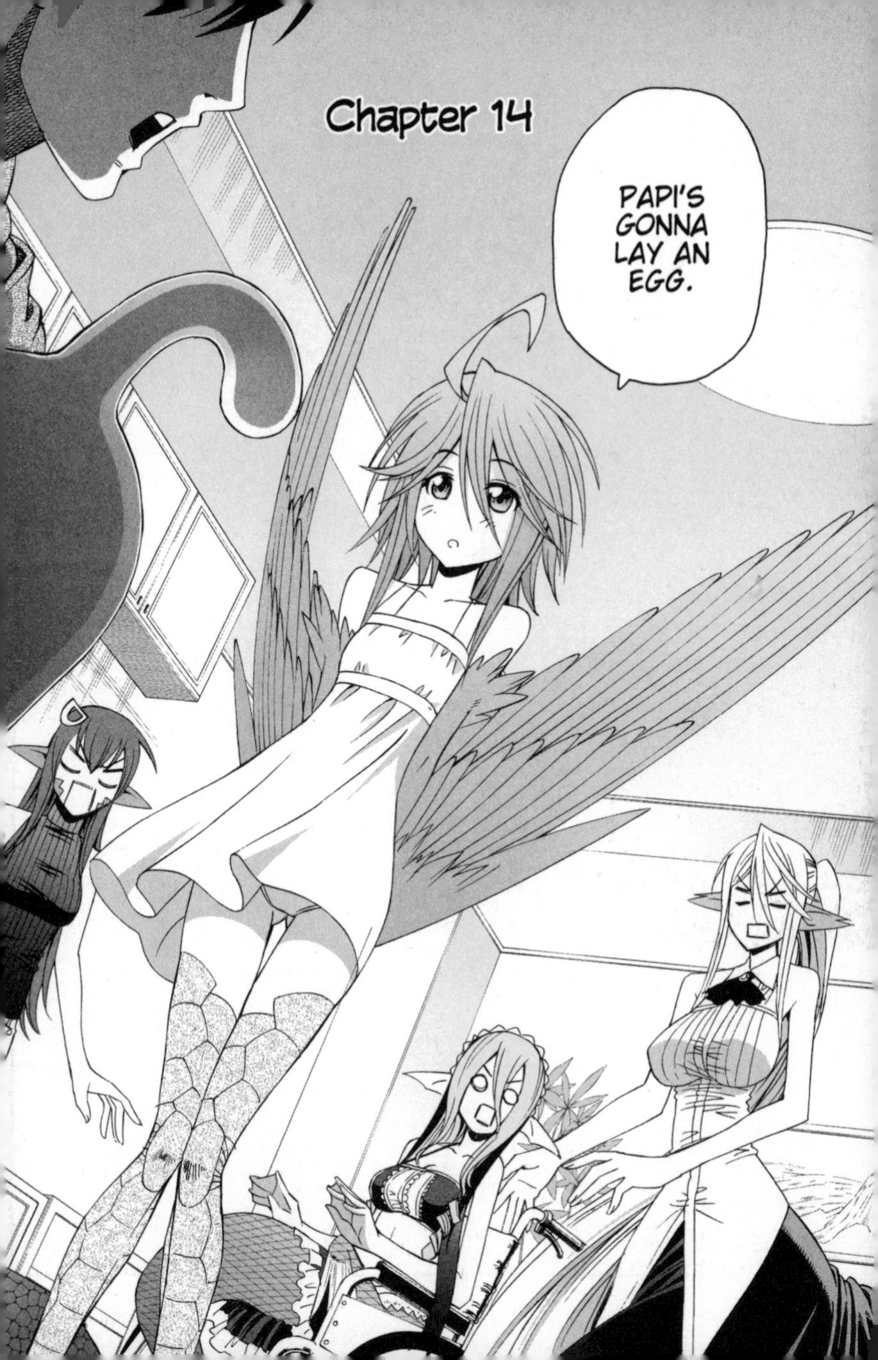
PAPI'S GONNA LAY AN EGG.

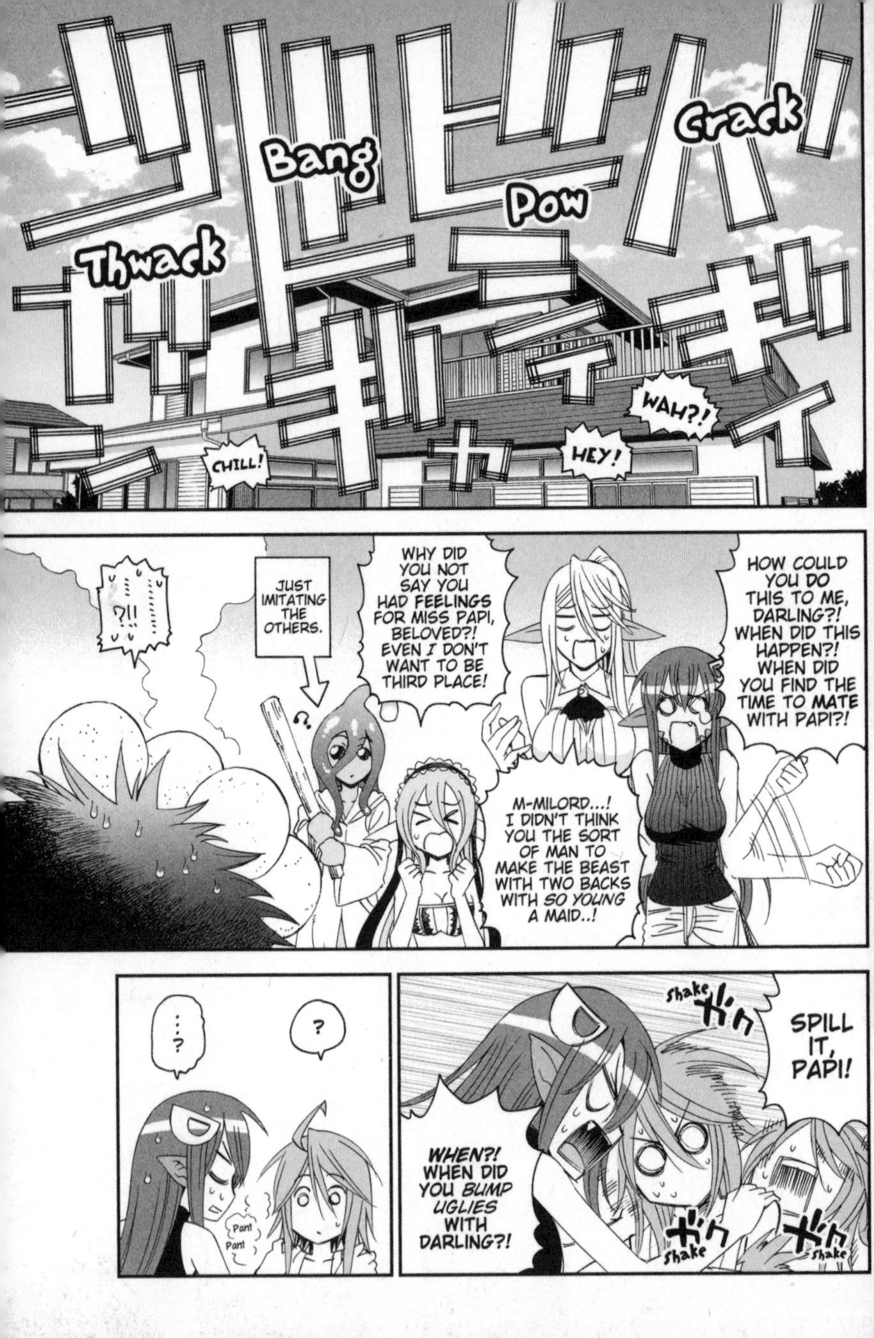
Crack
Pow
Bang
Thwack
WAH?!
HEY!
CHILL!
HOW COULD YOU DO THIS TO ME, DARLING?! WHEN DID THIS HAPPEN?! WHEN DID YOU FIND THE TIME TO MATE WITH PAPI?!
WHY DID YOU NOT SAY YOU HAD FEELINGS FOR MISS PAPI, BELOVED?! EVEN *I* DON'T WANT TO BE THIRD PLACE!
JUST IMITATING THE OTHERS.
?!!
M-MILORD...! I DIDN'T THINK YOU THE SORT OF MAN TO MAKE THE BEAST WITH TWO BACKS WITH *SO YOUNG* A MAID..!
shake
SPILL IT, PAPI!
WHEN?! WHEN DID YOU *BUMP UGLIES* WITH DARLING?!
shake
shake
?
...?
Pant
Pant

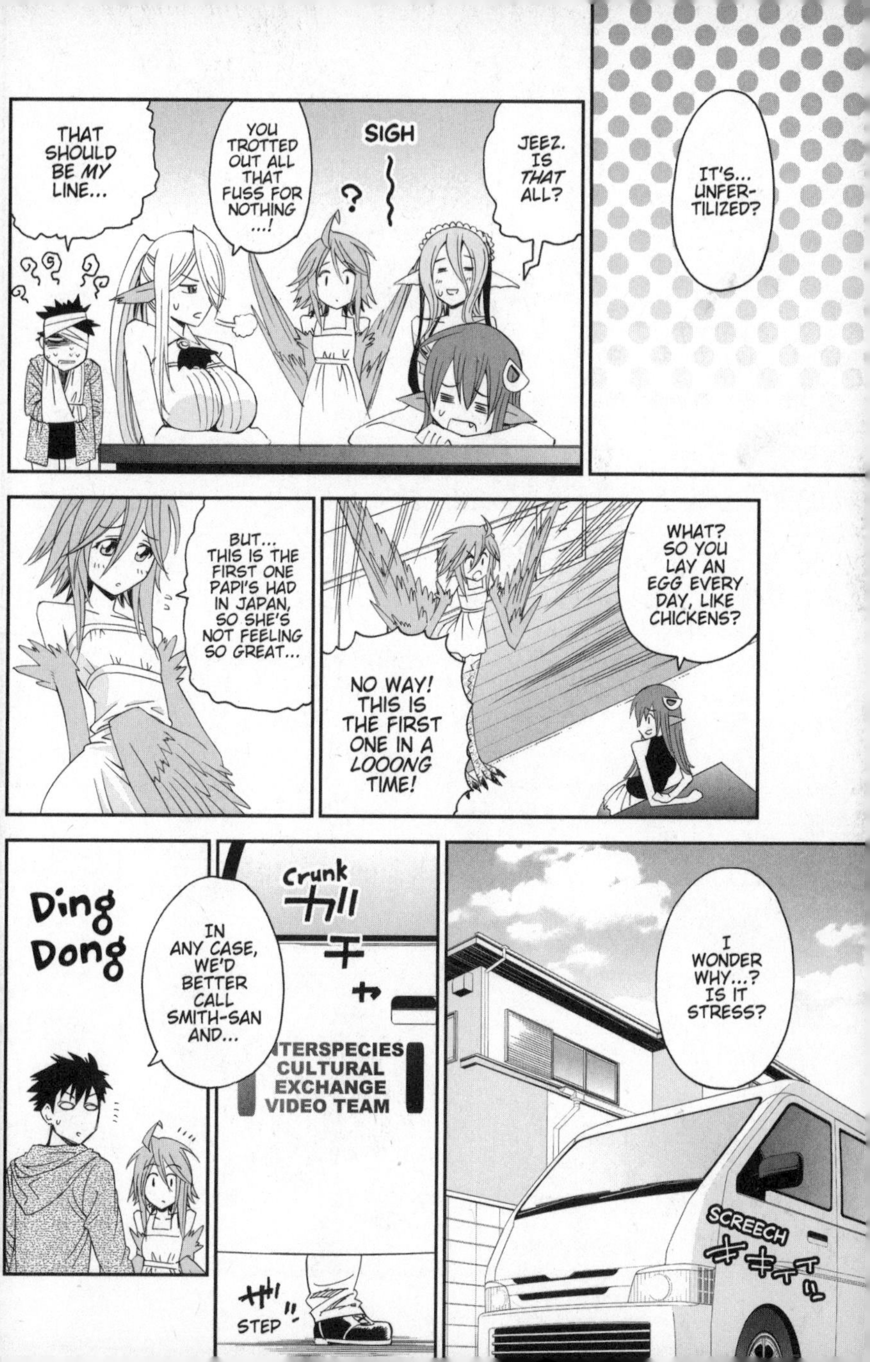
IT'S... UNFER-TILIZED?
JEEZ. IS THAT ALL?
SIGH
?
YOU TROTTED OUT ALL THAT FUSS FOR NOTHING ...!
THAT SHOULD BE MY LINE...
WHAT? SO YOU LAY AN EGG EVERY DAY, LIKE CHICKENS?
NO WAY! THIS IS THE FIRST ONE IN A LOOONG TIME!
BUT... THIS IS THE FIRST ONE PAPI'S HAD IN JAPAN, SO SHE'S NOT FEELING SO GREAT...
I WONDER WHY...? IS IT STRESS?
SCREECH
Crunk
INTERSPECIES CULTURAL EXCHANGE VIDEO TEAM
STEP
IN ANY CASE, WE'D BETTER CALL SMITH-SAN AND...
Ding Dong

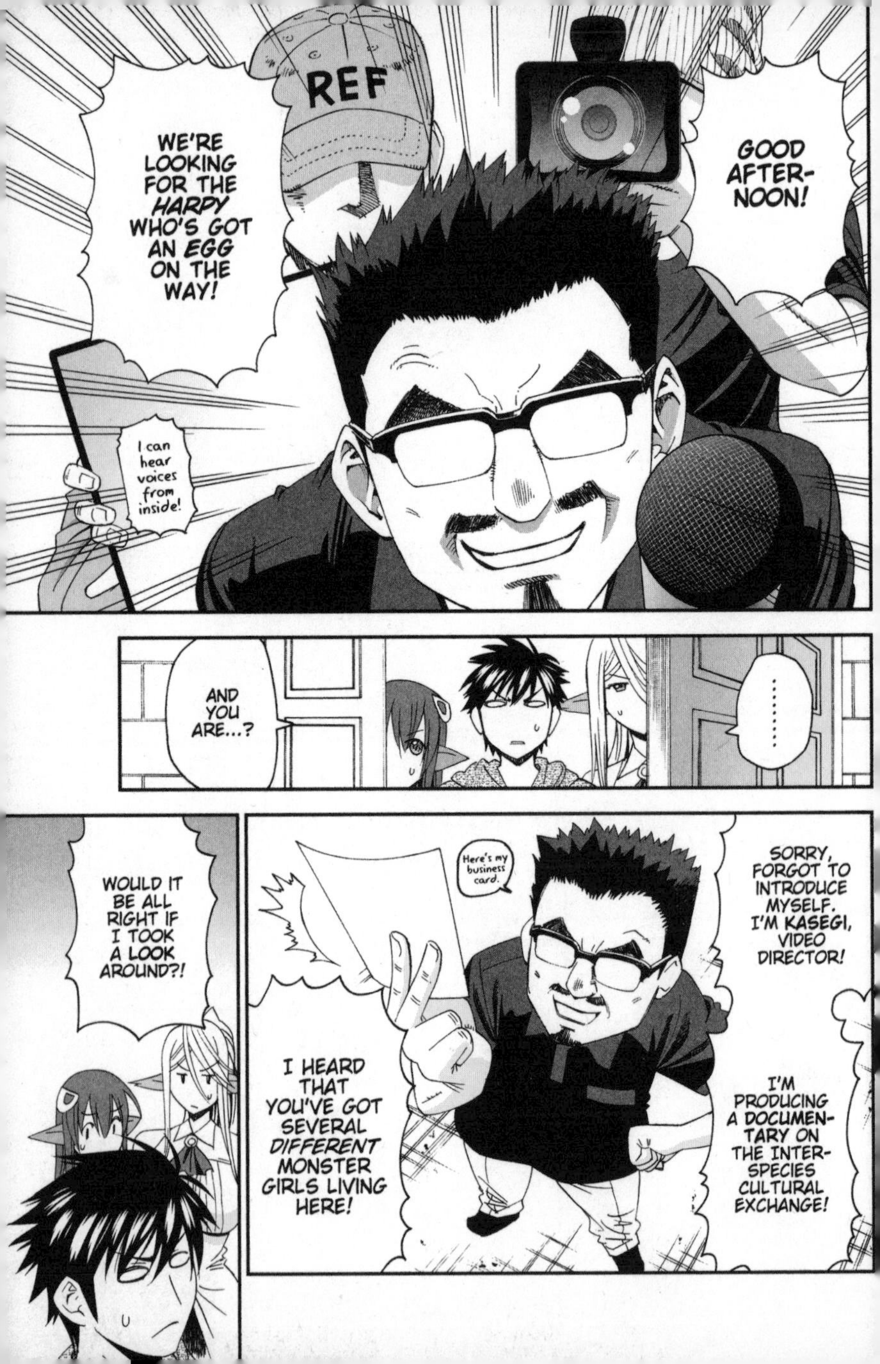
GOOD AFTER-NOON!
REF
WE'RE LOOKING FOR THE *HARPY* WHO'S GOT AN *EGG* ON THE WAY!
I can hear voices from inside!
......
AND YOU ARE...?
SORRY, FORGOT TO INTRODUCE MYSELF. I'M KASEGI, VIDEO DIRECTOR!
Here's my business card.
I'M PRODUCING A DOCUMENTARY ON THE INTER-SPECIES CULTURAL EXCHANGE!
I HEARD THAT YOU'VE GOT SEVERAL *DIFFERENT* MONSTER GIRLS LIVING HERE!
WOULD IT BE ALL RIGHT IF I TOOK A LOOK AROUND?!

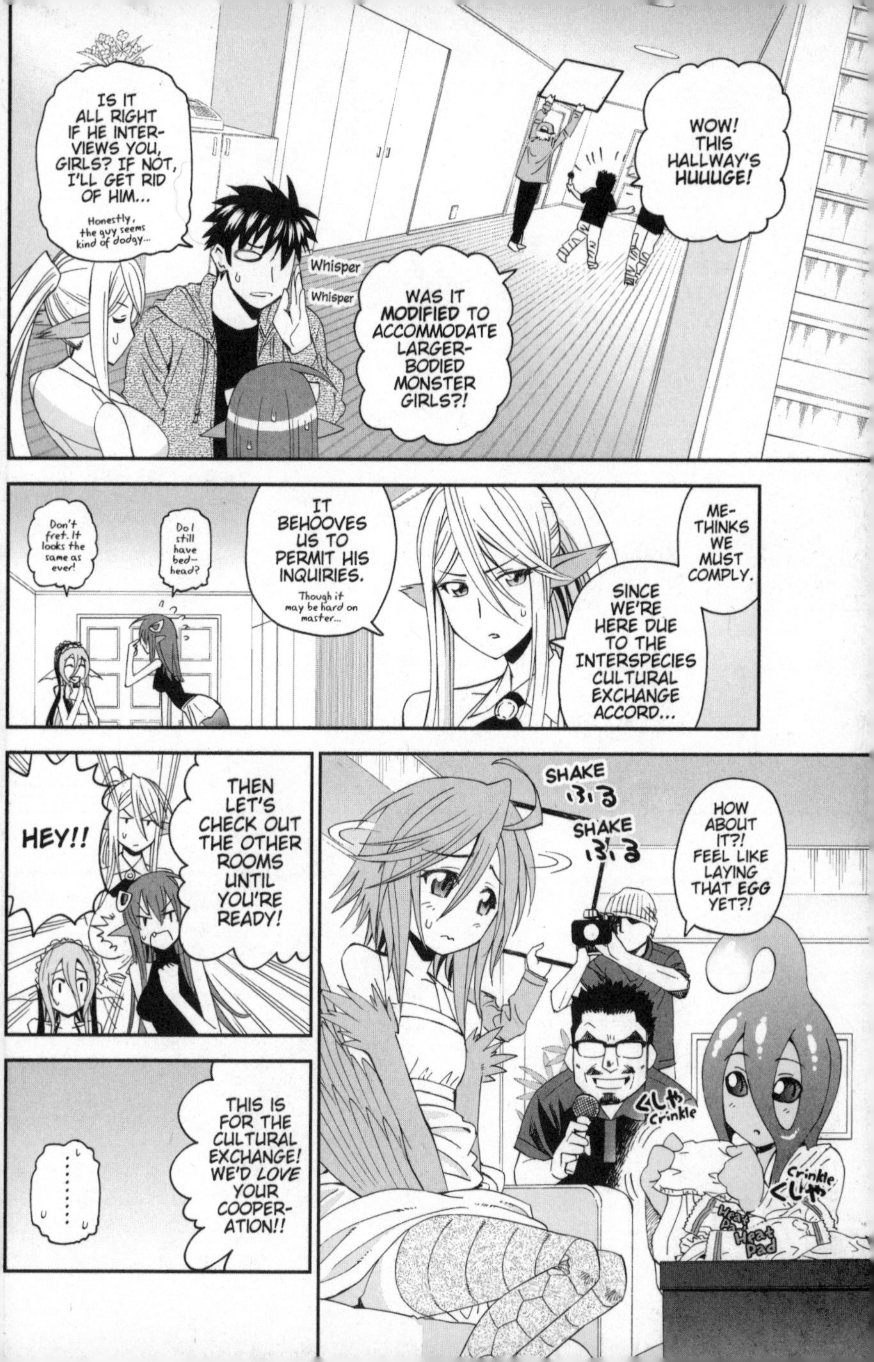
WOW! THIS HALLWAY'S HUUUGE!
WAS IT MODIFIED TO ACCOMMODATE LARGER-BODIED MONSTER GIRLS?!
Whisper
Whisper
IS IT ALL RIGHT IF HE INTER-VIEWS YOU, GIRLS? IF NOT, I'LL GET RID OF HIM...
Honestly, the guy seems kind of dodgy...
ME-THINKS WE MUST COMPLY.
SINCE WE'RE HERE DUE TO THE INTERSPECIES CULTURAL EXCHANGE ACCORD...
IT BEHOOVES US TO PERMIT HIS INQUIRIES.
Though it may be hard on master...
Do I still have bed-head?
Don't fret. It looks the same as ever!
SHAKE ふる
SHAKE ふる
HOW ABOUT IT?! FEEL LIKE LAYING THAT EGG YET?!
くしゃ Crinkle
Crinkle くしゃ
Heat Pad
Heat Pad
THEN LET'S CHECK OUT THE OTHER ROOMS UNTIL YOU'RE READY!
HEY!!
THIS IS FOR THE CULTURAL EXCHANGE! WE'D LOVE YOUR COOPERATION!!
....

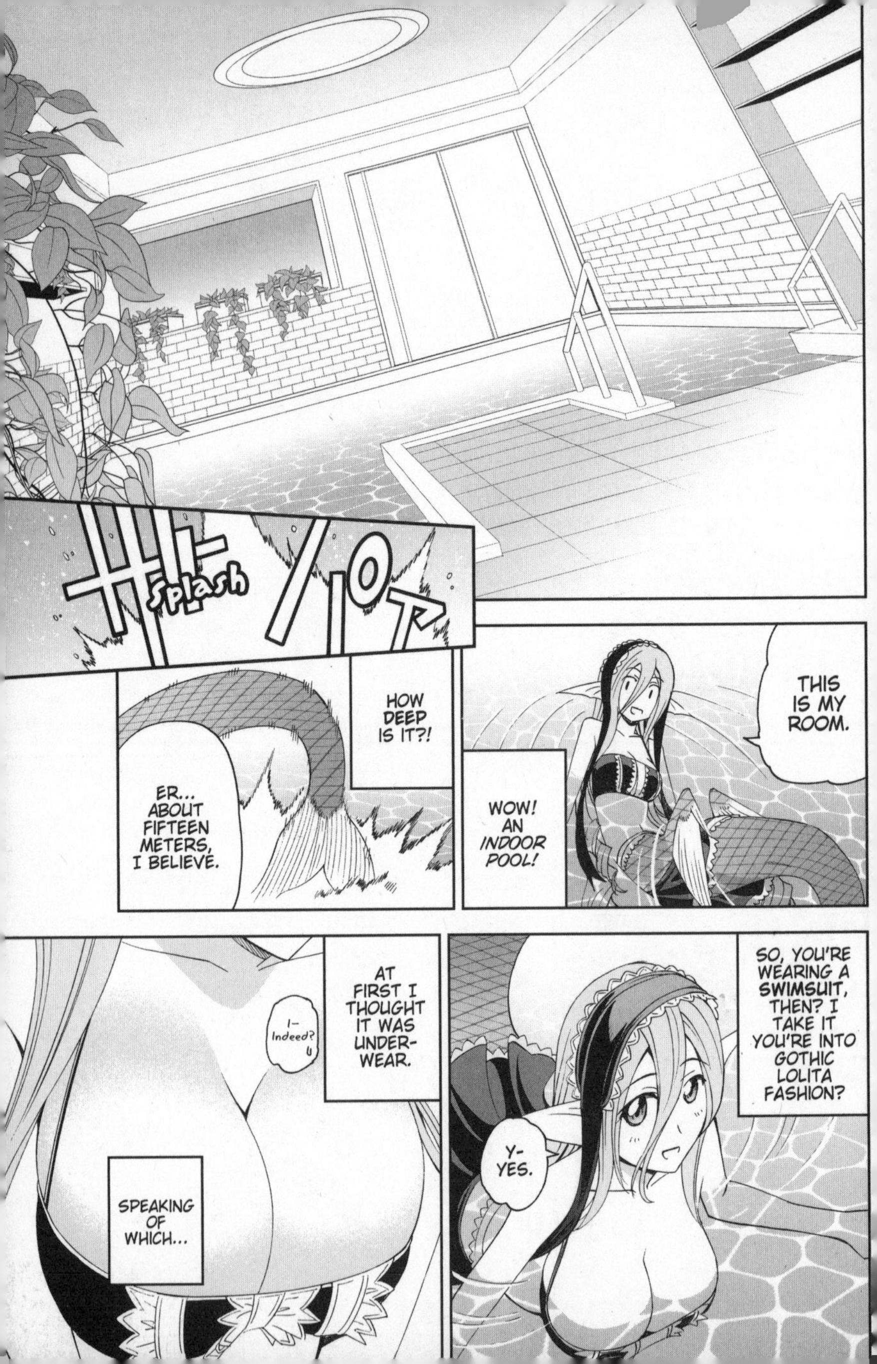
Splash
THIS IS MY ROOM.
WOW! AN INDOOR POOL!
HOW DEEP IS IT?!
ER... ABOUT FIFTEEN METERS, I BELIEVE.
SO, YOU'RE WEARING A SWIMSUIT, THEN? I TAKE IT YOU'RE INTO GOTHIC LOLITA FASHION?
Y-YES.
AT FIRST I THOUGHT IT WAS UNDER-WEAR.
I-Indeed?
SPEAKING OF WHICH...

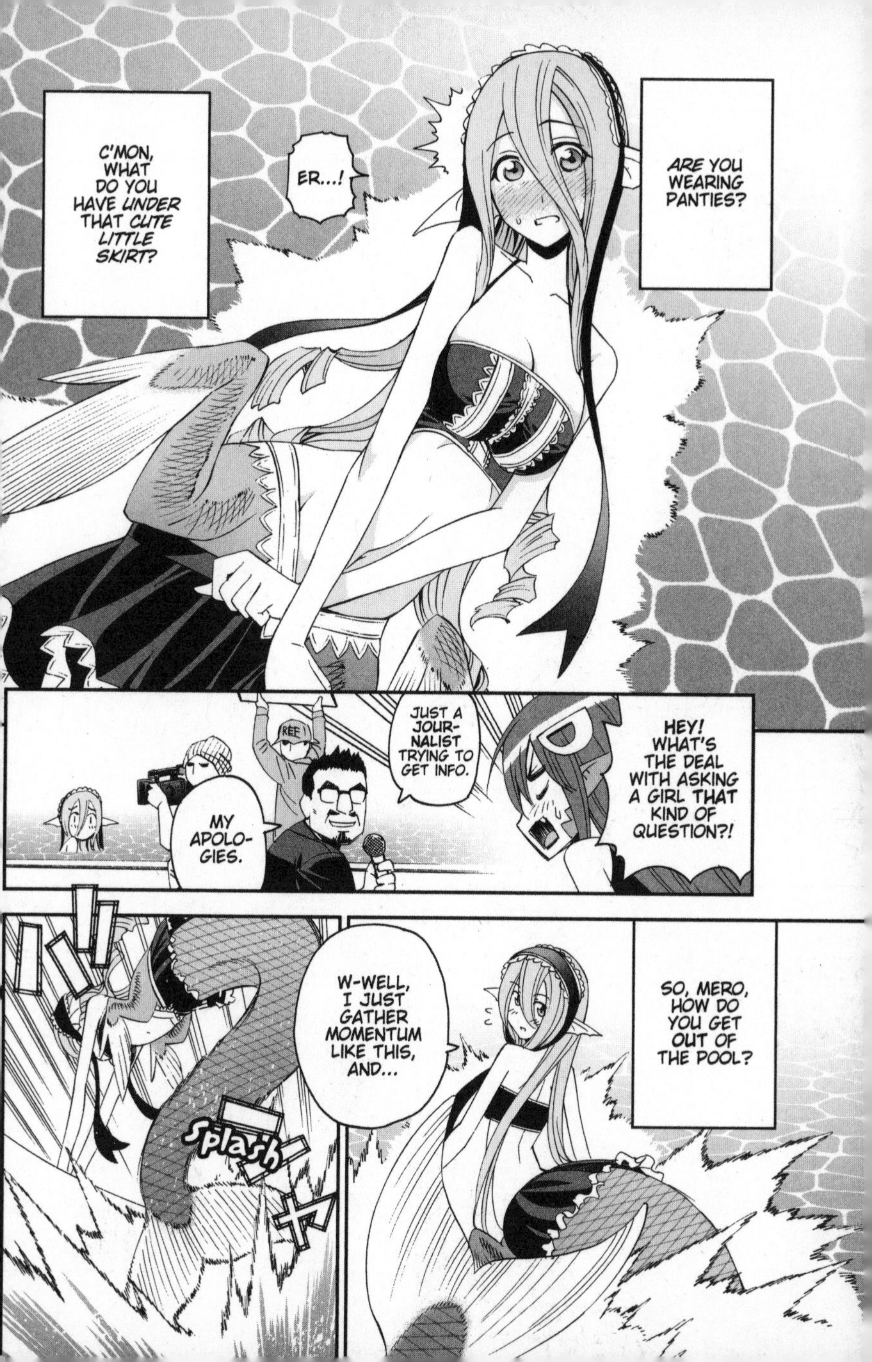
ARE YOU WEARING PANTIES?
ER...!
C'MON, WHAT DO YOU HAVE UNDER THAT CUTE LITTLE SKIRT?
HEY! WHAT'S THE DEAL WITH ASKING A GIRL THAT KIND OF QUESTION?!
JUST A JOURNALIST TRYING TO GET INFO.
REF
MY APOLOGIES.
SO, MERO, HOW DO YOU GET OUT OF THE POOL?
W-WELL, I JUST GATHER MOMENTUM LIKE THIS, AND...
Splash

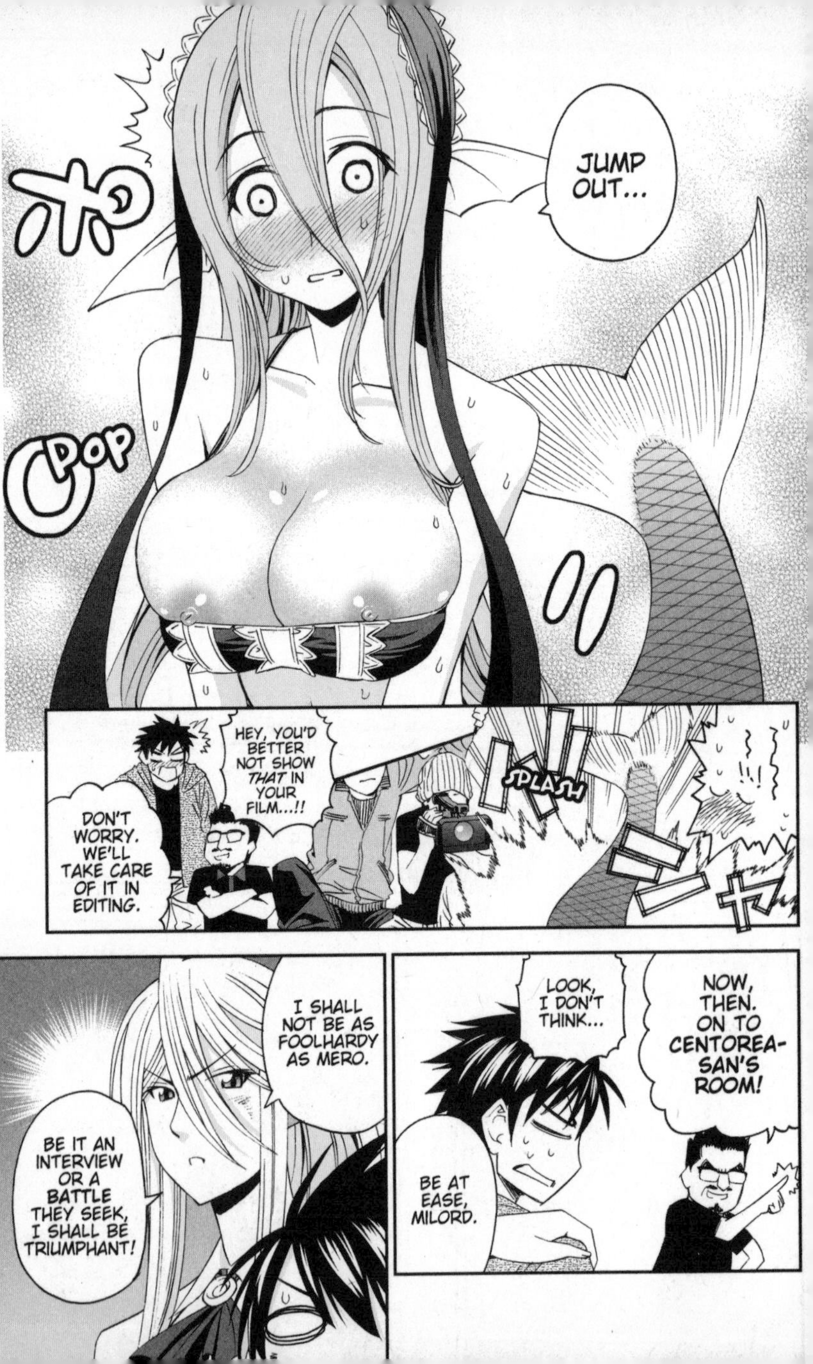
JUMP OUT...
POP
SPLASH
HEY, YOU'D BETTER NOT SHOW *THAT* IN YOUR FILM...!!
DON'T WORRY. WE'LL TAKE CARE OF IT IN EDITING.
NOW, THEN. ON TO CENTOREA-SAN'S ROOM!
LOOK, I DON'T THINK...
BE AT EASE, MILORD.
I SHALL NOT BE AS FOOLHARDY AS MERO.
BE IT AN INTERVIEW OR A BATTLE THEY SEEK, I SHALL BE TRIUMPHANT!

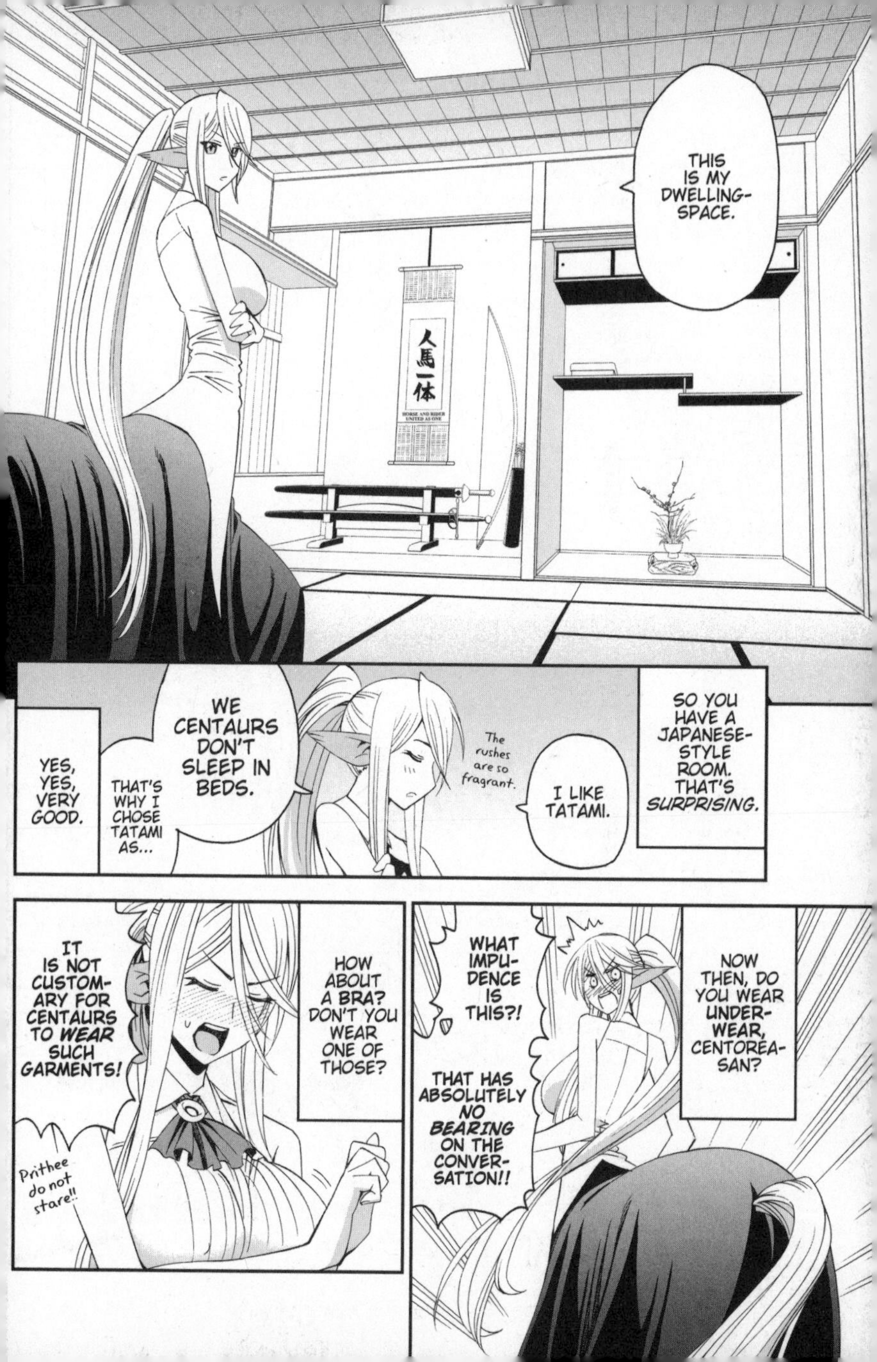
THIS IS MY DWELLING-SPACE.
人馬一体
HORSE AND RIDER UNITED AS ONE
SO YOU HAVE A JAPANESE-STYLE ROOM. THAT'S *SURPRISING*.
I LIKE TATAMI.
The rushes are so fragrant.
WE CENTAURS DON'T SLEEP IN BEDS.
THAT'S WHY I CHOSE TATAMI AS...
YES, YES, VERY GOOD.
NOW THEN, DO YOU WEAR UNDER-WEAR, CENTOREA-SAN?
WHAT IMPU-DENCE IS THIS?!
THAT HAS ABSOLUTELY *NO BEARING* ON THE CONVER-SATION!!
HOW ABOUT A BRA? DON'T YOU WEAR ONE OF THOSE?
IT IS NOT CUSTOM-ARY FOR CENTAURS TO *WEAR* SUCH GARMENTS!
Prithee do not stare!!

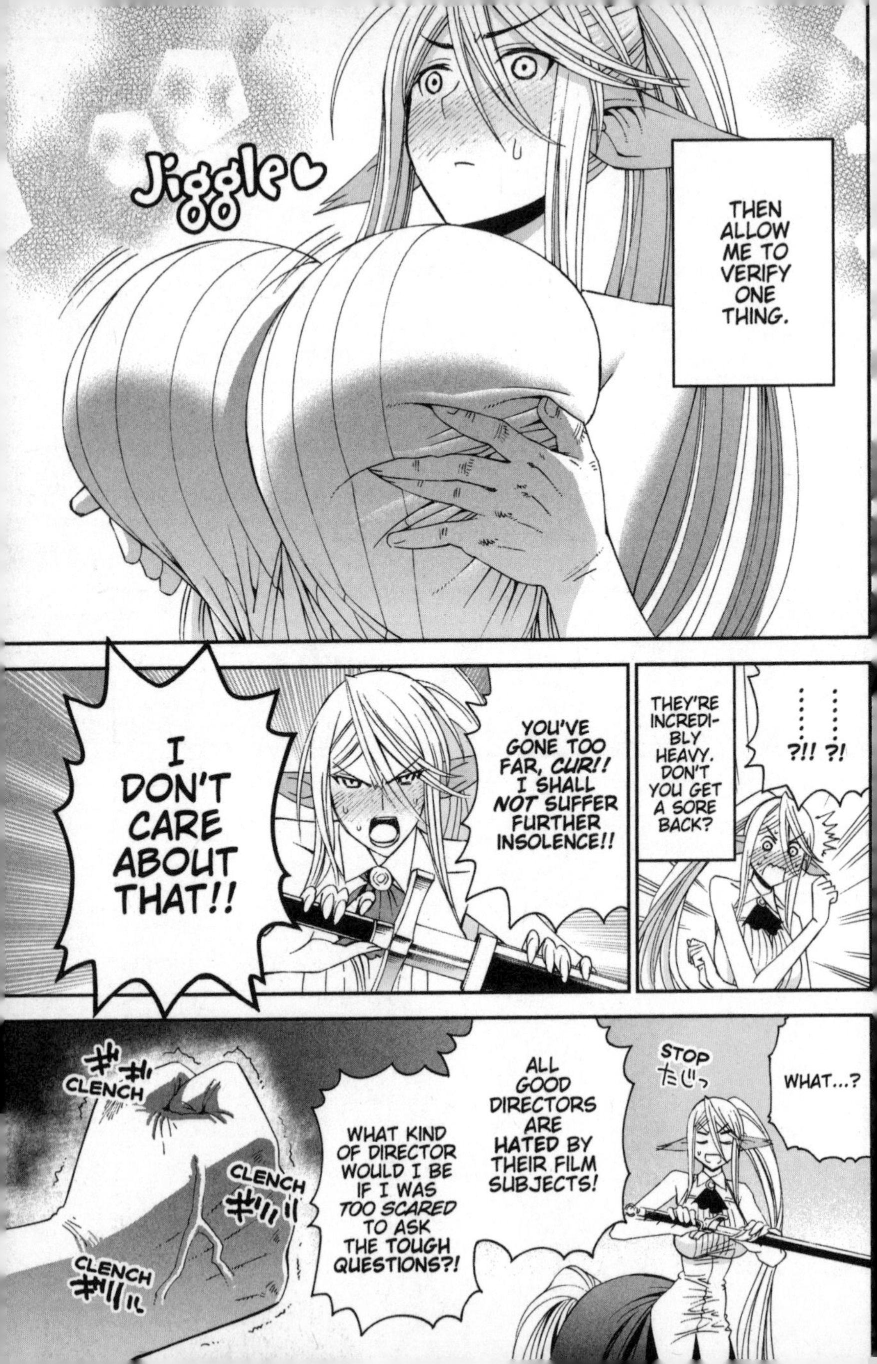
THEN ALLOW ME TO VERIFY ONE THING.
Jiggle♥
......?!! ?!
THEY'RE INCREDI-BLY HEAVY. DON'T YOU GET A SORE BACK?
YOU'VE GONE TOO FAR, CUR!! I SHALL NOT SUFFER FURTHER INSOLENCE!!
I DON'T CARE ABOUT THAT!!
WHAT...?
STOP
たじっ
ALL GOOD DIRECTORS ARE HATED BY THEIR FILM SUBJECTS!
WHAT KIND OF DIRECTOR WOULD I BE IF I WAS TOO SCARED TO ASK THE TOUGH QUESTIONS?!
ギギ
CLENCH
CLENCH
ギリリ
CLENCH
ギリル

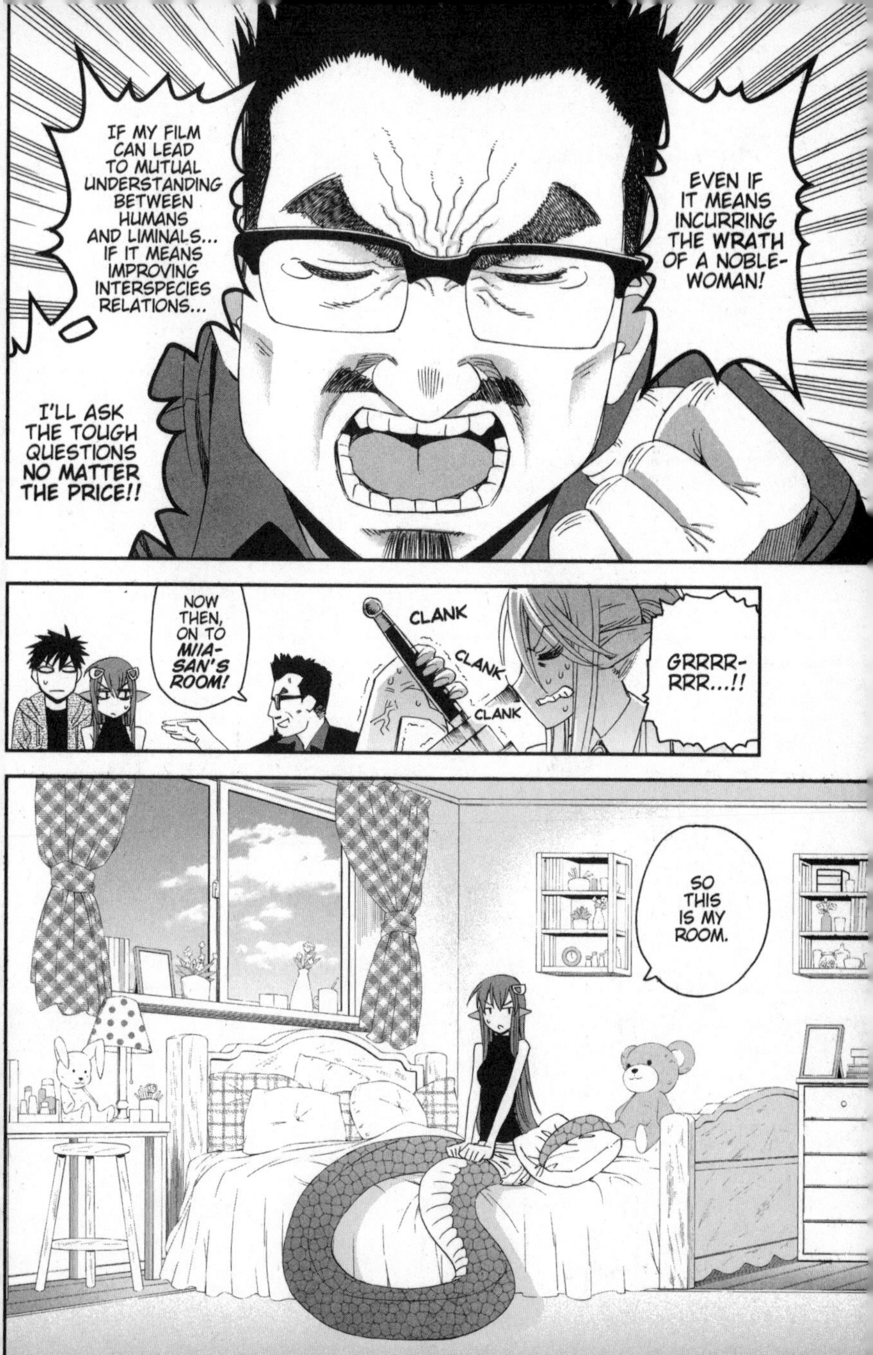
EVEN IF IT MEANS INCURRING THE WRATH OF A NOBLE-WOMAN!
IF MY FILM CAN LEAD TO MUTUAL UNDERSTANDING BETWEEN HUMANS AND LIMINALS... IF IT MEANS IMPROVING INTERSPECIES RELATIONS...
I'LL ASK THE TOUGH QUESTIONS NO MATTER THE PRICE!!
GRRRR-RRR...!!
CLANK
CLANK
CLANK
NOW THEN, ON TO MIIA-SAN'S ROOM!
SO THIS IS MY ROOM.

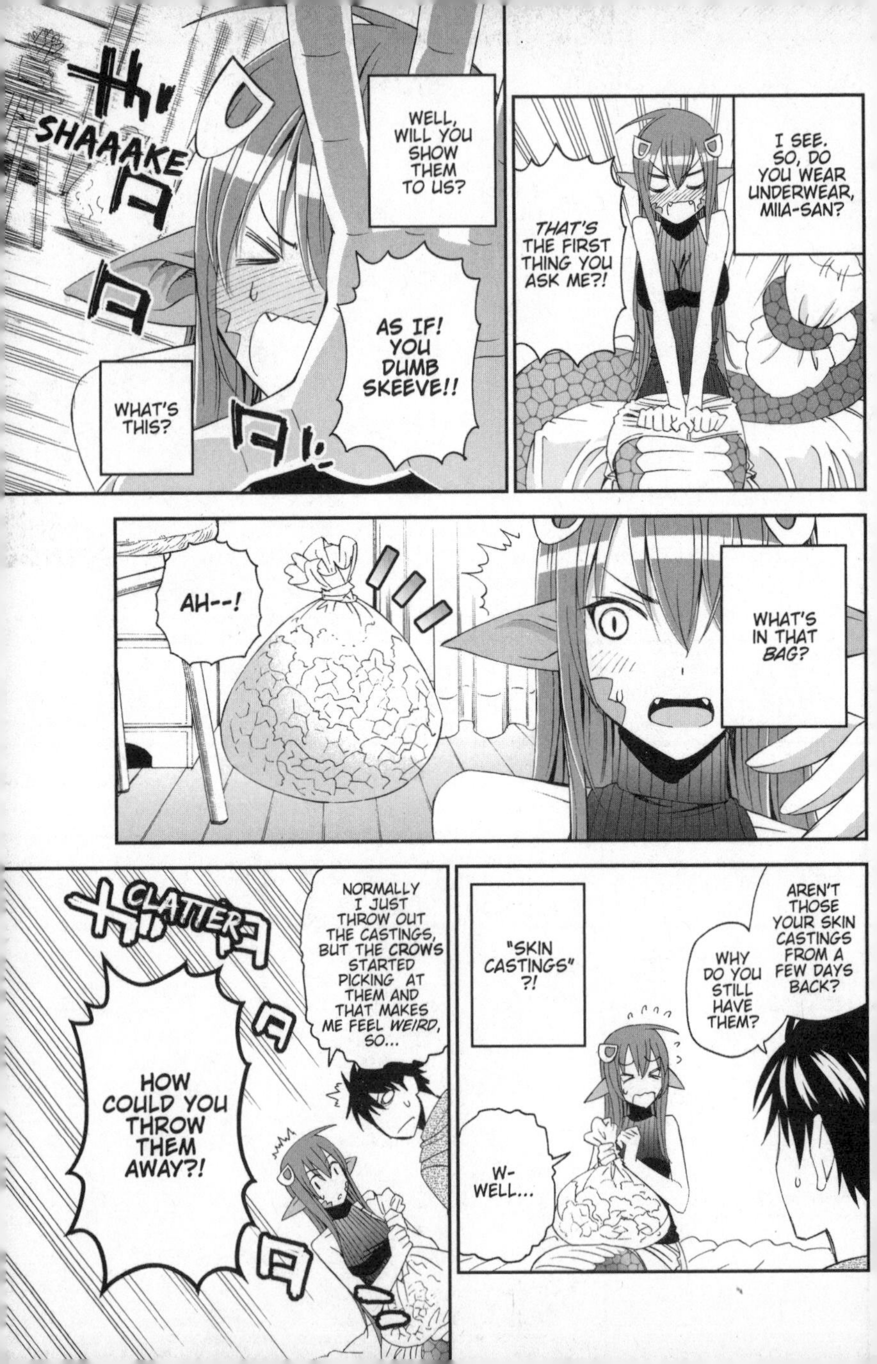
I SEE. SO, DO YOU WEAR UNDERWEAR, MIIA-SAN?
THAT'S THE FIRST THING YOU ASK ME?!
WELL, WILL YOU SHOW THEM TO US?
AS IF! YOU DUMB SKEEVE!!
SHAAAKE
WHAT'S THIS?
WHAT'S IN THAT *BAG?*
AH--!
AREN'T THOSE YOUR SKIN CASTINGS FROM A FEW DAYS BACK?
WHY DO YOU STILL HAVE THEM?
"SKIN CASTINGS"?!
W-WELL...
NORMALLY I JUST THROW OUT THE CASTINGS, BUT THE CROWS STARTED PICKING AT THEM AND THAT MAKES ME FEEL *WEIRD*, SO...
CLATTER
HOW COULD YOU THROW THEM AWAY?!

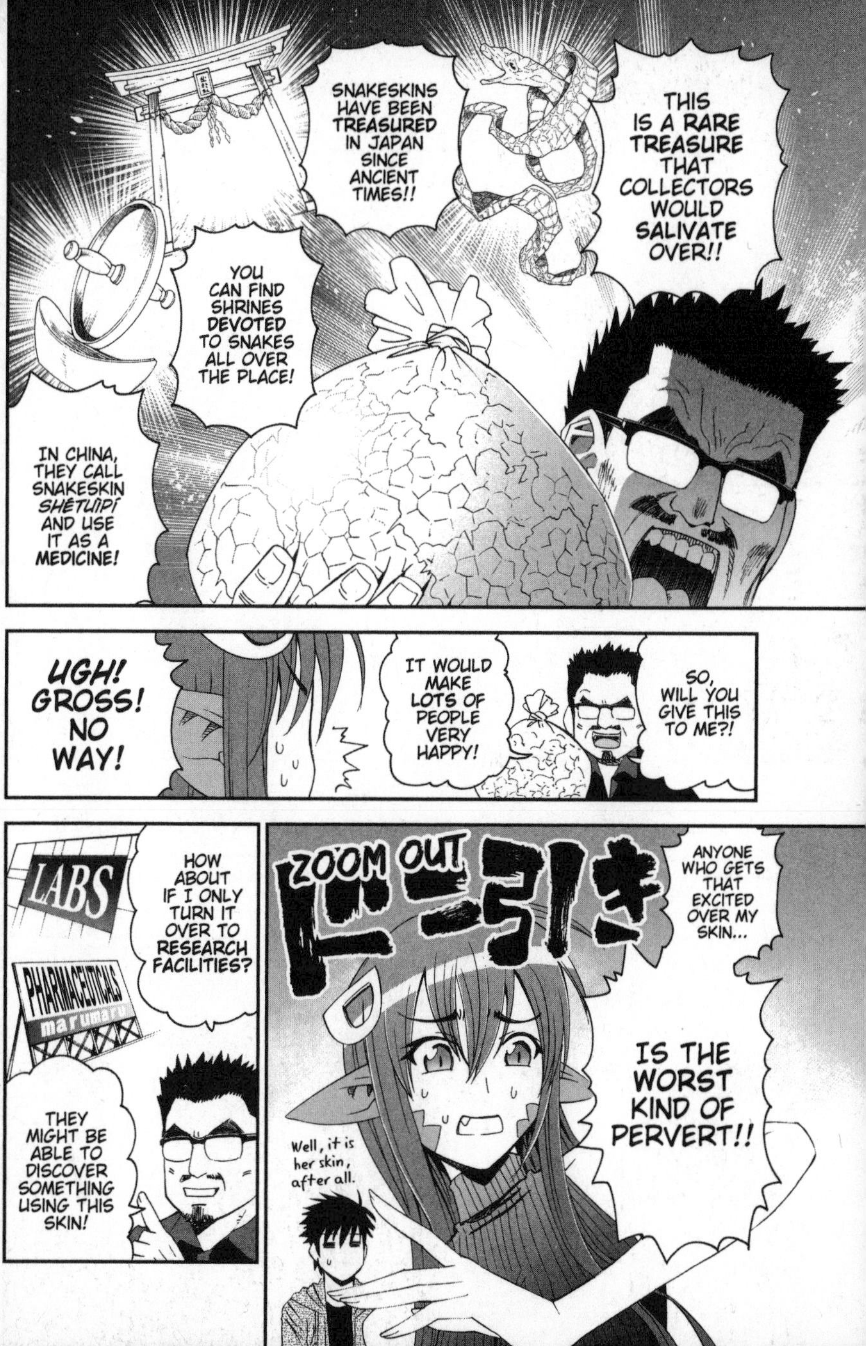
THIS IS A RARE TREASURE THAT COLLECTORS WOULD SALIVATE OVER!!
SNAKESKINS HAVE BEEN TREASURED IN JAPAN SINCE ANCIENT TIMES!!
YOU CAN FIND SHRINES DEVOTED TO SNAKES ALL OVER THE PLACE!
IN CHINA, THEY CALL SNAKESKIN *SHÉTUÌPÍ* AND USE IT AS A MEDICINE!
SO, WILL YOU GIVE THIS TO ME?!
IT WOULD MAKE LOTS OF PEOPLE VERY HAPPY!
UGH! GROSS! NO WAY!
ANYONE WHO GETS THAT EXCITED OVER MY SKIN...
ZOOM OUT
IS THE WORST KIND OF PERVERT!!
Well, it is her skin, after all.
HOW ABOUT IF I ONLY TURN IT OVER TO RESEARCH FACILITIES?
LABS
PHARMACEUTICALS
marumaru
THEY MIGHT BE ABLE TO DISCOVER SOMETHING USING THIS SKIN!

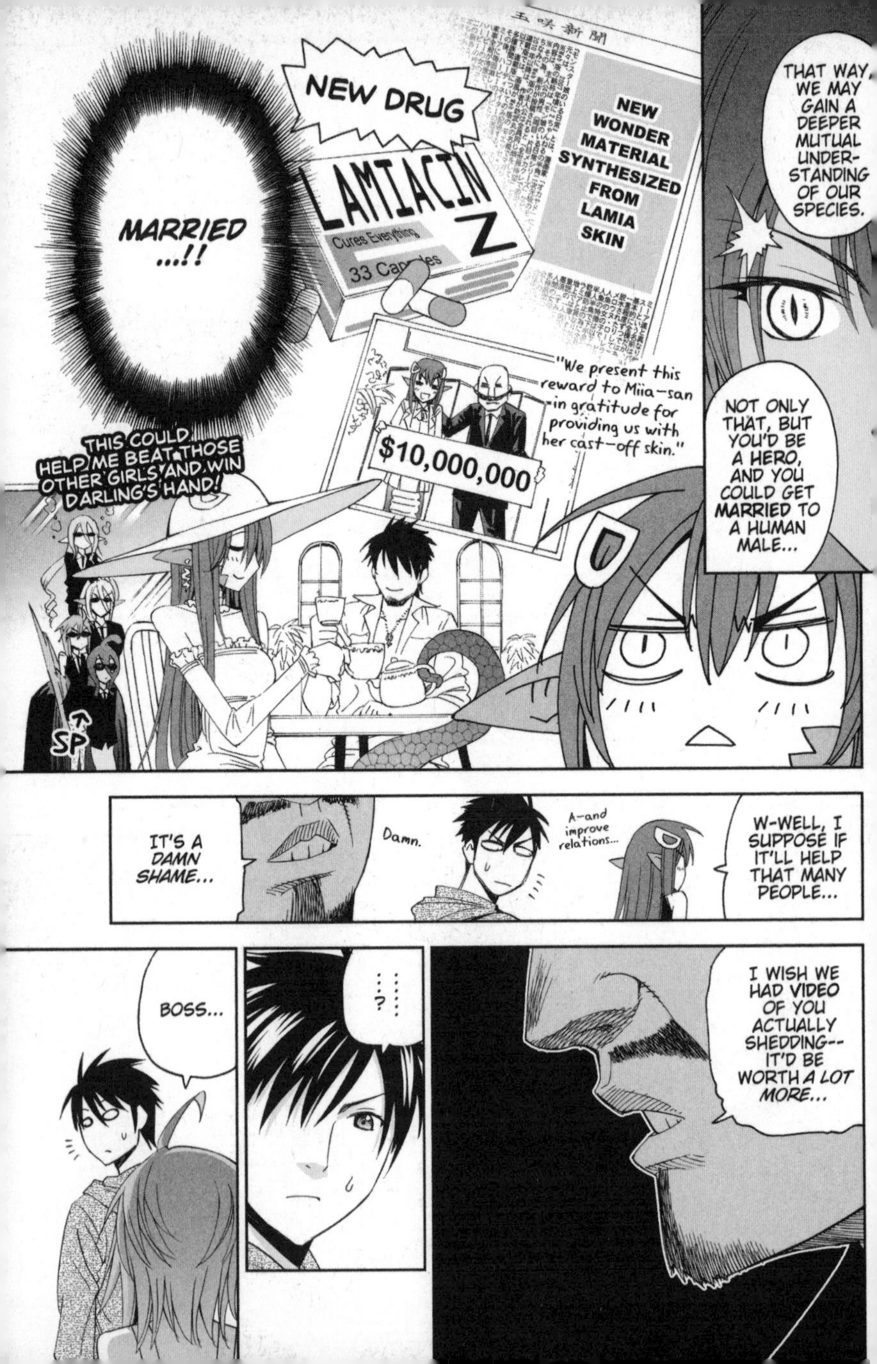

THAT WAY, WE MAY GAIN A DEEPER MUTUAL UNDER-STANDING OF OUR SPECIES.
NOT ONLY THAT, BUT YOU'D BE A HERO, AND YOU COULD GET MARRIED TO A HUMAN MALE...
MARRIED ...!!
NEW DRUG
NEW WONDER MATERIAL SYNTHESIZED FROM LAMIA SKIN
LAMIACIN Z
Cures Everything
33 Cap
"We present this reward to Miia-san in gratitude for providing us with her cast-off skin."
$10,000,000
THIS COULD HELP ME BEAT THOSE OTHER GIRLS AND WIN DARLING'S HAND!
SP
W-WELL, I SUPPOSE IF IT'LL HELP THAT MANY PEOPLE...
A-and improve relations...
Damn.
IT'S A DAMN SHAME...
I WISH WE HAD VIDEO OF YOU ACTUALLY SHEDDING-- IT'D BE WORTH A LOT MORE...
......?
BOSS...

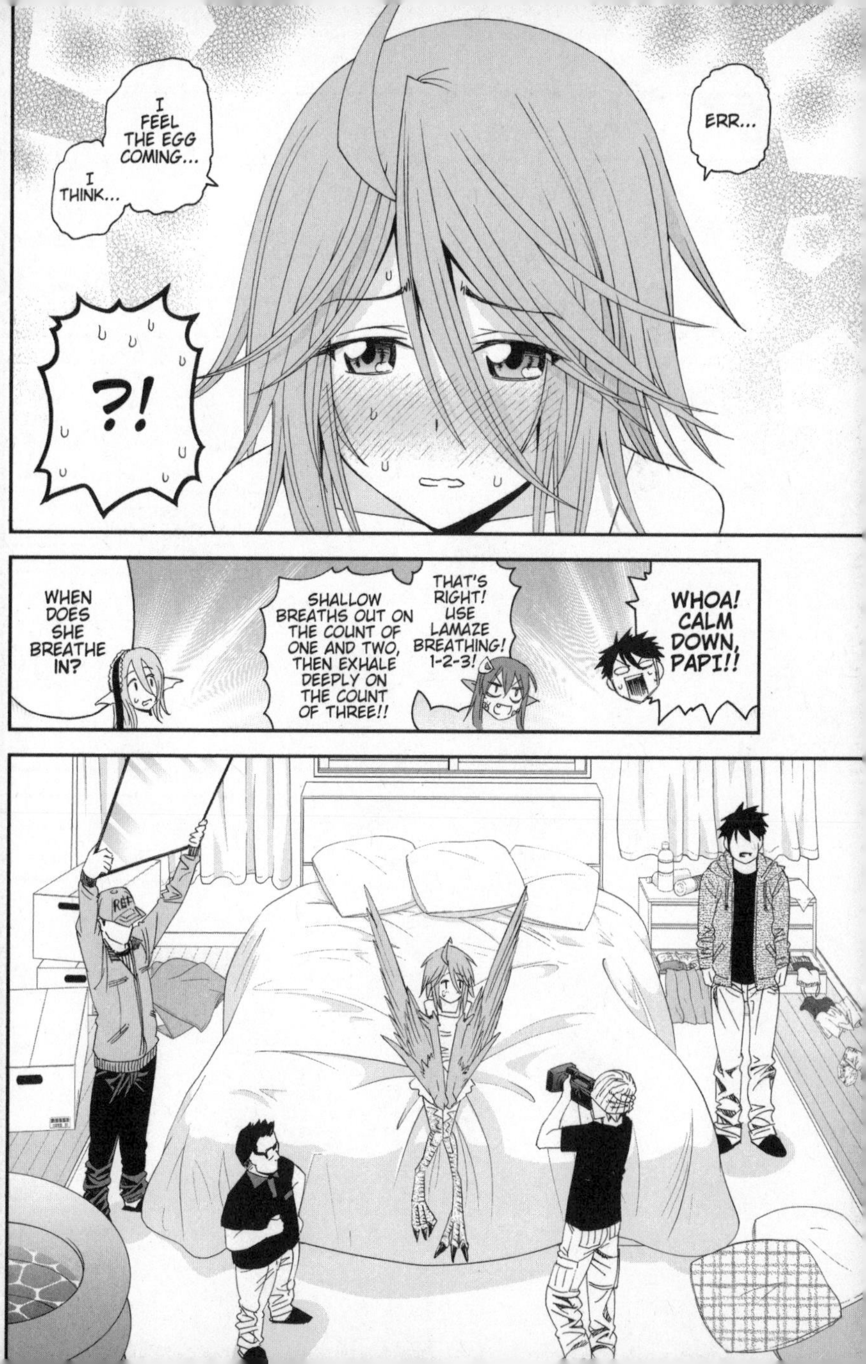
ERR...
I FEEL THE EGG COMING...
I THINK...
?!
WHOA! CALM DOWN, PAPI!!
THAT'S RIGHT! USE LAMAZE BREATHING! 1-2-3!
SHALLOW BREATHS OUT ON THE COUNT OF ONE AND TWO, THEN EXHALE DEEPLY ON THE COUNT OF THREE!!
WHEN DOES SHE BREATHE IN?

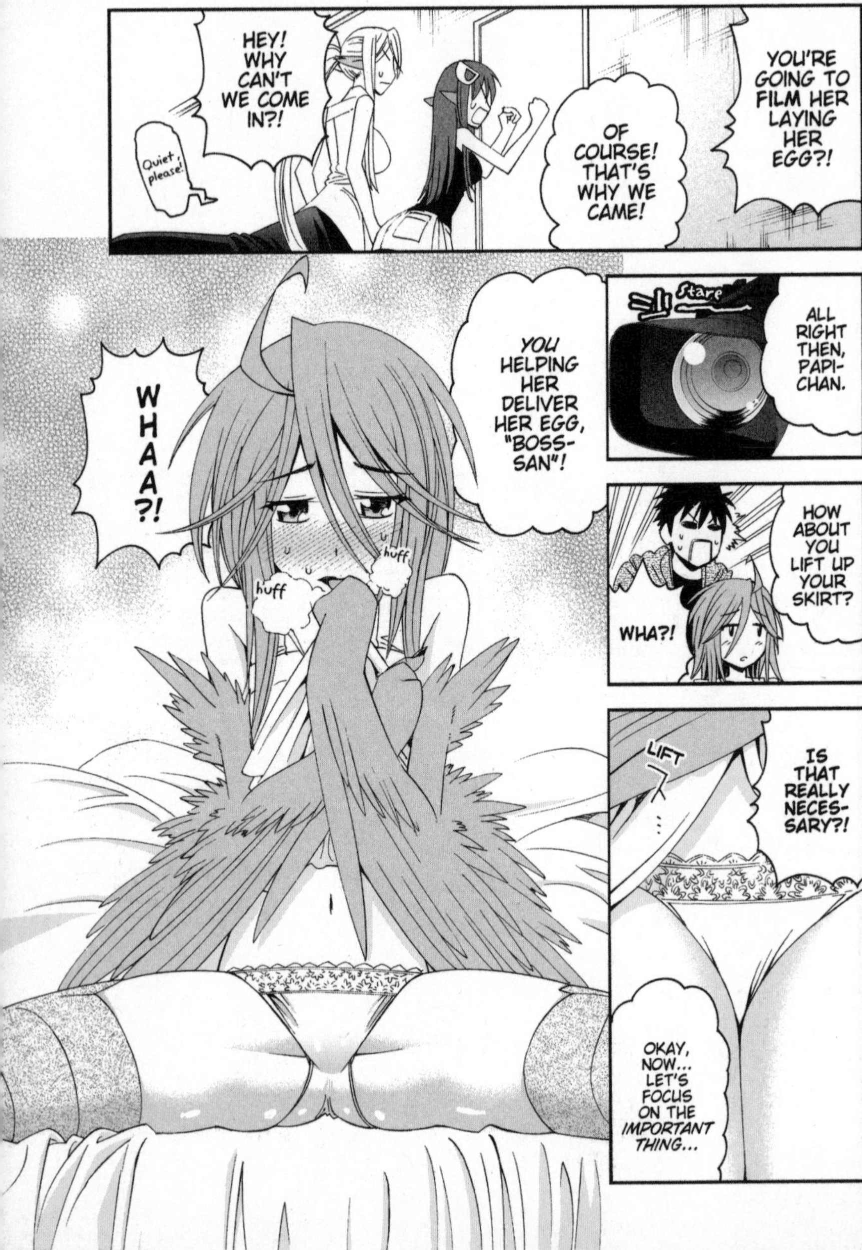

YOU'RE GOING TO FILM HER LAYING HER EGG?!
OF COURSE! THAT'S WHY WE CAME!
HEY! WHY CAN'T WE COME IN?!
Quiet, please!
Stare
ALL RIGHT THEN, PAPI-CHAN.
HOW ABOUT YOU LIFT UP YOUR SKIRT?
WHA?!
IS THAT REALLY NECESSARY?!
LIFT
OKAY, NOW... LET'S FOCUS ON THE *IMPORTANT* THING...
YOU HELPING HER DELIVER HER EGG, "BOSS-SAN"!
WHAAA?!
huff
huff

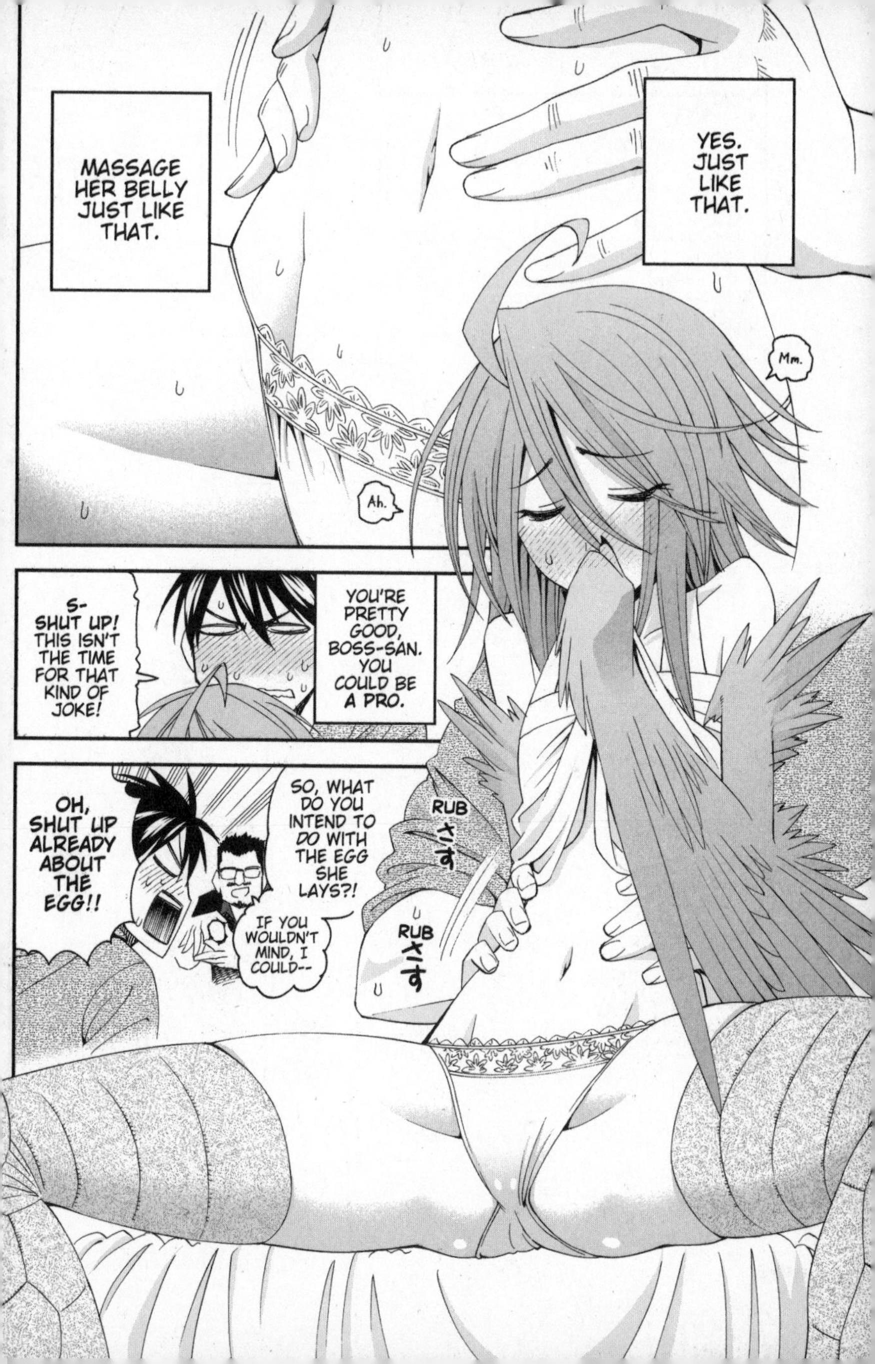

YES. JUST LIKE THAT.
MASSAGE HER BELLY JUST LIKE THAT.
Mm.
Ah.
YOU'RE PRETTY GOOD, BOSS-SAN. YOU COULD BE A PRO.
S-SHUT UP! THIS ISN'T THE TIME FOR THAT KIND OF JOKE!
RUB さす
RUB さす
SO, WHAT DO YOU INTEND TO DO WITH THE EGG SHE LAYS?!
OH, SHUT UP ALREADY ABOUT THE EGG!!
IF YOU WOULDN'T MIND, I COULD--

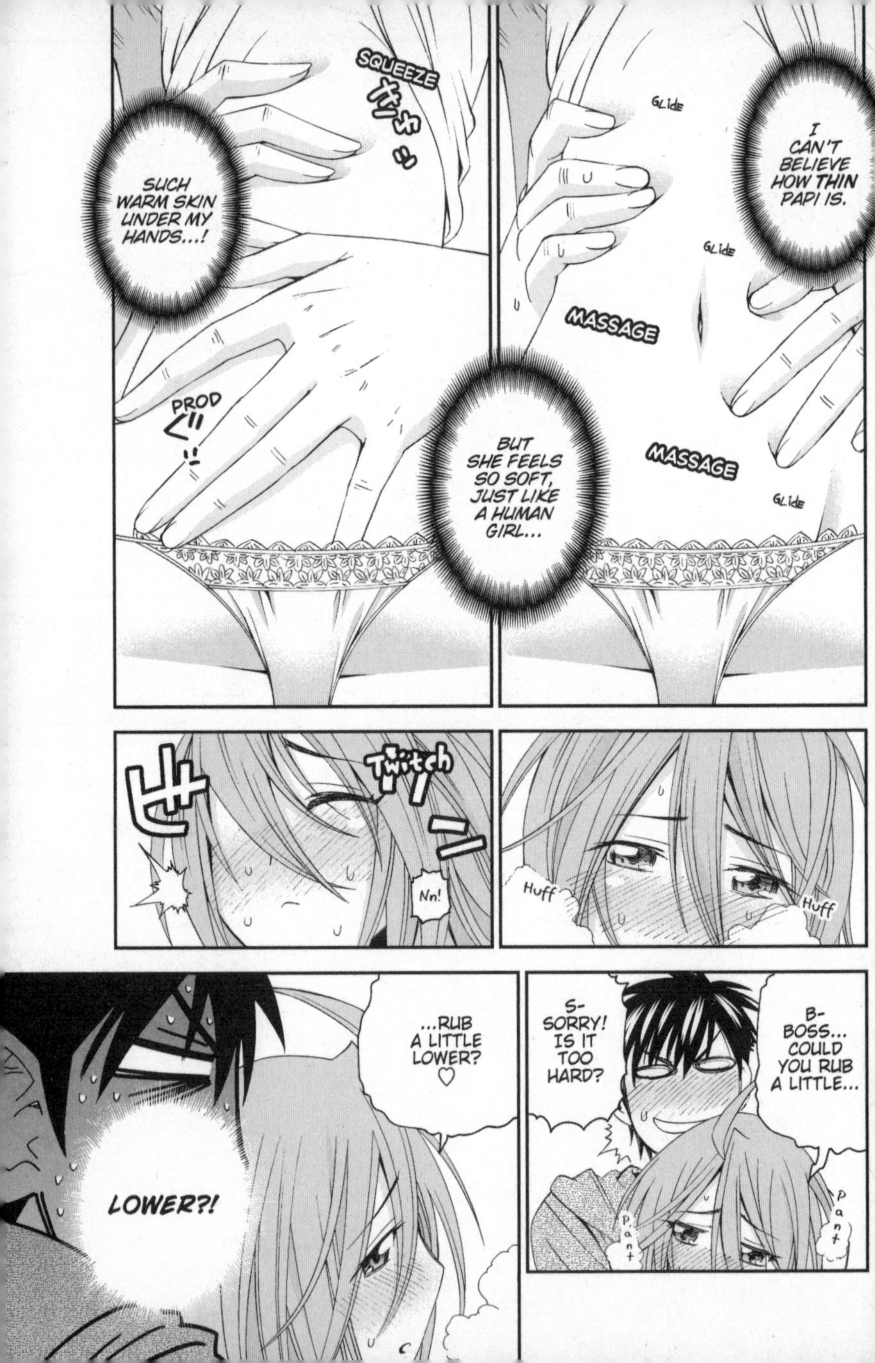
GLIDE
I CAN'T BELIEVE HOW THIN PAPI IS.
GLIDE
MASSAGE
MASSAGE
GLIDE
BUT SHE FEELS SO SOFT, JUST LIKE A HUMAN GIRL...
SQUEEZE
SUCH WARM SKIN UNDER MY HANDS...!
PROD
Huff
Huff
Twitch
Nn!
B-BOSS... COULD YOU RUB A LITTLE...
S-SORRY! IS IT TOO HARD?
Pant
Pant
...RUB A LITTLE LOWER? ♡
LOWER?!

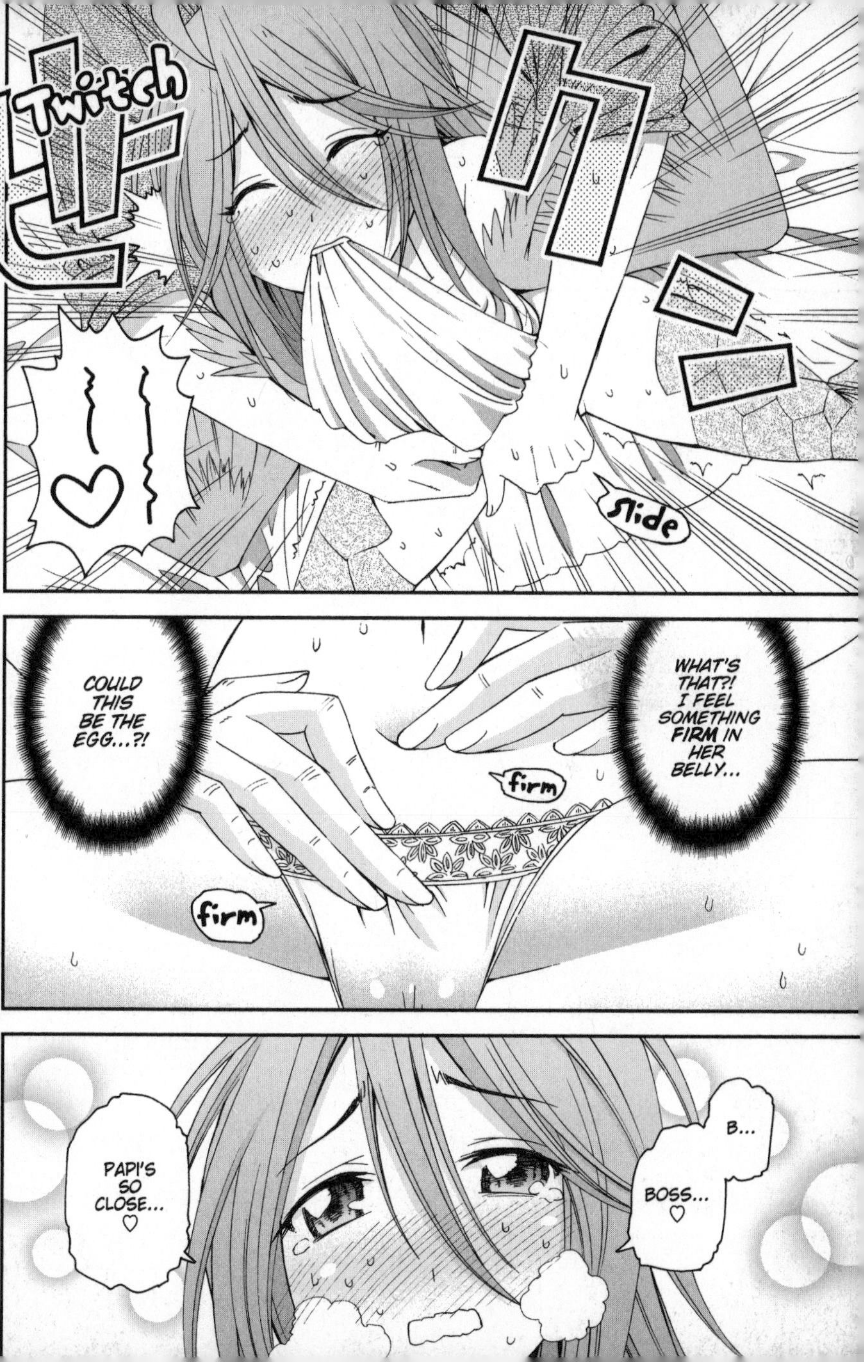
Twitch
slide
WHAT'S THAT?! I FEEL SOMETHING **FIRM** IN HER BELLY...
firm
COULD THIS BE THE EGG...?!
firm
B...
BOSS... ♡
PAPI'S SO CLOSE... ♡

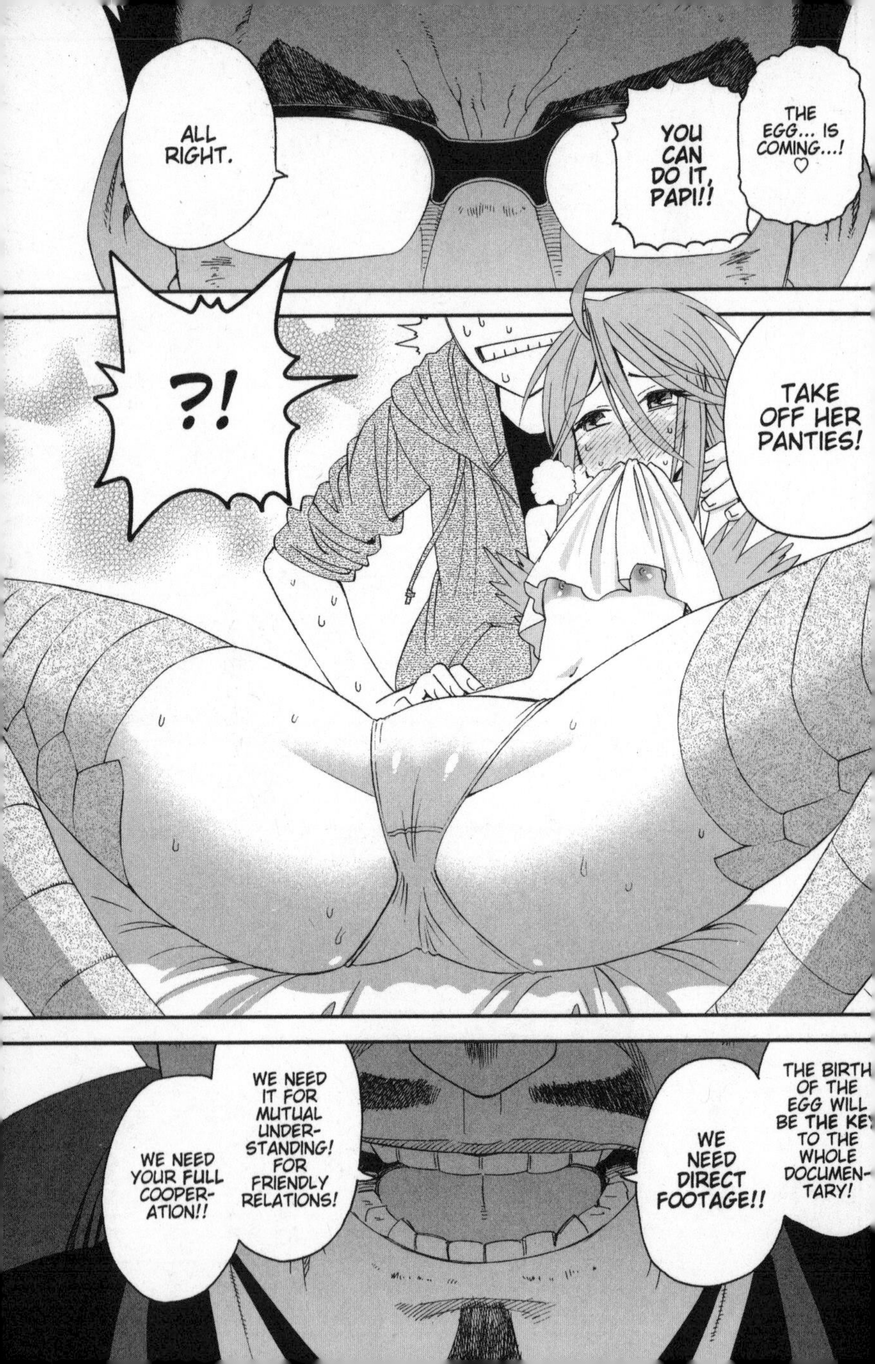
THE EGG... IS COMING...! ♡
YOU CAN DO IT, PAPI!!
ALL RIGHT.
TAKE OFF HER PANTIES!
?!
THE BIRTH OF THE EGG WILL BE THE KE TO THE WHOLE DOCUMENTARY!
WE NEED DIRECT FOOTAGE!!
WE NEED IT FOR MUTUAL UNDERSTANDING! FOR FRIENDLY RELATIONS!
WE NEED YOUR FULL COOPERATION!!

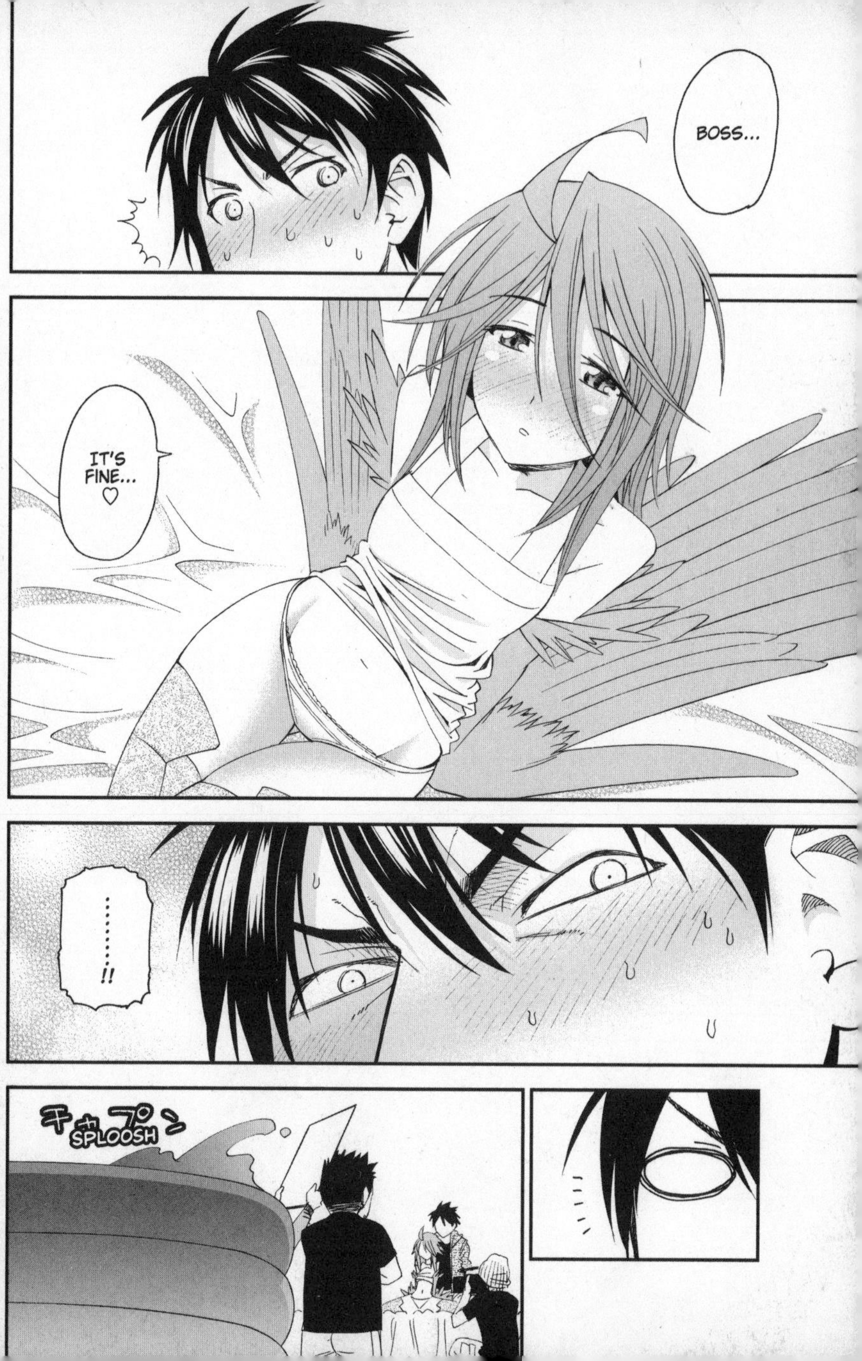
BOSS...
IT'S FINE... ♡
........!!
チャプン
SPLOOSH

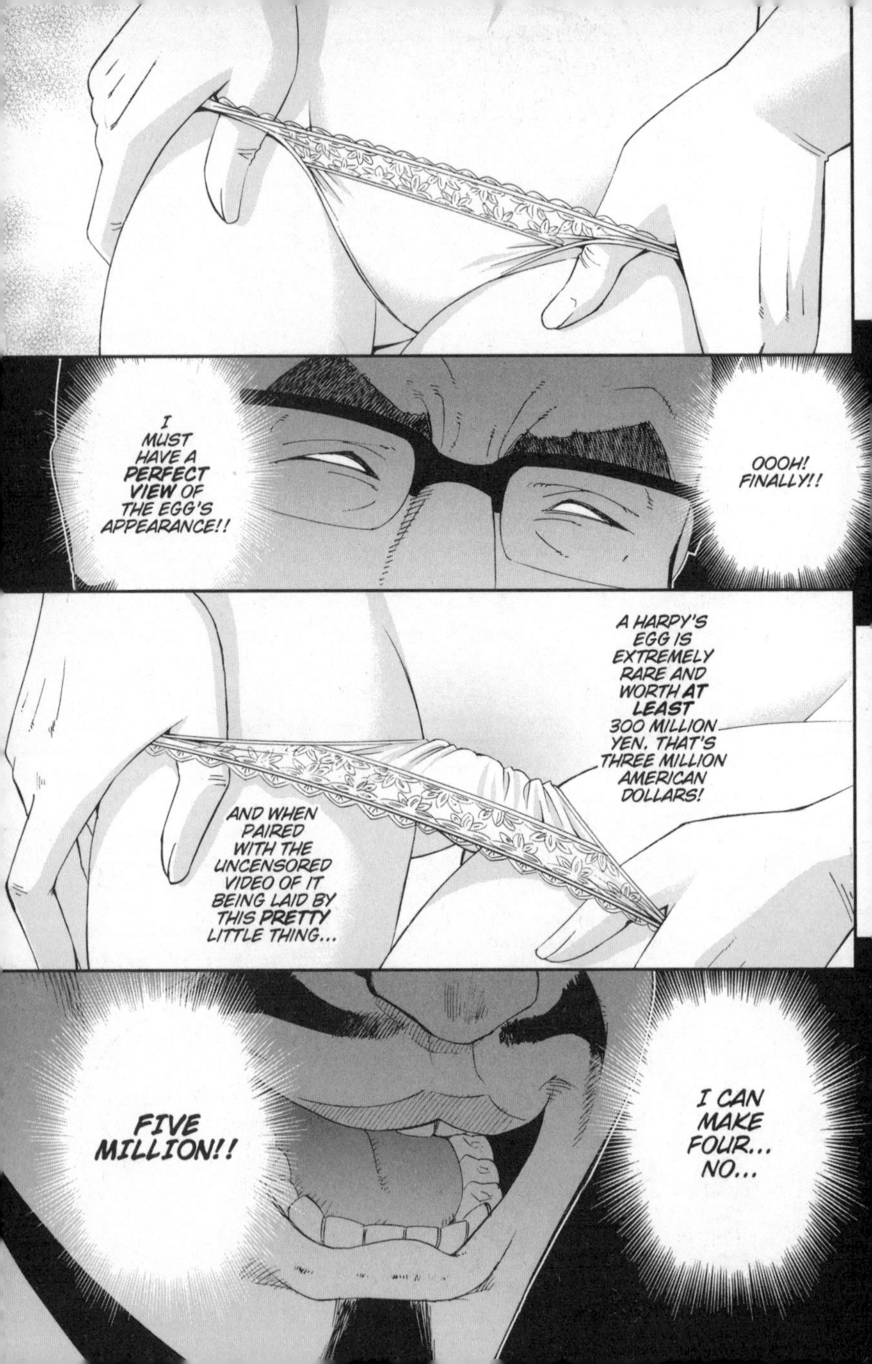
OOOH! FINALLY!!
I MUST HAVE A PERFECT VIEW OF THE EGG'S APPEARANCE!!
A HARPY'S EGG IS EXTREMELY RARE AND WORTH AT LEAST 300 MILLION YEN. THAT'S THREE MILLION AMERICAN DOLLARS!
AND WHEN PAIRED WITH THE UNCENSORED VIDEO OF IT BEING LAID BY THIS PRETTY LITTLE THING...
I CAN MAKE FOUR... NO...
FIVE MILLION!!

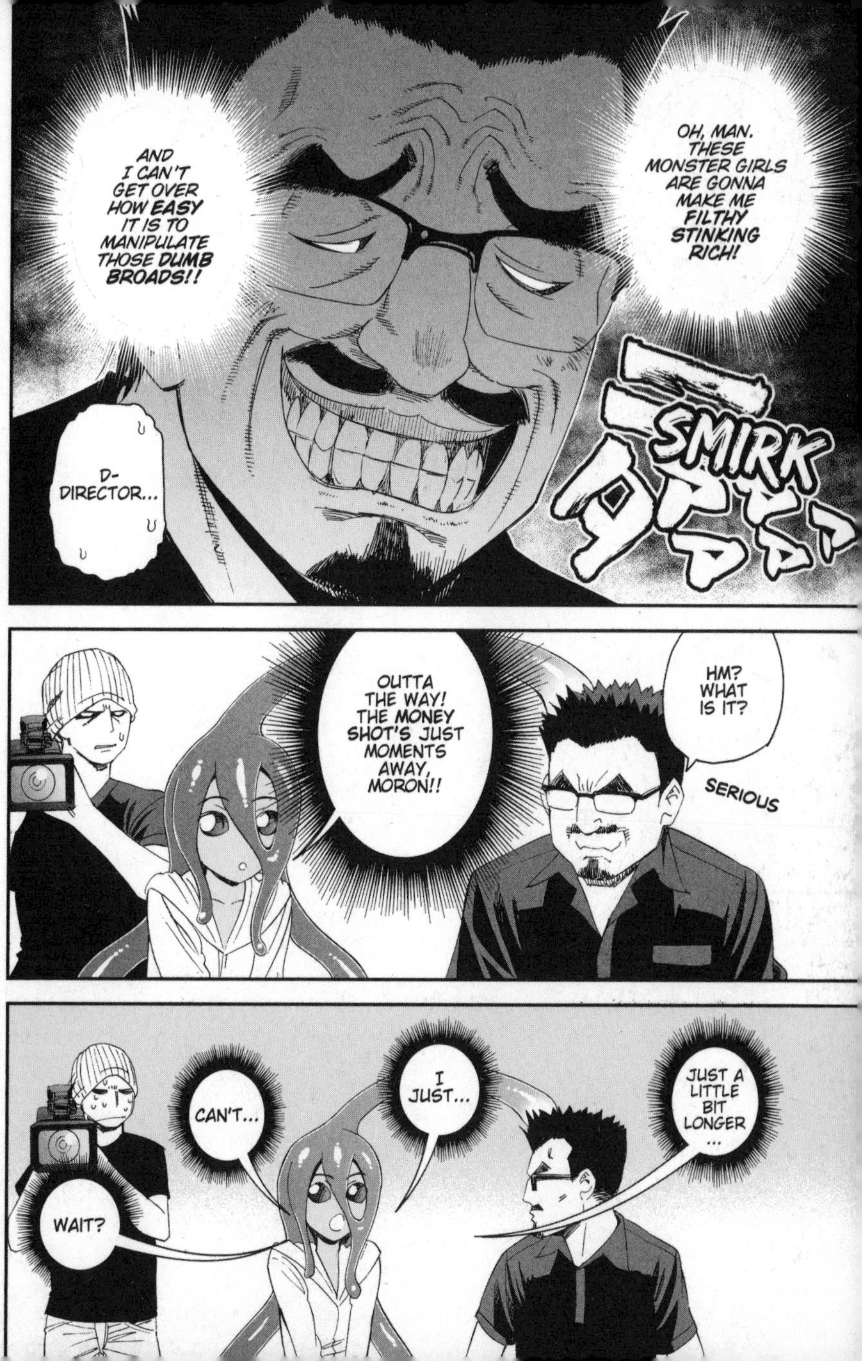
OH, MAN. THESE MONSTER GIRLS ARE GONNA MAKE ME FILTHY STINKING RICH!
SMIRK
AND I CAN'T GET OVER HOW EASY IT IS TO MANIPULATE THOSE DUMB BROADS!!
D-DIRECTOR...
HM? WHAT IS IT?
SERIOUS
OUTTA THE WAY! THE MONEY SHOT'S JUST MOMENTS AWAY, MORON!!
JUST A LITTLE BIT LONGER ...
I JUST...
CAN'T...
WAIT?

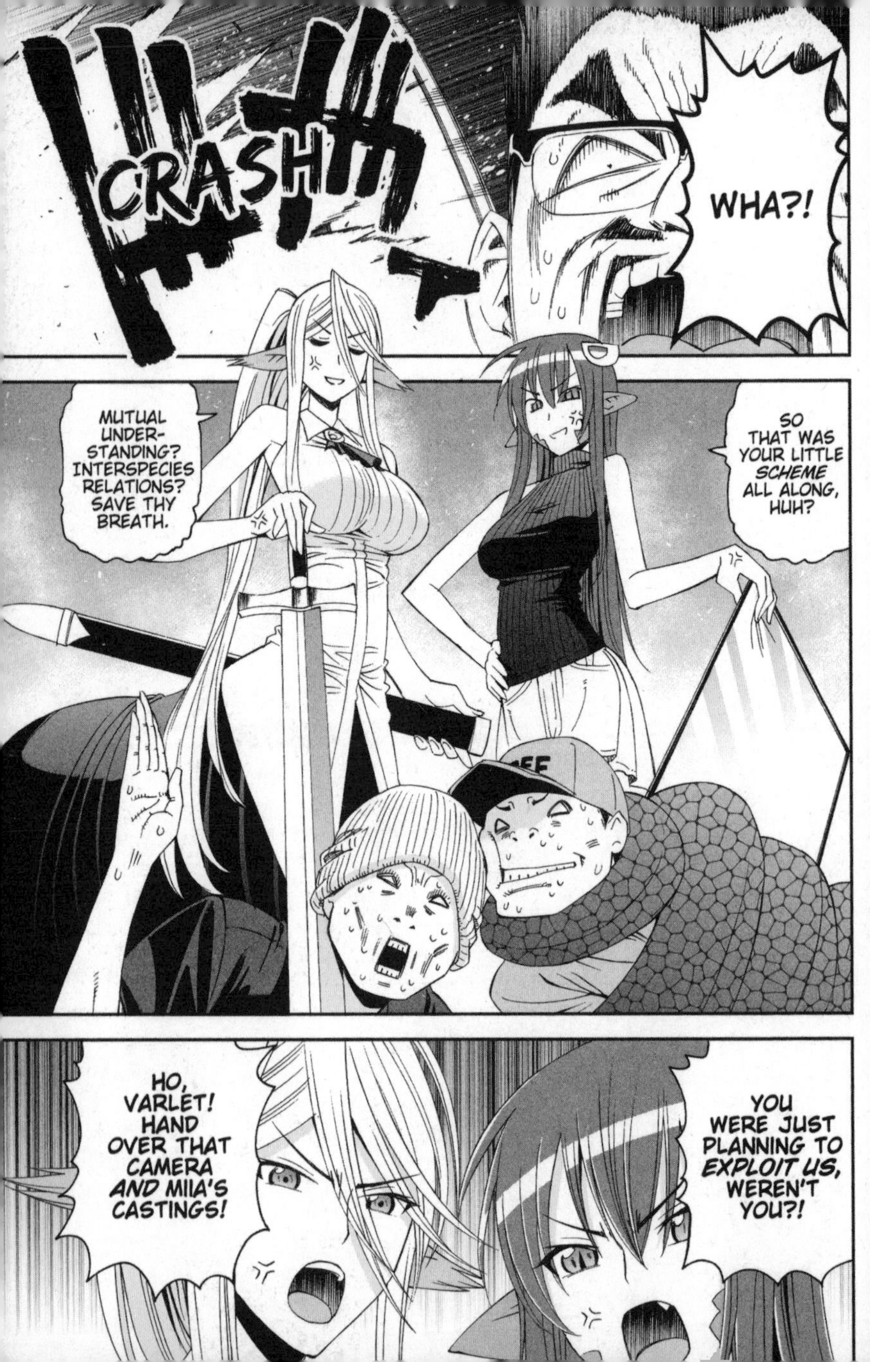
WHA?!
CRASH
SO THAT WAS YOUR LITTLE *SCHEME* ALL ALONG, HUH?
MUTUAL UNDER-STANDING? INTERSPECIES RELATIONS? SAVE THY BREATH.
YOU WERE JUST PLANNING TO *EXPLOIT US*, WEREN'T YOU?!
HO, VARLET! HAND OVER THAT CAMERA *AND* MIIA'S CASTINGS!

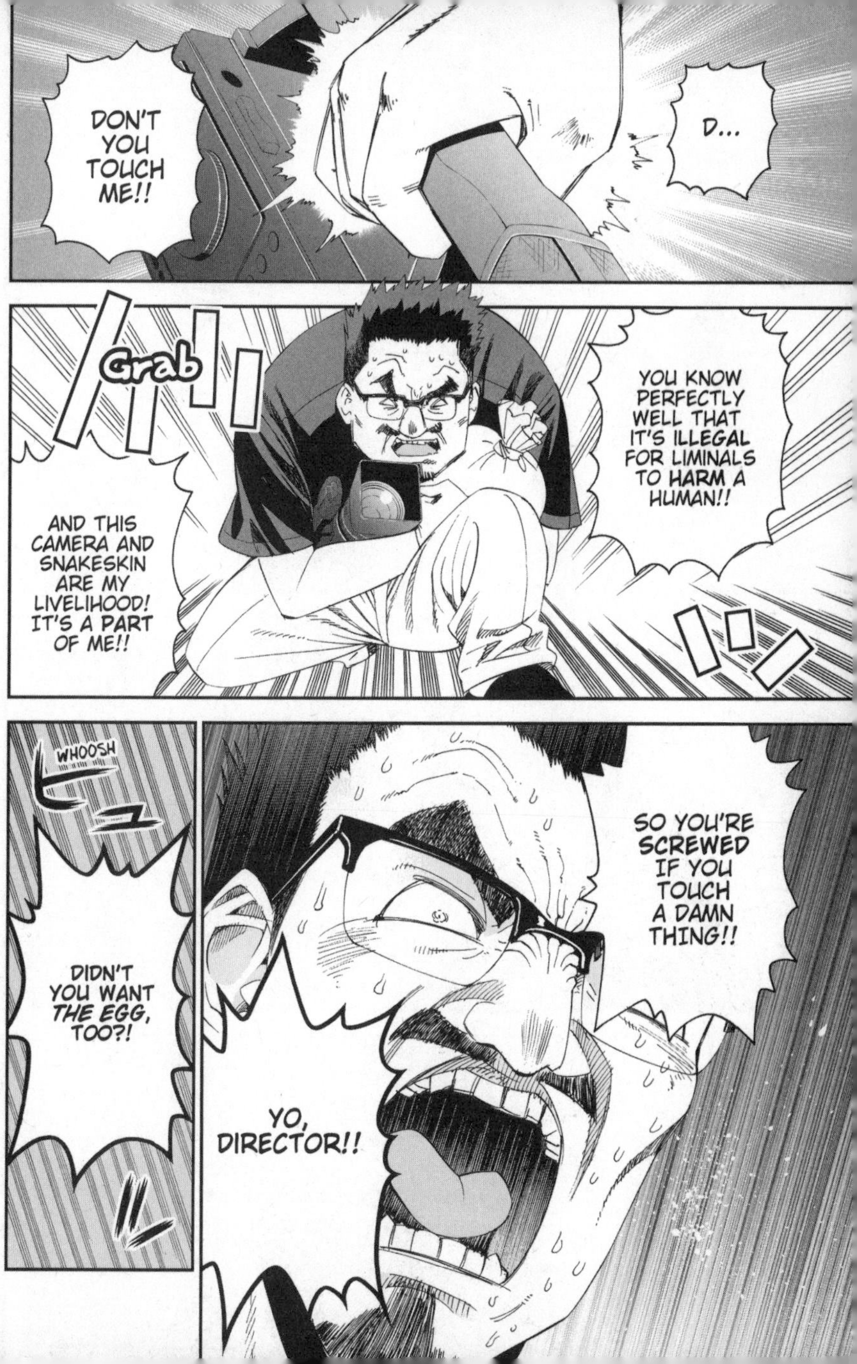
D...
DON'T YOU TOUCH ME!!
YOU KNOW PERFECTLY WELL THAT IT'S ILLEGAL FOR LIMINALS TO HARM A HUMAN!!
Grab
AND THIS CAMERA AND SNAKESKIN ARE MY LIVELIHOOD! IT'S A PART OF ME!!
SO YOU'RE SCREWED IF YOU TOUCH A DAMN THING!!
YO, DIRECTOR!!
WHOOSH
DIDN'T YOU WANT *THE EGG*, TOO?!

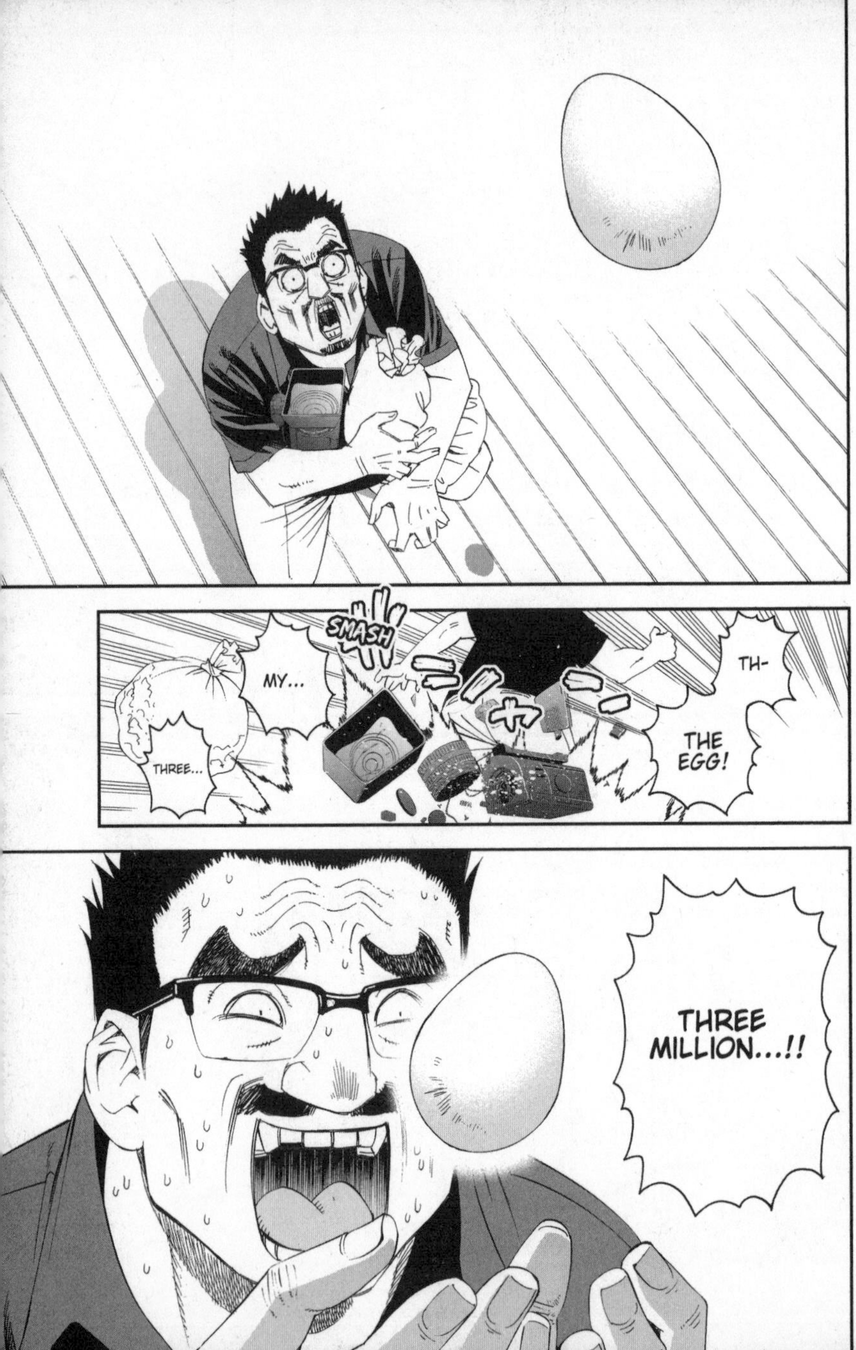
TH-
THE EGG!
SMASH
MY...
THREE...
THREE MILLION...!!

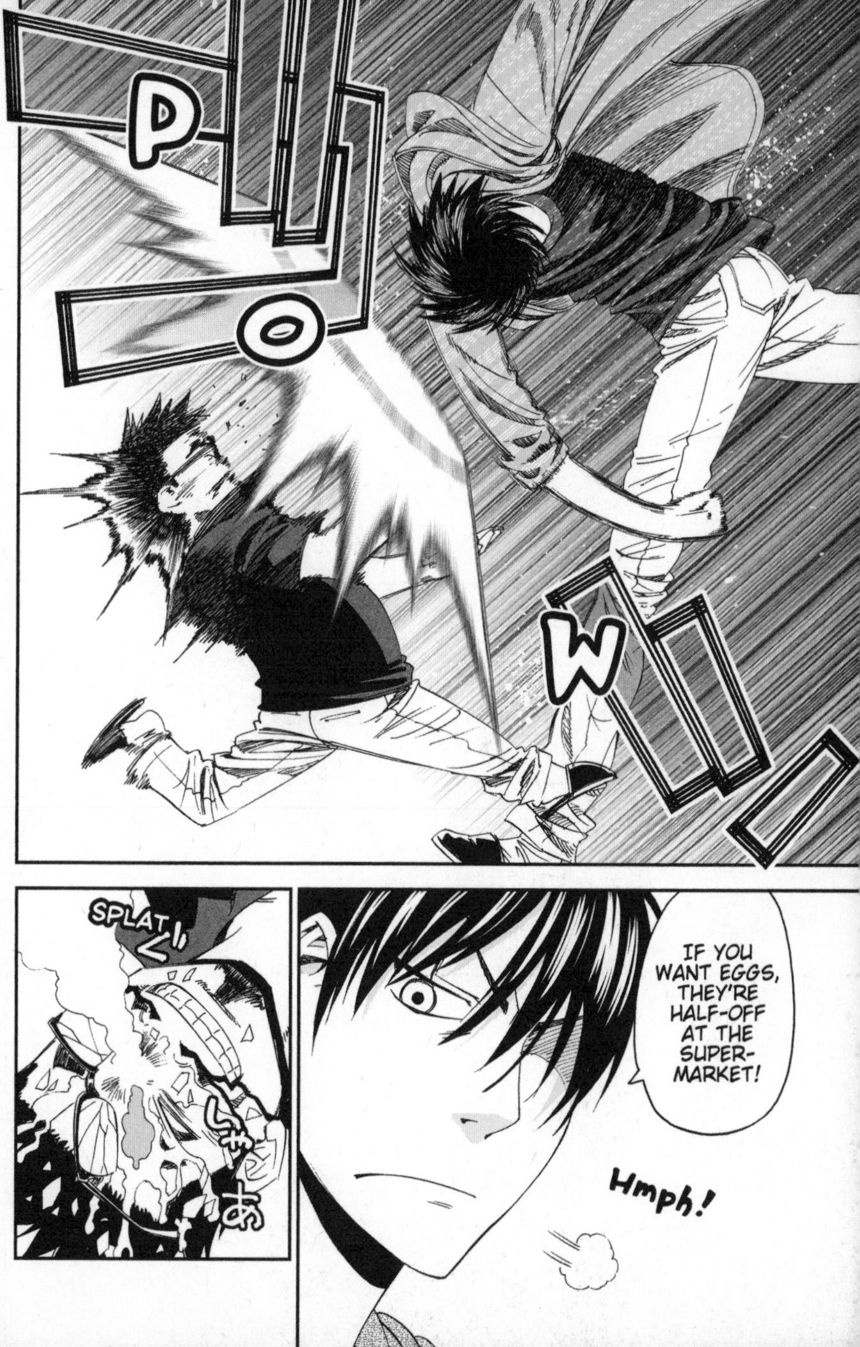
POW
IF YOU WANT EGGS, THEY'RE HALF-OFF AT THE SUPER-MARKET!
Hmph!
SPLAT

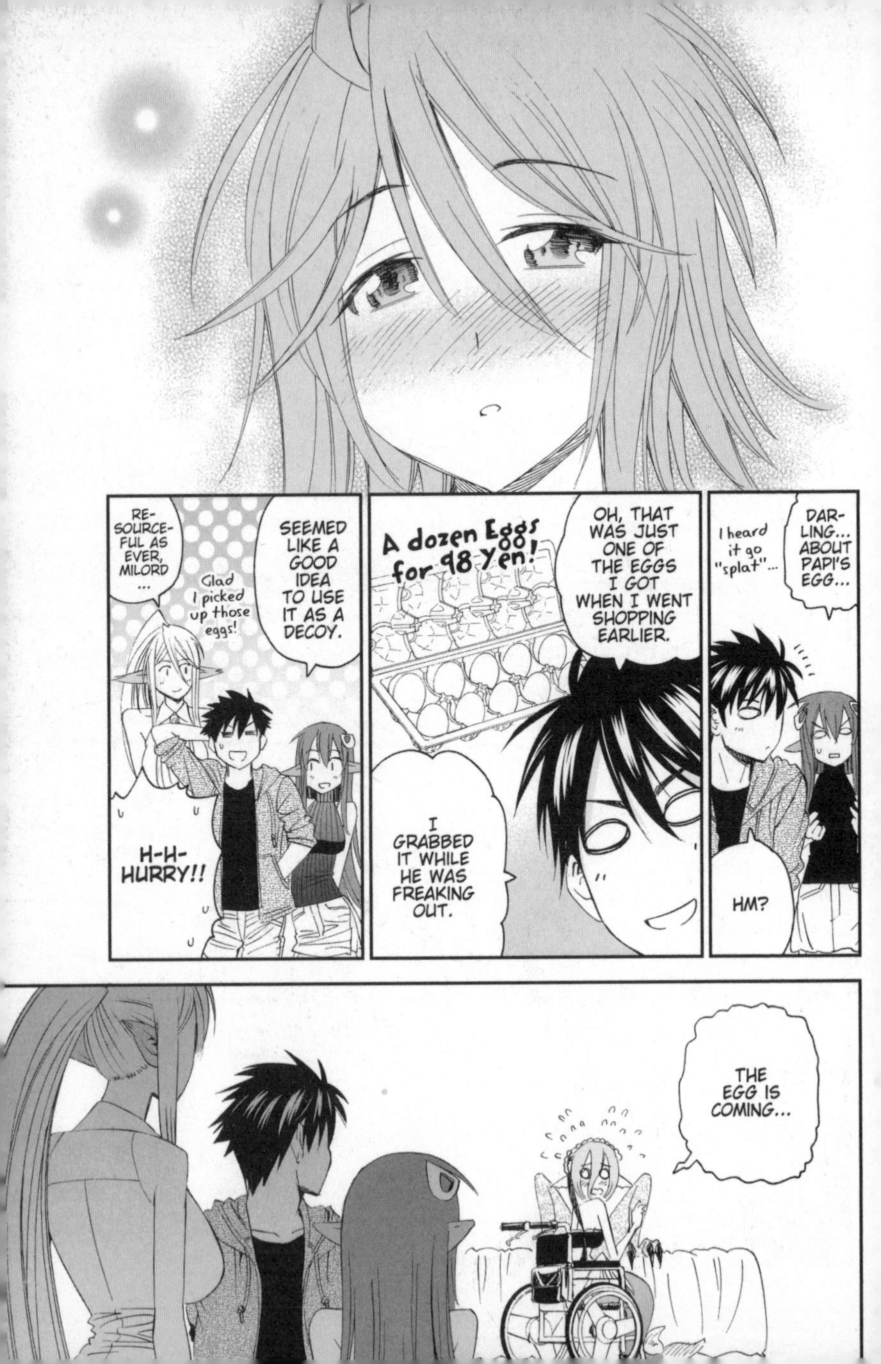
DARLING... ABOUT PAPI'S EGG...
I heard it go "splat"...
HM?
OH, THAT WAS JUST ONE OF THE EGGS I GOT WHEN I WENT SHOPPING EARLIER.
A dozen Eggs for 98 Yen!
I GRABBED IT WHILE HE WAS FREAKING OUT.
SEEMED LIKE A GOOD IDEA TO USE IT AS A DECOY.
RE-SOURCEFUL AS EVER, MILORD...
Glad I picked up those eggs!
H-H-HURRY!!
THE EGG IS COMING...

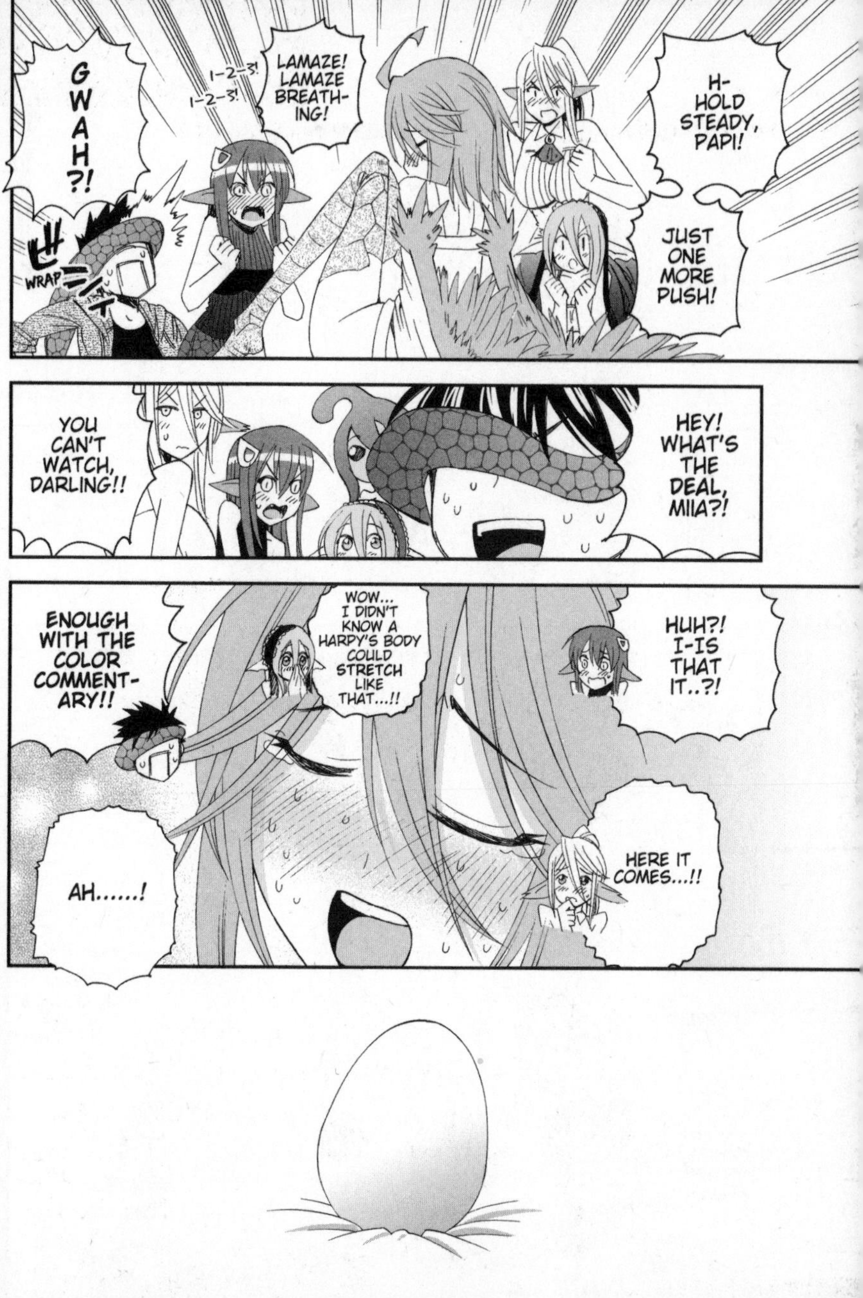
H-HOLD STEADY, PAPI!
JUST ONE MORE PUSH!
LAMAZE! LAMAZE BREATHING!
1-2-3! 1-2-3!
GWAH?!
WRAP
HEY! WHAT'S THE DEAL, MIIA?!
YOU CAN'T WATCH, DARLING!!
HUH?! I-IS THAT IT..?!
WOW... I DIDN'T KNOW A HARPY'S BODY COULD STRETCH LIKE THAT...!!
ENOUGH WITH THE COLOR COMMENT-ARY!!
HERE IT COMES...!!
AH......!

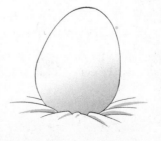

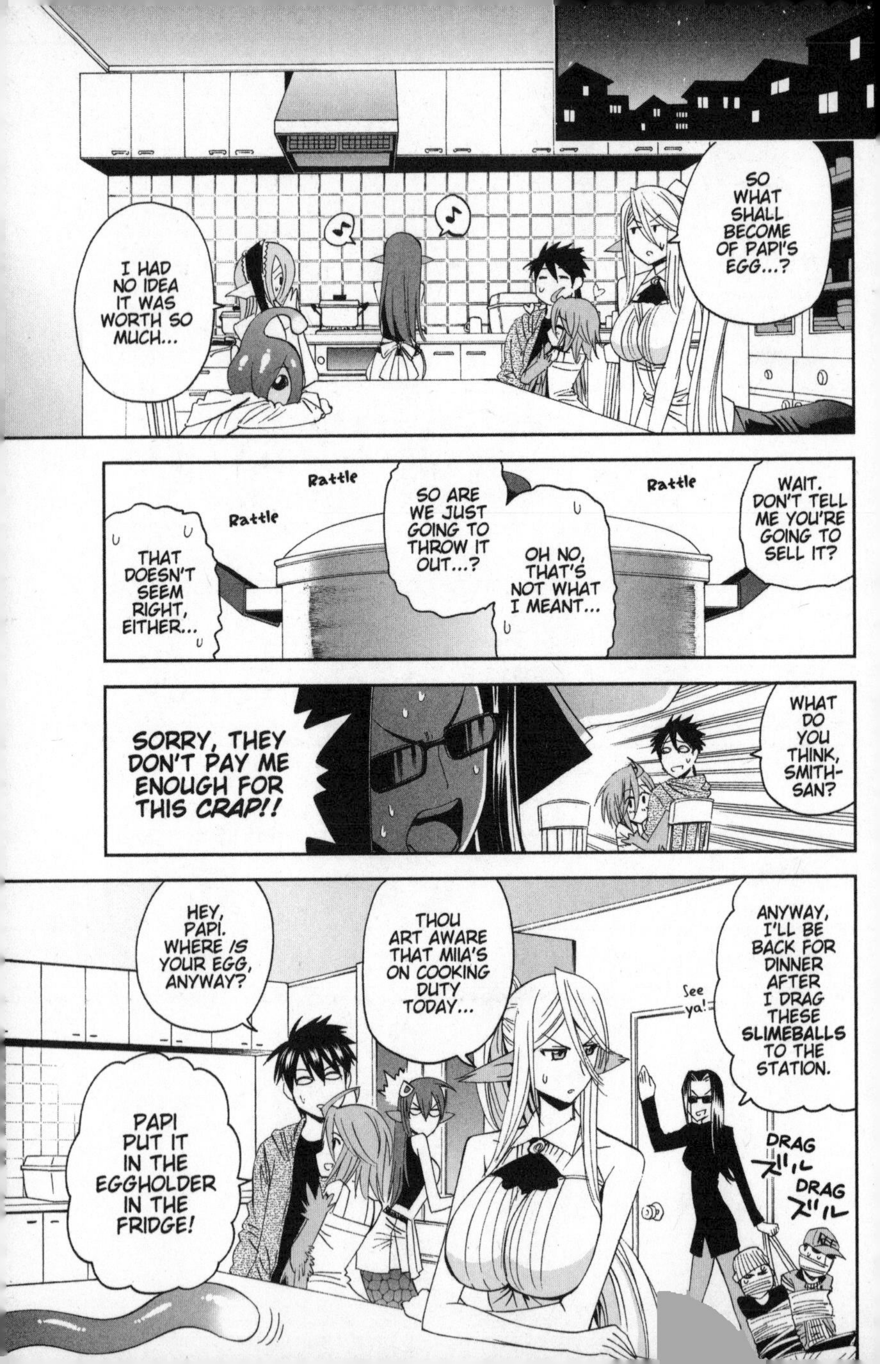
SO WHAT SHALL BECOME OF PAPI'S EGG...?
I HAD NO IDEA IT WAS WORTH SO MUCH...
WAIT. DON'T TELL ME YOU'RE GOING TO SELL IT?
Rattle
OH NO, THAT'S NOT WHAT I MEANT...
SO ARE WE JUST GOING TO THROW IT OUT...?
Rattle
Rattle
THAT DOESN'T SEEM RIGHT, EITHER...
WHAT DO YOU THINK, SMITH-SAN?
SORRY, THEY DON'T PAY ME ENOUGH FOR THIS *CRAP!!*
ANYWAY, I'LL BE BACK FOR DINNER AFTER I DRAG THESE SLIMEBALLS TO THE STATION.
See ya!
DRAG ズル
DRAG ズル
THOU ART AWARE THAT MIIA'S ON COOKING DUTY TODAY...
HEY, PAPI. WHERE *IS* YOUR EGG, ANYWAY?
PAPI PUT IT IN THE EGGHOLDER IN THE FRIDGE!

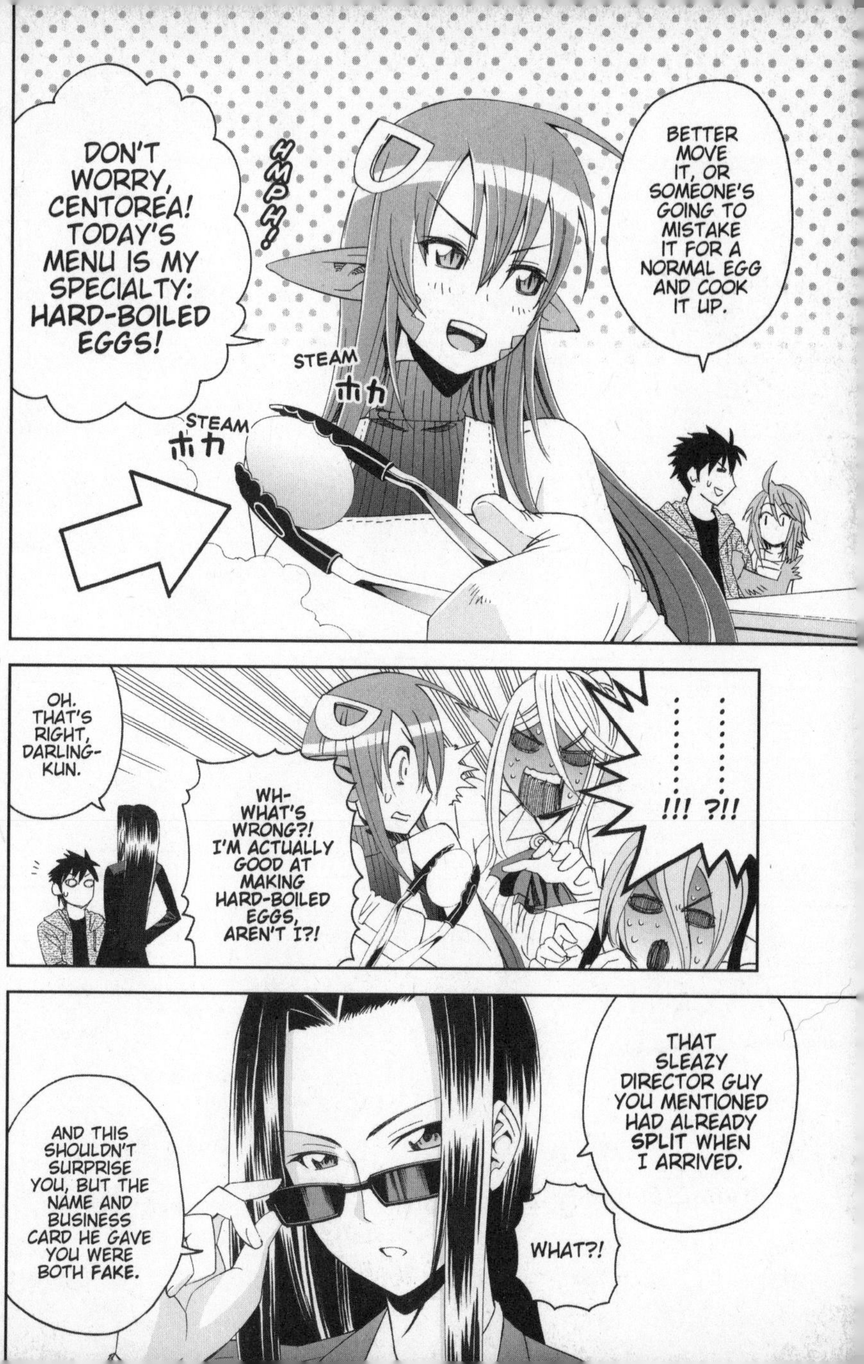
BETTER MOVE IT, OR SOMEONE'S GOING TO MISTAKE IT FOR A NORMAL EGG AND COOK IT UP.
HMPH!
DON'T WORRY, CENTOREA! TODAY'S MENU IS MY SPECIALTY: HARD-BOILED EGGS!
STEAM
ホカ
STEAM
ホカ
......
......
!!! ?!!
WH-WHAT'S WRONG?! I'M ACTUALLY GOOD AT MAKING HARD-BOILED EGGS, AREN'T I?!
OH. THAT'S RIGHT, DARLING-KUN.
THAT SLEAZY DIRECTOR GUY YOU MENTIONED HAD ALREADY SPLIT WHEN I ARRIVED.
WHAT?!
AND THIS SHOULDN'T SURPRISE YOU, BUT THE NAME AND BUSINESS CARD HE GAVE YOU WERE BOTH FAKE.

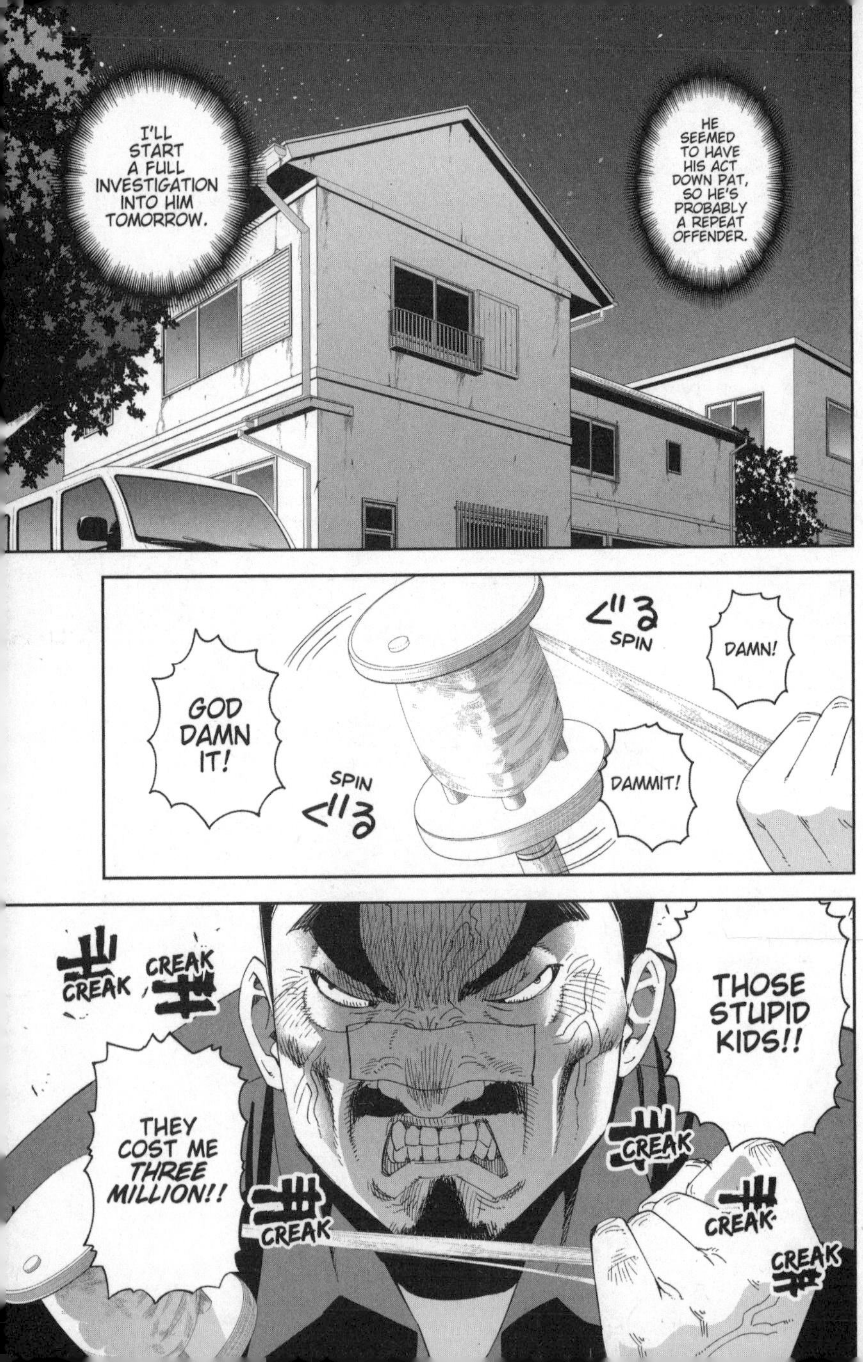
HE SEEMED TO HAVE HIS ACT DOWN PAT, SO HE'S PROBABLY A REPEAT OFFENDER.
I'LL START A FULL INVESTIGATION INTO HIM TOMORROW.
DAMN!
ぐる
SPIN
DAMMIT!
GOD DAMN IT!
SPIN
ぐる
THOSE STUPID KIDS!!
CREAK
CREAK
THEY COST ME THREE MILLION!!
CREAK
CREAK
CREAK
CREAK

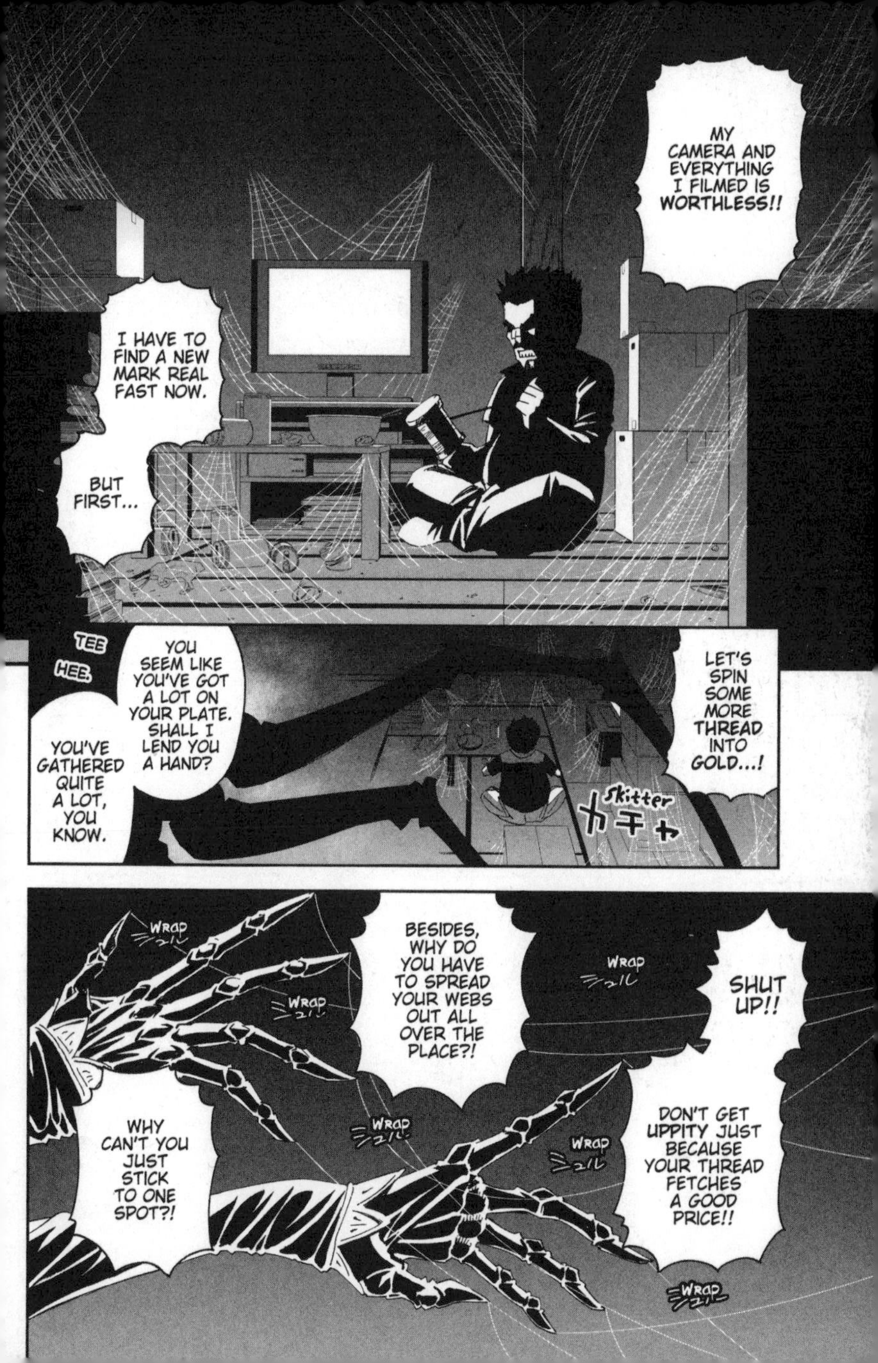
MY CAMERA AND EVERYTHING I FILMED IS WORTHLESS!!
I HAVE TO FIND A NEW MARK REAL FAST NOW.
BUT FIRST...
LET'S SPIN SOME MORE THREAD INTO GOLD...!
Skitter
カチャ
YOU SEEM LIKE YOU'VE GOT A LOT ON YOUR PLATE. SHALL I LEND YOU A HAND?
TEE HEE.
YOU'VE GATHERED QUITE A LOT, YOU KNOW.
SHUT UP!!
Wrap
DON'T GET UPPITY JUST BECAUSE YOUR THREAD FETCHES A GOOD PRICE!!
Wrap
BESIDES, WHY DO YOU HAVE TO SPREAD YOUR WEBS OUT ALL OVER THE PLACE?!
Wrap
Wrap
WHY CAN'T YOU JUST STICK TO ONE SPOT?!
Wrap
Wrap

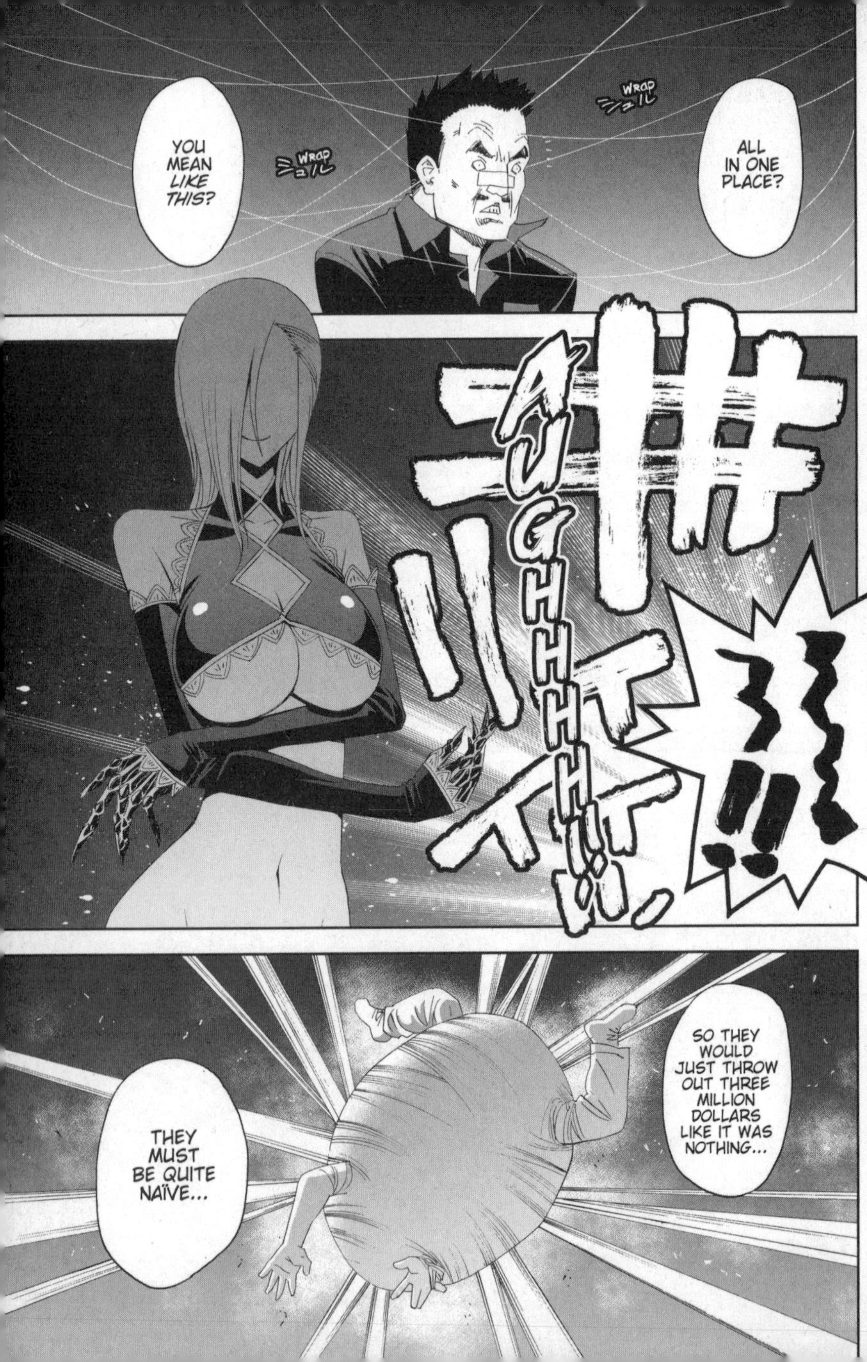
ALL IN ONE PLACE?
Wrap シュル
Wrap シュル
YOU MEAN LIKE THIS?
AUGHHHHHH!!!
SO THEY WOULD JUST THROW OUT THREE MILLION DOLLARS LIKE IT WAS NOTHING...
THEY MUST BE QUITE NAÏVE...

A HYPOCRITE DRESSING UP IN SAINT'S CLOTHING...

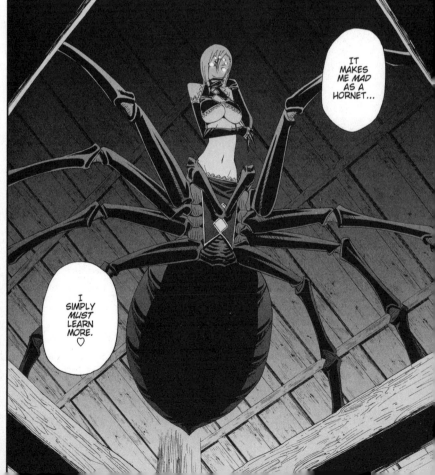

IT MAKES ME *MAD* AS A HORNET...

I SIMPLY *MUST* LEARN MORE. ♡

Monster Musume

Everyday Life with Monster Girls

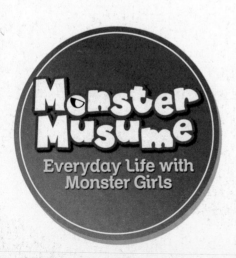

Undead

Zombina's Secrets

161CM B 85

58KG W 58

H 87

E CUP!

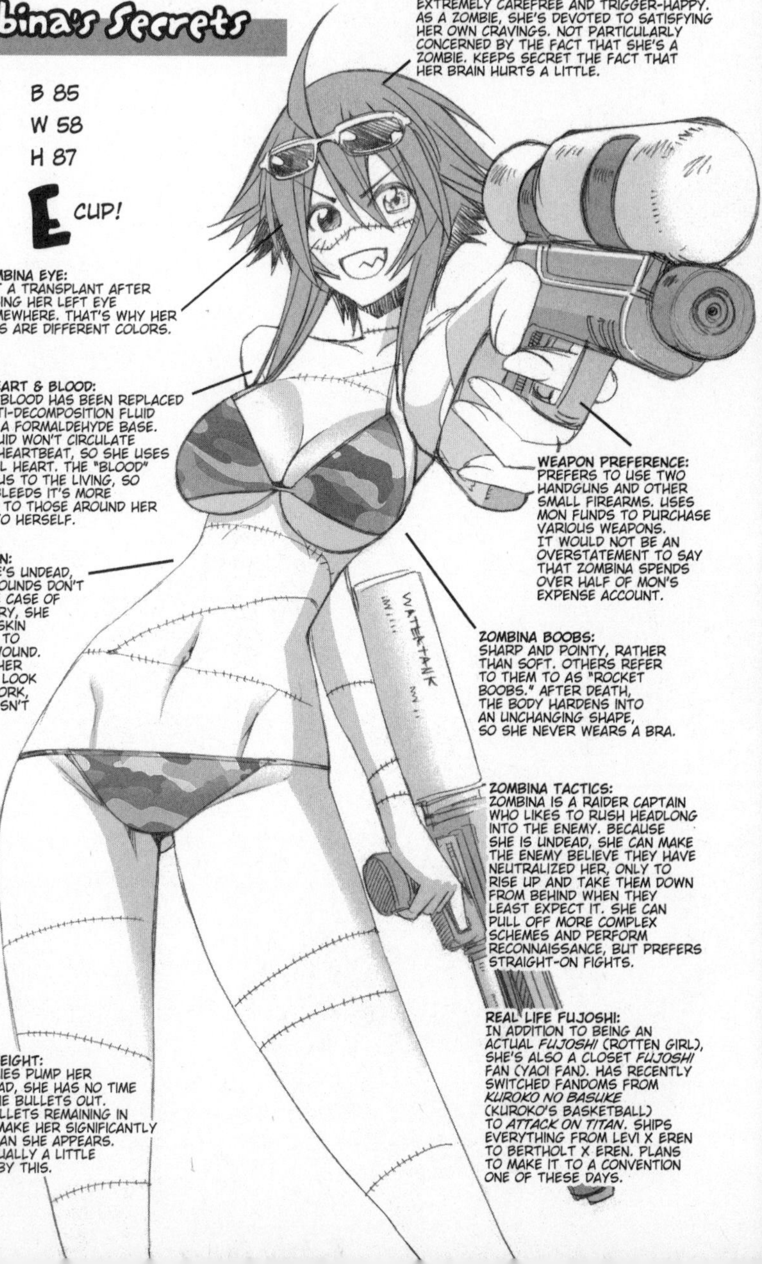

WATERTANK

ZOMBINA PERSONALITY:
EXTREMELY CAREFREE AND TRIGGER-HAPPY. AS A ZOMBIE, SHE'S DEVOTED TO SATISFYING HER OWN CRAVINGS. NOT PARTICULARLY CONCERNED BY THE FACT THAT SHE'S A ZOMBIE. KEEPS SECRET THE FACT THAT HER BRAIN HURTS A LITTLE.

ZOMBINA EYE:
GOT A TRANSPLANT AFTER LOSING HER LEFT EYE SOMEWHERE. THAT'S WHY HER EYES ARE DIFFERENT COLORS.

ZOMBINA HEART & BLOOD:
ALL OF HER BLOOD HAS BEEN REPLACED WITH AN ANTI-DECOMPOSITION FLUID MADE FROM A FORMALDEHYDE BASE. BUT THE FLUID WON'T CIRCULATE WITHOUT A HEARTBEAT, SO SHE USES AN ARTIFICIAL HEART. THE "BLOOD" IS HAZARDOUS TO THE LIVING, SO WHEN SHE BLEEDS IT'S MORE DANGEROUS TO THOSE AROUND HER THAN IT IS TO HERSELF.

WEAPON PREFERENCE:
PREFERS TO USE TWO HANDGUNS AND OTHER SMALL FIREARMS. USES MON FUNDS TO PURCHASE VARIOUS WEAPONS. IT WOULD NOT BE AN OVERSTATEMENT TO SAY THAT ZOMBINA SPENDS OVER HALF OF MON'S EXPENSE ACCOUNT.

ZOMBINA SKIN:
BECAUSE SHE'S UNDEAD, ZOMBINA'S WOUNDS DON'T HEAL. IN THE CASE OF SEVERE INJURY, SHE REQUIRES A SKIN TRANSPLANT TO COVER THE WOUND. THIS MAKES HER ENTIRE BODY LOOK LIKE PATCHWORK, BUT SHE DOESN'T MIND IT.

ZOMBINA BOOBS:
SHARP AND POINTY, RATHER THAN SOFT. OTHERS REFER TO THEM TO AS "ROCKET BOOBS." AFTER DEATH, THE BODY HARDENS INTO AN UNCHANGING SHAPE, SO SHE NEVER WEARS A BRA.

ZOMBINA TACTICS:
ZOMBINA IS A RAIDER CAPTAIN WHO LIKES TO RUSH HEADLONG INTO THE ENEMY. BECAUSE SHE IS UNDEAD, SHE CAN MAKE THE ENEMY BELIEVE THEY HAVE NEUTRALIZED HER, ONLY TO RISE UP AND TAKE THEM DOWN FROM BEHIND WHEN THEY LEAST EXPECT IT. SHE CAN PULL OFF MORE COMPLEX SCHEMES AND PERFORM RECONNAISSANCE, BUT PREFERS STRAIGHT-ON FIGHTS.

ZOMBINA WEIGHT:
WHEN ENEMIES PUMP HER FULL OF LEAD, SHE HAS NO TIME TO TAKE THE BULLETS OUT. ALL THE BULLETS REMAINING IN HER BODY MAKE HER SIGNIFICANTLY HEAVIER THAN SHE APPEARS. SHE IS ACTUALLY A LITTLE BOTHERED BY THIS.

REAL LIFE FUJOSHI:
IN ADDITION TO BEING AN ACTUAL *FUJOSHI* (ROTTEN GIRL), SHE'S ALSO A CLOSET *FUJOSHI* FAN (YAOI FAN). HAS RECENTLY SWITCHED FANDOMS FROM *KUROKO NO BASUKE* (KUROKO'S BASKETBALL) TO *ATTACK ON TITAN*. SHIPS EVERYTHING FROM LEVI X EREN TO BERTHOLT X EREN. PLANS TO MAKE IT TO A CONVENTION ONE OF THESE DAYS.

Ogre

Tionishia's Teasers

227CM B 160

SECRET☆KG W 72

H 119

P CUP!

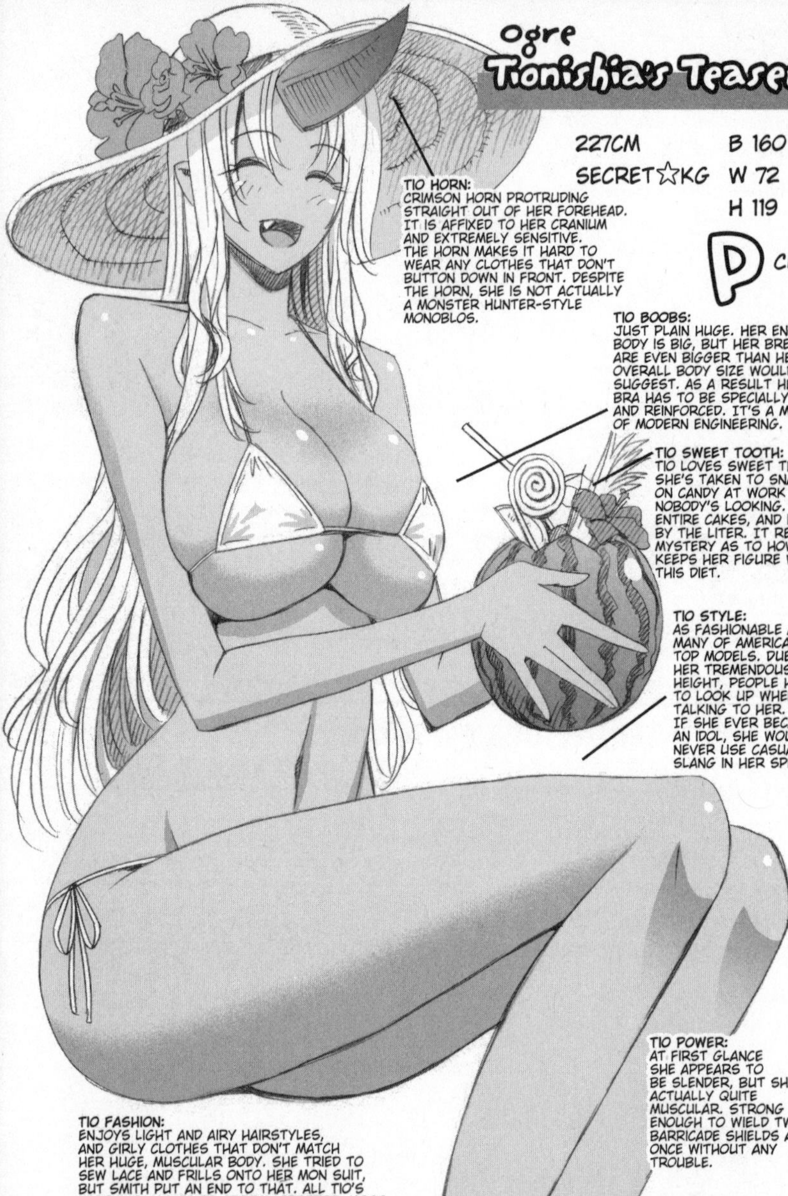
TIO HORN:
CRIMSON HORN PROTRUDING STRAIGHT OUT OF HER FOREHEAD. IT IS AFFIXED TO HER CRANIUM AND EXTREMELY SENSITIVE. THE HORN MAKES IT HARD TO WEAR ANY CLOTHES THAT DON'T BUTTON DOWN IN FRONT. DESPITE THE HORN, SHE IS NOT ACTUALLY A MONSTER HUNTER-STYLE MONOBLOS.
TIO BOOBS:
JUST PLAIN HUGE. HER ENTIRE BODY IS BIG, BUT HER BREASTS ARE EVEN BIGGER THAN HER OVERALL BODY SIZE WOULD SUGGEST. AS A RESULT HER BRA HAS TO BE SPECIALLY MADE AND REINFORCED. IT'S A MARVEL OF MODERN ENGINEERING.
TIO SWEET TOOTH:
TIO LOVES SWEET THINGS. SHE'S TAKEN TO SNACKING ON CANDY AT WORK WHEN NOBODY'S LOOKING. EATS ENTIRE CAKES, AND ICE CREAM BY THE LITER. IT REMAINS A MYSTERY AS TO HOW SHE KEEPS HER FIGURE WITH THIS DIET.
TIO STYLE:
AS FASHIONABLE AS MANY OF AMERICA'S TOP MODELS. DUE TO HER TREMENDOUS HEIGHT, PEOPLE HAVE TO LOOK UP WHEN TALKING TO HER. IF SHE EVER BECAME AN IDOL, SHE WOULD NEVER USE CASUAL SLANG IN HER SPEECH.
TIO POWER:
AT FIRST GLANCE SHE APPEARS TO BE SLENDER, BUT SHE'S ACTUALLY QUITE MUSCULAR. STRONG ENOUGH TO WIELD TWO BARRICADE SHIELDS AT ONCE WITHOUT ANY TROUBLE.
TIO FASHION:
ENJOYS LIGHT AND AIRY HAIRSTYLES, AND GIRLY CLOTHES THAT DON'T MATCH HER HUGE, MUSCULAR BODY. SHE TRIED TO SEW LACE AND FRILLS ONTO HER MON SUIT, BUT SMITH PUT AN END TO THAT. ALL TIO'S CLOTHING HAS TO BE SPECIAL ORDERED. MOST OF HER EARNINGS GO TO CLOTHING AND ACCESSORIES, WHICH IS A MAJOR CONCERN FOR HER.

Cyclops
Manako's Eye-openers

148CM B 73
33KG W 54
H 75
A CUP

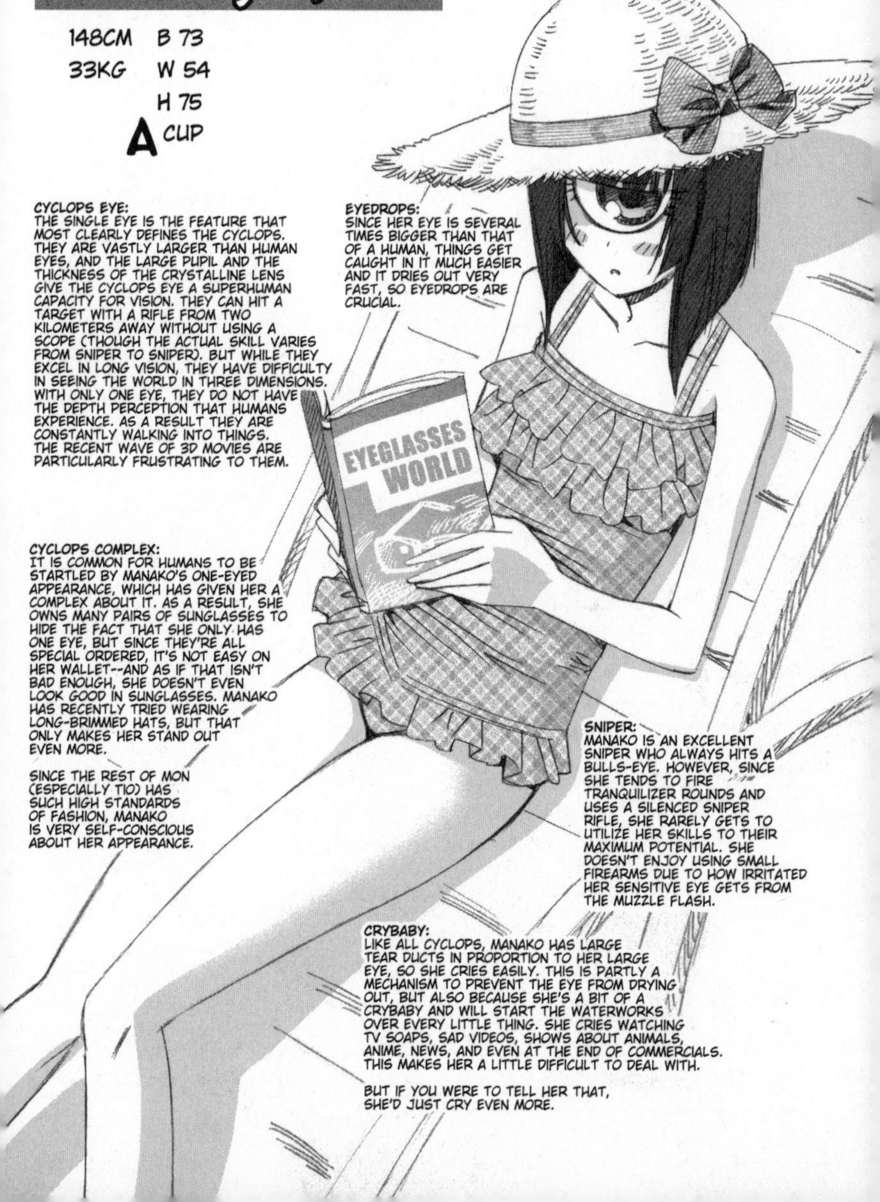
EYEGLASSES WORLD

CYCLOPS EYE:
THE SINGLE EYE IS THE FEATURE THAT MOST CLEARLY DEFINES THE CYCLOPS. THEY ARE VASTLY LARGER THAN HUMAN EYES, AND THE LARGE PUPIL AND THE THICKNESS OF THE CRYSTALLINE LENS GIVE THE CYCLOPS EYE A SUPERHUMAN CAPACITY FOR VISION. THEY CAN HIT A TARGET WITH A RIFLE FROM TWO KILOMETERS AWAY WITHOUT USING A SCOPE (THOUGH THE ACTUAL SKILL VARIES FROM SNIPER TO SNIPER). BUT WHILE THEY EXCEL IN LONG VISION, THEY HAVE DIFFICULTY IN SEEING THE WORLD IN THREE DIMENSIONS. WITH ONLY ONE EYE, THEY DO NOT HAVE THE DEPTH PERCEPTION THAT HUMANS EXPERIENCE. AS A RESULT THEY ARE CONSTANTLY WALKING INTO THINGS. THE RECENT WAVE OF 3D MOVIES ARE PARTICULARLY FRUSTRATING TO THEM.

EYEDROPS:
SINCE HER EYE IS SEVERAL TIMES BIGGER THAN THAT OF A HUMAN, THINGS GET CAUGHT IN IT MUCH EASIER AND IT DRIES OUT VERY FAST, SO EYEDROPS ARE CRUCIAL.

CYCLOPS COMPLEX:
IT IS COMMON FOR HUMANS TO BE STARTLED BY MANAKO'S ONE-EYED APPEARANCE, WHICH HAS GIVEN HER A COMPLEX ABOUT IT. AS A RESULT, SHE OWNS MANY PAIRS OF SUNGLASSES TO HIDE THE FACT THAT SHE ONLY HAS ONE EYE, BUT SINCE THEY'RE ALL SPECIAL ORDERED, IT'S NOT EASY ON HER WALLET--AND AS IF THAT ISN'T BAD ENOUGH, SHE DOESN'T EVEN LOOK GOOD IN SUNGLASSES. MANAKO HAS RECENTLY TRIED WEARING LONG-BRIMMED HATS, BUT THAT ONLY MAKES HER STAND OUT EVEN MORE.

SINCE THE REST OF MON (ESPECIALLY TIO) HAS SUCH HIGH STANDARDS OF FASHION, MANAKO IS VERY SELF-CONSCIOUS ABOUT HER APPEARANCE.

SNIPER:
MANAKO IS AN EXCELLENT SNIPER WHO ALWAYS HITS A BULLS-EYE. HOWEVER, SINCE SHE TENDS TO FIRE TRANQUILIZER ROUNDS AND USES A SILENCED SNIPER RIFLE, SHE RARELY GETS TO UTILIZE HER SKILLS TO THEIR MAXIMUM POTENTIAL. SHE DOESN'T ENJOY USING SMALL FIREARMS DUE TO HOW IRRITATED HER SENSITIVE EYE GETS FROM THE MUZZLE FLASH.

CRYBABY:
LIKE ALL CYCLOPS, MANAKO HAS LARGE TEAR DUCTS IN PROPORTION TO HER LARGE EYE, SO SHE CRIES EASILY. THIS IS PARTLY A MECHANISM TO PREVENT THE EYE FROM DRYING OUT, BUT ALSO BECAUSE SHE'S A BIT OF A CRYBABY AND WILL START THE WATERWORKS OVER EVERY LITTLE THING. SHE CRIES WATCHING TV SOAPS, SAD VIDEOS, SHOWS ABOUT ANIMALS, ANIME, NEWS, AND EVEN AT THE END OF COMMERCIALS. THIS MAKES HER A LITTLE DIFFICULT TO DEAL WITH.

BUT IF YOU WERE TO TELL HER THAT, SHE'D JUST CRY EVEN MORE.

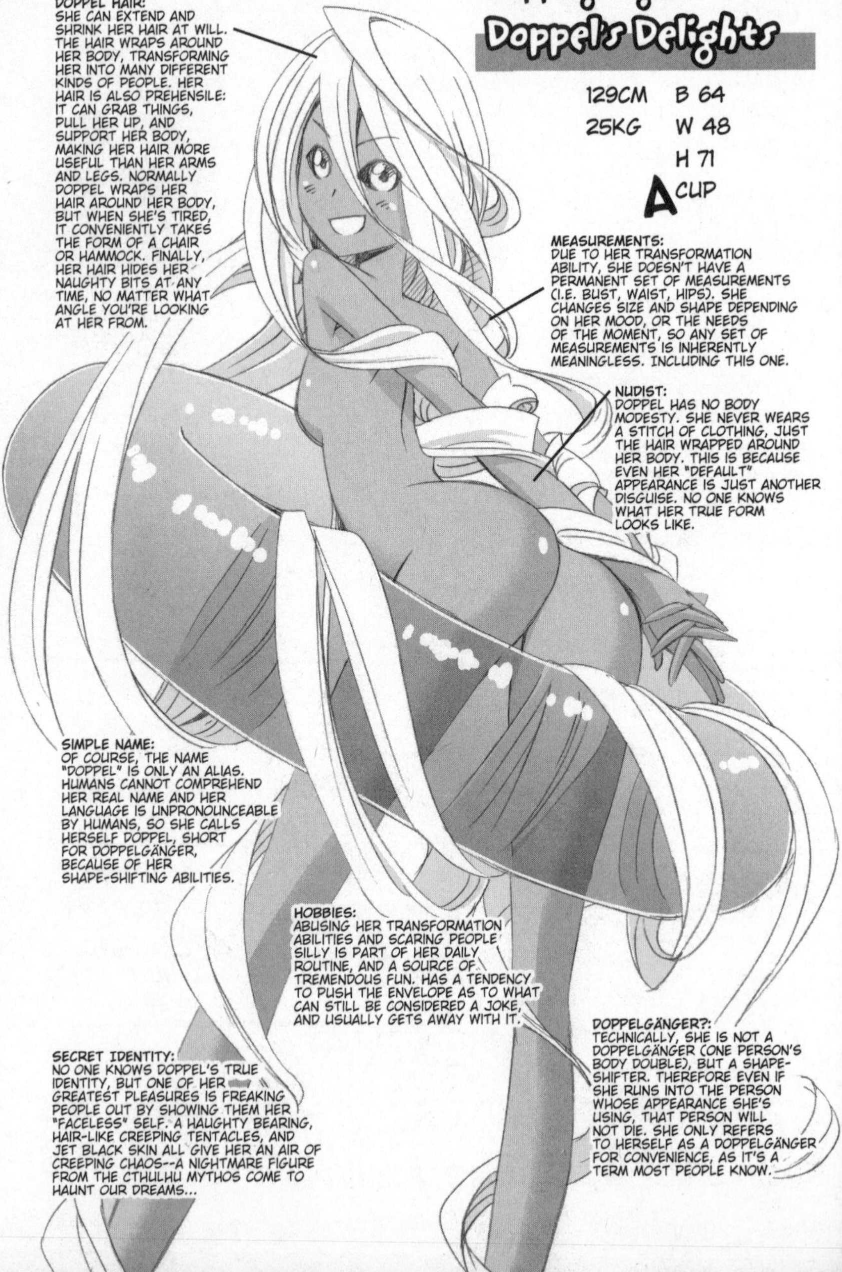

Doppelgänger

Doppel's Delights

129CM B 64
25KG W 48
H 71
A CUP

DOPPEL HAIR:
SHE CAN EXTEND AND SHRINK HER HAIR AT WILL. THE HAIR WRAPS AROUND HER BODY, TRANSFORMING HER INTO MANY DIFFERENT KINDS OF PEOPLE. HER HAIR IS ALSO PREHENSILE: IT CAN GRAB THINGS, PULL HER UP, AND SUPPORT HER BODY, MAKING HER HAIR MORE USEFUL THAN HER ARMS AND LEGS. NORMALLY DOPPEL WRAPS HER HAIR AROUND HER BODY, BUT WHEN SHE'S TIRED, IT CONVENIENTLY TAKES THE FORM OF A CHAIR OR HAMMOCK. FINALLY, HER HAIR HIDES HER NAUGHTY BITS AT ANY TIME, NO MATTER WHAT ANGLE YOU'RE LOOKING AT HER FROM.

MEASUREMENTS:
DUE TO HER TRANSFORMATION ABILITY, SHE DOESN'T HAVE A PERMANENT SET OF MEASUREMENTS (I.E. BUST, WAIST, HIPS). SHE CHANGES SIZE AND SHAPE DEPENDING ON HER MOOD, OR THE NEEDS OF THE MOMENT, SO ANY SET OF MEASUREMENTS IS INHERENTLY MEANINGLESS. INCLUDING THIS ONE.

NUDIST:
DOPPEL HAS NO BODY MODESTY. SHE NEVER WEARS A STITCH OF CLOTHING, JUST THE HAIR WRAPPED AROUND HER BODY. THIS IS BECAUSE EVEN HER "DEFAULT" APPEARANCE IS JUST ANOTHER DISGUISE. NO ONE KNOWS WHAT HER TRUE FORM LOOKS LIKE.

SIMPLE NAME:
OF COURSE, THE NAME "DOPPEL" IS ONLY AN ALIAS. HUMANS CANNOT COMPREHEND HER REAL NAME AND HER LANGUAGE IS UNPRONOUNCEABLE BY HUMANS, SO SHE CALLS HERSELF DOPPEL, SHORT FOR DOPPELGÄNGER, BECAUSE OF HER SHAPE-SHIFTING ABILITIES.

HOBBIES:
ABUSING HER TRANSFORMATION ABILITIES AND SCARING PEOPLE SILLY IS PART OF HER DAILY ROUTINE, AND A SOURCE OF TREMENDOUS FUN. HAS A TENDENCY TO PUSH THE ENVELOPE AS TO WHAT CAN STILL BE CONSIDERED A JOKE, AND USUALLY GETS AWAY WITH IT.

SECRET IDENTITY:
NO ONE KNOWS DOPPEL'S TRUE IDENTITY, BUT ONE OF HER GREATEST PLEASURES IS FREAKING PEOPLE OUT BY SHOWING THEM HER "FACELESS" SELF. A HAUGHTY BEARING, HAIR-LIKE CREEPING TENTACLES, AND JET BLACK SKIN ALL GIVE HER AN AIR OF CREEPING CHAOS--A NIGHTMARE FIGURE FROM THE CTHULHU MYTHOS COME TO HAUNT OUR DREAMS...

DOPPELGÄNGER?:
TECHNICALLY, SHE IS NOT A DOPPELGÄNGER (ONE PERSON'S BODY DOUBLE), BUT A SHAPE-SHIFTER. THEREFORE EVEN IF SHE RUNS INTO THE PERSON WHOSE APPEARANCE SHE'S USING, THAT PERSON WILL NOT DIE. SHE ONLY REFERS TO HERSELF AS A DOPPELGÄNGER FOR CONVENIENCE, AS IT'S A TERM MOST PEOPLE KNOW.

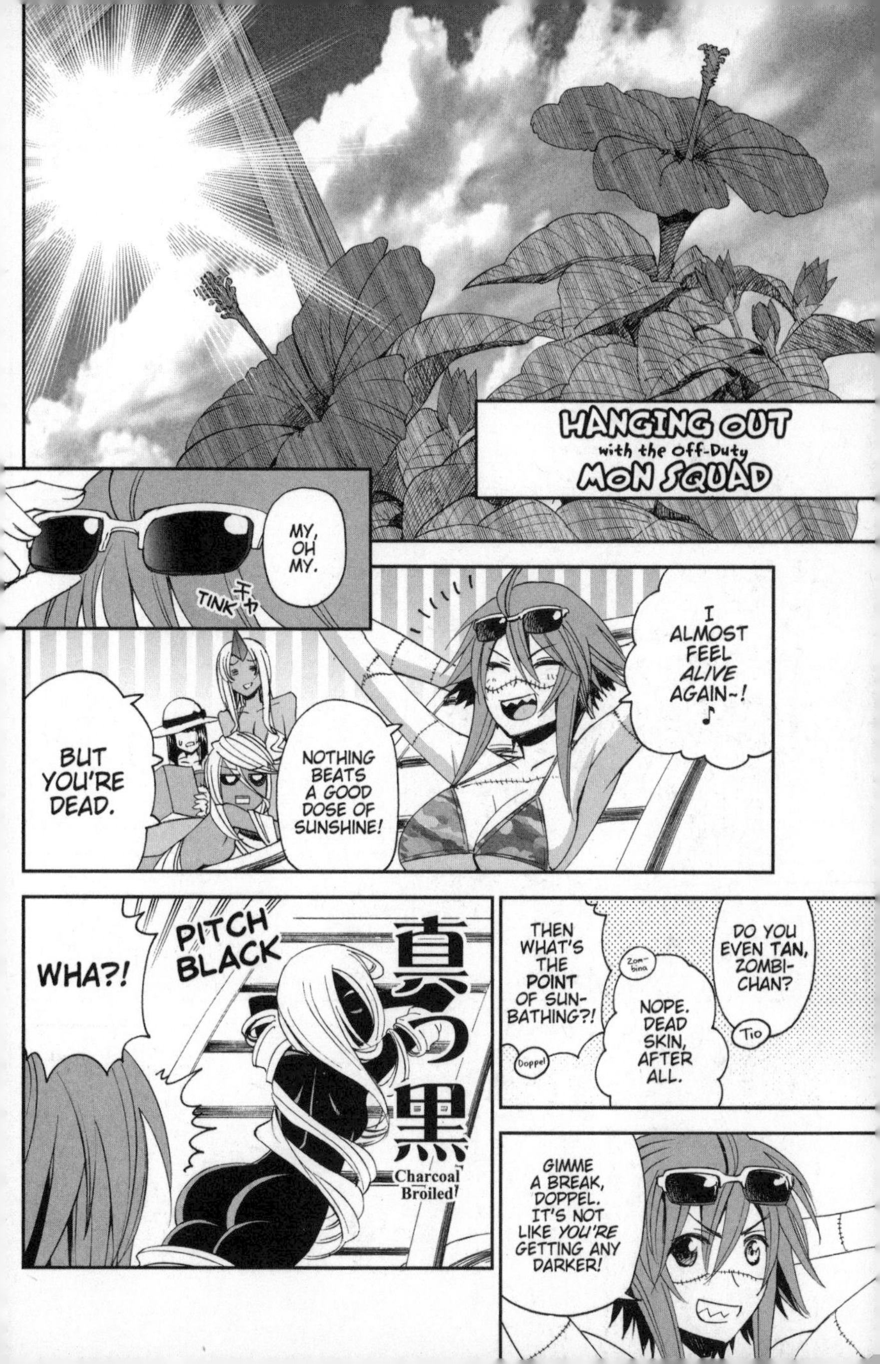
HANGING OUT
with the Off-Duty
MON SQUAD
MY, OH MY.
TINK
チャ
I ALMOST FEEL ALIVE AGAIN~! ♪
NOTHING BEATS A GOOD DOSE OF SUNSHINE!
BUT YOU'RE DEAD.
DO YOU EVEN TAN, ZOMBI-CHAN?
Tio
NOPE. DEAD SKIN, AFTER ALL.
Zombina
THEN WHAT'S THE POINT OF SUN-BATHING?!
Doppel
GIMME A BREAK, DOPPEL. IT'S NOT LIKE YOU'RE GETTING ANY DARKER!
WHA?!
PITCH BLACK
真っ黒
Charcoal Broiled!

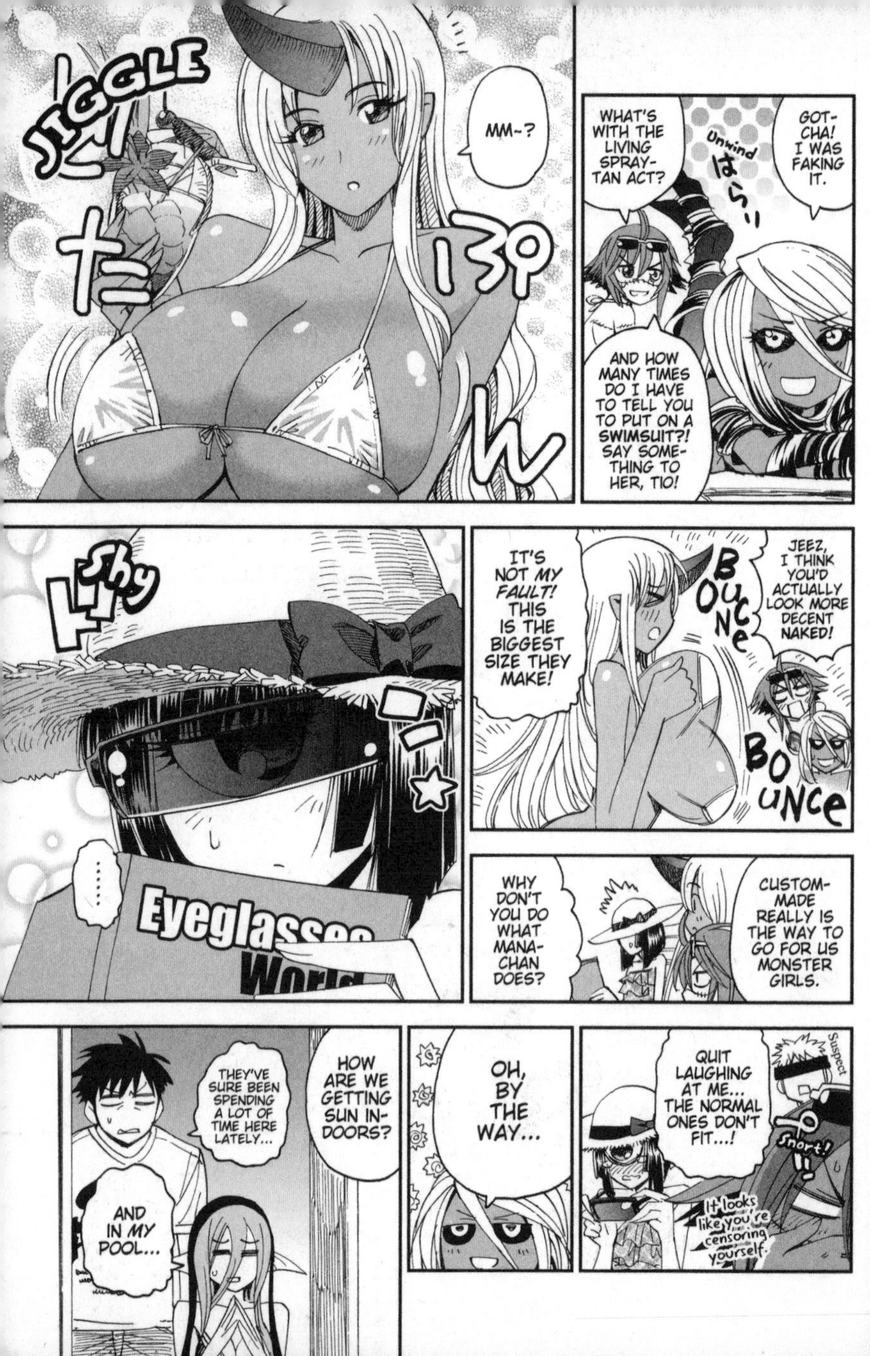
GOT-CHA! I WAS FAKING IT.
Unwind
はらり
WHAT'S WITH THE LIVING SPRAY-TAN ACT?
AND HOW MANY TIMES DO I HAVE TO TELL YOU TO PUT ON A SWIMSUIT?! SAY SOME-THING TO HER, TIO!
MM~?
JIGGLE
JEEZ, I THINK YOU'D ACTUALLY LOOK MORE DECENT NAKED!
BOUNCE
IT'S NOT *MY FAULT!* THIS IS THE BIGGEST SIZE THEY MAKE!
BOUNCE
CUSTOM-MADE REALLY IS THE WAY TO GO FOR US MONSTER GIRLS.
WHY DON'T YOU DO WHAT MANA-CHAN DOES?
Shy
......
Eyeglasses World
Suspect
QUIT LAUGHING AT ME... THE NORMAL ONES DON'T FIT...!
Snort!
It looks like you're censoring yourself.
OH, BY THE WAY...
HOW ARE WE GETTING SUN IN-DOORS?
THEY'VE SURE BEEN SPENDING A LOT OF TIME HERE LATELY...
AND IN MY POOL...

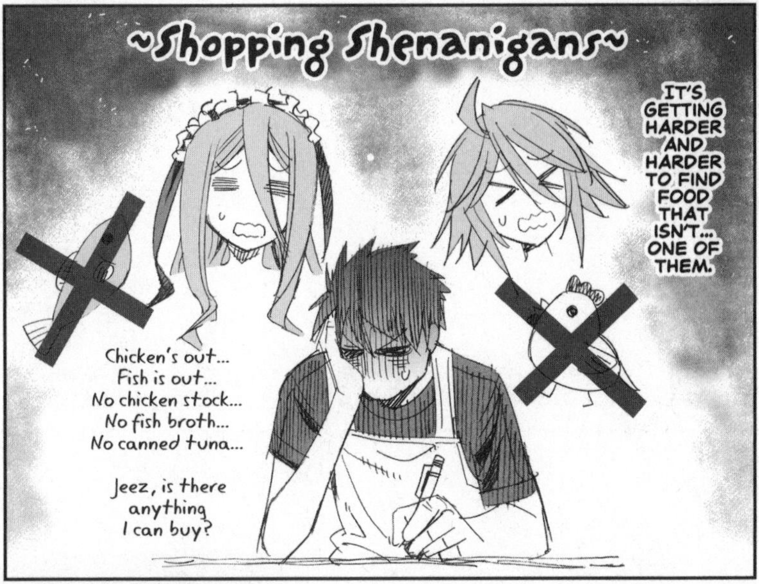
~Shopping Shenanigans~
IT'S GETTING HARDER AND HARDER TO FIND FOOD THAT ISN'T... ONE OF THEM.
Chicken's out... Fish is out... No chicken stock... No fish broth... No canned tuna...
Jeez, is there anything I can buy?

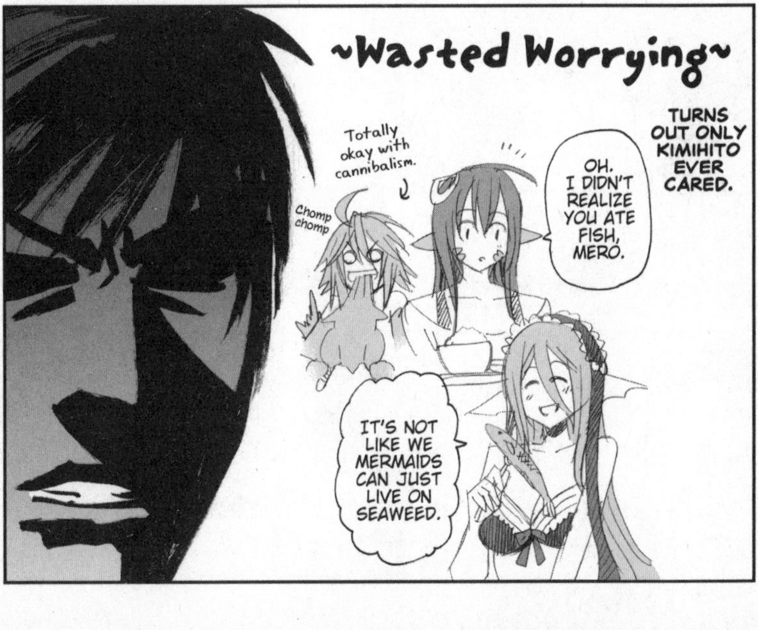
~Wasted Worrying~
TURNS OUT ONLY KIMIHITO EVER CARED.
OH. I DIDN'T REALIZE YOU ATE FISH, MERO.
Totally okay with cannibalism.
Chomp chomp
IT'S NOT LIKE WE MERMAIDS CAN JUST LIVE ON SEAWEED.